PERSONAL RELATIONSHIPS AND PERSONAL NETWORKS

LEA's Series on Personal Relationships
Steve Duck, Series Editor

For more information on LEA titles, please contact Lawrence Erlbaum Associates, Publishers, at www.erlbaum.com

PERSONAL RELATIONSHIPS
AND PERSONAL NETWORKS

Malcolm R. Parks
University of Washington

Routledge
Taylor & Francis Group

NEW YORK AND LONDON

First published by
Lawrence Erlbaum Associates, Inc., Publishers
10 Industrial Avenue
Mahwah, New Jersey 07430

This edition published 2013 by Routledge
711 Third Avenue, New York, NY 10017
2 Park Square, Milton Park, Abingdon, Oxfordshire OX14 4RN

Routledge is an imprint of the Taylor & Francis Group, an informa business

Cover design by Tomai Maridou

Cover art by Jason Laramie

Library of Congress Cataloging-in-Publication Data

Parks, Malcolm Ross.
Personal relationships and personal networks / Malcolm R. Parks.—
1st ed.
p. cm. — (LEA's series on personal relationships)
Includes bibliographical references and index.
ISBN 0-8058-0327-0 (cloth : alk. paper)
ISBN 0-8058-6104-1 (pbk. : alk. paper)
ISBN 1-4106-1438-7 (e book)
1. Interpersonal relations. 2. Social networks. I. Title. II. Series.

HM1106.P367 200
302.3'4—dc22   2006003201

                                                                      CIP
10 9 8 7 6 5 4 3 2 1

Contents

Series Foreword

Steve Duck, Series Editor
University of Iowa

Since its inception, the Personal Relationships series from Lawrence Erlbaum Associates has sought to review the progress in the academic work on relationships with respect to a broad array of issues, and to do so in an accessible manner that also illustrates its practical value. The LEA series already includes books intended to pass on the accumulated scholarship to the next generation of students and to those who deal with relationship issues in the broader world beyond the academy. The series thus not only comprises monographs and other academic resources exemplifying the multidisciplinary nature of this area, but also books suitable for use in the growing numbers of courses on relationships and in the growing number of professions that deal with relationship issues.

The series has the goal of providing a comprehensive and current survey of theory and research in personal relationships through the careful analysis of the problems encountered and solved in research, yet it also considers the systematic application of that work in a practical context. These resources not only are intended to be comprehensive assessments of progress on particular "hot" and relevant topics, but also have already shown that they are significant influences on the future directions and development of the study of personal relationships and application of its insights. Although each volume is well centered, authors all attempt to place the respective topics in the broader context of other research on relationships and within a range of wider disciplinary traditions. The series already offers incisive and forward-looking reviews and also demonstrates the broader theoretical implications of relationships for the range of disciplines from which the research originates. Collectively, the volumes include original studies, reviews of relevant theory and research, and new theories oriented toward the understanding of personal relationships, both in themselves and within the context of broader theories of family process, social psychology, and communication.

Reflecting the diverse composition of personal relationship study, readers in numerous disciplines—social psychology, communication, sociology, family studies, developmental psychology, clinical psychology, personality, counseling, women's studies, gerontology, and others—will find valuable and insightful perspectives in the series.

Apart from the academic scholars who research the dynamics and processes of relationships, there are many other people whose work takes them up against the operation of relationships in the real world. For such people as nurses, the police, teachers, therapists, lawyers, drug and alcohol counselors, marital counselors, the priesthood, and those who take care of the elderly, a number of issues routinely arise concerning the ways in which relationships affect the people whom they serve and guide. Examples are (a) the role of loneliness in illness and the ways to circumvent it; (b) the complex impact of family and peer relationships on a drug-dependent's attempts to give up the drug; (c) the role of playground unpopularity on a child's learning; (d) the issues involved in dealing with the relational side of chronic illness; (e) the management of conflict in marriage; (f) the establishment of good rapport between physicians and seriously ill patients; (g) the support of the bereaved; (h) the correction of violent styles of behavior in dating or marriage; and even (i) the relationships formed between jurors in extended trials, as these may influence a jury's decisions. Each of these is a problem that may confront some of the aforementioned professionals as part of their daily concerns and each demonstrates the far-reaching influences of relationship processes on much else in life that is presently theorized independently of relationship considerations.

Malcolm Parks' volume on social networks is a timely example of the ways in which this series seeks to promote the academic and theoretical developments that have been occurring in the field of personal relationships while also showing the practical value of such work. Networks surround and enfold us all, whether networks of friends, neighborhood connections, networks in the workplace, families, societies, or nations. The influence of networks is broad and deep, as Parks shows, and many activities that we have all too often assumed to be "individual decisions" are in fact subtly affected by network forces. For example, the selections of friends and romantic partners is often assisted, facilitated, or rendered possible in the first place by our connections with third parties who make the introductions. At work and elsewhere, "what we know" depends on "who we know" and the means of spreading information through networks is a well studied phenomenon finding new expression these days in the market interest in word of mouth (WOM), by which information about products spreads through networks of acquaintances and so influences purchasing choices. In his presentation of research on network influence and network operation, Parks offers an up-to-the-minute analysis of these issues and updates our understanding of the role of networks on personal relationship that have all too often been seen simply (and simplistically) at the dyadic level of analysis. The broader ramifications of the work in practical terms are also significant for all of us. None of us escapes network influence and the better we understand it, the better we can either resist or enhance it.

The book is a fine combination of academic writing and the delightfully humane, skillfully blending high levels of analysis with a truly inspiring and insightful flow that addresses the real-life practical implications and applications of the issues with some profound insights and wry observations. It is a welcome addition to the series and moves the field forward in all senses that the series has sought to do.

Preface

PERSONAL RELATIONSHIPS AND PERSONAL NETWORKS

Think about your best friend for a moment. Picture that person and what makes that relationship important to you. Or, think about a romantic partner and what makes that relationship important to you. Then picture the other people who are important to you, to whom you feel close or particularly connected. Together, these people make up the core of your personal social network. Now suppose we asked your friend or romantic partner to do the same exercise—to think of the people to whom he or she felt particularly close. Imagine who these people might be. Perhaps your friend or romantic partner would list some of the same people you did. The list might also contain other people you know less well, along with some you may only know of, and some you may not know at all.

These thought exercises bring us to the heart of what this book is about. The number of close personal relationships a person has at any one time varies widely, but the number is usually small—typically less than 10 to 20 people. Yet, as I illustrate in the opening chapter, these relationships profoundly shape our sense of self-worth, have a significant impact on mental and physical health, and are linked to a variety of larger social and economic phenomena in ways we rarely consider. Because of this, the study of personal relationships has attracted a growing number of students, researchers, and professionals with applied interests. They come from a wide variety of disciplines including communication, psychology, sociology, anthropology, family studies, clinical psychology, public health, nursing, education, and social work. Although the book presents original research, I have endeavored to write in a way that makes the findings accessible and draws out implications that may be applied across many of these disciplines. In addition, I have attempted to speak on a practical level to those seeking to be more thoughtful and effective in their own personal lives.

My goal is to advance a largely unexplored perspective on personal relationships. Efforts to understand friendships, romantic relationships, and other personal relationships have traditionally focused on the individual characteristics of the participants (e.g., personality, attractiveness), the way these characteristics match up (e.g., similarity, compatibility), or the pattern of interaction between the participants themselves (e.g., whether self-disclosure is reciprocal, how conflicts are managed).

What is missing, and what this book is about, is research linking the participants' feelings and actions within a given personal relationship to the larger social context surrounding it. Our personal relationships do not exist in isolation from one another. Instead they make up a social network or context that in turn becomes inextricably linked to the initiation, development, maintenance and dissolution of any given relationship within it.

To see how this happens, we first need to identify the essential dimensions along which relationships change as they develop or deteriorate. Once we know this, then we can consider which elements of social networks might be most relevant for understanding personal relationships. Both of these issues are addressed in the second chapter. This chapter lays the foundation for a social contextual theory of personal relationships. One of the central tenets of this theory is that relationships exist in communication. They are made, unmade, and remade in the interactions between the participants.

The social contextual perspective provides a new way to think about some of the most basic questions about how relationships form. Why do particular people meet? How do relationships get started? As the research presented in chapter 3 demonstrates, people who begin relationships may have been moving toward each other in a larger social network long before they actually meet for the first time. Moreover, their first meeting and their first steps along the path toward a close relationship are often greatly influenced by the actions of network members.

Social network factors continue to be closely linked with the development of personal relationships long after the participants meet. The studies presented in next two chapters (chaps. 4 and 5) demonstrate that social network factors are highly associated with the development of both friendships and romantic relationships. Participants in both types of relationships feel closer, more committed, and communicate more frequently when they also have greater amounts of contact with the members of each other's personal networks and when they believe that network members support their relationship.

The studies presented in the chapters that follow (chaps. 6 and 7) explore the generality of the social contextual perspective. Are social network factors involved in the personal relationships of adolescents and young adults in the same way? Does the social contextual model apply equally well to romantic relationships and same-sex friendships? Are there important sex differences in the relational development, in contact and support from network members, and in the association between relationship and network factors? Do network factors play a different role in relationships among people from different ethnic groups than they play in relationships among people of the same ethnic group? The answers to these questions contained several surprises, but also showed that the social context model was applicable to a number of different types of people and relationships.

Interactions with and among network members are actually far more complex than most of our theories suppose. That complexity is the subject of chapter 8. Relational participants do not simply react to network members. Instead they actively "work the network" by drawing on a wide range of strategies to manage the dilemmas of life in the network setting, to promote the desired image of their relationship, and to cope with network members whom they dislike, but cannot avoid.

The social contextual perspective also gives us new insights about how relationships deteriorate and end. Turnover in personal relationships, even close ones, is widespread. Yet, from a social contextual perspective, many relational endings are not really endings, but rather transformations into another kind of relationship. In chapter 9, we explore how social networks are involved in the deterioration of personal relationships as well in the transformation of some relationships into other types of relationships. This chapter completes the circle, showing how the changes at the ends of relationships restructure social networks in ways that promote the creation of new relationships.

The final chapter begins with a brief summary of the key findings and a general model of linkages between relational development and social network factors. It then turns to the question of what drives change in relationships. Is it driven primarily by the participants themselves or is it driven by the changes in the networks surrounding the relationship? The answer is both, but social contextual theory offers a surprising interpretation of what that means. The answer not only addresses a fundamental theoretic issue in the social sciences, but also gives us a way to link the microsocial world of personal experience to the macrosocial world of global society. This is not intended as a purely abstract exercise. The bulk of the final chapter is devoted to practical implications for how we can enhance our skills for working in networks, become better parents, more effectively help those in need, more effectively pursue goals in business and civic life, and reduce hostility between groups. Cultivating a network perspective ultimately helps us appreciate that we are more connected to the world than we think and that our personal choices as social actors have power and consequence far beyond what we imagine.

ACKNOWLEDGMENTS

A brief comment about terminology is warranted. For the most part, I have used the term *sex* when referring to specific, direct comparisons of male and female subjects and *gender* when referring to differences or similarities more generally. This will strike some as confusing. Some would advocate gender as the preferred term, whereas others would prefer to use sex when referring to biological differences and gender when referring to differences shaped by social and cultural forces. However, as I argue in chapter 7, advances in research are rapidly blurring traditional distinctions between the biological and the social. This, in turn, calls into question efforts to establish meaningful distinctions between sex and gender.

This book itself is the result of a long and complex set of interactions within a network. It reflects the good fortune to be raised by parents who both valued and modeled thoughtful argument and good conversation. It is legacy to early mentors—Joe Ayres, Roosevelt Martin, Bill Wilmot, Gerry Miller. Tom Farrell always drew me into discussions of the larger implications of my work. This book would not have been possible without the assistance, insight, and energy of my students. Many of them generously gave me permission to use the examples and stories that enriched my own thinking. No one deserves more credit than Lee Eggert, who was not only instrumental in helping me collect two of the data sets, but also first saw the potential of a larger project. Karen Barnes, Charlotte Stan, Mara Adelman, Lisa Riveland, and April Trees were also instrumental in gathering data. Daena Goldsmith was generous with data and insights for chapter 8. Jason Laramie brought the models to life with his illustrations, while Jerry Herting and Elaine Thompson guided me on a number of technical features of the analysis.

Every book is a triumph of persistence over distraction and this one more than most. Along the way, my career shifted from researcher/teacher to academic administrator. Although there is no better place to hone one's appreciation of the complexities of social networks than in the senior administration of a modern public research university, my new responsibilities took me far from this project. So I am especially grateful for all that Alvin Kwiram and Craig Hogan did to encourage and support its completion. This work would also not have been possible without the contributions of Arthur Whiteley and all the others who built and staff the Helen Riaboff Whiteley Center at Friday Harbor. I am particularly indebted to Steve Duck, whose encouragement and insights far exceeded all hopes for a series editor. Gratitude flows to my wife, Monica, most of all. She knew when to ask and when not to ask about my progress; when to encourage, when to make room, and when to take me away. This book is dedicated to Monica and to my daughter Ellen.

Framing Personal Relationships

We humans are social animals down to our very cells. Nature did not make us noble loners. Instead we are in our most natural state when we are with families, lovers, enemies, friends, acquaintances, fellow workers, leaders, followers, and all the rest who light the constellations of human affiliation. Our social character is much more than a matter of living arrangements. It is the essence of what we are, as Pasternak (1958) emphasized in *Doctor Zhivago*:

> What is it about you that you have always known as yourself? Your kidneys? Your liver? Your blood vessels? No. However far back you go in your memory, it is always in some external, active manifestation of yourself that you come across your identity—in the work of your hands, in your family, in other people. You in others—this is your soul. This is what your consciousness has breathed and lived on and enjoyed throughout your life … You have always been in others and you will remain in others …. This will be you—the you that enters the future and becomes part of it that enters the future and becomes part of it. (p. 60)

Often the things that we hold closest in our lives remain the most elusive. So it is with our personal relationships. For some, personal relationships represent mysteries that either cannot or should not be unraveled. Some prefer the mystery, believing that a scholar's understanding will somehow spoil their personal relationships. Scientific research, however, is no more likely to spoil personal relationships than understanding the principles of refraction is likely to spoil the beauty of a rainbow. If anything, the history of science teaches us that the quest for scientific understanding enriches our appreciation and fills us with new wonder.

Scientific research over the past 40 years, and especially over the last 20, has indeed enriched our appreciation of the role played by close relationships. I begin with a survey of some of those findings in this chapter. I will not fully summarize the research in any one area but I will show that close relationships are central among our public values, pivotal in larger societal arenas, and critical to our mental and physical health. In the next section of the chapter, I review the basic perspectives available for the understanding of personal relationships. These perspectives have also evolved over time. Although a healthy diversity of views remains, I believe there is increasing recognition that our personal relationships do not exist in isolation from one another. Understanding how our personal relationships influence one another and how changes in one relationship are linked to the participants' other relationships is the goal of this book. I introduce what I call the *social contextual perspective* at the end of this chapter and explicate it in greater detail in chapter 2.

THE SIGNIFICANCE OF PERSONAL RELATIONSHIPS

Public Values and Personal Relationships

In the most direct sense, personal relationships are important because we think they are. It is certainly true that both the individual and society depend on many types of relationships besides close ones and that personal development and creativity often flourish during periods of comparative social isolation (Parks, 1982; Storr, 1988). Nonetheless, most people still view their personal relationships as the primary centers of meaning and well-being in their lives. Close relationships contribute to our lives in ways that financial success, social status, and physical health do not (Chapple & Badger, 1989). Public opinion polls over the last 30 years consistently show that nothing ranks ahead of relationships with family and friends as sources of meaning in people's lives (e.g., Moore, 2003).

The belief that personal relationships are vital extends across all age groups. Young people, for instance, often believe that divorce, loss of friends, and other disruptions in their personal relationships will have long-lasting negative effects on their lives (Riesch, Jacobson, & Tosi, 1994). Looking back over their lives, the elderly often point to their close relationships as their greatest sources of satisfaction and accomplishment (Long, Anderson, & Williams, 1990).

Our public discourse regularly honors these values. Former First Lady Barbara Bush, for example, delivered this eloquent reminder in her 1990 commencement speech to the graduates of Wellesley College:

> As important as your obligations as a doctor, a lawyer or a business leader may be, your human connections with spouses, with children, with friends, are the most important investment you will ever make. At the end of your life, you will never regret not having passed one more test, not winning one more verdict or not closing one more deal. You will regret time not spent with a husband, a child, a friend, or a parent. (Butterfield, 1990, p. 1)

The significance we attribute to personal relationships extends far beyond polling results and public exhortations. It reaches down to our basic beliefs about the forces that cause illness. In their now classic study of heart attack victims Croog and Levine (1977) found that nearly one third believed that marital problems had been a major cause of their heart attack. And just over one third of the victims who had children believed that difficulty with the children had been an important contributor to their illness. These views were shared both by male victims and their spouses. These beliefs were also persistent, showing up again in a survey a year after the original heart attack. Most important, these beliefs were well placed. As I show in a later section, more recent research has demonstrated that there is indeed a link between disrupted patterns of personal relationships and physical health.

Personal Relationships in Society

Most of us think of our personal relationships as just that—personal. Yet our closest relationships have public as well as private dimensions and, as such, are tied to societal issues that transcend the individual concerns of participants. Some connections are obvious. Most children are raised within the context of a set of personal relationships. Beyond this, however, our personal relationships are tied to larger societal concerns in at least four arenas. They are primary sites of economic decision making and consumption. They play a special role in the process of organizational innovation. They act as reference points and training grounds for participation in larger social institutions. Finally, their disruption creates massive social service costs that are paid by society as a whole.

Personal Relationships and Consumer Activity. Personal relationships are big business. Forecasts of Valentine's Day spending appear each year in business publications. The impact of world events is duly noted, as in 2003, when newspapers predicted rising prices for Valentine's Day chocolate as the result of civil war in the Ivory Coast, the world's largest cocoa producer (Hagenbaugh, 2003). Efforts to market the holiday extend to nearly every corner of the consumer economy. Traditional gifts of chocolate and flowers are joined by jewelry, private dinners, exotic trips, and occasionally, downright odd gifts. A few years ago, for instance, one company offered a "Love Me Doo" manure service for organic gardeners on Valentine's Day (Krafft, 1994). Groups once thought outside the Valentine's Day market, such as homosexual males, are increasingly targeted by advertisers (Newman & Nelson, 1996). Even modest gestures become monumental in the aggregate. In 2005, for example, Americans exchanged over 200 million Valentine's Day cards, nearly one card for every person in the total U.S. population. And according to the National Retail Federation, Valentine's Day spending in the United States in 2005 exceeded $13 billion (Weber, 2005). Valentine's Day is second only to Mother's Day in terms of restaurant business and flower sales. Almost half of adult Americans send Mother's Day greetings and over one third of those with middle or higher incomes send flowers (Waldrop, 1990, 1992). Total retail flower sales in the United States were estimated at $18.5 billion in 2001 and, according to consumer tracking surveys, over 90% of these sales were intended for people with whom the buyer had a close relationship ("Size of Floral Industry," 2003). To give one last example, Mother's Day, Father's Day, and school graduations combine to make late spring the second busiest period, after Christmas, for sales of books (Kinsella, 1996). In short, the "relational holidays" represent major retail events, not just in the United states, but in many other countries as well (e.g., McMurdy, 2003).

Weddings, too, are significant economic events in the United States as well as other countries with burgeoning consumer economies. Commercial wedding services that arrange ceremonies, presents, photographs, and banquets have boomed in the growing economies of India and China (Basu, 2005; Yang, 1994). Between 1997 and 2002, for example, the average cost of a wedding in Shanghai nearly doubled to $18,000 in U.S. dollars ("Wedding Costs," 2002). Families in the oil rich United Arab Emirates frequently take out loans and borrow from friends in order to meet the social expectation for an extravagant wedding. The problem became so severe that the government established a fund to curb the impact of rising marriage costs on families (K. Evans, 1996).

Weddings are very big business in the larger consumer economies of the world, particularly in Japan and United States. Estimates of average wedding costs in Japan vary dramatically with some exceeding $100,000. The most conservative guesses are that wedding costs in Japan are typically no more than expensive weddings in the United States. Estimates of the average cost of a wedding and honeymoon in the United States hover between $20,000 and $30,000 ("Wedding and Honeymoon Statistics," 2003). One way to appreciate these figures is to consider that the amount Americans spend on weddings each year exceeds the gross domestic products of approximately two thirds of the countries in the world.

Aside from the wedding itself, the decision to marry has economic consequences for home sales, the sales of major and minor appliances, and the sales of truckloads of other consumer goods. Ironically, the decision to divorce sometimes produces exactly the same economic consequences. And because most people remarry, the divorce business and the wedding business are locked together in a yin and yang of unending economic consumption.

Whole industries have grown up around our desire to appear physically and hence relationally attractive. In 2001, Americans spent $6.9 billion on cosmetic surgery (National Clearinghouse of Plastic Surgery Statistics, 2001). They also spent $52.7 billion on personal care and cosmetic products and an additional $39 billion on weight loss programs and products ("Personal Care," 2001; "U.S. Weight Loss," 2002). Skin-care products alone generated over $50 billion in worldwide sales in 2004 (Tsiantar, 2005). Certainly some of this money can be attributed to valid health concerns, but much more of it can fairly be attributed to the desire to establish or maintain personal relationships with others.

Close personal relationships also influence spending in more subtle ways. People often decide where to shop or what services to purchase on the basis of advice from friends and family. For instance, the choice of holiday gifts for friends or family members is typically based on suggestions from third parties or on perceptions of how giving the gift will appear to others in one's social circle (Lowrey, Otnes, & Ruth, 2004). Although people may say they select physicians on the basis of their expertise and the way they manage their practices, it appears most of the information used to make these judgments comes from the opinions of friends and relatives ("Picking Physicians," 1986).

These examples only hint at the complex interplay between economic choices and personal relationships. We try to change relationships through purchases of products and services that have been carefully crafted and advertised to appeal to, or perhaps create, our relational ideals. We celebrate relationships through consumption. We compete in order to improve our status in the eyes of close friends and relatives. We seek the advice of close friends and relatives before spending our money. All these linkages between economic choice and personal relationships are experienced as private matters, but in the aggregate, they have profound effects on the economy as a whole.

Personal Relationships and Organizational Innovation. Personal relationships also play a pivotal role in the way that new goods, services, and ideas are created. Innovation fires the engines of modern consumer economies. Organizations must innovate on a more or less continuous basis if they are to survive ever increasing global competition, accelerating technological change, and ever more demanding consumers.

Different kinds of relationships are important at different points in the innovation process. The simple spread of information about new ideas seems to be facilitated best by the media and by our weaker, less personal relationships, our "weak ties" (e.g., Granovetter, 1973; E. M. Rogers, 2003). But there is a large difference between simply hearing about a new idea and developing a new product or service. In the workplace innovation occurs most frequently as a collective process. Even the mythic lone inventor must convince others to implement, manufacture, market, and sell his or her innovation. Thus innovation becomes rooted in talk about new ideas. By definition, however, talking about new ideas entails risk and uncertainty. Discussing a new idea opens one to the possibility of disagreement and rejection. As a result, talk about new ideas tends to be quite selective in the workplace. People are likely to limit such discussions to those they already trust, to their closer, more personal relationships.

This idea is illustrated nicely by a series of studies by Albrecht and her colleagues (Albrecht & Hall, 1991a, 1991b; Albrecht & Ropp, 1984). They examined innovation talk in several different kinds of organizations including a school system, a research unit, a hospital, an electronics manufacturing plant, a social service agency, and an engineering firm. In each case they found that up to two thirds of the talk about new ideas occurred in more personal work relationships. The willingness to talk about new ideas was strongly correlated with trust and the willingness to share personal and social interests. Studies of innovation in other countries also point to the importance of informal relationships in industrial firms (Kivimäki et al., 2000). Friendships appear to play a particularly critical role in helping people locate new sources of information, reformulate problems, and validate their ideas (Cross, Rice, & Parker, 2001).

These findings not only underscore the importance of personal relationships in the workplace, but also help explain why more formal innovation programs such as "integrated product teams" or "quality circles" often fail when they are imposed on workers who do not already have established relationships with one another. Nor is it enough simply to create common spaces where informal interaction can occur and then hope that innovation will follow. Organizational leaders must take an active role in supporting the underlying relational environment that ultimately promotes innovation.

Personal relationships play one final role in the innovation process. They usually supply the money. Although a deal of attention has been given to the role of venture capital firms in supporting new companies, the fact is that most of the financial backing for new companies comes from the founders' friends and families. Only 12% of America's fastest growing private companies in 2000 had received venture capital during their early phases. The rest relied on money raised through personal contacts. Overall, founders and their friends and families contributed just over 70% of the $144.6 billion dollars invested in new companies in the United States in 2001 (Bygrave, 2003).

Personal Relationships and Socialization. Perhaps the most obvious way in which personal relationships are linked to greater societal concerns is through their role as agents of socialization. They act as training grounds and reference points for participation in larger social systems (Goode, 1982). Family supervision and attachment, for example, appear to be among the best predictors of whether male adolescents will engage in criminal activity (e.g., Goldstein, Davis-Kean, & Eccles, 2005; Hoffmann, 2003). Family supervision and attachment are also among the best predictors of whether adolescents smoke, drink, or use drugs (e.g., Augustyn & Simons-Morton, 1995; D. R. Wright & Fitzpatrick, 2004).

Family and friends remain primary reference points for us even as adults and even in areas where society already has institutions to guide us. In one survey of over 18,000 American women, for example, 90% said that they would seek out a friend if they needed guidance on a moral issue. About 33% said they would also turn to their husbands. Only about 3% said they would consult a member of the clergy ("Clergy Not a Big Help," 1989). Clergy and other formal helpers also lagged far behind family and friends when 1,000 corporate executives were asked to whom they would turn if they faced ethical questions ("What Bosses Think About Corporate Ethics," 1988). Only 1% said that they would turn to a member of the clergy. Although many (44%) of these executives reported that they relied only on themselves, nearly an equal number (39%) named either friends or spouses as their most trusted confidants.

Personal Relationships and Social Costs. On the negative side, disrupted personal relationships pose serious social and economic costs that all citizens pay in the form of lost productivity and higher taxes. Although easily illustrated, the overall magnitude of these costs is difficult to determine. This is partly because relational disruptions fan out to produce myriad social effects. A divorce, for example, may increase the demand for counseling services, community supported child care, and medical assistance. Depending on the circumstances, it may also create new demands on everything ranging from the schools to child welfare services. Beyond this, new demands for social services for the elderly may be created when divorces among their adult children take time and money that might have been used to aid them.

The social costs of disrupted relationships are also difficult to quantify because our measures of relational disruption are so imprecise. Most calculations of social effects of relational disruption are based on comparisons of married persons to separated or divorced persons. The standard assumption is that an intact marriage, no matter how dysfunctional, is less disrupted than a relationship characterized by separation or divorce. Although this may be true generally, it ignores the fact that intact, but dysfunctional, conflict-ridden relationships also create significant costs for society as a whole. Thus our procedures are inadequate and, if anything, probably underestimate the true social costs of disrupted personal relationships. Even so, the costs of disrupted or inadequate personal relationships can be seen in at least two areas: productivity in the workplace and performance in the classroom.

Private life and work life are not separate social worlds; they interpenetrate in nearly every way. Difficulty on the job, for example, has long been recognized as a source of marital difficulties (Komarovsky, 1971; Westman, 2001). By the same token, satisfaction and productivity on the job are linked with the availability and stability of personal relationships. People with supportive families and co-workers are more likely to show up for work, enjoy their jobs, and be committed to remaining on the job (L. A. King, Mattimore, D. W. King, & Adams, 1995; Parker & Kulik, 1995). Conversely, separation, divorce, and low marital quality are associated with absenteeism, greater job stress, and lower job satisfaction (Keller, 1983; S. J. Rogers & May, 2003). Moreover, the stress surrounding a divorce is often manifested as difficulty in the workplace (Schultz & Henderson, 1985). Men and women alike report greater job satisfaction when their spouses are supportive, but spousal support may have a greater impact on women's job satisfaction whereas co-worker support may be more important for men (Krokoff, 1991; Roxburgh, 1999).

The costs of disordered personal relationships also extend into the classroom. Although there are numerous age and gender differences, as well as extenuating circumstances, the picture that emerges from the research is relatively consistent (Allison & Furstenberg, 1989; M. D. R. Evans, Kelley, & Wanner, 2001; Guttmann, Geva, & Gefen, 1988; Ham, 2004; Nielsen, 1993). Children whose parents are divorced or have other difficulties with personal relationships present the school system with a wide range of emotional, behavioral, and disciplinary problems. Beyond whatever real problems they bring to school, children whose parents are divorced are perceived in negative terms by students and teachers alike, thus raising the additional problems created by negative self-fulfilling prophecies.

Academic performance and adjustment suffer when children experience disordered family relationships. Compared with children from intact families, for example, children whose parents are divorced experience greater test anxiety, give up sooner on tasks, and are more likely to miss school (Guttmann, 1987; Guttmann, Amir, & Katz, 1987; Reid, 1984). These children generally have lower grades and score lower on aptitude and achievement tests (Allison & Furstenberg, 1989; Kaye, 1988; Mednick, Baker, Reznick, & Hocevar, 1990). Although divorce may have become less stigmatizing in recent decades, the negative impact of divorce on academic achievement appears to have increased rather than decreased (M. D. R. Evans et al., 2001; Reifman, Villa, Amans, Rethinam, & Telesca, 2001).

Ultimately we all share in the economic costs of children's disordered relationships. The immediate costs include higher initial training requirements for educators, money for remedial programs, money for counseling programs, and money for increased disciplinary needs. In addition we should count both the education lost by the children from disordered families and the education lost by other children while teachers minister to the needs of children from disordered families. These costs fan out into all sectors of society, displaying themselves most visibly in the higher prices needed to support a less productive, less innovative workforce, in higher social service costs, in higher insurance premiums, and in higher taxes.

In sum our personal relationships are not retreats from society. Rather they are junctions through which the social and economic life of our society pulses. This is not to adopt a privatized or tribal view of society. Society exists in both personal and impersonal relationships. But our personal relationships do function as hubs of economic decision making and marketing, as sources of new ideas for organizations, as training grounds and reference points for participation in larger social institutions, and, when they are inadequate or become disordered, as sources of social and economic costs that we all pay.

Personal Relationships and Health

Inadequate or disordered interpersonal relationships can kill, sometimes slowly, sometimes swiftly. Although the idea that physical and mental well-being are linked to the quality of social life dates from antiquity, the connection has been demonstrated in convincing fashion by research in the life and social sciences over the last 40 years. Classic works, such as Alexander's (1950) *Psychosomatic Medicine*, perpetuated the idea that specific psychological conflicts were associated with specific diseases. Although this view is still influential in the popular press, researchers have now moved beyond this rather mechanical model. In fact the entire concept of a *psychosomatic disease* may be misleading because it implies that some diseases have psychological components while others do not (Plaut & Friedman, 1981). It is more accurate to think of interpersonal and psychological factors as altering the person's susceptibility to illness or injury in general rather than as causing specific types of disease.

By the late 1980s, research evidence on the dangers of inadequate or disordered personal relationships was as strong as the evidence against cigarette smoking was when the United States government issued its first warnings in 1964 (J. House, Landis, & Umberson, 1988). But even this comparison is probably conservative. More linkages come into view when we fully liberate ourselves from the biomedical and psychosomatic models.

I believe that there are at least five interrelated pathways linking the quality of our personal relationships with our physical and mental health. Disrupted or inadequate personal relationships are associated with: (a) social skill deficits, (b) violence and suicide, (c) stress-induced illnesses of the cardiovascular system, (d) malfunctions in the immune system, and (e) risky health practices.

Social Skill Deficits. As social animals, we are born with a strong foundation for the acquisition of social skills. Yet additional learning and practice are required for nearly all of the social skills needed to manage complex interactions—perspective-taking, turn-taking, regulating emotional expression, constructing persuasive strategies, managing conflict, and so on. Interactions with family and peers in childhood and adolescence are among the most important arenas in which we develop these skills. When these early relationships are disordered, then important learning opportunities are lost or distorted and a variety of illnesses may result. This means that many illnesses, particularly mental illnesses, can properly be thought of as interpersonal illnesses (Segrin, 2001).

The damaging effects of interactions with those with poor social skills can be found all across the literature on mental illness. Children who are rejected by their parents, for example, are more likely to have difficulty regulating their own emotional expression and engaging in interaction (Cohn, Campbell, Matias, & Hopkins, 1990). Similarly, parents who are simultaneously highly controlling and yet unable to express affection toward their children may be setting their children up for lifelong deficits in social skills that manifest themselves in a wide range of mental health and relational problems (Hudson & Rapee, 2000). Adolescents with a history of negative interactions with parents, for example, are more likely to behave coercively and abusively with dating partners years later (K. J. Kim, Conger, Lorenz, & Elder, 2001).

This is not to suggest that people are necessarily victims of their early relationships. Early relationships matter, but critics have rightly faulted approaches to mental illnesses that place too much importance on childhood relationships (e.g., Coyne, 1999). Regardless of when they occur, interpersonal relationships serve as arenas for developing or damaging social skills. They are "rolling laboratories" in which the level of skills found in relationships at one point in life help determine the level of skills in relationships at the next point. Social skill deficits can thus be self-perpetuating.

In some cases, it is not merely the lack of positive models that leads to mental and physical illness, but the presence of negative models. Sexual abuse, for instance, is thought to be a precursor to eating disorders partly because it reduces its victims' sense of social competency (Mallinckrodt, McCreary, & Robertson, 1995). It is no wonder, then, that physical and sexual abuse in childhood are strongly linked to mental and physical illnesses across the adult life cycle (Dinwiddie et al., 2000).

Violence and Suicide.   Violence and abuse in personal relationships pose profound problems for society (for a survey, see Harvey & Weber, 2002). Those with inadequate or dysfunctional personal relationships are particularly susceptible to violence, either by their own hand or the hands of others. Some simply carry violent patterns from previous relationships. Violence in dating relationships, for example, is linked both to a history of family violence and to having friends who treat their dating partners abusively (Arriaga & Foshee, 2004). Similarly, spouses in violent marriages frequently grew up in families with a history of violence and abuse (Bergman & Brismar, 1993). Even nonviolent families may fail to provide positive models of conflict management. Parental neglect and divorce are also precursors of violence and abuse in young adults' romantic relationships (Billingham & Notebaert, 1993; Straus & Savage, 2005). People in dysfunctional relationships are themselves more likely to be victims of violence. They may have more people mad at them, but they may also just be more vulnerable and isolated. For example, school children who do not have a reciprocated friendship are more likely to be bullied by their classmates (Boulton, Trueman, Chau, Whitehand, & Amatya, 1999). More generally, data both from the United States and other countries indicates that people who are divorced or separated are far more likely to be homicide victims than people who are married (Lynch, 1977; M. Wilson & Daly, 1993).

Over a century ago Durkheim (1897/1951) hypothesized that people committed suicide because they were no longer integrated into the larger social institutions that give their lives meaning. Although we now consider suicide from a number of different perspectives, it is clear that being or feeling disconnected from friends and family contributes to suicide. Some of the most disturbing evidence comes from counselors who report that suicidal behavior among elementary school children is frequently a response to the divorce, illness, or death of parents or other significant relatives (D. E. Matter & R. M. Matter, 1984). In her study of people whom the police had rescued from suicide in Vienna, Margarethe von Andics (1947) painted the attempted suicide as a person who was either unable to form lasting relationships or unable to recover from their loss. More broadly based studies also support the link between suicide and inadequate or disordered personal relationships (Beautrais, Joyce, & Mulder, 1996; Trout, 1980). Demographic data reveals that divorced people have consistently had higher suicide rates over the last 25 years than people who are married, despite the fact that divorce has become more socially acceptable during that time (Stack, 1990).

Cardiovascular Disease. Poor personal relationships break people's hearts—literally. A large and varied body of evidence testifies to the effects of dysfunctional, inadequate personal relationships on cardiovascular disease. The conflict-laden, aggressive, unsupportive, and unsupportable "Type A" personality was formally recognized as a risk factor in coronary disease by the National Blood, Heart, and Lung Institute in the early 1980s. Global personality types, however, are crude measures because they are so far removed from social interaction itself. And indeed, the evidence linking Type A behavior to cardiovascular disease is far from consistent (Suls & Wan, 1993).

More powerful predictors of cardiovascular disease emerge when we look at the give and take of the social support process. Cardiovascular activity appears to be quite sensitive to changes in the nature of interpersonal communication (Lynch, 1985). Blood pressure changes less in reaction to stress, for example, in children whose family communication patterns are open and emotionally expressive, than in families where interpersonal communication is closed (L. B. Wright et al., 1993). Adult men reported less angina pectoris (severe pain radiating from the heart area to the left shoulder and arm) when they perceived their wives as supportive than when they perceived their wives as unsupportive (Medalie & Goldbourt, 1976).

All this implies that death from cardiovascular disease should be more common among those with disrupted or inadequate personal relationships. And indeed it is. Studies in a number of countries consistently reveal that cardiovascular disease is both more common and more likely to be fatal among people who experience high levels of family conflict, are divorced, separated, have few friends, and/or who have little involvement in informal and formal groups (Ebrahim, Wannamethee, McCallum, Walker, & Shaper, 1995; Orth-Gomer et al., 2000; Rosengren et al., 2004). These are not small risk factors. High psychosocial stress poses risks as great as high blood pressure and obesity.

The exact mechanism by which psychosocial stress increases the risk of heart disease is not yet well understood. Several researchers have found evidence linking psychosocial stress to abnormalities in vessel walls, constricted blood flow, inflammation, increased clotting, and a reduced ability to break down clots (Kop et al., 2001; Lewthwaite, Owen, Coates, Henderson, & Steptoe, 2002; von Kanel, Mills, Fainman, & Dimsdale, 2001). Another promising line of research has found that people with chronic social stress experience premature cell aging, another factor implicated in heart attacks (Brouilette, Singh, Thompson, Goodall, & Samani, 2003; Epel et al., 2004).

Immune System Malfunctions. The immune system is our body's private physician, curing and protecting us from a host of diseases (Desowitz, 1987). Although the complex interplay of the immune system's components is far from understood, research over the last 40 years demonstrates convincingly that disruptions in significant relationships cause significant disruptions in the immune system. This effect takes at least two forms: immunosuppression and autoimmune disease.

In everyday language, we would say that a person experiencing immunosuppression has a low resistance to disease. The ability to form an immune response to foreign cells or toxins entering the body is reduced. This occurs in large part because of disruptions in the various neuropeptides, neurotransmiters, and neuroendocrines that regulate immune responses (Fleshner & Laudenslager, 2004). People are simply more likely to get sick during periods of interpersonal stress because their immune systems are not as effective at warding off and recovering from disease. This was illustrated quite clearly in an early study by Meyer and Haggerty (1962) who tracked respiratory infections in 16 families over the course of a year. They found that respiratory illnesses were four times more common during periods of stressful family interaction than during less stressful periods.

Studies conducted over the past 30 years have consistently shown that chronic stress reduces immunity (Segerstrom & G. E. Miller, 2004). Immunosuppression has been associated with a variety of interpersonal and psychological conditions including depression, loneliness, family conflict, role conflict, separation from family and peers, divorce, and bereavement (Kaplan, 1991). Moreover, the consequences of this immunosuppression can be fatal. Divorced people are, for example, are far more likely to die of pneumonia than married people (Lynch, 1977).

The second major effect of interpersonal factors on the immune system is to stimulate autoimmune disease. In these diseases the body attacks itself. The immune system fails to distinguish properly between what is self and what is foreign. Consequently, the immune system produces antibodies that mistakenly injure the body's own tissue. The onset and severity of autoimmune diseases appears to vary with interpersonal events. Rheumatoid arthritis, for instance, progresses more rapidly and is more disabling among people who experience high levels of anger, depression, or stress (Latman & Walls, 1996; Solomon, 1985). These emotional disturbances may be caused by a variety of factors, of course, but the most common stressor identified in the literature is disrupted relationships with spouses or parents. Conversely, the presence of supportive relationships, especially ones in which the interaction helps the sufferer feel in greater control of his or her disease, is associated with better coping and less severe episodes (e.g., Evers, Kraaimaat, Geene, Jacobs, & Bijlsma, 2003; Holtzman, Newth, & Delongis, 2004).

Just as a lack of support worsens autoimmune disease, the disease itself limits social participation. Thus people with rheumatoid arthritis report significant reductions across the entire range of their social activities (P. P. Katz, 1995). For some, the net result is a vicious cycle of increasing social isolation and worsening disease.

Risky Health Practices.

Poor interpersonal relationships promote, or at least fail to discourage, risky and plainly destructive behavior. Failure to seek needed health care or to follow treatment regimens are common forms. People whose friends and family are unsupportive, for example, are less successful when it comes to smoking cessation, taking high blood pressure medication, maintaining control over diabetes, and losing weight (Gorin et al., 2005; Hanson, De Guire, Schinkel, & Kolterman, 1995; Umberson, 1987).

People may also be more prone to engage in risky activities or to engage in activities in unsafe ways if they lack commitments to positive personal relationships. For example, recently separated or divorced people are nearly three times more likely than married people to be involved in a traffic accident (Lagarde et al., 2004). Divorced parents or parents who are distracted by relational problems may provide less supervision and instruction to their children, making their children more susceptible to accidents, injury, or unsafe sexual practices. Teenagers who come from families with poor supervision and cohesiveness, for example, are more likely to drink and drive than teenagers whose parents provide better supervision (Augustyn & Simons-Morton, 1995). Another study found that a greater proportion of 12- to 14-year-olds from recently divorced families had engaged in sexual intercourse than from intact or stepparent families (Flewelling & Bauman, 1990).

Even in intact families, poor mother–daughter communication is among the most powerful predictors of teenage pregnancy (Adolph, Ramos, Linton, & Grimes, 1995; Silva & Ross, 2002).

Death from drug and alcohol abuse is far more common among people with disordered personal relationships (Risser, Bonsch, & Schneider, 1996). Disordered relationships are both the product and cause of drug and alcohol abuse. Certainly some people do cope with their relational inadequacies and losses by turning to drugs and alcohol. Compared to children from intact families, children from divorced families are more likely to try drugs and alcohol, to have drug and alcohol problems, and perhaps worst of all, to perpetuate the entire cycle by having greater difficulty forming stable relationships of their own (Flewelling & Bauman, 1990; Jeynes, 2001; Needle, Su, & Doherty, 1990).

The cycle continues when these people become parents themselves. The children of parents who abuse alcohol or drugs are at far greater risk for accidents and injuries. A study of house fires in Scotland between 1980 and 1990, for instance, indicated that parental alcohol abuse was a significant contributor to the death of children (Squires & Busuttil, 1995). Another study in the United States reported that children whose mothers were problem drinkers were over twice as likely to have serious accidents and injuries as children whose mothers are not problem drinkers. The risks were even higher when both parents were problem drinkers or when the problem drinker was also a single mother (Bijur, Kurzon, Overpeck, & Scheidt, 1992).

These findings remind us that negative social and health outcomes typically appear together—drinking, school problems, violence, suicide, psychological disorders, and so on. Yet to the extent that these problems are the consequence of low interpersonal skills and poor social relationships, all can be addressed by interventions that that build communicative skills and provide a social support network. Indeed, programs that focus on exactly these factors have proven successful in enhancing self-esteem, improving school performance, decreasing drug use, and reducing suicide potential among adolescents (e.g., Eggert, Thompson, Herting, Nicholas, & Dicker, 1994; E. A. Thompson, Eggert, Randell, & Pike, 2001).

Personal relationships, then, are much more than private arrangements. They are linked to the physical and mental health of their participants and, by virtue of the social and economic roles they play, to the vitality of society as a whole. This recognition has grown slowly as the study of personal relationships has evolved over the past 100 years.

THEMES IN THE STUDY OF PERSONAL RELATIONSHIPS

It is easy to imagine that the first piece of advice one human being ever gave another was about a personal relationship. Certainly the current deluge of popular press advice on relationships has a long history, dating at least from the early part of the 1800s (Gadlin, 1977). One would think that popular interest, combined with their critical role in health and society, would have made personal relationships among the most important objects of social scientific inquiry. Unfortunately concerted social scientific research on personal relationships is a recent development, even in comparison to the rather youthful character of the social sciences as a whole.

Personal relationship research grew by accretion from so many disciplinary tributaries that it is difficult to identify the first social scientific study. The beginnings of social psychology are often grounded in Lewin's experimental studies of groups in the 1930s, but the history of the study of personal relationships predates the rise of social psychology. It is sometimes dated to the work of German social theorist Georg Simmel at the turn of the 20th Century. Certainly Simmel's (1922/1955, 1950) contributions were and remain influential. Their impact can be found in many works including this one. However, Simmel's work was primarily based on insight and example. It was not until the 1930s that any appreciable body of data-based studies accumulated. The most influential studies of personal relationships during this era dealt with adjustment in marriage (Bernard, 1934; Burgess & Cottrell, 1939).

During the next 50 years, personal relationship research struggled for coherence. Until the early 1970s, research was fragmented into enclaves devoted to specific types of relationships, like marriage or friendship. There had been little effort to integrate these disparate bodies of work into a general theory of relationships. Among the first works to do so were McCall and Simmons' (1966) work on identity in relationships, M. S. Davis' (1973) text on intimate relationships, Levinger and Snoek's (1972) relationship-oriented view of interpersonal attraction, Altman and Taylor's (1973) social penetration theory, and the developmental theories of interpersonal communication articulated by Berger and Calabrese (1975) and Miller and Steinberg (1975). It would be another decade before the first journal devoted to the generic, interdisciplinary study of personal relationships was launched in 1984, the *Journal of Personal and Social Relationships*.

The evolution of research on personal relationships has followed three main tracks. We might call these "paradigm shifts," although that would be generous in its estimation of disciplinary coherence. Moreover, this was evolution without extinction. All of the earlier species of relationship studies are still well represented in current journals. Nonetheless, three shifts in the study of personal relationships are apparent and have converged to create the basis for my own work: (a) the shift from intrapsychic to interpersonal explanations, (b) the shift from studying contrived relationships to studying intact relationships, and (c) the shift from studying relationships in isolation to studying them in social context.

From Intrapsychic to Interpersonal Explanations

Much of the early work on personal relationships reflected the individualistic, intrapsychic perspective that permeated both psychotherapy and social psychology in the first part of the 20th Century. Early social psychologists, like F. Allport (1924), assumed that interpersonal activities could be reduced to the individual level. Prevailing psychoanalytic perspectives took this reduction one step further by locating the roots of individual behavior in intrapsychic processes. This bias toward the interior world of the individual took several forms, forms that can still be seen in research and theory today. The most pervasive of these was the preference for explaining social behavior in terms of a series of relatively fixed personality traits. If one person was more successful in personal relationships than another, it was probably because of some inherent trait or skill. Indeed this was exactly the form of argument adopted by Terman and Wallin (1949), when they argued that some people simply had a higher "marital aptitude" than others. This view implied that there were no bad relationships, only bad people. Bergler (1948), for instance, proposed that divorce was always caused by personality defects. Without extensive psychotherapy before they remarried, divorcing individuals would continue to be attracted to people who were also defective in one way or another.

Explaining success in personal relationships in terms of individual traits and attitudes also took less extreme forms. One enduring example is the research on personality similarity and attraction. Here success was explained by the compatibility or match of personality traits that each individual brought to the relationship. In spite of initial support (Dymond, 1954), much of the explanatory force of the research disappeared down a series of conceptual and methodological rabbit holes. Problems ranged from mixed findings to debates over how subjects and theorists judged personality similarity in the first place. As it turned out, it was less important that partners actually had similar personalities than it was that they believed they were generally similar in personality and attitudes (Berscheid & Walster, 1978) The explanatory success of matching theories of relational success has generally been quite limited. In spite of this, commercial dating services continue to sell themselves with promises of the perfect match. Even if these services were generally successful, however, theories of the perfect match would be open to criticism because of their essentially fatalistic nature. They imply that the fate of the relationship is cast at the outset by the match of individual characteristics, thereby excusing us from responsibility for daily action and subtly discouraging efforts to improve relationships over time.

It was not until the 1970s that the processes by which people carried on their relationships became a major topic of research (Altman & Taylor, 1973; G. J. McCall & Simmons, 1966). Similar shifts were occurring at about the same time in several other social scientific areas. Piaget's essentially individualistic view of cognitive development, for example, was being extended by new perspectives that underscored the importance of the child's interpersonal interactions from birth onward (Stern, 1985; Youniss & Smollar, 1985). Personality theories that relied on relatively fixed traits began to give way to conceptualizations that recognized both the interactive origins and the variability of social behavior across relational settings (Carson, 1969; Magnusson & Endler, 1977).

If the broader shift from intrapsychic explanation to interpersonal explanation had parents, they might well be symbolic interactionism and the social psychiatric movement. Symbolic interactionism portrayed the self as a social construction, as a fluid entity to be negotiated with others in the give and take of interaction. Although the social view of the self can be seen clearly in the earlier work of Cooley (1902) and Mead (1934), personal relationship research has been most directly influenced by Erving Goffman's (1959, 1967) insightful, often playful, discourses on the tactics of self-presentation and interaction management. Two aspects of Goffman's work left indelible marks on the study of interpersonal relations. First, Goffman and his followers reversed the intrapsychic agenda, placing interaction in the foreground and the individual's inner dynamics in the background. Goffman relocated the driving force of action from inside the individual to the outside encounter. Second, in doing so, Goffman and his followers recognized that encounters were inherently scenes of tension and self-contradiction and therefore required recurring negotiations of "face." It was not the individual, but the encounter that was problematic.

The social psychiatric movement and its relatives also gave an important push to the shift from intrapsychic to interpersonal explanation. Over a half century ago Karen Horney (1937) pioneered the view that mental health problems are responses to interpersonal events rather than purely intrapsychic phenomena. But it was Harry Stack Sullivan (1953) who most explicitly realigned psychiatry with the study of interaction. Sullivan's shift from the "immutably private" to the world of interaction was amplified by Jurgen Ruesch and the members of what is commonly called the Palo Alto School. Beginning with *Communication: The Social Matrix of Psychiatry*, Ruesch and Bateson (1951) brought the more interactive, process-oriented perspective of communication theory to psychotherapy. The Palo Alto School not only contributed significant work in psychotherapy, but also created classic statements placing interpersonal communication processes at the center of our understanding of marriage, and group relationships (Bateson, 1958; Lederer & Jackson, 1968; Watzlawick, Beavin, & Jackson, 1967).

From Contrived to Intact Relationships

Until about 20 years ago, the vast bulk of research on interpersonal processes was conducted in laboratory settings and involved imagined or contrived interactions. Aside from the often-ignored studies on marriage and the family, most researchers were content to study simulated interactions. Subjects were often merely asked to imagine what they would say or how they would act. Actual interaction was rarely examined and, when it was, it usually occurred in the laboratory between people whose relationship had been created just prior to the beginning of the experimental trial.

Whatever its appeal, research on simulated interaction and contrived relationships has been disappointing empirically. Among the first casualties were the small group studies that were popular from the 1940s through the early 1960s. Most of the groups used to study power relations, problem solving, cohesion, and other interpersonal variables suffered from a triple artificiality: no history, no future, and no social context. They were simply aggregations of people temporarily thrown together in a laboratory. They never really functioned as a group. Furthermore, the findings derived from these pseudo-groups did not apply well to genuine groups outside the laboratory (Argyle, 1969; Golembiewski, 1962).

Researchers continued to focus on contrived interaction even as they shifted topics in the mid-1960s. One of the most important of these topics was interpersonal attraction. Until the early 1980s, however, the great majority of studies on attraction were limited to initial attraction processes, usually in laboratory or imagined settings. Few dealt with established relationships and their processes. Byrne's studies on attitude similarity and interpersonal attraction epitomized research in this period (D. Byrne, 1961; D. Byrne & Nelson, 1965). Similarity was manipulated in these studies by providing subjects with information about how their attitudes matched those of another person. Once given this information, subjects were asked how attracted they were to the other person. The other person was a "phantom stranger"—he or she did not actually exist. In spite of its considerable successes, more recent findings have raised serious questions about the value of this method (Sunnafrank, 1991). For one thing, the degree of actual attitude similarity did not prove to be strong a predictor of attraction outside the laboratory. More recent studies have also shown that the attitude similarity–attraction relationship prior to interaction could be eliminated or attenuated by what went on when strangers actually started conversing.

The overriding problem is that it is difficult to model social relationships in the laboratory in a complete enough way to yield valid predictions about how people behave in intact relationships outside the laboratory. Methods like the phantom stranger do not merely leave things out, they result in a distorted picture of the way people interact. Duck and Barnes (1992), for example, point out that the phantom stranger method misrepresents the communication process between strangers in real settings. It presents a great deal of information that participants do not usually exchange all at once and certainly do not exchange with anywhere near the clarity of Byrne's experimental manipulations. Whatever position one takes in the debates on methods like the phantom stranger, it must be acknowledged that they signal a widespread dissatisfaction with studies that fail to examine interaction in intact relationships. While defending his laboratory methods of the 1960s, by the 1990s even Bryne had become an advocate of research on "extended, longitudinal interactions, including close relationships" (D. Byrne, 1992, p.195).

Once researchers began looking at intact relationships in the early 1980s, it soon became apparent that much of what had previously passed for stable individual qualities was actually quite variable across relational settings. Supposedly traitlike qualities, like social anxiety, were often shown to manifest themselves quite differently in interactions with people one knew well than with acquaintances (Parks, 1980). Scholars from a variety of disciplines began emphasizing the enhanced variability in basic psychological processes that was introduced by relational differences. Hinde (1987) provided two notable examples. In one he demonstrated that a child's style of attachment varied from one parent to the other and with the level of stress in the family as a whole. In the other example, Hinde showed that the cognitive procedures one uses for solving Piagetian tasks like number constancy depend on factors like the child's relationship with the experimenter.

The shift away from studying contrived interaction to studying close personal relationships following the mid-1970s was not only a result of empirical successes and failures, but may also have been the product of changing student and faculty populations. By the mid-1970s, the leading edge of the large post-World War II Baby Boom was beginning to assume faculty positions, while the trailing edge was driving college enrollments to record levels, especially for women who became the fastest growing segment of the student population in the early 1970s (Jones, 1980). The influx of such a large group of people, people who according to Erikson's (1968) developmental model should have been intensely concerned with issues of identity and intimacy by virtue of their age, could not help but influence the course of research. It is probably not a coincidence, for example, that *intimacy* first became a category in *Psychological Abstracts* in the early 1970s and that the number of articles indexed in this category grew steadily through that decade.

From Decontextualized to Contextualized Relationships

One more shift was necessary before we could truly begin to understand personal relationships. Once we begin to study actual relationships, it becomes apparent that they do not exist in a social vacuum. They are embedded in a broader social context. Unfortunately the vast bulk of research on personal relationships, especially in social psychology, has ignored the importance of contextual factors. This is ironic, given that contextual thinking in social psychology can be traced at least as far back as Lewin's field theory (Lewin, Adams, & Zener, 1935). Though he is regarded as the father of experimental social psychology, Lewin always wanted psychology to shift its focus from individual psychophysical phenomena to the broader interpersonal context. But most researchers forgot Lewin's (1952) reminder that interpretations of behavior must account for the context in which the behavior occurred. One notable exception, perhaps the first longitudinal field study of an interpersonal network, was Newcomb's (1961) 2 year study of the young men living in a house at the University of Michigan. Nonetheless, the influence of contextual and cultural themes waned as researchers became more dependent on undergraduate subject populations and laboratory methods following World War II (Backman, 1980).

By the mid-1970s, social psychology had reached what some characterized as a "crisis of confidence" (Elms, 1975; J. S. House, 1977). One of the most forceful skeptics was Gergen (1973), who pointed to inconsistent and ambiguous findings in social psychology as reason to turn away from the scientific model. However, Gergen's critique was directed at a social psychology that we can tell in hindsight was predestined to yield inconsistent and ambiguous findings. Experimental subjects rarely knew one another and usually played artificial roles in novel, poorly described settings that contained few lasting consequences. The lesson of the so-called crisis in social psychology was not that human behavior is unpredictable, but rather that people behave in unpredictable ways when they are stripped out of their social context and deprived of the rules and relationships in which their behavior is grounded.

Including the social context in research in a meaningful way has proven to be a elusive task for researchers. One pitfall has been the tendency to conceptualize the social context in terms of the participants' demographic characteristics such as age, race, gender, and ethnic background. These characteristics may (or may not) influence the context in a given case, but they never fully constitute it. They fail to capture the dynamic, communicative nature of real social contexts. Another pitfall has been the tendency to conceptualize the social context wholly in terms of one particular relationship (e.g., a friendship pair or marital couple). Taking a social contextual perspective, however, requires that we examine not only relationships, but also relationships among relationships.

Social context is created by and exists in the communication within and between relationships. Terms like *culture*, *ethnicity*, *social structure* and *personality* have meaning only to the extent that they can be found in ongoing communication between people. Precursors to this perspective have been around for some time. During the first third of the 20th Century, for example, Charles Horton Cooley advanced a social contextual view of self-concepts. Selves and their social context where fully interdependent in Cooley's vision (1902):

"… the individual is not separable from the human whole, but a living member of it, deriving his life from the whole through social and hereditary transmission as truly as if men were literally one body" (p. 35).

Relationships, no less than individuals, are intertwined with social contexts. If we were to expand Cooley's (1902) individual perspective to the larger relational level, we might express the social contextual view this way: "… no relationship is separable from the human whole, but a living element of a larger network of relationships; deriving its life course not only from character of its individual participants, but also from its ties to the relationships that surround it."

The image of social context as a network was probably first advanced in Georg Simmel's (1922/1955) essay on the "web of group affiliations." Network concepts can be found in a number of other early works as well (see Freeman, 1996), but two of the most influential views of networks grew out of sociometry and social anthropology.

The sociometric movement is usually associated with J. L. Moreno and his book, *Who Shall Survive*, first published in 1934 (Moreno, 1953). Two aspects of Moreno's work have had lasting influence in the study of personal relationships. First, like Lewin, Moreno emphasized that the actions of individuals could not be understood apart from the social context in which they occurred. He explicitly differentiated his theory of interpersonal relations from social psychology which he criticized for treating individuals as isolated units. Second, Moreno's maps of how people were linked within groups ("sociograms") provided the foundation for most contemporary procedures for visualizing and analyzing social network structure (Mitchell, 1979). As they elaborated Moreno's "sociometric" analysis, later researchers advanced a new set of mathematical concepts for the description of social systems (e.g., Harary, Norman, & Cartwright, 1965), as well as new theoretic insights about small group behavior (e.g., A. Bavelas, 1948; Festinger, Schachter, & Back, 1963). This work also formed the basis for new understandings of critical social processes like the diffusion of innovations (Coleman, Katz, & Menzel, 1957; Rapoport, 1956).

Another stream of network thinking flowed out of the social anthropological research on kinship and family structures in the 1950s. This work often focused on relationships in tribal settings or in geographically isolated communities (e.g., Barnes, 1954; Fortes, 1949). Nonetheless, the social anthropologists left two important legacies for the study of personal relationships. First, they were among the first to conceptualize the structure of a group or society as a *social network* (e.g., Radcliffe-Brown, 1952). Second, they were the first to recognize that behavior inside any one relationship may be influenced by the structure of the participants' surrounding social network. Elizabeth Bott's (1971) investigation of network influences on English family structure is the classic statement of this theme.

Social network research perspectives enliven wooden demographic categories and allow us to speak of the social context in terms of relationships among relationships. Unfortunately researchers have only occasionally recognized the potential for social network thinking to advance our understanding of personal relationships (e.g., Felmlee, 2001; Milardo, 1982; Ridley & Avery, 1979; Sprecher, Felmlee, Orbuch, & Willetts, 2002; Surra & Milardo, 1991). Even today, the vast majority of studies reported in leading research journals do not look beyond individual and relational factors.

SUMMARY AND OVERVIEW

"Human nature," Mead (1934) reminded us, "is something social through and through, and always presupposes the truly social individual" (p. 229). We are human only in relationship to others and personal relationships are the most important relationships of all. People across cultures share the belief that family and friends are the primary sources of meaning and satisfaction. This private value for close relationships has been transformed into a market value in consumer economies. Not only does a significant portion of the modern economy depend on decisions made in personal relationships, but personal relationships themselves have become important targets of advertising and marketing. Goods and services of all kinds are marketed with appeals to the belief that buyer will become a more attractive, successful relational partner. Relationships themselves become commodities (for a related view, see Hochschild, 2003). The importance of personal relationships fans out into larger institutions in several other ways. Even in very large bureaucracies, innovation and change are usually discussed first in the closer, more personal relationships among fellow workers. In addition, personal relationships act as reference points and training grounds for participation in larger institutions. When personal relationships are disrupted, society pays the price in terms of reduced productivity in the workplace and dramatic increases in social service costs. I meant it quite literally when I began the chapter by claiming that people were social animals down to their very cells. Sociability is not only abstract and metaphoric; it is also physiological. Thus it should not be surprising to discover that disruptions in our most involved social relationships are associated with a variety of threats to physical health.

Acknowledging the importance of close relationships is not the same as understanding how they develop and change over time. As I have noted, the evolution of academic interest in close relationships has followed a rather tortuous path. Over the last century, especially during the last 35 years, social scientists have moved toward a more dynamic, contextually situated view of personal relationships, but much work remains to be done. The present volume is aimed at enlarging our understanding of how the fate of any one personal relationship becomes intertwined with the fate of the network of relationships surrounding it. In chapter 2, I set the conceptual and theoretic stage for the research studies that dominate the remaining chapters of the book. I offer a conceptualization of that elusive term, *relationship*, describe the essential dimensions of personal networks, and propose a theoretic perspective for understanding the ways that relationships and networks influence each other. In the chapters that follow, I report a number of studies on how personal relationships are initiated, how friendships and romantic relationships develop and are managed over time, and on how they sometimes deteriorate.

CHAPTER TWO

Inside Relationships and Networks

Personal relationships are everywhere—the two old friends exchanging stories over coffee, that knot of teenage girls giggling over boys at the mall, the young lovers cooing in the corner of the café, the couple bickering in the car beside us at the intersection, the colleagues debating the details of some task, the elderly couple talking inaudibly at the table next to ours in the restaurant. How can we possibly understand something so varied?

The first challenge is to identify some underlying set of characteristics common to all these relationships. The concepts we select must also reflect the fact that relationships change over time. Consider our young lovers in the corner of the café, for example. Many things will influence the course of their relationship. Some are more widely recognized than others. In this book I will focus on a set of factors that is usually overlooked. These involve the ways that our young lovers relate to each other's friends, family, and other social contacts. Whether her mother likes the young man may be important. Whether his friends are introduced to her friends may be important. Whether others accept them as a couple will be important. Indeed, as we see in chapter 3, it is likely that social network factors have already contributed to our couple making it as far as they have. To understand how networks and relationships influence each other, however, we must add two things to our discussion of the dimensions of relationship structure. The first is a parallel discussion of the characteristics of social networks that are most relevant for the development, maintenance, and deterioration of personal relationships. The second is a theoretic perspective that connects relationships and networks.

INSIDE RELATIONSHIPS

Relationships as Communication

Relationships live in communication. They are made, unmade, and remade in the communicative practices of their participants. Even the noun, "relationship," tends to reify "the unfinished business of relating" (VanderVoort & Duck, 2000, p. 3). If it were not so cumbersome, I would refer to "personal relatings" rather than "personal relationships" throughout the book. Relationships also certainly exist in the emotions, physiological states, reflections, expectations, and memories of individuals as well as in the roles, rules, symbols, and rituals of culture. But I wish to reverse the background and foreground between the communication process and these standard psychological and sociological categories. For me, communication stands in the foreground. It is the generative force. Communication changes cognition and emotion, creates and reproduces social structure, and, in doing so, makes their meaning real for the self and others.

Scholars most often think of the communication process in terms of the way we use language. This is particularly true of those who look at the communication process through the disciplinary lens of psychology or sociology. Regardless of their disciplinary origin, these views of the communication process typically focus on the use of language in relationships. They might, for instance, focus on the simple frequency of communication or the frequency of certain types of talk such as self-disclosure as indices of relationships (e.g., Derlega, Metts, Petronio, & Margulis, 1993; Dindia, 1997). Others would note the significance of the verbal narratives or stories that both summarize and direct personal relationships (e.g., Bochner, Ellis, & Tillmann-Healy, 1997; Harvey, Orbuch, & Weber, 1992). Some would observe how our experience of relationships is shaped by more specific linguistic forms such as metaphors (e.g., Baxter, 1992; Duck, 1994). Still others would emphasize that our speech not only regulates how we enact established behavioral patterns, but also creates new patterns (Searle, 1969). Entire relationships may be constituted in speech events such as "joking around," "getting to know," "breaking bad news," "talking about problems," "making up," and so on (Goldsmith & Baxter, 1996).

For communication scholars, however, speech and conversation are models for a more general disciplinary perspective on human behavior that includes but extends far beyond a concern with particular linguistic forms. The "things" of communication (words, facial expressions, stories, etc.) are not what defines the communication perspective. Rather, the communication perspective is defined by its concern with the *process* of human interaction and its consequences. The core element in this process is interpersonal influence. The study of communication is about how people influence one another both intentionally and unintentionally. Anyone who studies the interpersonal influence process is by definition studying communication. When Aristotle (1954) defined *rhetoric* as the ability to discover "in a given case all the available means of persuasion" (p. 24), he was articulating a core disciplinary concern that has extended across 2500 years from the ancient study of rhetoric to the modern academic discipline of communication.

From this perspective, relationships represent structured interactions over time. Regardless of whether we are assessing the interaction directly or looking at one of its consequences, the assumption is that the relationship is sequentially created in the give and take of interaction. Because interaction is sequential and chronological, the pattern of interpersonal influence at one moment is simultaneously the context for behavior in the next. Communication is thus "structurating" (Giddens, 1984). The psychological states and social structure enacted at one moment are implicitly referenced or reproduced in the next.

False Starts in the Conceptualization of Relationship Change

The most useful conceptualizations of interpersonal relationships capture their dynamic qualities and describe their development, maintenance, and deterioration over time. Because the developmental perspective is still relatively new, however, many of our most common approaches to characterizing relationships fail to grasp it adequately. For example, presuming that relationships of greater duration are necessarily more developed is inherently misleading. The length of a relationship is rarely associated with its closeness, intimacy, satisfaction, and commitment (Berscheid, Snyder, & Omoto, 2004). Moreover, poorly developed, even dysfunctional relationships can be remarkably stable. To cite one particularly disturbing example, researchers have found that women in violent relationships were less likely to leave their abusive husbands if the husband was also an alcoholic (J. Katz, Arias, Beach, Brody, & Roman, 1995). They were more likely to excuse his violent outbursts as an effect of his disease, whereas abused women whose husbands were not alcoholics were more likely to hold them accountable and leave the relationship.

Another research strategy is to compare relationships in terms of broad social labels such as *acquaintance, friend,* or *best friend.* The assumption that these labels represent different levels of relational development unfortunately suffers from several shortcomings. First of all, people vary widely in how they use and interpret relational labels, both individually and across cultures (e.g., Gaines, 1995; Lin & Rusbult, 1995; Parks, 1976). In addition, there are gaps in the lexicon—some relationships are not well labeled and some stages of relationships are more elaborately labeled than others. For example, there are several labels to describe the development of romantic relationships (e.g., *just friends, dating, exclusive*), but no comparable labels to mark stages in their deterioration. The names we give to relationships are worthy of study in their own right, but they do not reflect the deeper patterns of the relational life cycle in a sufficiently systematic way.

Assessing change in relationships with single indicators such as satisfaction or attraction is also fraught with problems. Some of these problems are specific to the particular indicator selected. Satisfaction, for example, makes a poor indicator because it bears no necessary connection to movement across the relational life cycle. Participants may be satisfied or dissatisfied at any given point in their relationship and thus higher satisfaction does not necessarily imply a greater level of development. Moreover, satisfaction is heavily influenced by recent relational events and may not always reflect the overall state of the relationship (Flora & Segrin, 2003). Other indicators may also fail to capture adequately the larger process of relational change. Measuring attraction between relational partners, for instance, taps only one of several dimensions of relational life. General measures of "closeness" are probably the most useful single indicators because they are correlated with so many other dimensions of relational life (A. Aron, E. N. Aron, & Smollan, 1992; Parks & Floyd, 1996b). As useful as global assessments of closeness are, however, they lack the conceptual specificity needed for a thorough theoretic analysis of the relational life cycle. They summarize, but do not adequately illuminate the inner workings of relationships.

Dimensions of Relationship Change

The first task of a theory of relational life is to identify the specific dimensions along which interaction changes as relationships are created, maintained, and ended. If our interest is in the development of a general understanding of personal relationships, then our conceptual framework must be capable of encompassing many different types of relationships. There have been several notable efforts to identify specific, yet widely applicable dimensions of the relational development beginning with Altman and Taylor's (1973) seminal work. The dimensions identified below build on their work, others' efforts in the same vein (e.g., Huston & Burgess, 1979; H. H. Kelley et al., 1983), and my own work over the years (Parks, 1976, 1995, 2000; Parks & Eggert, 1991). These dimensions constitute a definition of the relational change process. The seven dimensions discussed below are: (a) interdependence, (b) depth or intimacy of interaction, (c) breadth or variety of interaction, (d) commitment, (e) predictability and understanding, (f) code change and coordination, and (g) amount of communication. The entire relational life cycle may be conceptualized in terms of changes in these dimensions. A relationship develops as they increase and deteriorates as they decrease. Relational change is rarely linear. Dimensions may change at different rates and in different directions. Participants may use "maintenance strategies" to sustain a given level of development or they may draw on "repair strategies" in an effort to return to a previous level of development.

Interdependence. The concept of *mutual influence* or *interdependence* lies at the core of nearly every approach to the relational life cycle (e.g., Altman & Taylor, 1973; H. H. Kelley & Thibaut, 1978; G. Levinger & D. J. Snoek, 1972; Rusbult,

Kumashir, Coolsen, & Kirchner, 2004). Three types of mutual influence are integral in the life of relationships (Parks, 2000). The first is *mutual behavior control* or "true" interdependence. It represents the degree to which each person's outcomes are influenced by the way her or his overt actions and internal states fit with the other's (H. H. Kelley & Thibaut, 1978). Two friends, for example, would be interdependent in this way if each person's preference for what to do when they go out together depended on the other person's preferences. A married couple would be interdependent in this way if each person's desire for, say, a particular meal on the weekend, varied with the other's desire for that same meal.

A second kind of interdependence occurs in *patterns of bilateral dependency*. Anna's appreciation of a movie may depend on how much Gary likes it, even though Gary's appreciation of the movie is not influenced significantly by whether Anna enjoyed it. At the same time, how much Gary enjoys dinner at his mother-in-law's house may depend greatly on how comfortable Anna is with her mother that day, while Anna's level of comfort with her mother on a given day is based on a long history of interaction and is rarely influenced by Gary's mood. Although each of these dependencies is unbalanced and unreciprocated, they come together to form a complex, higher order pattern of interdependency. Each is a thread that binds a pair together. A third form of interdependence is vital in the relational development process, even though it has generated comparatively less interest among traditional social psychologists and sociologists. This is *conversational interdependence*—the degree to which each person's utterances in a sequence depend on the other's. The degree to which partners are able to collaborate in the management of conversational topics marks the developmental status of their relationship as a whole. As they introduce, develop, and retire topics, relational partners are expressing not only a set of content concerns, but are also implicitly negotiating their identities in relation to one another. It is not surprising, then, that married couples whose interactions are more coordinated or synchronized are also more satisfied (Julien, Brault, Chartrand, & Begin, 2000). Conversational interdependence focuses on the give and take of ongoing conversation, on its true communicative character, in a way that outcome-based definitions usually do not. True interdependence, bilateral patterns of simple dependence, and conversational dependence are all interrelated, but conceptually distinct forms of interdependence. Together, they define the first and most essential feature of the relational life cycle. As they increase, a relationship develops. As they decrease, it deteriorates.

Patterns of interdependence also set expectations in motion. The potential consequences of such expectations were humorously noted by the novelist, Milan Kundera, in *The Book of Laughter and Forgetting* (1996):

> … every love relationship rests on an unwritten agreement unthinkingly concluded by the lovers in the first weeks of their love. They are still in a

kind of dream but at the same time, without knowing it, are drawing up, like uncompromising lawyers, the detailed clauses of their contract. O lovers! Be careful in those dangerous first days! Once you've brought breakfast in bed you'll have to bring it forever, unless you want to be accused of lovelessness and betrayal. (p. 51)

Although more than a single meal in bed may be required for their creation, patterns of exchange do, nonetheless, create expectations sets that resemble quid pro quo agreements (Weiss, Birchler, & Vincent, 1974). These contracts may be negotiated explicitly with verbal communication (e.g., "If you clear the table, I'll wash the dishes"). More often, however, they are negotiated nonverbally and implicitly. Their structure remains unspoken until one person fails to comply with the agreement. The ability to make, honor, and revise relational contracts is vital for the development of personal relationships. Without them, individuals will have difficulty managing complex patterns of interdependence associated with personal relationships of all kinds (Parks, 1976).

Interdependence is so central to our view of personal relationships that it is worth pausing to consider the upper limits of the concept. As I have noted, increasing interdependence implies increasing development. Very high levels of interdependence, however, are not always desirable. Some relationships may be *overdeveloped*. Their interdependence may drain the emotional and physical resources of the participants. Or, they may be overdeveloped from the standpoint of the social context they occupy (e.g., workers whose personal friendship interferes with their job responsibilities). In some cases patterns of interdependence become unhealthy for the participants. The popular clinical concept of codependency is a case in point. Although it has been marketed to the point of meaninglessness by the self-help industry, the general idea of neurotic dependence has a long and honorable history (see P. H. Wright & K. D. Wright, 1995). Over 50 years ago, for instance, Karen Horney (1942) wrote provocatively about the problems of the "morbidly dependent." Regardless of what the fashionable label may be, cases of excessive interdependence remind us that very high levels of development may not always be healthy or functional.

Depth or Intimacy of Interaction.

Depth or Intimacy of Interaction.   Following Lewin (1948), Altman and Taylor (1973) originally conceptualized the depth dimension of relationship development in terms of a personality model that viewed some aspects of the self as more central than others. As relationships develop, interaction moves from peripheral layers of the self toward more fundamental, core layers of personality. As they deteriorate, interaction retreats to the safer, more surface aspects of the participants.

Self-disclosure is often treated as a defining characteristic of relationship development (Derlega et al., 1993; Prager & Roberts, 2004). Although early approaches emphasized the importance of exchanging highly personal information in relationships (e.g., Jourard, 1971), more recent approaches have acknowledged the importance of exchanging less personal information both in the early development and ongoing conduct of close relationships (e.g., Derlega et al., 1993; Vangelisti & Banski, 1993). The bulk of communication is nonintimate even in highly developed relationships. For every intimate discussion of deep personal feelings, most married couples have many discussions of nonintimate topics such as where to shop, what to eat, what movie to see, where one placed a now missing object, and so on. Because of this, the overall level of disclosure is not strongly correlated with more general relational perceptions such as global closeness (e.g., J. B. Miller & Stubblefield, 1993). Thus, development is marked not so much by an overall shift in the level of disclosure as it is by a greater accessibility of private topics over time. More recent approaches have emphasized these process-oriented, communicative aspects of self-disclosure (e.g., Dindia, 1997, 2002).

The depth dimension has also been closely associated with intimacy. Intimacy has sometimes been conceptualized in terms of whether particular behaviors (e.g., sexual intercourse) or conversational topics (e.g., "lies I told my mother") have occurred in the relationship (e.g., D. A. Taylor, 1968). It is also common to equate intimacy with emotional attachment. Thus measures of attraction, liking, love, and other forms of attachment might be thought of as correlates of the depth dimension. Although these approaches are certainly legitimate, it may be more useful to view intimacy in terms of the overall process of interaction or as a product of an extended series of interactions. Thus, Clark and Reis (1988) defined intimacy as "process in which one person expresses important self-relevant feelings and information to another, and as a result of the other's response comes to feel known, validated, and cared for" (p. 628). Although the dyadic, communicative tone of this definition is laudable, at least one problem with the concept of *intimacy* remains. Intimacy is a cultural term that connotes sexual or romantic feelings. Thus, there are notable differences in the characteristics people ascribe to "close friends" and "intimate friends" (Parks & Floyd, 1996b). Asking people to describe the depth dimension in terms of intimacy may therefore result in an incomplete or skewed picture.

I conceptualize the depth dimension in terms of the subjective importance participants place on the topics they discuss and the behaviors they exchange. This conceptualization is consistent with Altman and Taylor's (1973) theoretic foundation and also can be applied to a wide range of relationships. The tendency to view depth in terms of positive affective intimacy is appropriate for many types of personal relationships, but leaves others out. Although it may work for friendship and romantic relationships, it does not apply well to business relationships. My definition would cover intimacy, but would also include depth in the sense of two business associates working on larger projects or taking greater risks together. Moreover, it would include cases of growing negative attachment. Business rivals whose competition expands into areas with higher stakes, for instance, could be said to have a deeper, more developed relationship. Animosity, like positive intimacy, follows a developmental path (Wiseman & Duck, 1995).

Variety or Breadth of Interaction.

As relationships develop, they also grow to encompass a greater variety of activities. The "breadth" or "richness" of interaction increases (Altman & Taylor, 1973). As they deteriorate, breadth decreases. Some refer to this dimension as the "diversity" dimension of relationships (Berscheid et al., 2004; Hinde, 1987; H. H. Kelley et al., 1983), while others describe increases in breadth in terms of a shift from a "uniplex" relationship to a "multiplex" or multistranded relationship (e.g., Mitchell, 1969). Regardless of the label, there are three general ways in which breadth may be conceptualized. In its most general sense, breadth represents the variety of behaviors or resources exchanged. The exchange matrix expands with development and contracts with deterioration. In Hays' (1984) study of same-sex friendships, for example, friends who grew closer over a 3-month period displayed a greater variety of behaviors across a greater range of categories (i.e., task sharing, assistance, expressing emotion, mutual disclosure) than friends whose relationship stagnated or terminated. Their relationship developed from having just a few "strands" of interaction to being multistranded or multiplex. Measurements of this aspect of breadth usually rely on participants' assessments of the variety of activities or resources they share either by means of global judgments or by means of checklists (e.g., Berg, Piner, & Frank, 1993; Berscheid, Snyder, & Omoto, 1989b, 2004).

Breadth may also be conceptualized in terms of the variety of conversational topics discussed in the relationship. As relationships develop the range of conversational topics expands. D. A. Taylor (1968), for instance, tracked the number of different topics discussed by newly paired college roommates over a three month period and found increases in both the number of non-intimate and intimate topics discussed. There are limits to breath, of course, that result from the participants' desires for privacy or from the simple fact that not all topics will be equally relevant for a given type of relationship. Nonetheless, the perception that any topic can be discussed binds the partners together. Once a relationship starts to deteriorate, both the perceived and actual range of topics discussed is likely to shrink. Topics which were once discussed are now actively closed off or "circumscribed" (Knapp & Vangelisti, 1999).

Finally, breadth may be conceptualized in terms of the variety of communicative contexts or channels used. As personal relationships develop, the participants interact in a greater variety of settings (Huston & Burgess, 1979). The workplace friendship that spreads to encompass settings beyond the workplace may be said to be more highly developed than one that remains anchored to its original setting. We also can think of breadth in terms of the expanding range of channels used for communication. Personal relationships started on the Internet, for example, often broaden over time to involve other channels including face-to-face contact (Parks & Floyd, 1996a; Parks & Roberts, 1998).

Commitment.   Commitment connects relationships to the past and the future. It is rooted in the memory of something already shared and the expectation that the relationship will continue into the future. Though they may have considerable interdependence, depth, and variety, personal relationships that lack commitment are usually found wanting. Novelists know this well. American writer, Edward Abbey (1988) described the uncommitted relationship as "too much of a now thing" (p. 364), while Kundera (1984) suggested that such displacement from the past and future resulted in "an unbearable lightness of being." Three different bases for commitment are typically identified in the literature—personal, moral, and structural (Adams & Jones, 1997; M. P. Johnson, Caughlin, & Huston, 1999). These are, respectively, (a) the personal desire to continue the relationship, (b) the belief that it ought to continue, and (c) the belief that external forces make it necessary to continue. Other approaches to psychological commitment include Levinger's (1991) cohesiveness model, Sternberg's (1986) triangular theory of love, and Rusbult's investment model (Rusbult, 1980). Although there are notable differences among these models, all of them share the common view that commitment is rooted in private judgments. External social structural factors, such as laws that make termination difficult, act to enhance commitment through constraint, but in the end commitment is only as real as it is perceived to be. Commitment of this type is typically assessed by asking people how long they want or expect a given relationship to last, how attached to it they are, or how much energy they would invest to maintain the relationship (e.g., Parks & Adelman, 1983; Rusbult, 1983).

Commitment is a communicative as well as psychological accomplishment. It is inferred from the way the participants negotiate behavior, exercise power, and set the emotional tone of their relationship (Ballard-Reisch & Weigel, 1999; Weigel & Ballard-Reisch, 2002). An individual's sense of commitment is a fluid indicator of how the inevitable tensions of relationships are being addressed, including contradictions fundamental to the structure of relationships such as being together or apart, open or closed (Sahlstein & Baxter, 2001). This is the *process* of committing rather than simply a sum of a how much one wants to, ought to, and has to maintain a relationship. Partners sometimes create secret interpretative tests to gauge the level of commitment emanating from each other's communication (Baxter & Wilmot, 1984; Bell & Buerkel-Rothfuss, 1990). It appears that relational partners rarely communicate explicitly about commitment, but when they do, it usually signals a turning point in the relationship or an effort to make relational repairs after a crisis (Knapp & Taylor, 1994).

Predictability and Understanding.   In order to manage the growing complexity of a developing relationship, participants must develop some level of understanding and agreement about what behaviors are desirable, about what responses the other is likely to have, and about how each person's actions fit into larger relational sequences (Parks, 1976). In short, they must become experts on one another (Planalp & Garvin-Doxas, 1994). The management of uncertainty figures prominently in nearly every major theoretic perspective on the relational life cycle. It plays the title role in uncertainty reduction theory (Berger, 1979; Berger & Calabrese, 1975). It plays a less explicit, but no less important, role in several other theories of close relationships as well (Altman & Taylor, 1973; H. H. Kelley & Thibaut, 1978; Prager & Roberts, 2004). In these and in other theories that locate the driving force behind relational change in the prediction of outcomes, the ability to obtain desirable outcomes and coordinate interpersonal exchange depends in part on the ability to make reliable forecasts of the partner's behavior and the consequences of one's own behavior.

Managing uncertainty requires considerably more than the mechanistic acquisition of information. People change. Situations change. People move in and out of each other's presence. The need to reestablish predictability is ongoing. As interdependence becomes more complex, predictability and understanding become both more crucial and more difficult to maintain (Ickes & Simpson, 1997). Making sense of the other is important, but it is also important that one feels understood and validated by the other person in the relationship (Laurenceau, Rivera, Schaffer, & Pietromonaco, 2004; Reis & Shaver, 1988). On the other hand, people often behave in ways that seem to run counter to the general pursuit of predictability and understanding. They seek novelty, change, excitement, and adventure. They complain when relationships become too predictable as well as when they are not predictable enough. The presence of contradictory desires and the communication patterns that go with them has been acknowledged by relationship theorists for a long time (Altman, Vinsel, & Brown, 1981; Baxter, 1988; Baxter & Montgomery, 1996; Simmel, 1950). Recognizing that people may wish for certainty and uncertainty at the same time, however, should not lead us to underestimate the importance of the management of uncertainty in the larger relational life cycle. The willingness to seek novelty, to be spontaneous, is often bounded by larger relational certainties. Indeed it may be precisely the predictability and security relational partners feel about the overall relationship that frees them to explore new activities.

That said, it is also worth emphasizing that the impact of uncertainty can not be evaluated in isolation (Brashers, 2001; Goldsmith, 2001). People not only estimate the likelihood of particular relational events, but they also have evaluations of whether those events are likely to be positive or negative. If the outcome is likely to be positive, then we seek to reduce uncertainty about it. But if the outcome is likely to be negative, then people may prefer not to reduce their uncertainty (e.g., W. A. Afifi & Weiner, 2004; Babrow, 2001; Brashers, 2001). If, for example, you are uncertain about your romantic relationship because you think your partner may wish to end it, you may prefer to live with the uncertainty for a time rather than to find out for sure that he or she is leaving. More generally, events that violate our expectations or otherwise increase uncertainty are likely to be satisfying only to the extent that they are rewarding (D. L. Kelley & Burgoon, 1991; Planalp & Honeycutt, 1985). In other words, although we may say we like surprises, we really only like nice surprises.

Pleasant surprises can be the source of significant arousal. As poet, Mona Van Duyn (1990) observed, to be "'in love' is to be taken by surprise" (p. 9). We are rarely content to leave such surprises unexplored, so each surprise restarts a cycle of uncertainty management. Or, as Kundera (1996) put it, "love is a continual interrogation" (p. 223).

The measures currently used by researchers do not adequately address these more complex aspects of the management of uncertainty and predictability, especially its often contradictory desires for predictability and novelty (Baxter & Montgomery, 1996; Knobloch & Solomon, 2002a, 2002b). Most measures emphasize simple accumulations of information or the relative level of confidence with which one feels he or she can predict and explain the partner's behavior (e.g., Gudykunst & Nishida, 1986; Parks & Adelman, 1983).

Communicative Code Change.   The structure of communication changes as relationships develop. It is not just that relational partners talk about different things as their relationship develops. They also talk about the same things differently. They create their own linguistic forms and cultural codes. Waller and Hill (1951) first observed this over 50 years ago in their studies of courtship:

> As a result of conversations and experience, there emerges a common universe of discourse characterized by the feeling of something very special between two persons .... They soon develop a special language, their own idioms, pet names, and jokes; as a pair, they have a history and a separate culture. (p. 189)

These changes are not unique to courtship, but rather are characteristic of the way personal relationships of all kinds develop. Three particular changes occur in communication codes as a relationship develops (Parks, 2000). The most widely recognized is code *specialization*. Partners specialize their use of language to create relationally unique nicknames, teasing insults, indirect requests and reproaches, and other personal idioms (Hopper, Knapp, & Scott, 1981). The number and variety of personal idioms used is positively related to

perceptions of satisfaction and closeness in same-sex friendships, dating relationships, and recently married couples (Bell, Buerkel-Rothfuss, & Gore,
1987; Bell & Healey, 1992; Bruess & Pearson, 1993). There is some evidence
that idiom use flattens out after the first few years of marriage, but it is not
clear why (Bruess & Pearson, 1993). It may be that the creation and use of personal idioms is more characteristic of the earlier portions of the developmental cycle. Or it may be that over time idioms become so woven into the
relationship that they are no longer easily recalled or recognized. In addition
to creating personal idioms, people in personal relationships often treat particular behaviors, events, objects, places, and cultural artifacts such as movies or
songs as specialized symbols of their larger relationship (Baxter, 1987; Oring,
1984). Referring to these relational symbols reinforces feelings of closeness
and unity in the larger relationship.

The boundaries of idiomatic speech and relational symbols, like those of
language more generally, are rarely sharp. Idioms and symbols developed in
one relationship may become more widely shared among the members of a
close social circle (Bell & Healey, 1992). As their use spreads, the functions
played by private language generalize from the dyad to the network, coming
to symbolize the solidarity of the friendship group as a whole as well as of the
dyadic friendships within it.

A second general change is the *abbreviation* of communicative codes as
personal relationships develop. What once may have required many words,
now requires few. What once may have required extensive gesturing is now
conveyed with less. The codes of close personal relationships become "restricted" in the sense described by Basil Bernstein (1964). The shared experiences and expectations that accumulate as a relationship develops allow the
speakers to forego extensive verbal elaboration. This more implicit conversational style is characterized by rapid topic shifts, incomplete expressions,
and frequent logical gaps in content (Hornstein, 1985). Code abbreviation
both exemplifies and drives relational development. The ability to communicate easily, implicitly, and with less attention to formal style reinforces the
relationship and spurs further development.

A third broad change in the structure of communication as relationships
develop is the *substitution* of nonverbal codes for language. Roommates, for
example, who once issued verbal traffic instructions as they negotiated their
too small kitchen are now able to negotiate the sharing of space with looks
and gestures. Over time, they have learned the dance so well that verbal instruction is no longer necessary. In other cases, awkward moments that once
might have required direct verbal discussion are noted and resolved at the nonverbal level. Although the substitution of nonverbal for verbal communication may be problematic for those who equate the amount of explicit verbal
communication with the quality of the relationship, code substitution creates
a richer texture to the communication and enhances participants' ability to

make tactical adaptations in the explicitness of their communication. Aside from this, the ability to share silence comfortably is often treated as a sign of intimacy and security (Knapp & Vangelisti, 1999). Ironically, however, the reliance on implicit, nonverbal forms of communication that reinforces the intimacy of the relationship can also pose dilemmas for it. When something cannot be negotiated at an implicit level, relational partners may be caught in the dilemma between wishing to be more explicit and fearing that the explicitness will call into question the unspoken trust upon which the relationship is built. Adelman and Siemon (1986) illustrated this when they observed that adult twins often face situations in which they must explicitly renegotiate their relationship (e.g., when one of them is about to marry), but feel that explicit talk somehow undermines their intimacy.

Little is known about what happens to code use when relationships come apart. We would expect that specialized language would be used less often and that code abbreviation and substitution should become problematic as relationships deteriorate. For instance, the partner who seeks to withdraw may stop responding to terms of endearment, thus leading the remaining partner to cling to such language even more tightly for the reassurance it once provided. In other cases, interaction can no longer be coordinated effectively with abbreviated codes and nonverbal codes because perspectives and motives are no longer shared. The resulting misunderstandings and conflicts only serve to heighten the participants' belief that their relationship is in trouble.

Amount of Communication. Development is often associated with increases in the frequency or amount communication (e.g., Berscheid et al., 1989b, 2004; H. H. Kelley et al., 1983). At first consideration, simple changes in the frequency of interaction per se would not necessarily appear to reflect changes in the "development" of the relationship. Repeating essentially the same encounter with a hairdresser or barber every 3 weeks rather than every 6 weeks would not seem to count as development. Yet something is happening even here. If nothing else, increasing the frequency of interaction with the hairdresser turns the customer into "a regular" and thus heralds additional layers of exchange and influence.

Changes in the amount of communication may take on special significance at particular points in the relational lifecycle. Early in relationships, participants may interpret increases in the amount of interaction as investments of time and energy on their behalf (Rusbult, 1980, 1983). Later on, spending more time together may be seen as a maintenance strategy (Acitelli, 2001; Canary & Stafford, 2001). Still later, one of the participants may attempt to dramatically reduce the amount of communication as a way of terminating the relationship without direct confrontation (Wilmot, Carbaugh, & Baxter, 1985).

Some relational events take on meaning in terms of the changes in the amount of communication that follow them. It is common for individuals to recall the history of their relationships as a series of "turning points" in which some critical event altered the relationship's trajectory (Baxter & Bullis, 1986). In some cases, the turning point itself represents a change in the amount of interaction between partners (e.g., "our first weekend together" or "she left for the holidays"). In other cases, it is the change in contact between the partners following a relational event that defines the turning point (e.g., partners avoid one another in the aftermath of a fight).

Relational Change in Perspective

The relational life cycle, then, may be conceptualized in terms of changes along seven dimensions: interdependence, depth, breadth, commitment, predictability, communication code use, and the amount of communication. Three features of this conceptualization should be emphasized before moving on to examine the nature of social networks. First, although the initial development of a relationship is usually paralleled by increases in emotional intensity, we should not assume that these emotions (affects) are always positive or that deterioration necessarily weakens them. The development of a bitter rivalry might be described using these dimensions. Indeed, in some cases, an observer working with this conceptualization might say that a relationship was actually developing when others would say it was deteriorating. The couple whose once placid marriage spirals into hostility and competition, for instance, may actually be more interdependent, display more varied and personal behaviors, and be more attached—in short, have a more developed relationship than they had previously. Although it is common to conceptualize intimacy in terms of positive involvement (Prager & Roberts, 2004), negative involvements can be quite intimate as well (Duck & Sants, 1983). There is no simple equation linking either the valence or the intensity of affect to the relational life cycle.

Second, the dimensions just outlined are intended to describe not only the development and deterioration of relationships, but also efforts to maintain and enhance them. Relationships are always vulnerable, perhaps more today than in the past, so it is not surprising that there is a growing literature on how they might be maintained and enhanced (e.g., Canary & Dainton, 2003; Harvey & Wenzel, 2001). When one looks at this literature, however, it becomes apparent that the activities needed to nourish an ongoing relationship are quite similar to those necessary to "grow" it in the first place. A. Aron, Norman, and E. N. Aron (2001) for instance, argue that sharing novel and arousing experiences will help a couple maintain their relationship. But it is also true that sharing a novel and arousing experience may have provided the spark that started the relationship in the first place, a fact that Aron himself had noted almost 30 years earlier in a classic study of attraction between strangers (Dutton & Aron, 1974).

Finally, this model differs from other approaches to the relational life cycle in that it does not attempt to slice the process into a sequence of discrete stages. Many insightful stage models of relational development and deterioration have been offered (e.g., Knapp & Vangelisti, 1999; Lewis, 1973a; Rollie & Duck, in press). Although these models are useful pedagogically and often have heuristic value, they have not been the object of a direct empirical test. There has been little attempt to verify the sequencing of stages or whether only one stage occurs at a time. Still, stage models do seem to capture the large shifts or "turning points" that people often report when summarizing the history of their relationships (e.g., Baxter & Bullis, 1986; Baxter & Pittman, 2001). Such abrupt shifts in relationships can, however, be viewed more parsimoniously as sharp quantitative changes in a common set of underlying dimensions than as beginnings or endings of discrete, qualitatively distinct stages.

INSIDE NETWORKS

Conceptualizing Networks

Let us revisit the people in my opening tableau of personal relationships. We could pick any of the relationships to introduce a social network perspective, but I'll focus on a pair of friends. Let's call them Helen and Julie. In the previous section, we explored concepts that might be used to describe their friendship. But Helen and Julie have other relationships, too. There are friends, casual friends, work associates, and distant relatives. There are people known only in a given setting—the woman at the veterinarian's office, the hairdresser, the checker at the supermarket. And at the edges of each woman's immediate social circle are the people whom Milgram (1977) called "familiar strangers." They are the individuals whom we encounter often and whose faces we recognize, but with whom we have never spoken and whose names we do not know. Together these various relationships constitute a social network that typically contains several hundred people (Killworth, Bernard, & McCarty, 1984).

One way to appreciate the theoretic importance of social networks is by analogy. George Herbert Mead (1934) observed, "Selves can only exist in defined relationship to other selves. No hard-and-fast line can be drawn between our own selves and the selves of others" (p. 164). What Mead and many others have said about the social character of the self is also true at higher levels of analysis. Just as selves do not exist apart from relationships, relationships do not exist apart from other relationships; that is, from networks. No hard-and-fast line can be drawn between the activities of one relationship and the activities of the other relationships to which it is connected. Helen and Julie's friendship will inevitably be colored by how the two of them relate to the rest of the people in their respective networks.

Viewing social relations from the vantage point of social networks is not, however, merely a way to link relationships to one another. Networks are the living tissue of culture and social structure. Cultural rules, norms, and rituals are meaningful only to the extent that they are *enacted and reenacted* in the actual communication patterns of individuals. The "structure" in social structure is what is contained in the patterned content flows of social networks. The "who talks to whom about what" is the living, the real part of culture and social structure. Looking at the content and structure of social networks in this way not only provides empirical grounding and an ontological foundation for concepts like *culture* and *social structure*, but it also addresses what White (1970) called the *aggregation problem*. This is the problem of linking the local, often personalized interactions to broader social structures and trends. Because network concepts provide theoretic transport between the micro- and macrolevels of analysis, they are uniquely suited for addressing the implications of personal relationships in the aggregate (Granovetter, 1973).

These more abstract points may be restated more simply if we go back to our friends, Helen and Julie. The life course of their friendship, I argue, is derived not only from the fit between their individual qualities, but also from the dynamics of their surrounding networks. And these networks themselves constitute the meaning Helen and Julie have for their cultural situation. Whatever is consistently enacted in that network of relationships, how Helen and Julie fit into those relationships, and how those relationships are linked to one another *will be* Helen and Julie's sense of their culture and of their place in it.

Sampling Networks

The total number of people with whom one has contact over any appreciable period of time is likely to be quite large. Because of this, researchers usually sample network members using one of two basic strategies. The most common strategy is to sample people who are significant for the subject in some way. Thus a network roster may be generated by asking respondents to list those individuals who are particularly important to them or to whom they feel close (e.g., M. P. Johnson & Milardo, 1984; Parks & Adelman, 1983). In other cases, researchers identify network members by asking respondents to list friends, members of their immediate family, or other individuals who have been designated as important by the researcher on a priori grounds (e.g., Laumann, 1973; Lewis, 1973b). In still other cases, network rosters have been generated by asking respondents to list people who served important functions for them, such as being a confidant or being someone who could be depended on for personal favors or with whom important matters are discussed (e.g., Fischer, 1982; Marsden, 1987; Milardo, 1989).

Another general strategy for sampling networks has been to include every one with whom the respondent has had a certain amount of interaction over a given period. This is might be done through direct observation or through survey methods such as asking respondents to list individuals whom they see regularly. Sometimes respondents are asked to create a record of their interactions with a log or diary or to respond to retrospective questions about their interactions within some specified period of time. In one study, for example, subjects were telephoned seven times during a 3-week period and were asked on each occasion to list the people with whom they had interacted voluntarily for 5 minutes or more during the previous 24 hours (Milardo, 1989).

The first strategy yields what has been called the *psychological network*, while the second approach yields an *interactive network* (Milardo, 1992; Surra & Milardo, 1991). Different methods can yield strikingly different results. Milardo (1989), for example, asked individuals to generate both their psychological and interactive networks and found that only 25% of the people listed appeared on both lists. Even so, the psychological network and the interactive network are probably not as distinct as these findings might suggest. There is certainly no reason to treat the interactive network as if it were real and the psychological network as if it consisted merely of "the interior furnishings of one's mind" (Milardo & Allan, 1997, p. 520). It is probably more useful to recognize that these are not different networks but rather different sectors or layers of the same overall network. People will appear in one and not the other only when there is a large disparity between their stated importance to the focal person and their frequency of communication with the focal person. In the case of the study in which the two network sectors had only 25% overlap in membership, for example, the researcher had restricted the interactive network to only those individuals with whom the respondent had communicated within the previous 24 hours. Restricting membership to such recent interactions undoubtedly maximized the differences between the two networks. After all, a network of psychologically significant people is still an interactive network at some level. People with whom one never or rarely interacts are unlikely to remain significant. Thus, the differences in sampling approaches, although important, should not be dramatized to the point of ignoring similarities. To one degree or another, all social networks are communication networks and, because of this, I use the terms interchangeably.

Moreover, the two strategies can easily be combined. Fischer (1977), for example, asked men to name "the three men who are your closest friends and whom you see the most often" (p. 45). Others have also advocated network rosters be constructed so as to contain the people who both interacted frequently with the respondent and who were socially or emotionally important to him or her (Burt, 1983).

The choice of sampling methods ultimately rests on the substantive focus on the research. No one method fits all cases. If one is interested in the effects of opposition or support from network members, for example, it may be more useful to look at the reactions of significant others because their support or opposition may have a greater impact than that of less important network members. If one is interested in the frequency of communication with members of the partner's network, it may be necessary to consider both the importance and frequency of contact when identifying network members. On the other hand, if one is interested in structural effects such as access to alternative partners or the level of overlap between individuals' networks, it may be more useful to focus on the interactive network because it better captures broader structures. A roster based entirely on one person's list of significant others may overlook important, but nonreciprocated links (Carley & Krackhardt, 1996; Kalmijn, 2003). For example, not everyone Bob lists as a friend will also list Bob as a friend and, moreover, Bob may fail to list people who list him as a friend. Because of these considerations, the research described in the chapters that follow will draw on several different strategies for identifying network members.

Network Factors in the Relational Life Cycle

Both the structure of linkages in a network and the content of the communication flowing through them are important if we are to understand the interplay of networks and relationships. Six aspects of network structure and content should be linked to the life cycle of personal relationships (Parks, 2000): (a) network distance, (b) network overlap, (c) cross-network contact, (d) cross-network density, (e) attraction to members of the partner's network, and (f) support for the relationship from members of one's own and one's partner's network. Some of these have long histories, whereas others are still awaiting detailed empirical exploration.

Network Distance.   Social networks act as relational maps that show how close or distant people are from one another. The people who have relationships are directly linked. Thus, our friends Helen and Julie will be directly connected—as illustrated in Fig. 2.1. However, Helen and Julie are also linked to others who are linked to still others. These people may have either direct or indirect linkages (i.e., have a relationship or not). Thus, Helen may know Kaisa, but Kaisa may not know Julie. Julie may know Ted, who in turn knows both Helen and Marie. Marie has met only Ted. The distance between any two unacquainted persons is determined by the number of links separating them. This characteristic has been variously labeled as *reachability* (Mitchell, 1969), *network proximity* (Parks & Eggert, 1991), and *distance* (Pattison, 1993; Surra & Milardo, 1991). Thus, the distance between Helen and Julie is one because they are separated by only one link. The distance between Kaisa and Ted is two—reflecting the fact that information from Kaisa must go through at least two links (via Helen) before reaching Ted. And the distance between Kaisa and Marie is two—reflecting that both Helen and Ted stand between them.

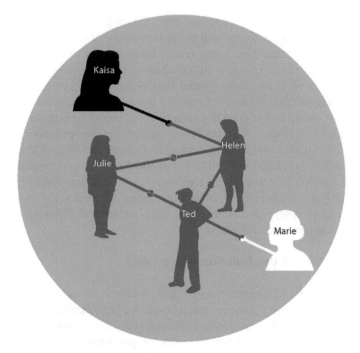

FIG. 2.1.   Social distance in networks.

Network distances greater than one represent indirect relationships. And, if one follows the indirect linkages far enough, it becomes reasonable to think of almost everyone as having indirect relationships with everyone else. Studies of this "small world effect" suggest that five to ten links are usually sufficient to connect randomly selected individuals even when they live great distances from one another (e.g., Dodds, Muhamad, & Watts, 2003; Milgram, 1967). For our purposes, however, the significance of indirect relationships lies in their potential for creating new relationships. In chapter 3, I explore how the network distance separating unacquainted persons is associated with their likelihood of initiating a direct, personal relationship.

Network Overlap.   Relationship development and deterioration are about the joining and separating of networks as well as individuals. Thus the degree of linkage between the participants' networks should be strongly correlated to the developmental status of their dyadic relationship (e.g., Kearns & Leonard, 2004; Milardo, 1982). The extent to which network members are connected to each other is generally reflected by the concept of *network density*. Density is usually measured as the ratio of the number of observed links between network members to the number of possible links (Barnes, 1969a).

The density of the total network created from the relational partners' contacts will, however, be of less interest than the density of the specific local sectors where the individual networks of the relational partners come into contact. Three aspects of this local density command attention. The first of these is network overlap—the number or proportion of people that are common members of the relational partners' individual networks. These are the people who are listed on the network rosters of both relational partners. Network overlap is illustrated in Fig. 2.2. In this example, Helen and Julie have each listed five people on their network rosters. Three of Helen's contacts are unique to her network (the contacts designated with an "h") and three of Julie's are unique (those designated with a "j"). Two people, however, appear on both lists. These members overlap (the contacts designed with "hj"). Thus, the network overlap would be calculated as .25 (2 joint members out of 8 total listed by the respondents).

Cross-Network Contact. Another kind of linkage between the partners' individual networks occurs when one partner begins to communicate with

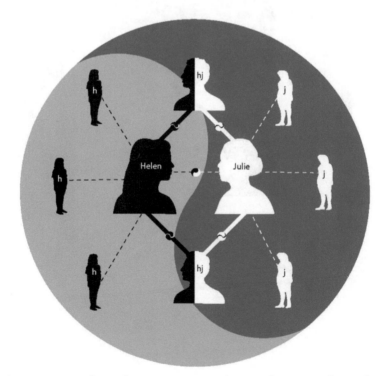

FIG. 2.2. Network overlap represents people named as network members by both partners.

the members of the other partner's network. This is cross-network contact (Parks, 2000) and is illustrated in Fig. 2.3 with solid lines. *Network overlap* and *cross-network* are distinct concepts, though they may be associated empirically. When each person lists the people that he or she sees most often, then the level of overlap will reflect the number of people common to both partners' lists, whereas cross-network contact will reflect the frequency of communication with everyone on the partner's list, even if they are not among one's own most frequent contacts. When each person lists their close friends, a given friend may appear on one respondent's list but not on the other's. Helen may list her friend, Ted, who, although not appearing on Julie's list of significant others, is still someone with whom Julie communicates regularly. Sampling networks according to the type or importance of relationships preserves the subtle, but potentially important, distinction between "our friend" and "your friend with whom I have contact." Cross-network contact is usually measured as the num-

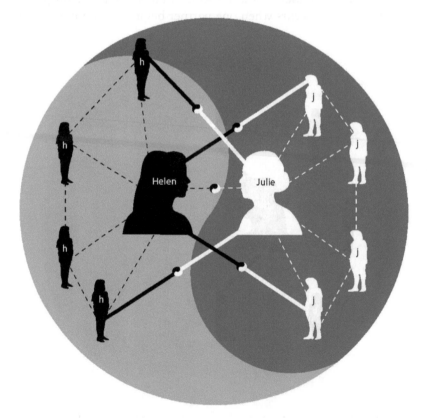

FIG. 2.3. Cross-network contact represents linkages between one partner and the unique members of the other partner's individual network.

ber or proportion of people in the partner's network one has met or as the average frequency of communication with known members of the partner's
network (e.g., Parks, Stan, & Eggert, 1983).

Cross-Network Density.   *Cross-network density* reflects the extent to which
members of each partner's network know and communicate with members of
the other partner's network (Parks, 2000). It can be measured as the proportion
of observed to potential cross-network linkages. The solid lines in Fig. 2.4 illustrate cross-network density. Helen and Julie each list four links. Not including
Helen and Julie, there are 28 possible linkages among members of the total network. But six are within Helen's network and six are within Julie's network, leaving the total number of potential cross-network contacts to be 16 (see Appendix
A for computational formula). Seven of these 16 are active in my illustration, so
observed the cross-network density is 7/16ths or approximately 44%.

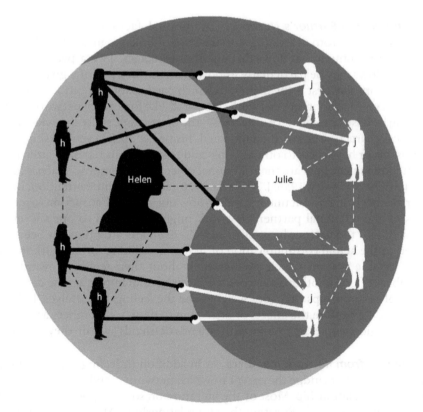

FIG. 2.4.   Cross-network density represents linkages between members of
each partner's network and members of the other partner's network.

Although the role of cross-network density has not been explored extensively in research on the relational life cycle, the concept is consistent with traditional network approaches to "clustering" between members of the partners' separate networks (Barnes, 1969b). A strict measure of cross-network density would require researchers to contact each separate network member. Just how formidable a challenge this can be was illustrated in a study by H. J. Kim and Stiff (1991). First, they found that perhaps as many as 20% of the couples in their sample where lost because one or both members refused to give access to network members. Even with a reduced sample of only 75 couples, however, nearly 1,000 network members were named. A simpler, but still useful, measure can be obtained by asking the partners themselves to estimate the level of cross-contact between the members of their individual networks. In one prototype, for example, we asked dating partners to create a grid in which one person's contacts were listed along the rows and the other's were listed in the columns. They were then asked to discuss together whether each possible combination of people had ever met and, if they had, how often they communicated with each other (see chap. 5, Appendix A).

Attraction to Partner's Network.   Additional factors come into view when we move from describing the structure of linkages in a network to describing the content that flows through those linkages. Two aspects of these content flows may be particularly important in the life cycle of a given dyadic relationship. The first is the degree to which participants are attracted to the members of one another's network. Like or dislike for a given network member can be based on a variety of factors—the personality, skills, knowledge, or physical characteristics of the individual, his or her social memberships and status, his or her access to other people and resources, and so on. Patterns of attraction in networks are the traditional object of sociometric analysis (e.g., Cartwright & Harary, 1956; J. A. Davis, 1970). Relatively little attention, however, has been directed at understanding how one's level of attraction to members of the relational partner's network might be related to one's level of attraction to the partner himself or herself. Even less attention has been devoted to the actual communication of liking or disliking for network members. Yet the way in which partners talk about their feelings toward the members of one another's network may well have an impact on the development of relationships that goes well beyond the feelings themselves. In later chapters, we explore the effects of attraction to network members as well as the strategies people use to cope with "friends of friends" whom they dislike.

Support from network members.   In addition to feelings of attraction, relational partners judge the extent to which network members are supportive of their relationship. Most of the literature on social support has focused on support for individuals rather than for relationships. Although support for the individual and support for the relationship often go hand in hand, it is easy to imagine cases in which they are at odds. One may support Helen as an individual, but be quite skeptical of her friendship with Julie. Sometimes network members believe that the best way for them to support the individual is to actively oppose the relationship. This happens, for example, when a network member worries that an individual's new acquaintance may become a "bad influence" on him or her. Conversely, network members may be very supportive of the relationship, but not very supportive of the individuals within it. Network members may, for instance, discourage one relational partner from doing something, say taking up a new hobby or social activity, by suggesting that it will damage the partner's relationship.

Social support networks have traditionally been viewed as buffers against the effects of stress or as channels for resources for the alleviation of stress (e.g., Gottlieb, 1983; LaRocco, House, & French, 1980). More recent approaches have emphasized that support often works by enhancing the recipient's sense of personal control over his or her circumstances (Albrecht & Adelman, 1987; Hobfoll, 1988; Spitzer, Bar-Tal, & Golander, 1995). But relationships may be supported or opposed by network members in many other ways including the symbolic reinforcement conveyed both explicitly through verbal comments and implicitly through social activities such joint invitations (Lewis, 1973b; Parks & Eggert, 1991). In a later chapter, we investigate the dilemmas relational partners face when they experience problems in their relationship and wish to obtain support from network members.

Most investigators have focused on the outcomes of the support process—that is, whether partners end up feeling that network members support their relationship. As important as these summary perceptions are, however, they fail to get at the full range of activities through which partners and network members negotiate what is known, presented, and expressed about the relationship. To give just one example, it appears that a couple's memory of the important turning points in their romantic relationship is often worked out as they share the story of their relationship with network members (Baxter & Pittman, 2001). This implies that, in many cases, relationship memories are actually distributed memories across a broader network.

SOCIAL CONTEXTUAL PRINCIPLES IN THE RELATIONAL LIFE CYCLE

Structure, Action, and Communication

Over the last 100 years, social scientists have increasingly recognized that to understand personal relationships, we must view them as interactive entities situated in a natural social context. My goal is to build on these developments using an approach that embeds the life cycle of relationships in the social context created by the participants' interactions with social network members.

The first challenge of constructing a social contextual theory of personal relationships is to reconcile two very different ways of explaining interpersonal behavior. These go by a variety of names, but are perhaps most often referred to as *structuralist theories* and *action theories* (see Fararo, 1989; Ritzer & Goodman, 2004; Waters, 1994).

Structuralists usually explain individual behavior in terms of larger social structures such as one's position in a network, one's role in a group, or membership in a social class or culture (e.g., Berkowitz, 1982; Blau, 1977a; 1977b). The roots of this tradition go back well over a century to Karl Marx's emphasis on the division of labor, Auguste Comte's view of institutions as church social organisms, and Emile Durkheim's idea that individuals are controlled by larger customs and values—what he called "social facts"—that are external to the individual. In each case, the explanation for why an individual acts in a particular way is to be found in something beyond the individual—something in a larger social structure that controls or shapes behavior. These views of individuals as essentially passive found their way into many of other theories, including several that sought to include some degree of individual choice such as Parsons' (1937) structural functionalism. They also found their way into social network thinking (e.g., Holland & Leinhardt, 1977a; Monge & Contractor, 2003; Scott, 2000). Thus individual behavior was the product, not so much of personal choice, but rather of the position one held in a larger social network. People who played the same roles or occupied the same location in a larger network were thought to behave in similar ways regardless of their other more individual qualities. Whether young people selected friends from other racial groups, for example, was shown to depend on the overall racial heterogeneity of the schools they attend as well as the degree to which school programs encouraged contact between races (e.g., Moody, 2001). Even when individual choice was acknowledged, as in Bott's (1971) classic work on marital role division, the overarching view was that interpersonal behavior was largely a function of external network structures.

The inner dynamics of personal relationships, on the other hand, have traditionally been studied from perspectives that emphasize individual variability and choice. These *action theories* also have a long history in the social sciences and rest on assumptions about human agency—that is, our ability as individuals to imagine alternative actions, to evaluate and form preferences among possible choices, and to respond selectively (Emirbayer & Mische, 1998; Fararo, 1989). In the case of Mead's (1934) symbolic interactionism, for example, the actions of individuals are explained by their personal choices, their idiosyncratic perceptual processes, and their interaction within a larger, personally perceived social world. Mead and those who followed prioritized personal meaning over social structure. This did not mean that social context was ignored. Indeed Mead himself was critical of those who ignored the social context. Nonetheless, Mead and his intellectual heirs (e.g., Blumer, 1969;

Goffman, 1959) explained interpersonal behavior in terms of individual interpretation and creativity rather than as a function of social roles that people simply absorbed from the environment.

Theories of social exchange also reflect the tenets of action theory. Classic exchange theories, like those of Homans (1961) and Thibaut and Kelley (1959), assumed that people rationally analyze and select among their options. Social relationships were conceptualized as patterns of ongoing exchange and interdependence. They developed and deteriorated in response to the participants' efforts to maximize their outcomes. Exchange theories have formed the foundation for several major contributions to the study of personal relationships, including Altman and Taylor's (1973) social penetration theory, Miller and Steinberg's (1975) theory of interpersonal communication, and H. H. Kelley and Thibault's (1978) theory of interdependence. Social exchange theories and symbolic interactionism, although differing in several ways, both explain the dynamics of personal relationships in terms of individual perception and choice (G. J. McCall & Simmons, 1966). Social context is usually ignored as a source of explanation for interpersonal behavior.

To explain the interplay of personal relationships and networks, however, it is necessary rethink the relationships between structure, action, and communication. Structuralist theories in their purest form reduce interpersonal relationships to cogs in a larger machine, discount personal choice, and fail to match our lived reality of personal action and meaning. Action theories, on the other hand, fracture our ongoing sense of social continuity and fail to recognize much beyond the interaction itself. These theoretic traditions have opposite, but equally limited conceptions of social structure, personal choice, and communication.

Marx (1963) observed, "men make their own history, but they do not make it just as they please" (p. 15). One obvious way to overcome the limitations of pure structuralist and pure action theories is simply to combine them into the sort of "constrained choice model" Marx's observation implies. In Parsons' (1937) theory of social action, for example, personal choice is constrained largely by the norms into which the individual has been socialized. In a more recent view, Fischer (1977) argue for a "choice-constraint" model, in which structural limitations provide a context in which individuals rationally sort out their choices as envisioned by exchange theory.

Although they avoid the limitations of pure structuralist and action theories, constrained choice models do not go far enough. We can provide a richer understanding of interpersonal behavior if we cast both individual choice and social structure within a broader communication perspective. What I call the *social contextual perspective* begins with the assumption that both interpersonal relationships and broader social structures are communication patterns. They have no existence apart from the communication practices in which they are enacted. In this view, social structure is no longer a relatively fixed stage upon which actors play out relatively scripted parts. Instead, both the individual's conception of self and the nature of the social context become determined through ongoing communication. Behavior at one point in time becomes the context for behavior at the next point in time and, in turn, that behavior both reflects the context of the previous point and becomes the context for behavior at the next point. Thus individual choices and social contexts mutually determine each other in chronological sequence.

This line of reasoning is implicit within general systems theory (see Buckley, 1967; Fielding, 1988), but has been more explicitly articulated in a number of recent sociological theories. These theories all take the position that social structure has no predetermined objective reality (Collins, 1998, 2004; Fuchs, 2001; Giddens, 1976, 1984; White, 1992). Instead, the structures of social life, whether they be identities or institutions are wholly determined by the interactions within a social network, or a region of a social network, at a particular point in time (Fuchs, 2001; White, 1992). Interactions that create or reinforce symbols of group membership and shared goals are particularly important. Collins (2004) argues that the interactions that produce these symbols are "interaction ritual chains"—in which the participants are focused so intensely on the same event that their behavior becomes interdependent at a physiological level. The symbols created in interaction rituals are infused with a sense of personal and group efficacy that is then circulated through broader social networks. Rituals, indeed interactions of all kinds, have thus a dual character, as Giddens (1976, 1984) observed in his theory of structuration. They express individual choice, but also create intentional and unintentional consequences that become the social structure upon which future behavior is predicated. Behavior thus reproduces structures and contexts. Giddens' approach, while emphasizing duality, actually reduces social structure to individual action and memory (Waters, 1994). One way around this is to argue that social behavior is shaped by communication with others and that, as a result, individual action and memory already reflects interactions beyond the individual (Collins, 2003; Mead, 1934). Put another way, the distinction between individual behavior and social structure is largely temporal, a product merely of focusing attention to different points in the same ongoing process.

Viewing behavior and context as parts of unified process is a radically different perspective than the one taken by traditional models of constrained choice. It first recognizes what Giddens (1976) called the "duality of structure." Social structures both constrain individual action and provide a set of resources that enable it. More important, instead of treating social structure as a given, the communication perspective taken here recognizes that social structure is itself generated through behavior. Culture, too, is created and maintained through interaction. Broader cultural values and expectations have no status beyond that conferred by the frequency of interactions that embody them. Although traditional models of constrained choice may acknowledge that social structure and culture change over time (e.g., changes in gender roles), they assume that the options for individual choice at any one point in time are relatively fixed. The theoretic view taken here embraces a more dynamic view of structure as something that is actively, often strategically, created by participants on an ongoing basis.

Relationships and Networks

The connections between the personal relationships and communication networks become much more interesting once we recognize the mutuality of individual action and social context. Participants' communication networks are not merely sources of influence, but are also resources that participants actively manipulate. Because of this, explanatory principles must incorporate both intentional actions and the unintended, often impersonal consequences that occur when individual actions ripple out into a social system and back again. No one explanatory principle will be sufficient to account for the diverse connections between personal relationships and their surrounding networks. We can, however, identify two major processes that function to link the life cycle of personal relationships to the dynamics of the participants surrounding networks. These are *relational sense-making* and *network structuring* (Parks, 2000; for a related discussion, see Sprecher et al., 2002). Each is previewed in the paragraphs to follow and explicated in greater detail in the studies covered in the chapters beyond.

Relational Sense-Making. To at least some degree, people are strategic about relationships—seeking to satisfy their needs and desires by deliberately moving into and out of relationships. In order to be successful, participants must be able to predict and explain each other's behavior with a reasonable level of accuracy. Sense-making thus becomes a tool for the deliberate conduct of relationships. In addition, relational partners often need to make sense of the unexpected consequences of their own or others' behavior within the broader social context. Sense-making activities are thus central to the relationship and may be found in several of the subprocesses that link the development and maintenance of personal relationships with social networks.

Linkages with network members open vast trade routes of information about the partner and the relationship (Parks, 2000). In some cases, relational participants may quite actively seek information from network members. They may seek information on how the partner has behaved in the past, explanations for the partner's behavior, and predictions of future responses. Network members may offer or be called upon to evaluate one's own predictions and explanations for relational events. Relational partners may actively seek contacts with network members who are thought to possess unique or particularly important knowledge that goes beyond what can be learned from the partner directly. Certainly, not all information acquisition is so deliberate. Network members reveal information about one another as a matter of course in everyday discussion. Even without explicit discussion, the relationships of network members create reference points against which partners may evaluate their own relationship. Married couples, for instance, commonly compare their marriage to the marriages of their friends (Titus, 1980). All of this implies that relational partners should be in a better position to manage their uncertainty about one another if they have direct and indirect contact with the partner's network. Increases in cross-network contact, network overlap, and perhaps even in cross-network density should therefore be positively related to the development and maintenance of personal relationships because of their contribution to the participants' sense-making activities. In one of our early analyses, for example, we found that cross-network contact was actually a better predictor of uncertainty in romantic couples than the amount of communication directly with the partner (Parks & Adelman, 1983). In another study, sense-making was found to be the most common reason that individuals disclosed private information about their romantic relationship to network members (Goldsmith, 1988).

Some of the most important information exchanged with network members deals with whether network members support or oppose the participants' relationship. As we will see in later chapters, the level of support from the members of one's own and one's partner's network is a powerful predictor of whether a personal relationship develops or deteriorates. A structuralist view of support would confine its effects to simple reinforcement. Relationships develop and are maintained only if they are selected and supported by network members. Although simple social reinforcement is obviously one factor, social support is also the object of extensive strategic activity by partners and network members alike. Participants and network members conspire to conceal, reveal, and distort information that may be challenging to their larger interests. Because their interests often do not coincide, the interactive dance between participants and other network members typically unfolds as a series of signals, interpretive offers, and inferred responses. In troubled relationships, network members may experience conflicts over whether to support the partner or the relationship. Network members may also face difficult decisions such as whether to confront a friend about her romantic partner's drinking problem or whether to express their ambivalence about their widowed parent's desire to find a new partner. And the relational participants may respond to these conflicts either by adopting communicative strategies that avoid explicit acknowledgment of the problem or by strategically seeking contacts with those network members who are most likely to share their views.

Human sense-making is often shaped and evaluated by the aesthetic principles of symmetry and balance. This is no less true in interpersonal relationships than it is in other realms of human endeavor. It is therefore not surprising that relational sense-making often revolves around such perceptions. It is more symmetrical or balanced if we like the people our partner likes. Balance theories predict that we should be more attracted to the partner whose friends we like (Heider, 1958; Newcomb, 1961). We should also be more attracted to members of the partner's network if we are attracted to the partner. Alternatively, if the partner's network contains people we strongly dislike, we either may back away from the partner or engage in a series of coping strategies that have the effect of denying or concealing the imbalance. These strategies will be explored in a later chapter. The point to be emphasized here, however, is that the principles of symmetry and balance predict that attraction to members of our partner's network should be related to the development of our own relationship with the partner.

In addition to broad principles like symmetry and balance, sense-making activities undoubtedly draw on more culturally or relationally specific expectations. In many societies, for example, people in close relationships expect to meet their partner's other close associates. In cultures where courting pairs are accorded considerable freedom and privacy, being introduced to the partner's parents is often a significant marker of relational development. Meeting the partner's friends, family, or close work associates satisfies a widely held social expectation and thus makes the relationship less uncertain. Failing to meet them after an appropriate period of time has passed, however, generally disrupts the sense-making process, casting doubts on the partner's feelings, on one's own desirability, and on the overall viability of the relationship.

Network Structuring.   Network factors are integral to the relational life cycle because they influence opportunities to meet, influence the amount and quality of interaction relational participants have, and regulate the availability of alternative relational partners. Network structuring occurs both through the strategic activities of the partners themselves and as an unintended consequence of their own and others' behavior.

The first and most important aspect of network structuring is its impact on whether prospective relational partners even meet. Given that we are all indirectly related, network distance (the number of links separating two unacquainted people) becomes an important determinant of whether a given pair of people will ultimately meet. This aspect of network structuring may occur passively as prospective partners are carried toward one another by shifts further out in their social networks. It may also occur quite deliberately as individuals manipulate their networks to increase access to prospective partners. These strategic activities may continue well after a new relationship is established. Participants will usually realign their networks so that opportunities to interact are maximized. They may, for instance, be drawn toward a more overlapping network because of its potential to create more opportunities to be together and to reduce the number of competing demands on their time. In this way, network structuring contributes to the maintenance and enhancement of personal relationships.

Active and passive network structuring are also evident in the deterioration of personal relationships. People in troubled relationships often actively manipulate their networks so as to restrict contact and access to information. They reduce network contact, sever overlapping relationships, and restrict contact with those who are likely to pass on information they wish to keep private. These changes, however, need not be deliberate. They could be unintended consequences of other actions, such as moving from one part of town to another, shifting work groups, changing jobs, or any number of other aggregated social changes over which the individual has little control. Either way, changes in the network structure surrounding a relationship should be tied to changes in the life of that relationship.

Network structure also regulates both the desirability and availability of alternative partners. The role of network factors as barriers to dissolution has long been recognized (Levinger, 1979). Individuals are less likely to meet and spend time with alternative partners when they share an overlapping network with their relational partner, when they regularly interact with the partner's network (cross-network contact), and when the members of their network interact regularly with the members of their partner's network (cross-network density). Contact with the partner's network may enhance the attractiveness of the partner if its members provide access to resources that would not otherwise be available. Participants in troubled relationships may reevaluate their desire to leave when confronted with the social costs of losing these connections. Moreover, supportive network members are unlikely to introduce the participants to alternative partners. Even subtle things like personalized communication patterns that become generalized across a circle of friends can serve to support the dyads within it. Interactions with and among network members thus create barriers to leaving, but they can just as easily hasten the demise of a relationship. Finally, once a relationship has ended, the structure of the individual's network may make it easier or harder to find new partners.

The Chapters Ahead

In the chapters that follow I turn to a series of studies that further explicate the social contextual principles outlined in this chapter. Extensive analyses covering several different data sets will be presented in these chapters, although I rely on appendices to carry the most technical material. I begin in the next chapter at the beginning of the relational life cycle, actually before it begins, and address the question of how relationships are initiated. Why do some people meet and begin relationships and others do not? In the two chapters after that I explore the development of friendships and romantic relationships. In order to provide the most comprehensive view, I not only reanalyze existing data, but also present new studies.

In the two chapters that follow, my concern will shift to examining the generality of the social contextual perspective. In the first, I examine the interplay of development and networks in different age groups and across different relationship types. In the second, I explore the role of gender and ethnicity in the social contextual perspective.

At that point we will return to the give-and-take of ongoing interaction to consider the complexities and dilemmas posed for relational participants as they deal with network members. How, for instance, do people manage information about the state of their relationship, particularly negative information? How do people cope with the members of the partner's network whom they actively dislike?

In the final chapters, I first complete our tour of the relational life cycle by considering the interplay of relational and network factors as personal relationships, particularly romantic relationships, deteriorate. And in the final chapter, I summarize the findings and consider their implications for the broader social issues confronting personal relationships.

Initiating Personal Relationships

The beginning of personal relationships, particularly romantic relationships, is often shrouded in an aura of luck and mystery. Popular advice columnist, Ann Landers (1996) put it this way in a note to her readers:

> Dear Readers: Do you believe in fate? Or is it just dumb luck—a matter of being in the right place at the right time? When I asked readers how they met their mates, I was struck by how frequently Cupid had arranged for them to be sitting next to one another .... An incredible number of people told me they just happened to be seated next to one another on a place, train, bus, roller coaster, street car or camel ride. (p. D3)

Ms. Landers went on to recount several stories of first meetings sent to her by her readers. One couple happened to have seats next to each other at a football game. Another met while donating blood at the Red Cross. Still another couple chanced to sit next to each other around the campfire at a club outing. Naturally the stories all have happy endings. The imagery is revealing: the woman who says that hers was a "lucky seat" on the plane, the reference to fate, even Ms. Landers' bow to Cupid. In each case the forces that first brought people together were outside their control, perhaps beyond their comprehension.

Something else is striking in these stories of relational genesis. There is often little reference to anyone other than the future partner. In some cases, the focus on the other person is so intense that everything else is perceptually blotted out. The hero of Goethe's (1774/1971), *The Sorrows of Young Werther*, expressed this sentiment shortly after being introduced to Lotte, the young woman with whom he was to fall tragically in love: "Since then, sun, moon, and stars may continue on their course; for me there is neither day nor night, and the entire universe about me has ceased to exist" (p. 32).

Luck, fate, the gods, and the suspension of natural law all exemplify the birth of romance. The power of these images, however, does not flow from their empirical reality. On the contrary, the power of romantic imagery flows from its transcendence, even denial of social and physical realities. The truth of romantic imagery stems from its emotional purity and motivational energy, not its descriptive accuracy. It makes the couple feel special, focuses them on each other, inspires gratitude, and fires mutual desire. Who would not be affirmed by having a lover describe meeting them as a blessing or a gift?

For those struggling to understand and improve their relationships, however, romantic imagery that emphasizes mystical explanations may in fact be detrimental. Telling lonely people that it is a matter of luck whether they find a friend or lover will not be very helpful. Telling them that they will find a relationship when it is "meant to be" offers little support and less guidance. These explanations are also troubling for scholars seeking to understand the relational life cycle. Indeed one measure of a successful social science is that it provides empirically grounded explanations for events that people once attributed to luck, fate, or other mysterious forces.

Unfortunately researchers have given surprisingly little attention to the process of relational initiation. Many of the studies that claim to address the process actually fail to do so. In the next section, I explore the reasons for this and then advance a social contextual perspective on relationship initiation in the sections that follow. These sections begin with the social contextual factors that have been recognized in the previous literature. These include *physical proximity effects*, *group norms* regarding partner choice, and what I refer to as *situational generalization*. The bulk of the discussion, however, is devoted to research reports on two additional social contextual factors: *social proximity effects* and *third party effects*.

PREVIOUS RESEARCH ON RELATIONSHIP INITIATION

The effects of physical proximity on relationship initiation have been recognized for over 70 years (e.g., Bossard, 1932; Kennedy, 1943). Important as it is, however, proximity in residential choice or work setting is not sufficient to account for initiation and early formation of relationships. With the exception of research on physical proximity effects, much of the research on attraction, initial interaction and relationship formation conducted over the past 35 years can be fairly criticized for failing to address the earliest stages of relationship formation or the natural social context of relationship initiation, or both.

Many of the longitudinal field studies on the development of relationships are actually studies of recently initiated relationships rather than of relationship initiation. Whether they examine the development of relationships between roommates, friends, or dating partners, researchers do not typically begin measurement until after the relational partners have already initiated their relationships and often had considerable interaction (e.g., Flora & Segrin, 2003; Hays, 1984; Milardo, 1982; Sprecher & Felmlee, 2000).

Laboratory studies of interpersonal attraction and initial interaction have also usually failed to address the actual process of initiation. In the typical procedure, researchers arbitrarily pair strangers for interaction in a laboratory setting (e.g., Simpson, Gangestad, & Biek, 1993; Snyder, Berscheid, & Glick, 1985). The participants may or may not be provided with information about one another in advance. One of the participants is a confederate in some cases. Regardless of the particular configuration, these designs suffer from two limitations. First, they focus on very recently initiated relationships rather than relationship initiation. These may be quite new relationships but they are nonetheless already initiated as the result of the investigator's actions. In addition, these designs rip the participants out of the social settings they naturally inhabit. This is most apparent in studies in which participants are paired randomly and told to "get to know each other" or, worse yet, told nothing. They are in effect given no information about one another, no realistic task or activity, and no natural contextual cues that will help them select and evaluate behavior.

In other cases, researchers have either attempted to create social contexts for interaction or have taken advantage of previously created, but highly specialized, social contexts. Perhaps the most dramatic example of the former is Altman and Haythorn's   (1965) study of relationship formation between pairs of men who were confined to a small room for 10 days. Less dramatic examples include the now classic studies of interpersonal attraction at student dances arranged by researchers (e.g., Walster, Aronson, Abrahams, & Rottmann, 1966). Sometimes researchers have examined relationship initiation in highly specialized contexts such as personal ads and commercial dating services (e.g., Green, Buchanan, & Heuer, 1984; Lance, 1998). As online computer services have grown, it was inevitable that researchers would also investigate computer-mediated settings as well (e.g., Donn & Sherman, 2002; Scharlott & Christ, 1995). Although these synthetic contexts are legitimate objects of study in their own right, they are not analogues for the more complex, consequential social environments in which people most often meet.

Studies that lack both a realistic social context and an actual interactive partner are even less informative. Research using D. E. Byrne's (1971) "phantom other" technique or variations on it falls into this category. Participants are typically instructed to form impressions of a nonexistent other purely on the basis of highly limited information provided by the experimenter. They may be given attitude information, pictures, or other information, but at no point is there any real interaction with another person (e.g., Hahn & Blass, 1997; Snyder et al., 1985). It is doubtful that designs such as these tell us much at all about the ways that relationships actually come into being or even about their early development. The fact that participants in these studies appear to use the information they are given in predictable ways does not necessarily suggest that they seek or use similar information in actual encounters. Instead, it may only suggest that people will rely heavily on the few scraps of information they have left when they are placed in socially impoverished environments.

Particular attitudes or personality variables may seem vitally important, not because they really are, but because the researcher has systematically stripped away so many other factors that influence relational initiation in natural settings. Indeed, looking at how people meet in real settings reveals a far different picture than the one derived from these studies.

BEYOND THE MYTH OF THE OPEN FIELD

In her remarkable family history, *Wild Swans*, Jung Chang tells the story of three generations of women in 20th Century China. She relates how her parents had to seek the permission of the Communist Party in their town before they began to court in the late 1940s. She also tells how, a generation later in the 1960s, the youthful Red Guards vilified couples who had met outside the confines of party and family. She tells of a schoolteacher who was publicly beaten for having behaved immorally. The evidence of her immorality was that she had first met her husband on a public bus. In parts of China, as in most other places in the world, relationship initiation occurs in a relatively "closed field" (Murstein, 1970). The choice of relational partners is limited by a variety of social mechanisms including norms, surveillance, and physical segregation.

In the United States and other Western cultures, on the other hand, relationship initiation is widely presumed to occur in an "open field", in which individual choice is maximized and larger social influences are minimized. The contrast between these two models of relational choice is illustrated dramatically by the juxtaposition of Jung Chang's account of the Chinese woman who was publicly beaten with Ann Landers' happy tales of Cupid arranging for lovers to meet for the first time by chance.

Such striking cultural differences, however, lead us to overestimate the degree of openness in Western cultures. Their openness is relative. Strictly speaking, there is no such thing as a pure "open field" when it comes to relational choices. There are only degrees of being closed. The distinction is more than semantic. If we say nothing affects our relational choices, that they are completely free, then we miss an entire set of contextual factors that can be shown to influence those choices.

STARTING RELATIONSHIPS IN CONTEXT

The social and physical context in which relationships form is much more than a passive backdrop for individual choices. It contains a series of factors that influence who meets whom. Some of these factors are beyond the control of the individual, whereas others are resources that individuals manipulate for their own ends. Some of these factors have been recognized, if not fully appreciated, in the previous literature. These include physical proximity effects and group norms regarding partner choice. The way in which affective reactions to situations may generalize to become attached to the people in those situa-

tions has also been occasionally acknowledged. Each of these is now discussed, along with research on two other social contextual factors, social
proximity effects and third-party effects.

Physical Proximity

Probably the most widely recognized contextual factor in the initial meeting
of strangers is sheer physical proximity. Indeed physical proximity has been
recognized as a force in relational initiation for so long that we rarely review or
question the evidence behind the claim. Yet the classic studies are worth reex-
amining both for what they can and cannot tell us.

In one of the first of these studies, Bossard investigated the distance between the residences of couples applying for marriage licenses in Philadelphia
during the first 5 months of 1931. A total of 5,000 applications were examined
and the distance in city blocks between the applicants was calculated. Results
indicated that most of the applicants lived close to one another. Just over 25%
lived within three blocks and just over 40% lived within 10 blocks of each other
at the time they applied for the marriage license. The majority lived within 20
blocks. Although Bossard concluded that these findings demonstrated the
role of residential proximity in mate selection, later investigators noted that it
would be more telling to determine how far apart the applicants lived when
they first started dating. Data on this issue were provided by Clarke (1952) in
interviews with 431 couples who applied for marriage licenses in Columbus,
Ohio during the summer of 1949. Of the 281 couples in the final sample, 61%
lived within 20 blocks of each other when they first started dating. Nearly 25%
lived within four blocks of each other.

Other studies have given us a more detailed picture of the effects of proximity
on relational initiation. Studies of neighborhoods and housing complexes showed
that people tended to socialize more with proximal than with distal neighbors
(Caplow & Forman, 1950; Festinger et al., 1963). Within a given building, people
are more likely to select people who live or work close by as friends than people
who are more removed in distance (e.g., Loether, 1960). Proximity may play a particularly important role in settings where residents vary widely by age and race.
Friendships between dissimilar people are often restricted to those who live very
close to one another (Nahemow & Lawton, 1975).

That people must be in physical proximity in order to meet face-to-face is,
of course, a truism. This, coupled with a consistent pattern of findings over
several decades, accounts for the prominence given to physical proximity in
discussions of relational initiation. Certainly architectural and temporal structures that place some people in closer proximity than others influence opportunities for relationships. This seems so obvious that the role of physical

proximity is no longer questioned or even researched. Unfortunately, there are significant problems with explanations based on physical proximity.

The early findings are not as powerful as they are often assumed to be by later writers. Nearly half of the couples in Bossard's (1932) data, for example, lived more than 20 blocks apart and just under 20% lived in different cities. Approximately 35% of those in Clarke's (1952) Columbus sample lived in different cities. To make matters worse, these studies often threw out couples for whom calculating distance was difficult. Clarke, for example, threw out the 35% who lived in different cities. Removing the people who lived farthest from each other quite obviously biased the results toward an overestimation of the effects of physical proximity. This is not to say that physical proximity is unimportant, but it does suggest that we need to question whether physical proximity is as significant a factor in relationship initiation as it is routinely presumed to be.

At best, physical proximity is a necessary, but not sufficient, condition for relationship initiation and development. A study of friendship formation in an apartment complex, for example, revealed that, although proximity accounted for initial contacts between people, it did not account for which ones became friends once contact had occurred (Snow, Leahy, & Schwab, 1981). More generally, showing that a large percentage of those who start dating or who marry live within a few blocks of one another does not explain why they started dating each other rather than any number of other potential partners within the same geographic radius.

Finally, for many people, physical proximity is no longer even a necessary condition for relationship initiation. The importance of residential propinquity diminishes as the proportion of the population having personal access to automobiles increases. Indeed one effect of the changes in communication and transportation technology in the 20th Century may have been to lift relationships from the confines of physical proximity. Modern suburbanites, for example, use these technologies to maintain functional, but geographically dispersed, social networks (Wellman, 1979). Computer-mediated social environments provide total liberation from physical proximity as a force in relationship initiation. The social venues of the Internet make it easy for people to meet and initiate relationships without regard for the physical location of the parties relative to one another. On the Internet, there is no difference between being one block away and being one continent away. The initial studies of relationship development in computer-mediated settings indicate that the vast majority of users do indeed initiate personal relationships there (Parks & Floyd, 1996a; Parks & Roberts, 1998). Thus although physical proximity is an often an important contextual factor in the initiation of personal relationships, it is clearly not the only contextual factor of importance and may in some cases be losing its influence altogether as changes in technology allow more widespread movement and communication.

Group Norms

Only a few of the people who are available for relationships are ever considered as possible relational partners. The larger "field of availables" is screened to a narrower "field of eligibles" and then to a still narrower "field of desirables" (Kerckhoff, 1974; Winch, 1958). This winnowing occurs as people make rapid cognitive appraisals about whether a given person is an appropriate or acceptable prospect. People who do not make it into the field of eligibles are not thought of possible partners. On the other hand, there is often a defining moment in the initiation process when one starts consciously to consider someone as a possible relational partner. This person has made it into the field of desirables. Choices about who is counted among the field of desirables reflect group norms as well as a series of more idiosyncratic factors. These norms operate as criteria for inclusion and are widely diffused throughout the individual's social group. In effect, they become part of the social context.

Chief among these norms is the norm of similarity or homogamy. People tend to pick relational partners who are similar to them along a remarkable number of dimensions. When it comes to selecting a mate, group norms typically favor the selection of someone who is similar in age, ethnicity, socioeconomic status, education, and religion (e.g, Hayes & Jones, 1991; Joyner & Kao, 2000; Kalmijn, 1991, 1994, 1998; Kalmijn & Flap, 2001; Vera, Berardo, & Vandiver, 1990). There is also some evidence to suggest that people usually select someone who is similar in weight and physical appearance (Chambers, Christiansen, & Kunz, 1983; Schafer & Keith, 1990). In places with considerable racial and linguistic diversity, such as South Africa, similarity in language may be critical in mate selection as well (Maconachie, 1988).

There are exceptions to the rule of homogamy, but even they may show the presence of strong social norms. In many cultures, it is expected, for example, that the male will be taller than his female partner. This expectation is relatively easy to satisfy given that males are generally taller than females. Nonetheless it appears that more than simple probability is at work. Gillis and Avis (1980), for instance, found that males were taller than females in 719 of the 720 North American couples they studied—far more often than would be expected by chance alone.

Social and cultural change usually means a transformation of group norms governing the selection of relational partners. Although the content of the norms may change, the presence of norms of some type does not. Analyses of census data and national surveys in Europe, for instance, indicate that although religious similarity has declined in importance, similarity in educational attainment has become a more important factor in mate selection over the last 40 years (Kalmijn, 1993).

Situational Generalization

A third situational factor in the initiation of personal relationships has been recognized in the literature on attraction and personal relationships. Its impact has been explored less frequently than the effects of physical proximity and group norms. Nonetheless, the idea that affective responses to situational factors may generalize to influence the feelings the participants have for one another is well recognized.

Perhaps the best known kind of situational generalization is the effect of stress on affiliation and attraction. Research has long demonstrated that people are more likely to affiliate with one another if they find themselves together in a stressful situation (Schachter, 1959). Sharing a stressful situation can cause people to see others as more attractive and motivate them to initiate interaction. This effect was demonstrated dramatically in Dutton and Aron's (1974) study of how young men reacted to meeting a young woman while walking across a bridge over the Capilano River near Vancouver, British Columbia. In the experimental condition, the men were asked to cross a narrow wooden footbridge suspended 230 feet above the river. The bridge swayed and wobbled and had only low handrails. In the control condition, men were asked to cross a bridge upstream. This bridge was wider, better constructed, had high handrails, and was only 10 feet above a small tributary to the main river. As the men crossed the bridges, they were met by a young woman who explained that she was doing a study on how scenic attractions affected "creative expression." She asked them to fill out a short survey and write a brief story based on a picture of a woman. She also offered to tell the subjects more when she had more time and offered her phone number. When Dutton and Aron scored the stories for sexual content, they found that the men who had crossed the higher, more dangerous bridge wrote stories with more sexual imagery than the men who had crossed the lower, safer bridge. Moreover, the men who had been experienced greater stress were more likely to accept the woman's phone number and to actually call her later.

Real life examples often take the form of a shared adventure. Karen, one of my students, told how she had gotten together with John. She wrote:

> I lived in Colorado this past winter. One day I went hiking and skiing into the backcountry with a group that included John. It was a beautiful, clear day with two feet of fresh powder. They took me to a run called the "killer slide" where there were three big rocks that you could jump off of. This was both exciting and scary for me. I had never jumped off anything that big. I

wanted to do it and looked to others for support. Jumping off these rocks and skiing in the backcountry was an intense and exhilarating experience. There was a bond between us because of what we had just experienced. It made the trust and rely on the group, especially John.

The characteristics of situations may generalize to influence relationships even if they are not particularly stressful. One form occurs when people share a common set of positive outcomes. Kim, another student, told this story about her friend, Kara, Kara's boyfriend, Rick, and Rick's roommate, Brian:

> ... one Friday night last January Kara and I decided to go bowling together. Kara got Rick to bring Brian. There were no fireworks at first, but as the evening went on it got better. We decided to have teams, Kara and Rick vs. Kim and Brian. This was a crucial event that really brought us closer. We were able to encourage one another and celebrate together. We beat them so it was a positive note to end the date on. We went out again and have ever since. We are getting married in November.

These examples illustrate how the characteristics of the context may "rub off" on the participants. Sometimes the positive aspects of the context reinforce the relationship. In other cases, as Dutton and Aron (1974) suggested, negative aspects of the context may create anxiety that is cognitively relabeled as attraction. The opposite can occur, too. A string of negative events on a first date, for instance, may well leave the participants with a sour taste for the relationship. Although we don't yet understand the factors that determine whether the generalization has positive or negative consequences, it is clear that the physical context in which people meet plays a role in relationship initiation.

Social Proximity Effects

Social networks act as maps that allow us to plot how people are related to one another in social space. Several different structural features of networks are involved in the life cycle of individual relationships (i.e., network distance and overlap, cross-network contact and density). From the standpoint of relational initiation, however, it is the concept of *network distance* that reveals the most. Network distance, as we observed in the previous chapter, refers to the number of links separating any two people.

The fact that nearly everyone is linked indirectly creates what Milgram dubbed the "small world phenomenon" and accounts for the fact that total strangers often find they know the same person. For example, Kyle, one of my students, told me about meeting a fellow traveler named Joost in a youth hostel in London. Joost lived in Amsterdam. Joost and Kyle talked through the evening, describing their travels and their lives in Seattle and Amsterdam.

Joost mentioned that about a year before, he had met another American who had been visiting Holland. A few more comments uncovered the fact this American came from the same part of the country as Kyle. Joost then mentioned that his American friend attended a small college in New York. Kyle mused that his best friend from high school also attended a small college in New York. One question led to another and, before long, they both realized they were talking about the same person. Kyle and Joost, although living half a world away and meeting seemingly by chance, discovered that they shared a mutual friend. They were only one link apart in a global social network.

Although we may think of such meetings as the fruit of luck or chance, they are often the product of social proximity effects. Social proximity effects occur when a change in individuals' structural location relative to one another in a social network alters their probability of meeting. The general principle is that as the number of links separating any two people decreases, their probability of meeting increases. It may not be obvious how this principle could account for the meeting between my student and his Dutch friend, but in other cases we can see clearly how social proximity effects shape the relational terrain.

Consider the case of Christine and Sam, a couple I met at a dinner party hosted by a friend. Sam and Christine were in their early thirties had been married for just over a year. Over the course of dinner, they told me a bit about how they had met. About 8 years before, Sam had worked with a friend of Christine's brother, Mike. Within a couple of years, Sam and Christine's brother met on a project. They became friends and continued working together. Apparently Mike never mentioned his sister to Sam, who was married to someone else at the time. But as time passed, Mike and Sam became closer. Sam's marriage fell apart and he devoted himself to new projects in his banking business. One of these projects was in the town where Christine lived. Sam needed someone to assist with the public relations and advertising work for his new bank and asked Mike for suggestions. Mike suggested his sister. Sam met her and hired her. Christine was not intimidated either by his brashness or by the fact he came from a very prominent family. She said that the fact he was a friend of her brother's always allowed her to see beyond his status and business demeanor. Work soon turned to romance and the rest, as they say, is history.

But it is the prehistory of their relationship that is most interesting at this point. That prehistory was defined by a change in the structure of their social network. Sam meets Mike's friend, Sam meets Mike, Sam meets Christine. Each meeting reduces network distance and increases the likelihood of the next meeting. Participants in a dynamic social structure are "pulled" or "carried" toward one another in this way. One can imagine a social tectonics with participants drifting on the "plates" created by local network densities. As links are forged between some participants, the plates and the relationships making them up are realigned. Some relationships are lost; others are born.

Social proximity effects could be observed most clearly if we were able to follow changes in the network structure of a large number of people over time. Creating such data sets, however, has proved to be a daunting task and we are thus forced to rely on results gleaned from more restricted lines of research. One of these is the research on the transitivity of emotion by structural sociologists (e.g., J. A. Davis, 1970; Hallinan, 1974; Holland & Leinhardt, 1977b; Louch, 2000). The central prediction was that positive sentiments would be transitive across a social network. That is, if A likes B and B likes C, then A will come to like C. Several different types of studies yielded evidence consistent with this prediction. J. A. Davis (1970), for example, examined patterns of liking and friendship choice in 742 groups drawn primarily from school classrooms and college residences. He began by extracting all possible three-person relationships out of each group (e.g., a 20-person group would contain 1,140 different combinations of three persons). He then examined the pattern of sentiments in these groups and found that transitivity occurred in a far greater number than would be expected by chance.

Others observed that the transitivity of positive sentiments should predict the course of friendships over time. Two people are more likely to become friends if they already have a friend in common and tightly linked friendship groups should be more stable in their membership than loosely linked groups (Hammer, 1980; Louch, 2000). Data consistent with both these predictions emerged from a longitudinal study by Salzinger (1982), who followed Harvard students' friendship networks for several months. She found that tightly linked clusters where most people named each other as friends were remarkably stable over time. When new friends were added, they were most likely to come from the ranks of those who were friends of existing friends.

These findings got me thinking about the role of social proximity effects in initiating relationships. If social proximity effects occurred, then people who become friends or romantic partners should have had one or more common contacts prior to meeting for the first time. I turned to four large data sets collected with Lee Eggert to test this hypothesis (see Appendix A). These data sets are described more fully in the chapters that follow, so here I focus only on the data related to the proximity hypothesis. The data sets covered 858 participants who reported on either a same-sex friendship ($n = 478$) or a premarital romantic relationship ($n = 380$). Relationship type was crossed with age group, so that approximately 40% of the participants came from a suburban high school and 60% from a university. Respondents were instructed to obtain a list of the partner's four closest kin and eight closest nonkin contacts. Once this list was obtained, respondents were asked to indicate which of the people on the partner's list they had met *prior* to meeting their partner for the very first time.

The results were consistent with the social proximity hypothesis. Two thirds (66.3%) had indeed met at least one member of their partner's network of family and close friends prior to meeting their partners for the first time. Close to half (47.3%) had met between one and three members of the partner's close circle before meeting the partner. Some (13.2%) had met between four and six, while a few (5.8%) had met over half of the people in the partner's close circle of friends and family. Social proximity effects appeared to occur equally for men and women and across age groups.

A number of qualifications should be noted. Because the analyses were retrospective rather than prospective, they could not provide the most direct evidence of proximity effects. In addition, the results might be biased because they were based on the partner's current network rather than the network at the time of the first meeting. If people were more likely to retain those who knew the respondent as part of their network over time, as I predict they would, then my estimate may be inflated. On the other hand, there are also biases running in the opposite direction. For one thing, we looked at only half the picture. We tallied the number of prior contacts the respondent had in the partner's network, but not the number of prior contacts the partner had in the respondent's network. Both are relevant. Moreover, we only examined the 12 closest contacts in networks that are probably far more extensive. The 33.7% of respondents who did not have prior contact with the partner's closest circle of friends and family might well have had prior contact with the partner's less intimate friends and family.

In spite of their limits, these findings as well as the findings from earlier sociometric studies of friendship choice are consistent with the idea that reductions in the network distance separating people are associated with increases in the probability of them meeting and developing a relationship. The fact that people often have common acquaintances before they meet for the first time has also been corroborated by a study in the Netherlands. Using a national sample of married and cohabitating couples, Kalmijn and Flap (2001) found that just over 46% had common friends before they met and just over 14% said that members of their immediate families had known each other before they met for the first time.

One of the most intriguing findings in our studies is that social proximity effects vary across relationship types. Although both friends and romantic partners usually had contact with people in their future partner's network prior to meeting the partner for the first time, people in romantic relationships had more extensive contact. In fact they had prior contact with almost twice as many people in their prospective partner's network as people in same-sex friendships ($Ms = 2.68$ vs. 1.40, $p < .0001$). This difference was most pronounced among college-age respondents. Put another way, young people, especially college-age people, tend to select romantic partners from those who are socially close. They are willing to develop friendships from those who are not quite so close in social space; that is, they "reach" further for their friends than for their romantic partners. It is not clear why this should be so or whether a similar pattern would emerge in other age groups. One possibility may be the differential importance placed on friendships and romantic relationships. If participants view a romance as a greater potential source of vulnerability and stress, they may be more likely to select romantic partners from among those who are more connected as a way to reduce the perceived risks. Another possibility is that people are more sensitive to whether other people in the network support a romance than to whether they support a friendship.

Third-Party Effects

Relationships may also be initiated through the deliberate actions of third parties. Unlike the more passive social proximity effects, third-party effects are usually intentional and, we discovered, frequently occur at the request of one of the potential beneficiaries. This finding emerged from a study that explored the role of third parties in the initiation of dating relationships and is reported here for the first time in print. The study was conducted with Karen Barnes, then one of my graduate students.

Owing to the lack of research in the area, we began with a series of semistructured interviews. We had originally intended to ask about "matchmaking" strategies. Although matchmaking can be found in some ethnic communities in the United States and Europe and in a number non-Western countries, formal matchmaking as a topic is nearly absent from the social scientific literature (for exceptions, see Knight, 1995; Rockman, 1994; Wang & Chang, 2002). Our respondents had strong negative connotations for the concept of matchmaking. Instead they preferred to talk about their role as "helpers." Once we shifted to this term, it became apparent that young adults not only helped each other out, but also had a wide range of strategies for doing so. We then developed a survey designed to explore the experience of giving and receiving help. We began by asking respondents if they had helped at least one other couple initiate a dating relationship within the previous 12 months. If they had, additional items solicited information as to when the helping occurred, the nature of the relationship between the helper and the recipients, whether the recipients were aware of the helper's efforts, what strategies were used, and whether the helper felt responsible and successful. The second section paralleled the first except that the respondents were asked about help they had received rather than help they had given. The survey was administered to 260 women and 177 men who attended the University of Washington. They ranged in age from 17 to 65, but most were between 18 and 26 ($M = 21.82$, $SD = 4.53$). These data allowed us to address several basic questions about the helping process.

How Often Does Third-Party Help Occur?   Over half (55%) of the respondents in the total sample said that they had helped at least one other couple "get a romantic relationship started" in the last year. Those who had helped reported helping an average of nearly three couples during the previous 12 months. On the other side of the coin, nearly two-thirds (64%) of those who had started a new romantic relationship within the past year said that they had assistance from one or more third parties. Moreover, they had typically received help from more than one person ($M = 2.02$ persons, $SD = 1.23$). Thus most people who initiated a new romantic relationship had the assistance of third parties and most people had played the role of helper more than once in the previous year. Third-party help in relationship initiation is prevalent.

Who Helps and Who is Helped?   Several factors differentiated helpers and nonhelpers. As a group, those who helped tended to have larger, more densely interconnected networks of close friends than those who did not help. Respondents who belonged to a fraternity or sorority were far more likely ($\chi^2 = 26.49$, $p < .0001$) to be helpers than nonhelpers (72% vs. 28%), whereas those who did not belong to these groups were more evenly split between helpers and nonhelpers (46% vs. 54%). Belonging to a fraternity or sorority might have the effect of increasing network size and density to the point where one has more opportunities to play the role of helper, but it might also encourage a more positive attitude toward helping. There were also several significant attitudinal differences between helpers and nonhelpers. Compared to those who did not, those who offered help were generally more confident in their ability to help, more likely to think that their friends and relatives would want their help, and less concerned with the potential risks of helping,

Helpers tended to be younger than nonhelpers ($M = 21.04$, $SD = 2.77$ vs. $M = 22.78$, $SD = 5.90$). Although this difference was significant ($p < .001$), my guess is that it represents the effects of marital status rather than age alone. The majority of single people had been helpers in the last year (58% vs. 42%), whereas the opposite was true of married people (29% vs. 71%), and separated or divorced individuals (40% vs. 60%). These differences were also significant ($\chi^2 = 11.34$, $p < .01$), but the relatively small proportions of married, divorced, and separated people in the sample (10% total) made it difficult to parse out the relative impacts of age and marital status. It may be that marriage reduces the opportunity to be a helper by moving one into a network containing fewer single people. Married people tend to have married friends (Verbrugge, 1977).

The differences between recipients and nonrecipients mirrored those between helpers and nonhelpers. Although recipients and nonrecipients did not differ in the size of their friendship networks, recipients reported having more densely connected networks. Recipients also tended to be somewhat younger than nonrecipients ($M = 20.55$, $SD = 2.37$ vs. $M = 21.83$, $SD = 4.32$; $p < .05$). Although 81% of the members of fraternities and sororities had received help from third parties, only 50% of nonmembers had received such help ($\chi^2 = 19.77$, $p < .0001$).

There were, however, few attitudinal differences between recipients and nonrecipients. They did not differ in their assessment of their need for help from others, their general willingness to accept help when it became available, their willingness to go out on a blind date, or in the degree they worried about whether accepting help would cause them to lose control of the relationship. Only one attitude significantly distinguished between recipients and nonrecipients ($t = 2.18$, $p < .05$). Those who accepted help from third parties were somewhat less concerned ($M = 2.62$, $SD = 1.46$, 7-point scale) about looking "too desperate" than those who had not received help ($M = 3.10$, $SD = 1.52$).

Recipients and helpers also had a number of things in common. One explanation for this similarity is that the people who give help have a higher probability of receiving help themselves. And indeed, additional analyses indicated that giving and receiving help were related ($\chi^2 = 17.69$, $p < .0001$). Although helpers and nonhelpers differed on a number of attitudinal items, there were relatively few differences in the attitudes of recipients and nonrecipients. This might suggest that the helping process depends more on finding the right kind of person to give help than on being the right kind of person to receive help.

One of the most striking findings was the lack of sex differences. Men and women were equally likely to play the role of helper. They were equally likely to be the recipients of help. Popular materials and cultural stereotypes frequently assign the helper role to women, suggesting that men are not relationally oriented. By the same token, men are often viewed as less relationally skilled and presumably therefore more in need of help. These findings suggest that there are no sex differences in who seeks or provides help in starting relationships.

How Are Helpers and Recipients Related?

In order to understand better the social topography of third-party help, we examined how the helper was linked to the people who received the help. We did this by asking helpers and recipients to designate the relationships between them: immediate family, relative outside the family, close friend, friend, acquaintance. This allowed us to map the relationships between helpers and recipients.

Patterns involving immediate family members or kin beyond the immediate family were the least common—making up only 7% of the cases. Kin were only minimally involved in the helping process. Cases in which the helper was equally close to each of the recipients were also less common. The helper was a close friend to both of the recipients in only 12% of the cases and a friend to both in only 10% of the cases. One reason for these numbers being low may be that close friends of close friends, as well as friends of friends, are likely to have already met on their own. The least common of the three "equal" relational patterns was the one in which the help of was only an acquaintance of both parties (1%).

By far the most common patterns were those in which the helper was closer to one of the recipients than the other. And the most common of these (35% of the total) was the one in which the helper was a close friend to one recipient and a friend of the other. Patterns in which the helper was close friend to one recipient and an acquaintance of the other were also common (22%). Patterns in which the helper was a friend of one recipient and an acquaintance of the other were less common (13%). Together, however, these patterns of unequal attachment totaled to 70% of the total cases.

Helpers, it appears, do not merely bring potential romantic partners together. They also bring together previously unconnected parts of their own social networks. They are acting as "network bridges." The bridges they create in the structure of their networks most often link close friends with friends or with acquaintances. Very short bridges (e.g., close friend to close friend) are uncommon as are very long bridges (e.g., acquaintance to acquaintance, immediate family to acquaintance).

Are the Recipients Aware of the Help They Receive?

The findings challenged several common stereotypes about third-party helpers. Although helpers are often perceived to be acting "off-stage" without the knowledge of their targets, the findings suggest just the opposite. Helpers reported that one or both recipients were aware of their activities in 83% of the cases, while those who reported receiving help said that either they, their partners, or both had been aware of the helper's activity in 79% of the cases. Interestingly, the question of whether both members of the recipient couple were aware of the helper's activities depended on who was reporting. Whereas 70% percent of the recipients said that both had been aware of the third-party helper's activities, only 39% of the helpers realized that both recipients were aware of what they were doing. Third parties may underestimate how obvious their activities are or they may fail to appreciate that the recipients may talk among themselves about their activities.

One of the most common images of what third parties do is the dinner to which the host has invited two single people. Neither has been told much, if anything, about the other and the result is an awkward, unwanted meeting between strangers. Although such scenes probably occur, our results paint a far different picture. Instead of being hapless victims of meddling hosts, most recipients deliberately sought the assistance of third parties. In nearly half (45%) of the cases, helpers reported that they had been directly asked to help by one or both of the recipients. Even in the absence of a direct request, the majority of helpers (64%) reported that one or both recipients had hinted that the helper's assistance was desired. Of course, these perceptions may be distorted by the helpers' wish to see themselves as helpers rather than meddlers. On the other hand, most hints were apparently not very subtle—most were rated as "obvious" or "very obvious" by helpers. Together these findings demonstrate that people actively use their networks as resources for relationship initiation. Far from being passive, unwitting recipients, people deliberately seek the help of third parties.

What Strategies Do Third Parties Use?

Respondents classified the types of help they had given or received according to the 14 strategies portrayed in Table 3.1. Helpers and recipients generally reported similar patterns of strategy use. The percentages of helpers and recipients who reported using each strategy were, for example, within 10% of each other for 13 of the 14 strategies. We grouped these strategies into three broader categories: *attraction manipulations, direct initiations,* and *direct assists.*

The most common strategies involved statements by the third party that had the effect of increasing the prospective partners' attraction to each other. This was most often accomplished simply by making positive comments about one person to the other. Jim, one of our respondents, used this strategy when he helped two friends get together: "I began talking about the good qualities of each to both Dean and Liz. I told him that Liz was absolutely the best looking and sweetest girl I'd ever met. I told her that Dean was a nice guy who wouldn't even try to kiss her on the first date."

Attraction manipulations sometimes took the form of downplaying or reframing potentially negative information. When Cindy, another of our respondents, was about to meet Mike, one of her friends told her, "He may seem a little hesitant, but don't worry because he's just a bit shy." Third parties also manipulate attraction by noting and reinforcing similarities between the prospective partners. When Kari wanted to get her friend, Suzanne, together with her boyfriend's cousin, for example, she "emphasized everything they had in common such as having the same hair color, loving chocolate, having the same fun personality, and sharing the same kind of middle-class upbringing." Telling one person how much the other likes him or her is another strategy third parties use to manipulate attraction. Sometimes these statements are embellished in creatively persuasive ways. One illustration comes from Melanie, who reported what her friend Sara said to her when she saw Melanie out with Michael: "Melanie, I think Michael really likes you. Did you see how dressed up he is? I know him and he wouldn't do that for just *anyone.*" Later Sara told Melanie that her boyfriend, Casey, said, "John thinks you're so funny and pretty." All these statements have the cumulative effect of increasing the prospective partners' attraction to each other.

In other cases, third parties take direct action to initiate the relationship. These *direct initiations* (see Table 3.1) take several forms. It is common to arrange for both parties to be in the same place at the same time. One of our respondents, for example, encouraged his friend to take the same bus as a young

TABLE 3.1

Strategies Used by Third-Party Helpers in Romantic Relationships

Strategy type: What the third party did.	Percentage of helpers reporting (n = 242)	Percentage of recipients reporting (n = 129)
I. Attraction manipulations		
Said good things about one potential partner to the other.	86%	91%
Told one or both persons how well they would get along.	60%	57%
Told one or both persons how interested the other was in him or her.	50%	67%
Told one or both how much they had in common, how similar they were.	45%	51%
Put one person's negative qualities in a positive light when talking to the other.	25%	23%
Had someone else say positive things about one person to the other.	21%	20%
II. Direct initiations		
Arranged for both persons to be in the same place at the same time so that they would meet.	37%	47%
Introduced them to one another for the first time.	37%	46%
Arranged for the potential partners to meet through a "double date."	33%	27%
Arranged for the potential partners to meet through a "blind date."	17%	17%
III Direct assists		
"Coached" one person on how to approach or what to say to the other.	49%	43%
Provided information (e.g., name, phone) to one person so he/she could contact the other.	39%	46%
Asked one person questions that the other requested, then relayed answers back.	36%	41%
Solved some problem that was making it difficult for them to get together.	21%	20%

woman he knew. The surest form of direct initiation is certainly the personal introduction. Other researchers have also reported that this is a common way for romantic relationships among young people to begin (Laumann, Gagnon, Michael, & Michaels, 1994). One of our respondents provided this example:

> About two weeks ago I went to the golf course with my boyfriend. I was walking round each hole with him when I noticed this great looking guy. One week later I was in a popular bar with my best friend Julie. Julie had just broken up with her boyfriend and I thought it would be good for her to talk with this guy. Eventually he came over and said he recognized me from the golf course. We talked and I learned that his name was Jeff and that he was a business major. "Oh," I said, "you should meet my friend Julie—she's a business major, too." I motioned Julie to come over and introduced them.

Although third parties sometimes arrange "blind dates," it is more common for them to arrange "double dates." Even with these, the third party may use several additional strategies to convince the prospective partners to go along with the idea. Sally's account of her efforts to start a relationship between her friends, Tracy and Craig, illustrates this:

> My sorority had a "double date dance." I asked Tracy to be my "double" and she needed a date. I instinctively knew that Tracy and my boyfriend's good friend Craig would have a super time together. Although she wasn't thrilled at the idea of being set up ("he'll think I'm desperate, Sal!"), she reluctantly consented after I built up what a great guy Craig is and told her everything he had going for him. The dance turned out to be a lot of fun and my prediction turned out to be true. Tracy and Craig hit it off.

Third parties also help prospective partners in a variety of ways that we grouped together in a category called *direct assists* (see Table 3.1). The most common form occurred when the third party "coached" one or both recipients on how to approach the other. Our respondents, for example, frequently told one person how to dress for a date and what topics to discuss. Sometimes the advice was diffuse ("don't dress like a dork") and sometimes it was quite specific ("He likes plaid and you look great in that plaid shirt"). Third parties play important roles as information sources and relays. They give one person the name or phone number of the other. Often they seek more detailed information on behalf of one or both members of the prospective couple. The level to which such efforts sometimes extend is illustrated nicely in this account from a 21-year-old female:

> I became attracted to Dave while he still had a girlfriend. However, I knew that their relationship was having problems. Also, my roommate was friends with a girl in the same sorority as his girlfriend Jane. My roommate,

Eileen, knew that I liked Dave so when she talked to Jane's friend, she would nonchalantly ask her questions about Jane and Dave's relationship. Then she would report back to me. Eileen was my informant.

Third-party activity is not usually so clandestine. Indeed, in many cases, third parties revealed to one partner that they had been asked to inform on them by the other. This happened, for example, when Loren told her friend Marilyn that "Robert has been asking about you." Loren went on to reveal exactly what Robert had asked and, in turn, Marilyn wanted to know a number of things about Robert before she would go out with him. In this way, third parties facilitate relationship initiation by acting as information relays.

What Are the Outcomes of Third-Party Assistance?   Helpers and recipients generally had different concerns when it came to judging the success of help attempts. Helpers were asked to estimate their percentage of perceived successes. Helpers reported that they had "accomplished what they had intended" in slightly over half (53%) of their attempts. About 30% of the helpers believed that they had been successful in all of their attempts, while about 26% reported that they had not been successful in any. Helpers generally did not feel responsible for the fate of the relationships they helped foster. However, the more strategies a helper employed, the more responsible he or she felt for the way the recipients' relationship turned out ($r = .42$, $p < .001$). And the more strategies a helper used, the more involved he or she perceived the recipient couple to become ($r = .24$, $p < .001$). This finding might reflect a bias for helpers to assume that they had done more and to take more credit for relationships that turned out well. I suspect it also reflects a temporal, cyclic process. If the initial help attempt is unsuccessful, it is unlikely that additional help will be requested or offered. On the other hand, if initial help seems to be successful, the helper may offer or be asked to provide additional help. This in turn helps facilitate the new relationship, enhances the helper's perception of responsibility, and may lead to further assistance. In such cases, the helper may play a continuing, albeit secondary, role in the unfolding relational development process.

Recipients did not share this perspective. There was no significant correlation between the number of strategies helpers were perceived to use and the recipients' perceptions of how involved the ensuing relationship had become. Obviously we can only speculate from these data, but it is likely that recipients are biased toward underestimating the degree of helper involvement in successful relationships. They may also be biased toward overestimating the degree of helper involvement in unsuccessful relationships.

Whatever the ultimate outcome, however, people who received third-party help dated much more extensively than those who did not. Respondents were asked to indicate how extensively they had dated during the previous year. As the results portrayed in Table 3.2 suggest, there was a strong positive associa-

TABLE 3.2

Dating Frequency and Receiving Third-Party Help

Frequency of dating in previous 12 months	Received third-party help	Did not receive third-party help
Dated extensively (several different people)	75%	25%
Dated somewhat	57%	43%
Did not date	29%	71%

tion between the frequency of dating activity and the receipt of help from third parties ($\chi^2 = 14.46$, $p < .001$).

Through their helping activities, network members offer a resource for people who would otherwise not go out as often. It is also possible that those who already wish to go out frequently simply learn to take advantage of third-party help. Regardless of who initiates the assistance, however, it is apparent that those who received third-party assistance had more active social lives than those who did not. This study also makes it clear that third-party help is incredibly common. Helpers have a wide range of strategies to bring potential partners into contact, to enhance attraction, and to assist them once they meet. People may be quite creative in applying these strategies, although they rarely operate behind the recipients' backs. Helpers in this study appeared to be working more or less openly with at least one, of not both, of the recipients in the majority of cases.

SUMMARY

Personal relationships in industrialized cultures, especially romantic relationships, are presumed to form in an "open field" characterized by luck and personal choice. The prevailing mythologies in these cultures emphasize romanticized images of chance, fate, and divine intervention. But in spite of their appeal, romanticized images of the open field fail to describe the processes by which interpersonal relationships are actually born. The failure to look beyond the myth of the open field has hampered social scientific efforts to understand how relationships are initiated. Worse, it has also made it more difficult for people who are shy or lonely to establish relationships with others. By ignoring the social context, the myth of the open field causes these people to overlook potentially important resources and supports at their disposal.

When we look more closely, we find that the formation of new relationships is facilitated by a variety of factors found in the social context in which the participants are embedded. A few of these, such as the effects of physical proximity and the role of shared group norms, have been recognized for some time. Others, such as the relationally facilitative effects of shared and emotionally charged situations, have been recognized in only limited ways. But others have been overlooked almost completely. These include the role of what I call *social proximity effects*—the tendency for participants' relative locations within social network structure to influence their likelihood of meeting. They also include *third-party effects*, in which network members play a more active role in the initiation of relationships. Although the role of "matchmaker" has been recognized for generations, the far more general impact of the informal, often more subtle help given by third parties has gone largely unexplored. The research I have described in this chapter underlines the importance of these social contextual influences and resources in the formation of new relationships. In the next several chapters I explore how these and other social context influences contribute to the further development of friendships and romantic relationships.

CHAPTER FOUR

Becoming Friends

Friendships are remarkably similar across culture and time. There is variety, yet friendship retains its common and essential elements across nearly all settings. Although friendships may have served a richer set of political and economic functions in ancient times, a friendship in Greek or Roman times would still be recognized as such today (Konstan, 1997). Plutarch observed that true friends, unlike flatterers, were willing to point out our faults. His observation rings as true today as when it was written nearly 2,000 years ago.

The essential elements of friendship include its voluntary nature, its mutual candor, its loyalty, its emphasis on shared activity, and its noticeably personal character. Compared to other relationships, even family and marital relationships, friendship is more fully shaped by the distinctive interests and characteristics of its participants (Kurth, 1970; Suttles, 1970). Friendship thus stands apart from our obligations to other roles and institutions. Friendship has been described as an "interstitial institution," filling the spaces between more formal groups. In business, for example, friendships between people in different companies play a critical role in the creation of new commercial alliances and other links between businesses (Appleyard, 1996; Olk & Elvira, 2001). Friendships make a distinctive contribution to our sense of well-being as well. Women and men, particularly men, with no friends or few friends are more likely to experience anxiety, depression, and other forms of mental distress (Hintikka, Koskela, Kuntula, Koskela, & Viinamäki, 2000).

The life course of any one friendship will be shaped by many different individual, environmental, situational, and dyadic factors (Fehr, 1996, 2000). In chapter 3, we saw how social contextual factors help determine who meets whom and whether they begin a relationship. In this chapter we see how the social context continues to influence and be influenced by the development of relationships. In chapter 2, I outlined a general model for describing the relationship development and social network (contextual) factors that should be related to development. My goal in this chapter is to put portions of the model to the test and see how well they describe the development of same-sex friendships in two age groups: high school age adolescents and college age young adults. Although I provide brief overviews of the methods behind each study, the emphasis here is on what we learned rather than on how we learned it.

Our focus in these studies was on the formation of same-sex friendships between the ages, generally, of 14 and 23. Opposite-sex friendships are common and there is excellent research being done on them (e.g., Monsour, 2002). Nonetheless, large-scale social surveys have consistently demonstrated that the majority of friendships are between people of the same sex (e.g., Kalmijn, 2002; Marsden, 1987; McPherson, Smith-Lovin, & Cook, 2001).

Although every period in life is of interest, the years spanning adolescence and early young adulthood are particularly pivotal from the standpoint of interpersonal relationships. During this period, young people emerge from their families to form their first adult relationships. Although children begin acquiring peer contacts by about age 3, the proportion of peers rises steadily until, somewhere between the ages of 14 and 17, the majority of the individual's significant social contacts are outside the family (Feiring & Lewis, 1988; Vondra & Garbarino, 1988). The first close friendships appear in adolescence and are the focus of vast amounts of teenage concern and energy (Blyth & Traeger, 1988; Shulman, Laursen, Kalman, & Karpovsky, 1997). These relationships are important in their own right, but are also important because they act as gateways to other settings and relationships, including romantic relationships (Connolly, Furman, & Konarski, 2000). As further transitions occur in early adulthood, the ability to relinquish or redefine adolescent friendships and to form new friendships in new settings become major developmental tasks (e.g., Paul & Brier, 2001).

FRIENDSHIP DEVELOPMENT IN ADOLESCENCE

Studying Friendship Development in Adolescents

To study how same-sex friendships develop among adolescents, my colleague, Lee Eggert, and I turned to a group of 204 high school students in a middle-class Seattle suburb. The methods are more fully described in Appendices A and B, but it is worth noting that most participants were between 15 and 17 years of age. There were more females (66%) than males in the study. Although the majority of participants (80%) were European American, seven other ethnic or racial groups were represented in the sample. Students were asked to fill out a series of surveys about one of their same-sex friendships. The average friendship had started about a year before the study, although some were very new (less than 2 weeks) and others had been formed in kindergarten or grade school. The surveys asked questions not only about the friendship itself, but also about how the people in their own and their partner's social network viewed the relationship. Students were asked to list the four members of their family and the eight people outside the family (nonkin) to whom they felt the closest and to obtain a similar list of network contacts from their friend.

These surveys contained questions regarding many, but not all, of the various relational and network characteristics described in chapter 2. Responses to individual items (indicators) were grouped together to form more general measures (factors) of these characteristics. These factors included general measures of commitment, communication, communication with members of the partner's network (cross-network contact), and support. Items measuring support for the relationship from network members were grouped according to whether the support was perceived to come from members of the subject's own network or from members of the partner's network. The surveys also included questions about how much subjects liked their partner's family and friends, but these items were not sufficiently correlated to combine into a more general measure or factor in the primary analysis. I will, however, discuss them separately. The remaining questions or scales were combined to produce a global factor that might be described as *closeness* (Parks & Floyd, 1996b). It consisted of six scales measuring perceptions of liking, perceived similarity, love, uncertainty reduction, interpersonal solidarity, and satisfaction with communication. Although these scales are rather general, they do contain items that tap several of our developmental factors, including interdependence, breadth, depth, and predictability.

A Model of Friendship Development in Adolescence.

In order to test the social contextual model of friendship development, we needed to determine the associations among and between three factors describing the development of the friendship (commitment, closeness, communication with partner) and three factors describing activities in the friends' network (amount of communication with the partner's network, support from the subject's own network, support from the partner's network). This was done using confirmatory factor analysis. This procedure not only provides specific tests of particular associations and a test of the overall model, but also lends itself to a straightforward summary for readers less interested in the technical details of the analysis.

Two or more specific indicators were used to define or estimate each of these factors. Communication with the partner's network, for example, was estimated using four different indicators: (a) the number of family members that the subject had met, (b) the number of nonfamily or friends that the subject had met, (c) how often the subject had communicated with people in the partner's network in the last 2 weeks, and (d) how often the subject communicated with them generally. In total, a set of 19 indicators was used to estimate the six factors (see Appendix A).

Many different models were evaluated—45 in all—before finding one that appeared to best fit the data. Further technical information about these analyses and the final model can be found in Appendix B. Our greatest interest is in the top layer of the final model. This layer deals with the associations among the three relational factors and the three network factors. It is displayed in Fig. 4.1.

With just a bit of explanation, those who are not statisticians should be able to interpret the findings. The circles represent the relational and network factors and the numbers inside the curved lines are correlations that tell us how strongly any given pair of factors is connected. Correlations may range from –1.0 to +1.0, where 1.0 means the strongest possible association and zero means that there is no relationship at all between the two things being measured. For example, the positive correlation of .64 between commitment and closeness means that as one increases, the other generally does as well. If the correlation were negative, it would imply that as commitment increased, closeness went down or that as commitment decreased, closeness increased. The particular findings are

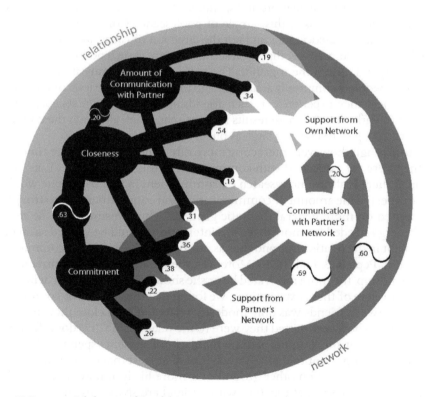

FIG. 4.1.   Adolescent friendships.

now discussed. I begin with the associations among the relational factors, turn to the associations among the network factors, and then move to the associations between the network and relational factors.

Associations Among Relational Factors.   Within the friendship itself, the strongest correlate of closeness in these findings was commitment ($r = .63$, $p < .0001$). Closeness undoubtedly influences commitment, but increases in commitment may lead to greater closeness as well. For one thing, friends may not risk higher levels of self-disclosure and interdependence until they feel committed to the friendship. In addition people may express their commitment in ways that enhance their own feelings of closeness. In one study, people reported that they demonstrated commitment to their partner by showing affection and respect, providing support, and expressing a willingness to work through problems in the relationship (Weigel & Ballard-Reisch, 2002). Showing all of these behaviors to a friend should not only enhance the friend's sense of closeness, but should enhance one's own as well.

Talking with the friend more and spending more time together were also associated with closeness in this sample of adolescents. Correlations, however, measure only the associations and not the direction of cause and effect. So we could just as accurately say that adolescents who are close tend to talk more often and spend more time together. The amount of communication between younger people is commonly assumed to go together with the level of intimacy or closeness they experience in their friendships (Bigelow & LaGaipa, 1980; Eggert & Parks, 1987). These results support that belief, although the correlation ($r = .20$, $p < .05$) is not a large as one might otherwise expect.

Surprisingly, however, interacting more often and spending more time together were *not* associated with commitment in this sample ($r = .11$, *ns*). Although there is almost no research on commitment in friendship, one would have expected the amount of communication and commitment to be strongly associated on more general theoretic grounds. The investment of the time and energy needed for more extensive interaction should be viewed as an investment in the relationship and thus as one basis for feeling more committed (e.g., Bui, Peplau, & Hill, 1996). Moreover, the greater one's commitment to the friendship, the more motivated he or she should be to spend time with the friend. In spite of these expectations, we found that the amount of communication between friends was only modestly related to how close they felt and unrelated to how committed they were to the relationship. It is doubtful that this means that the amount of time high school students spend with their friends is unimportant to them. Rather, it may suggest that commitment and closeness are judged on other grounds. Or more likely, it may simply imply that opportunities to get together with a friend are shaped by many factors besides how close or committed one feels to the friend.

Associations Among Network Factors.   The network factors were them-selves associated in interesting ways. The two support measures were signifi-cantly correlated ($r = .60$, $p < .0001$). The more one group supported the friendship, the more the other group supported it. The level of support per-ceived from the partner's network was also highly correlated with the level of contact the subject had with network members ($r = .69$, $p < .0001$). Members of one's own network and members of the partner's network are probably more likely to support the friendship if they think that the other group is supportive. And they are likely to withhold support if they find that the other group is unsupportive. By the same token, adolescents are likely to be introduced to or seek out members of the partner's network who support the friendship.

This is probably a good juncture to emphasize that perceptions of sup-port may be quite selective and highly managed. One may be introduced only to supportive friends and family and shielded from those who might op-pose the friendship. One may also be guided toward a misperception of sup-port by a partner who does not wish, for example, to let on how much her father disapproves of the friendship. Or her father may not express his disap-proval for this particular friend and prefer instead to think that his daughter will soon see the friend's faults without his intervention. The management of information within the larger network is obviously a major topic and is addressed in more detail in chapter 8.

There may also be challenges in managing time and access in addition to the challenges of managing information. Unless the friends' networks are already highly overlapping when their friendship begins, it is likely that time spent with members of the partner's network will detract at least somewhat from time spent with members of one's own network. Family members may, for example, resent the amount of time the adolescent is spending with her new friend and his associates. This tension between net-work sectors might account for why the amount of communication with the partner's network is strongly associated with support from the part-ner's network ($r = .69$, $p < .0001$), but only very modestly associated with support from the subject's own network ($r = .20$, $p < .05$).

Associations Between Relational and Network Factors.   The central hypothesis of social contextual theory is that changes in any one relationship are intertwined with changes in the participants' surrounding social network. Relationships are not islands (Felmlee, 2001). The results displayed in Fig. 4.1 support this view by demonstrating that the level of development of friend-ships is broadly and significantly associated with social network characteris-tics. Some are stronger that others, but all of the linkages between adolescent friendship development and networks are statistically significant. They reflect how *relational sense-making* and *network structuring*—the two explanatory engines of social contextual theory—function to tie changes inside a friendship to changes in the participants' broader social networks. I will have more to say about these explanatory principles after I present the findings of the second study. For now, perhaps the best way to dig deeper into the findings is to consider each of the major linkages more fully.

Adolescents felt closer or more intimate with their friends when they had greater levels of contact with their friend's network. Though significant ($r = .19$, $p < .05$), the correlation was not a strong one. Nor were there any notable differences in the correlations among the individual indicators beneath these two factors. Stronger associations were found between closeness and support from network members. Subjects reported feeling closer to their friends when they perceived that the members of their own network and the members of their partner's network supported their friendship. Two more general features of this pattern are worth exploring further. First, although support from one's own network ($r = .54$, $p < .0001$) is somewhat more strongly associated with closeness than support from the partner's network ($r = .38$, $p < .0001$), both are relatively strong in comparison to the findings typical in the literature on personal relationships. This is striking, given the lack of attention paid to social network factors in this literature. Second, although it is tempting to think in terms of the positive effects of network support on relational development, we should also keep in mind that these findings also reflect the effects of opposition from network members. The low end of the relational support continuum is, after all, opposition to the relationship. An adolescent's relationship with a new friend may stall, for example, when he discovers that his current friends do not want to include the new friend in their social circle.

Network factors were clearly associated with the level of commitment adolescents felt for their friendships. These adolescents were more committed to a friendship when it was accepted and supported by their friends and family ($r = .36$, $p < .001$), by the partner's friends and family ($r = .26$, $p < .01$, and when they had a great deal of contact with the partner's friends and family ($r = .22$, $p < .05$).

The associations between commitment and the network factors probably reflect a two-way process. One is more likely to be committed to a relationship that is supported by a group of people who are close to you or to your partner and with whom you spend a good deal of time. By the same token, network members are probably more likely to express support for a relationship, or at least express their concerns less stridently, when they see that its participants are committed to one another.

Adolescents' friendships frequently seem all-consuming to parents and teachers. Yet others do have an impact on how much time an adolescent spends with a friend. Adolescents talked more often and spent more time with a given friend when they felt the friendship was accepted and supported by the partner's friends and family ($r = .31$, $p < .01$) and when they had a great deal of contact with the partner's friends and family ($r = .34$, $p < .001$). They also interacted more when members of their own network supported the relationship, although this was not as important a factor as support from the friend's network ($r = .19$, $p < .05$). And, as I noted earlier, the amount of interaction with the friend was not strongly related to how close or committed the friendship was. Before exploring this further, however, it may be useful to delve deeper into the networks themselves.

Friends Versus Family in Adolescent Friendships. So far we have distinguished only between the subject's own network and the partner's network. But within each of these groups, there is a further distinction between family and nonfamily (friends). Although there were not enough indicators to build these finer categories into the larger models, it may be instructive to ask two additional questions about them (see Table 4.1).

The first question is whether there are differences between friends and family in terms of how supportive they are seen to be, how likeable they are, and how often one communicates with them. The results of these tests are portrayed in Table 4.1.

To my surprise, family members were seen as significantly more supportive than friends, although support for the friendship was perceived to be relatively high across all the groups (all averaged above 7 on a scale that ranged from 2 to 10). Family members were seen as more supportive in both the subject's own network and in the partner's network. Additional analysis (not in the table) demonstrated that the subject's family was also seen as significantly more supportive than the partner's family and that the subject's friends were seen as significantly more supportive than the partner's friends. These results call into question two common, but contradictory, stereotypes about young

TABLE 4.1
Friend Versus Family Effects in Adolescent Friendships

Measure	Family Mean (SD)	Friends Mean (SD)	Difference
Support from own network (Scale: 2-10)	8.25 (1.39)	7.62 (1.40)	p < .001
Support from partner's network (Scale: 2-10)	7.29 (1.41)	7.07 (1.25)	p < .05
Liking for partner's network (Scale: 2-10)	5.68 (1.60)	6.12 (1.57)	p < .001
Communication with partner's network A (Scale: 0-14)	1.69 (2.14)	4.17 (3.32)	p < .001
Communication with partner's network B (Scale: 1-5)	1.75 (.98)	2.43 (1.11)	p < .001

people's friendships. One is that adolescents deliberately select friends who will annoy their family and please their peers. The opposing stereotype is that interpersonal life in high school affords little support and is frequently critical, if not downright brutal on occasion. Neither of these views seems to be correct. In this sample of adolescents, family members were seen as more supportive than friends, but even the friends were generally seen as supportive of the friendships we examined.

The remaining findings were somewhat less surprising, although no less significant. Subjects generally expressed only moderate levels of liking for members of their friend's network, but reported liking their friend's friends more than their friend's family members. Finally, subjects reported that they had more communication with their friend's friends than with members of their friend's family.

The second question is whether the correlations between the development indicators and the network indicators differed for friends and family. That is, did communication and support from friends have a stronger or weaker association with relational development than communication and support from family members did? To answer this question we compared each pair of network indicators (e.g., support from one's own friends vs. one's own family), using a series of statistical procedures known as multiple regressions. This allowed us to determine if closeness, communication with the partner, and commitment inside the relationship were more strongly associated with the friendship network or with the family network. Because of the large number of tests involved, I focus on the patterns in the findings rather than individual regression results.

The patterns that emerged underscored the importance of the friends, but family members also had a distinctive role to play. Support from friends, both in one's own network and in the partner's network, was generally more strongly associated with closeness than was support from family members. Support from friends in the network was also more strongly associated with the amount of communication between the partners than was support from family members. Moreover, the amount of communication with the partner was more strongly associated with how often one communicated with the partner's friends than with how often one communication with the partner's family. On the other hand, it was the amount of communication with the partner's family that was more strongly associated with closeness between the partners themselves. There were no friend/family differences in associations involving the liking or commitment measures.

Summary.   It is clear across the findings that the development of same-sex friendship among adolescents is firmly embedded in their existing networks of other friends and family members. The amount of interaction between a given pair of friends, as well as how close and committed they felt, was consistently associated with the support the friendship received from each other's friends and families as well as their own. No sector of the friends' combined network was unimportant, but further analyses suggested that perceptions of closeness and commitment were somewhat more strongly associated with support from one's own network than from the partner's network. The amount of interaction, on the other hand, was somewhat more strongly associated with the level of contact and support from the partner's network. Within the partners' combined network, interaction with and support from friends, rather than family, were more closely linked to the development of the friendship. This is precisely what we would expect in adolescence where the shift from family to peers is so pronounced. But there were surprises as well. It was the amount of interaction with the partner's family, not the partner's friends, that was correlated with how close the friendship was. Admission to the family circle may be seen as an intimate act in its own right, but it is also likely that closer, more involved friendships are likely to gain the attention of family members. Another unexpected finding was that the amount of communication between friends was not more strongly related to their closeness or commitment. We consider these findings in greater detail after considering the way friendships develop among young adults.

FRIENDSHIP DEVELOPMENT IN EARLY ADULTHOOD

Studying Friendship Development in Young Adults. The second study shifts our attention to a somewhat older group. The participants in this study were students or friends of students at the University of Washington. Almost all (95%) were between the ages of 18 and 23. This sample was relatively balanced for sex (43% male, 57% female) and slightly more diverse that the sample in the first study, although 63% identified themselves as European American.

The procedures were the same as those used in the first study (Appendix A). Participants completed surveys about one of their same-sex friendships and interactions with the social network surrounding it. The social network was defined, as before, in terms of the subject's 12 closest kin and nonkin as well as the partner's 12 closest kin and nonkin. Almost all of the "nonkin" were identified as friends, so I simply refer to the network of family and friends. The central relationship was the one between the subject and his or her friend. These friendships averaged almost 14 months in duration, although 35% had been initiated in the month before the data were collected and 10% had been initiated more than 3 years before data collection.

The measures were also the same as those used in the first study (see Appendix A). Once more, 19 different measures or indicators were used to assess three underlying factors defining friendship development (communication, closeness, and commitment) and three underlying factors defining characteristics of partners' social network (communication with the partner's network, support from the partner's network, and support from one's own network).

A Model of Friendship Development in Early Adulthood

Confirmatory factor analysis was again used to determine the associations between the three friendship development factors and the three network factors. Although I focus here on a nontechnical summary of the findings, more about the specific analyses as well as technical information on the final model can be found in Appendix B. In brief, the final model was derived by progressively testing a large number of models in order to obtain the best fit to the data. Although a model very much like the one that fit the high school friendship data was tried, the best-fitting model for these data turned out to be rather different. The top layer of the model is presented in Fig. 4.2. I work through it by first considering the links among the relational and network factors and then turn to discuss the linkages between the network and rela-

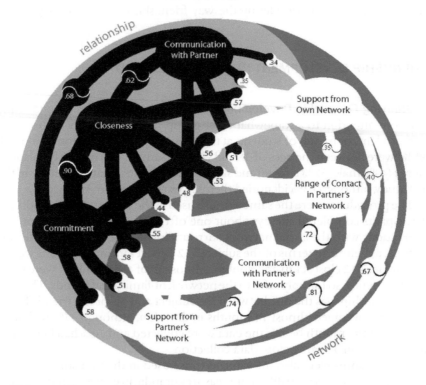

FIG. 4.2.　Young adult friendships.

tional factors. Once again, the numbers presented in Fig. 4.2 represent correlations between the factors.

Associations Among Relational Factors.

As Fig. 4.2 illustrates, the three factors we used to assess friendship among these young adults were all highly linked with one another. Perceptions of closeness were significantly correlated with the amount of communication $(r = .62., p < .0001)$ and commitment $(r = .90, p < .0001)$. Commitment and communication were high correlated as well $(r = .68, p < .0001)$. Thus, friends who communicated more often felt closer and more committed to the relationship. Or, put the other way, friends who felt close and were committed to the relationship communicated more often. These associations were generally stronger in the university sample than in the high school sample.

Associations Among Network Factors.

Perhaps the most striking difference between this model and the model for high school friends is that it has two cross-network communication factors rather than one. The same four indicators were split into two factors in this model: one factor representing how many people subjects had met in their partner's network and the other represented how often subjects communicated with them. These two aspects of cross-network contact were much more strongly correlated among high school students than they were among students of university age. I explore age differences in greater detail in chapter 6, but it is possibler that this difference reflects the more bounded character of the high school environment. Compared to a large public university, the high school campuses tend to be smaller, have fewer students, and offer a smaller range of courses and activities. High school students are thus more likely to spend time with the people they meet. On the other hand, because of their larger and more diverse environment, university students are more likely to know people that they do not interact with on a regular basis.

The four network factors were highly associated. The range of contact (number of people met) in the partner's network, although a distinct factor, was strongly correlated with how often the subject communicated with members of the partner's network. People who had met a greater number of their friend's family and friends, communicated with them more often as well $(r = .72, p < .0001)$. Meeting more people in the partner's network was strongly associated with greater support from the partner's network $(r = .81, p < .0001)$ and moderately associated with greater support from one's own network $(r = .35, p < .0001)$. Communicating more often with people in the partner's network as also strongly associated with greater support form the partner's network $(r = .74, p < .0001)$ and moderately associated with greater support from one's own network $(r = .40, p < .0001)$. Finally, there was a significant positive association between the extent to which members of the subject's own network and members of the partner's network were perceived to support the friendship ($r = .67$, $p < .0001$).

Associations Between Relational and Network Factors.
The addition of one more factor also means that network and relational factors are laced together in a richer set of ways. Indeed, as Fig. 4.2 illustrates, network communication and support and friendship are laced together in every possible way. All of the linkages tested significant and positive. Friendships that received greater support from network members were closer. This was true for support both from members of one's own network ($r = .57$, $p < .0001$) and from members of their partner's network ($r = .58$, $p < .0001$). Friendships that received greater support were also more committed. Again, this was true regardless of whether the support came from one's own network ($r = .56$, $p < .0001$) or from the partner's network ($r = .58$, $p < .0001$). These associations undoubtedly flow both ways. All things being equal, others are likely to be more supportive of a friendship that appears to be closer and more committed. By the same token, it is likely that those who were skeptical of the friendship will either warm to it or at least withhold further criticism if the friendship appears to be thriving.

Friends who communicated with each other more often also tended to meet a greater number of people in each other's network ($r = .35$, $p < .0001$) and to communicate with them more often ($r = .51$, $p < .0001$). This finding probably reflects a variety of factors ranging from the nature of informal talk itself to purely structural arrangements in the network. The more regularly friends talk, the more likely they will be to mention their other activities and relationships. Interpersonal relationships are so central to our lives that it is difficult to talk informally for very long without mentioning them. In this way talk provides an entree to the other's network. Beyond this, sometimes the only way to get to spend more time with a friend is join him or her in a joint activity with friends or family. But even this works both ways. Network members may invite the partner in order to get more time with their own friend or relative. These invitations can be motivated by several things, but one is certainly that time for face-to-face communication is finite and has to be rationed across a series of relationships. Getting together as a group is one of the few ways to beat the "zero-sum" problem in which time spent with one person results in time being taken away from another.

Friends communicated more often when they perceived that network members approved of their relationship. Support from both sides of the network was linked to how often friends communicated, but support from the partner's network ($r = .48$, $p < .0001$) was a somewhat better predictor than support from the subject's own network ($r = .34$, $p < .0001$). The processes that these findings reflect are not necessarily pleasant ones. It is tempting to think of network members supporting the relationship in positive ways (and they do), but the findings also represent the disruptive effects of unsupportive networks. Put simply, you are not likely to get as much time with your friend if his or her friends and family disapprove of your relationship. Making it difficult for the friends to spend time together is one of the strategies network members rely on to discourage unwelcome relationships.

Finally, the closer the friends' relationship, the more people they had met in their partner's network ($r = .53$, $p < .0001$) and the more often they communicated with them ($r = .44$, $p < .0001$). And, the more committed friends were to their relationship, the more people they had met in their partner's network ($r = .55$, $p < .0001$) and the more often they communicated with them ($r = .51$, $p < .0001$). Closeness and commitment are obviously motivators to spend time with the partner's friends and family. On the other hand, an unwillingness to spend time with other people who are significant to the partner calls into question the value placed on the partner. But it is probably even more complicated than this. The partner's network is not likely to be completely foreign territory. As we saw in chapter 3, by the time friends meet, they may already have considerable contact with each other's networks. In many cases, spending time with the partner's friends may simply mean spending time with one's other friends. Feelings of commitment and closeness may attach for the group as a whole as much as to any one relationship within it.

Friends Versus Family in Young Adult Friendships.   Two additional series of analyses were conducted to determine if there were differences in the way friends and family functioned regarding the friendship. The first set explored differences between friends and family in terms of how supportive they are seen to be, how likeable they are, and how often young adults communicate with them. Table 4.2 presents the results of these analyses.

Although the differences were not large, young adults generally reported that family members supported their friendships as much or even more than their other friends. This difference was significant in the case of the members of the subject's own network, but was not significant in the case of members of the partner's network. Apparently, young adults do not generally seek out close friends in an oppositional fashion. Support for the friendship across the various sectors of the subjects' and partner's network was rather high. The fact that family support is perceived to be so high is striking considering that young adults are very much in the process of establishing an independent identity.

The comparatively high level of support from family members may be the result of several factors. One, of course, is actual support. But it is also possible that people may overestimate the extent to which family members actually support a given friendship. Family members, like other network members,

TABLE 4.2

Friend Versus Family Effects in Young Adult Friendships

Measure	Family Mean (SD)	Friends Mean (SD)	Difference
Support from own network (Scale: 2-10)	7.83 (1.38)	7.62 (1.36)	p < .01
Support from partner's network (Scale: 2-10)	6.99 (1.18)	6.89 (1.11)	ns
Liking for partner's network (Scale: 2-10)	4.91 (1.23)	5.37 (1.25)	p < .001
Communication with partner's network A (Scale: 0-14)	.43 (.90)	2.12 (2.08)	p < .001
Communication with partner's network B (Scale: 1-5)	1.18 (.50)	1.74 (.80)	p < .001

may withhold or downplay negative reactions thus leading to an inflated sense of support. Or, the individual may bring cognitive biases that skew perceptions of support in a positive direction. Consider, for example, the possible effects of the biases in this seemingly innocuous statement: "I try not to think about what my mom would think of my drinking buddy, Mark. We get pretty wild, but I'm sure she'd like him if she really got to know him."

Young adults reported moderate liking for members of their partner's network. Predictably, however, they reported more liking for their friends' friends than for their friends' family members. Although members of the partner's network were perceived as generally supportive and at least moderately likeable, most young adults reports having little regular contact with their partner's family and friends. The mean ratings for both communication frequency measures were well below the midpoint of the scales (see Table 4.2). Communication with the partner's friends, however, was significantly more frequent than communication with members of the partner's family.

The final series of analyses focused on whether measures of network support, liking, and communication were associated with relational development in the same way across different sectors of the network. For example, we may ask if support from family members and support from friends are associated with relationship development in the same way. Answering questions like this requires calculation and comparison of a large number of correlations, so I focus on general patterns in the findings instead of individual test results. Generally speaking, network measures (support, liking, communication) were associated with relational development in the same way regardless of whether they were based on family members or friends. There were no differences in nearly three quarters of the comparisons. But there were some notable differences as well. The frequency of communication with one's partner, for example, was positively associated with support, liking, and communication with the partner's friends, but not with support, liking, and communication with either one's own family or the partner's family. In the same vein, perceptions of short-term commitment (staying friends for 3 more months), but not long-term commitment (staying friends forever), were positively associated with support, liking, and communication with the partner's friends, but not with support, liking, and communication with either one's own family or the partner's family. Put simply, how often young adults communicated with a friend, as well as how committed they were to continuing the relationship for at least the next few months, depended far more on perceptions of the partner's friends than on perceptions of the partner's family. In most cases, both friend and family measures for the partner's network were significantly and positively correlated with the development of friendship between young adults, but when differences were observed, they were always in the direction of greater influence of friends rather than of family.

FRIENDSHIP DEVELOPMENT IN SOCIAL CONTEXT

The development of a friendship is strongly associated with how the participants relate to each other's network of close friends and family. The results of the studies reported in this chapter indicate that this generalization holds true both for adolescents and for young adults. Friendships do develop somewhat differently in these two age groups and those differences should be noted before summarizing the larger similarities.

Perhaps the most striking difference occurs in how tightly the three developmental factors are related to each other. Commitment, closeness, and communication in young adult friendships are all strongly interrelated. In adolescent friendships, however, the frequency of communication and the amount of free time spent together are less strongly linked to feelings of closeness and commitment. Indeed, these communication measures were only modestly related to closeness and not related at all to commitment in adolescent friendships. Some have argued that environmental constraints on social relationships generally diminish as people move from adolescence into early adulthood (e.g., Laursen & Williams, 1997). Compared to adolescents, young adults have more direct control over a number of factors that influence the amount of communication they have with others. They are more likely to live on their own, have greater freedom to move about, and to set their own schedules. This gives them greater freedom to align their communication patterns with their relational preferences. They should be able to see their friends more often and to dedicate more of their free time to interaction. The result should be stronger correlations between relational factors like closeness and commitment and the various measures of communication. Put simply, although young adults still have obligations, they have greater freedom than adolescents to spend time with the people they want to.

This speculation may also help us explain why the network submodels differed in the two samples. The number of people known in the partner's network and the frequency of communication with them were assessed in both studies. The way these two communication indicators were related, however, differed for adolescents and young adults. In the adolescent sample, they were strongly correlated and formed a single factor. Although they were also positively correlated in the young adult sample, they did not form a single factor. It was necessary to treat the range of contact in the partner's network and the frequency of communication with known members of the partner's network as separate factors. Because they share a common social environment, adolescents may end up having more contact with the people they meet in their partner's social network. Young adults, however, may not be so compelled to communicate with members of the partner's network once they meet. As diversity and control increase, young adults may have a greater number of contacts, including contacts in the partner's network, with whom they do not communicate as often. This possibility is explored in more detail in chapter 6.

In spite of these differences, the findings of the two studies reported here suggest that network factors function in similar ways in the development of friendships among adolescents and young adults. Support from members of one's own network was positively associated with communication, closeness, and commitment in both adolescent and young adult friendships. Friendships that received higher levels of support from friends and family also displayed higher levels of closeness and commitment as well as more frequent communication. Although the correlations were slightly stronger in young adult friendships, they were positive and significant in both age groups. The same pattern emerged when we examined support from members of the partner's network. Friendships that received higher levels of support from the friend's family and friends also exhibited higher levels of closeness and commitment as well as more frequent communication.

These findings reflect the relationally affirming and reinforcing effects of social support from network members. Support functions to reduce uncertainty about the viability of the relationship and confirm the participants' positive judgments about one another. Knowing that a friendship is supported by others to whom one also feels close promotes cognitive symmetry or balance (Cartwright & Harary, 1956; Newcomb, 1961). In these ways, support from network members contributes to the *relational sense-making* that is essential if a friendship is to develop. As I noted in chapter 2, support also promotes relational development through *network structuring*. A friendship that is actively supported by other network members is not only more attractive, but it also more difficult to leave. The simple fact that others support the friendship makes it more difficult to use network members to contact alternative partners or even to express reservations about the friendship. Because support weaves the friendship into a larger social network, the benefits of development as well as the risks of disruption are spread to a wider group.

Relational sense-making and network structuring also help account for the strong relationship between how often one communicates with the partner's network and how often one communicates with the partner, how close one feels to the partner, and how committed one is to the partner. In both studies, people who communicated more often with their friend's family and friends also reported interacting more with the friend. They also reported feeling closer to the friend and more committed to the friendship. Friends gain both specific information and a frame of reference for the relationship through communication with members of their partner's network. These promote understanding within the friendship. Contact with the partner's network also structures contacts with the friend. Again, adolescents and young adults who have extensive contact with their friend's family and friends will not have as many relational alternatives as those who do not. Moreover, relationally untoward acts, such as complaining about the friend, are more likely to be monitored and reported when the individual is embedded in a shared social network.

The fact that communication and support from network members are so strongly linked to the development of friendship implies that we should reassess a number of our common conceptions about the friendships of adolescents and young adults. First, these findings underscore the importance of family influence. Although adolescents and young adults strive for autonomy, we should keep in mind that relationships with parents and other family members remain an important source of support. The results of both studies reported here bear witness to this point, as to the results of several previous studies (e.g., Shulman, Collins, & Knafo, 1997; Youniss & Smollar, 1985). Young people continue to be both concerned about and influenced by family members' opinions of their friendships. Both studies suggest that friendship development is closely linked to support from family members. This connection appears to be stronger and more consistent for young adults than for adolescents, but is never absent. More important, it is never negative. That is, although some of the analyses failed to find a significant relationship between support or communication with family members and friendship development, it was never the case that support or communication with family members was negatively related to friendship development. There was no evidence of reactivity effects. In other words, young people do not generally appear to be more attracted to friendships that are opposed by family members. Nor are they likely to lose interest in a friendship simply because they perceive that family members approve of it. Young people are not the contrarians they are sometimes portrayed to be. We can all think of exceptions, but the practical implication is that family members, indeed all network members, can generally proceed on the belief that their opinions of young people's friends really do matter.

This view might be challenged by arguing that adolescents and young adults carefully manipulate information and contacts to create support from network members. They may, for example, emphasize the friend's positive characteristics or his or her similarities with network members rather than the friend's bad habits or dissimilarities. Contact with network members thought to be unsupportive may be reduced, while contact with more supportive network members is increased. These and other information management strategies are explored further in chapter 8. For now, it is sufficient to note that the results probably reflect the effect of the friendship on the network as much as the network on the friendship. Each influences the other, but even this underscores the impact of the views of family and other network members. If they were not important to young people, adolescents and young adults would not make such an effort to manage them.

These findings also have practical implications for how we approach the problem of helping young people with inadequate or disrupted social relationships. Selman, Watts, and Schultz (1997), for example, pioneered relationship-based strategies for enhancing the psychosocial skills of young people so that they may express intimacy and autonomy more effectively. Their model reflects the importance of networks of relationships and implies that intervention with larger sections of the adolescent's network might reap even greater benefits. In pair therapy, adolescents are commonly paired by the clinician—usually to form some contrast in which each adolescent might learn from the other (e.g., the shy child with the aggressive child). Using intact network segments might not yield such marked contrasts, but it may be possible to identify individuals within a preexisting network who could benefit from one another's social skills. The positive effects of pair therapy might be more sustainable when the individuals involved are part of a shared, naturally occurring networks rather than a network constructed purely for clinical purposes.

We might also extend the findings reported in this chapter by more thoroughly examining the role of family members in friendship development. Parents and siblings may have distinct effects and play distinct roles. Siblings, for example, may be caught in the middle between efforts to enlist parental support for a questionable relationship and efforts by parents to enlist them as allies in opposing the relationship. More generally, positive relationships with siblings in early adolescence serve as a foundation for the development of close friendships outside the family in later adolescence (Yeh & Lempers, 2004).

These implications may extend to other types of relationships besides friendship. To consider how generally we may apply the theory of relationship development that emerges from these studies of friendship, we now turn to another type of personal relationship. In chapter 5, we consider the role of social context in the development of romantic relationships among adolescents and young adults.

CHAPTER FIVE

Becoming Romantic Partners

Reliance on peer relationships increases dramatically as individuals traverse the uncertain paths of adolescence and early adulthood. Same-sex friendships grow in importance during this period, as we saw in chapter 4. So, too, do opposite-sex friendships and a variety of other same-sex and opposite-sex relationships. Romantic relationships warrant particular attention because of the functions they serve and the risks they create. Although this chapter focuses on male-female romantic relationships, adolescence and early adulthood are often the time when gays and lesbians first experience same-sex romantic relationships. Before exploring what the social contextual model can say about the development of male-female romantic relationships, we should briefly note their functions and risks, as well as the broader social setting from which they arise.

Some adolescent and young adult romantic relationships lead to marriage, but most do not (Connolly & Johnson, 1996; Feiring, 1996). Yet even relatively short relationships can confer significant benefits on their participants. They are significant sources of social support in adolescence and early adulthood (Furman & Buhrmester, 1992). Romantic relationships affirm the adolescent's autonomy and may drive changes in relationships with friends and family (Erikson, 1968; Shulman, Collins, et al., 1997). They may influence scholastic achievement, career interests, and career opportunities (Furman & Shaffer, 2003). They offer opportunities to develop and test skills in opposite-sex relationships and thereby influence later relational choices. They leave a lasting frame of reference for evaluating future relationships.

Romantic relationships also pose major risks for young people. One of the most common health risks is sexually transmitted disease. Although people between the ages of 15 and 24 represent only 25% of the sexually experienced population, nearly half (48%) of all new cases of sexually transmitted diseases in the United States occur in this age group (Weinstock, Berman, & Cates, 2004). The lifetime medical cost of the nearly 9 million new cases affecting 15 to 24 year olds in 2000 has been estimated at $6.5 billion (Chesson, Blandford, Gift, Tao, & Irwin, 2004). Although less quantifiable, the suffering and disruption produced by sexually transmitted diseases are no less significant.

Teenage pregnancy and childbearing are also major risk factors. Nearly 25% of teenage women in the United States will become pregnant at least once before the age of 18 ("Adolescent Unintended Pregnancy," 1994). It is true that early childbearing is culturally sanctioned in some groups and that it should not automatically be seen as a disaster (Fessler, 2003; Geronimus, 2003). Nonetheless, significant personal and social costs accrue when the pregnancy is unintended or unwanted. Teen parents are far less likely to complete their schooling (Coley & Chase-Lansdale, 1998). The mother of the unintended or unwanted child is less likely to receive adequate health care before delivery and the child is likely to have poorer health outcomes following delivery, especially if the mother already has other children (Marston & Cleland, 2003). Unintended teen pregnancies also trigger a cascade of costs for social, health, and welfare services.

Young women who become pregnant are more likely to become victims of violence than young women who do not (Krulewitch, Roberts, & Thompson, 2003). Violence in adolescent dating relationships is, of course, a much more general problem. Estimates of the prevalence of dating violence vary widely depending on the ethnicity of the sample, the measures, and the time frame. Even so, at least 10% and perhaps as many as 50% of adolescents experience violence in dating relationships (Carver, Joyner, & Udry, 2003; Glass et al., 2003). Understanding how these relationships are linked to the participants' social networks may suggest more effective ways to prevent violence and victimization. Too often, network members are either unaware of abusive relationships or respond to them in ways that fail to assist or, worse, make it more difficult for the victims to escape an abusive situation (Mahlstedt & Keeny, 1993).

To understand problems such as these, it is helpful to remember that these early romantic relationships emerge as part of a larger transition in social network structure. The ground is prepared for romantic relationships in early adolescence when sexual segregation breaks down and boys and girls begin to interact more frequently with each other. Social scientists have recognized for more than 40 years that adolescent romantic relationships emerge from larger mixed-sex social groups or "crowds" (Dunphy, 1963). It was only recently, however, that researchers began to focus on the process by which this occurs. It appears that those with larger same-sex networks as they enter adolescence will develop a larger mixed-sex network over time. As the mixed-sex network increases in size in middle and late adolescence, romantic relationships begin to emerge (Connolly et al., 2000; Feiring, 1999). This change both provides an arena for learning about the other sex and a pool from which romantic partners can be selected.

The fact that networks influence the availability and onset of romantic relationships should not surprise us. We have already seen some of the roles network members play in the initiation of romantic relationships (chap. 3, this volume). Indeed the very idea that network members would *not* be involved in the formation and development of relationships between men and women is distinctively modern, romantic, and Western. The freedom of choice so readily assumed in Western discourse ignores the well-documented influence of religion, ethnicity, and social status on mating choices. Throughout most of history, unions between men and women were viewed as mechanisms by which families could form alliances and secure resources (Barzun, 2000). Even today, managed courtships and arranged marriages are still common in many parts of the world, including numerous ethnic and racial enclaves in North America and Europe (e.g., Jahn, 2003; Talbani & Hasanali, 2000).

My goal in this chapter is extend our understanding of the role network factors play in development of male-female romantic relationships among high school age adolescents and college age young adults. I present the results of three studies. The methods and measures used in the first two studies parallel those used for the studies of same-sex friendship in chapter 4. The third study extends the first two by examining a more complete set of network factors in a sample with greater ethnic and racial diversity. My discussion here will emphasizes the findings—readers will find more information on the methods and analyses in Appendices A and B.

ROMANTIC RELATIONSHIP DEVELOPMENT IN ADOLESCENCE

Studying the Development of Romantic Relationships in Adolescence

Until the mid-1980s, there was relatively little research on romantic relationships among adolescents. Most investigations of adolescent relationships centered on friendship and same-sex cliques (e.g., Hallinan, 1980). My colleague, Lee Eggert, and I considered this to be a significant gap in the literature, so we returned to the same middle-class suburban high schools in which we had studied friendship formation. A group of 135 students (88 females, 47 males) involved in dating relationships agreed to participate. Participants ranged in age from 15 to 19, but averaged just over 17 years of age. Most were European American (83%), but several other ethnic or racial groups were represented in the sample. The largest contingent was Native Americans, who made up nearly 6% of the total sample.

Participants were asked to fill out a series of surveys about their current dating relationship. The average duration of these relationships at the time of the survey was approximately 11 months, though almost 40% were less than 4 months old and very few (3%) were more than 3 years old. This probably reflects the fact that many of our subjects had only started dating within the last year or so, but is also consistent with longitudinal data indicating that only 8% of the romantic relationships reported by 9th graders lasted until the 11th grade (Connolly et al., 2000).

The data collection mirrored the materials and procedures used to study adolescent friendships (see Appendix A). Subjects completed a series of surveys containing both relational measures and reports on their own network as well as their partner's network. Nineteen separate measures were grouped to produce a series of relational and network factors. Scales measuring liking, loving, solidarity, perceived similarity, uncertainty reduction, and communication satisfaction were grouped together to form a global measure of closeness. This drew on several of the developmental factors identified in the second chapter, including depth, breadth, predictability, and interdependence. Other items were grouped to yield factors for commitment and communication. Network factors were also created to assess how much cross-network contact there was with members of the partner's network, as well as the level of support for the dating relationship subjects perceived from members of their own and their partner's network.

A Model of the Development
of Romantic Relationships in Adolescence

The analysis of the data also mirrored the analysis of the data on friendships. Direct measures were linked to factors that were, in turn, related to each other using confirmatory factor analysis. The goal was to discover a model that both fit the data well and made theoretic sense. Several dozen alternatives were evaluated before a good fit was found. Further technical information can be found in Appendix B. The present discussion centers on the final model's top layer, which is concerned with the associations among the various relational and network factors. The model is displayed in Fig. 5.1.

Once again, the circles represent the relational and network factors and the curved lines represent statistically significant linkages between factors. The correlations themselves are displayed as well. If there is no line linking a pair of factors, it means that they were not associated in a statistically significant way. Following the convention of chapter 4, I first discuss the associations among the relational factors, then turn to the associations among the relational factors, and finally discuss the associations between the relational and network factors.

Associations Among Relational Factors. Perhaps the most striking feature of this model of adolescent romantic relationships is the way that the three developmental factors were associated with each other. Predictably, commitment to the relationship and our composite closeness factor were strongly and positively linked ($r = .66, p < .0001$). That is, adolescents who reported greater loving, liking, solidarity, similarity, predictability, and satisfaction also expressed a stronger desire to continue the romantic relationship into the future. However, further analyses suggested a more complex picture. For

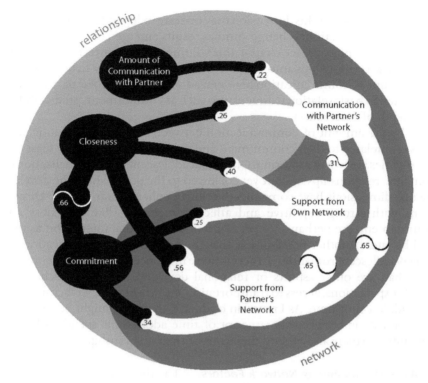

FIG. 5.1. Adolescent romantic relationships.

one thing, the closeness measures as a group were only marginally, though significantly, related to participants' short-term commitment to the relationship (i.e., expecting to be together for the next 3 months). Most, but not all, of the closeness measures were related to long-term commitment (i.e., expecting to get married someday). Perceived similarity, solidarity, predictability, and communication satisfaction were positively related to long-term commitment, but Rubin's (1970) measures of loving and liking were not. Thus, short-term commitment was only marginally dependent on closeness; whereas long-term commitment was more strongly related to closeness.

The most notable finding, however, was the relative lack of association between the amount of communication and both closeness and commitment. How often adolescent romantic partners saw each other and how much of their free time they spent together were not significantly related to how close they felt or how committed they were to the relationship. This does not imply that the amount of communication is unimportant. The amount of interaction between partners is, after all, one of the basic dimensions along which personal relationships change over time. Rather, these findings suggest that this dimension may operate independently of the other dimensions of relational change. Similar results emerged from our study of adolescent friendships (see chap. 4, this volume), so this pattern may be typical of close relationships among adolescents more generally. In both studies, the amount of communication between adolescents and their partners was unrelated to basic relational dimensions such as commitment, predictability, and depth of interaction.

Why the amount of communication between adolescent romantic partners is unrelated to their commitment and closeness is less clear. At least two possibilities are worth exploring. One is that adolescents' conceptualization of romantic relationships has not yet coalesced to the point where the developmental dimensions have come together into a coherent framework. Dimensions with strong cognitive and affective elements, like closeness and commitment, are perhaps not yet as grounded in actual interaction as they will be later. Another possibility is that the amount of communication between adolescent romantic partners is more influenced by environmental factors than are other aspects of relational development. School schedules, family expectations, access to transportation, and a host of other factors structure adolescents' time. As I noted in chapter 4, the result might be to reduce the connection between the amount of time adolescents spend with their romantic partners and other dimensions of their relationship.

Associations Among Network Factors. The three network factors were positively and significantly related to one another. Adolescents who reported that their friends and family supported their romantic relationship thought that their partner's friends and family did as well ($r = .65$, $p < .0001$). By the same token, adolescents who felt that their family and friends were unsupportive also reported that their partner's friends and family were unsupportive.

Support for the relationship from the partner's friends and family was a good predictor of how much interaction adolescents had with members of the partner's network ($r = .65$, $p < .0001$). Understandably, adolescents' tended to interact more with members of the partner's network if the network was perceived as supportive. Support for the relationship from members of the adolescent's own network was also positively related to the number of people known and the amount of interaction within the partner's network ($r = .31$, $p < .05$).

These associations, as I noted in chapter 4, undoubtedly reflect reciprocal influences. Supportive friends and family encourage interaction and interaction may encourage support ("Just meet him, you'll like him"). Beneath this generality, however, lays a host of more specific sequences and strategies. Support may diffuse as contact with the partner spreads from an initial group of supporters to the rest of the network. A supportive network member may attempt to rally support from a less supportive one ("Come on, mom, all of Eileen's friends like her new boyfriend"). Unsupportive members may be shunned and unsupportive interactions may be tactfully overlooked. These and other aspects of network management will be address in greater detail in chapter 8.

Associations Between Relational and Network Factors.

As Fig. 5.1 illustrates, social network factors are linked in one way or another, often multiple ways, to the development of adolescent romances. Support from the network and communication with the network influence these relationships both directly and indirectly. These effects are not unidirectional. As we will see, the developing relationship affects the network as well.

Adolescents felt closer to their romantic partners when they perceived that members of their own network ($r = .40$, $p < .01$) and members of their partner's work ($r = .56$, $p < .0001$) supported the relationship. Likewise, adolescents were more committed to romantic partners when they believed that their own network ($r = .25$, $p < .05$) and their partner's network ($r = .34$, $p < .01$) were supportive. Receiving support helps participants make sense of their relationship by confirming expectations, affirming their choice of partners, and removing worries about potential areas of conflict. Conversely, opposition, or even a noncommittal stance, may undermine commitment and closeness in adolescent romances by reducing the participants' confidence, distracting the partners from otherwise rewarding activities, and touching off conflict. Opposition and support also influence commitment and closeness by structuring flows of information as well as access to alternative partners and activities. Unsupportive friends may, for instance, fail to pass along positive comments made about the relationship by others in the network, may make it uncomfortable for the participants to recount positive experiences that reinforce the relationship, and may even disrupt the relationship by introducing an alternative partner. Romantic partners participate actively in this process. They manipulate information so as to cast the relationship in the best possible light. They may, for example, withhold information about a partner's negative attributes or spread information about the partner's positive qualities. Romantic partners may also manage contacts so that the partner is shielded from unsupportive network members (see chap. 8).

Closeness and commitment appear to be somewhat more strongly related to support from the partner's network than to support from one's own network. The differences are small ($.56$ vs. $.40$, $p < .05$, and $.34$ vs. $.25$, ns), but intriguing. Support from the partner's network may be less expected and thus more influential. Perhaps romantic partners simply have less direct access to the views of people in their partner's network than to those of people in their own. If so, judgments of support would rest on a greater inference and thus be subject to cognitive biases toward making them consistent with one's own view of the relationship.

Support also structures the participants' opportunities for interaction. A supportive network makes it easier for the partners to get together. Conversely, it makes it more difficult to use network members to contact alternative partners or even to express reservations about the friendship. Because support weaves the romance into a larger social network, the benefits of development as well as the risks of disruption spread to a wider group.

Surprisingly, support from network members was not directly related to how often the romantic partners communicated with each other. This was true regardless of whether the support was from one's own network or the partner's network. There was, however, a small but significant link ($r = .22$, $p < .05$) between how often an adolescent communicated with the romantic partner and how often he or she communicated with members of the partner's network. Spending more time with the partner may increase the likelihood of meeting the partner's friends and family either in terms of simple probability or because it may be necessary to spend time with the partner's network in order to get additional time with the romantic partner. Some of these joint interactions may be daunting (e.g., being invited to the boyfriend's home to share a holiday meal with extended family), while others may be merely annoying (e.g., being told that if you want the car to take your girlfriend to a movie, you have to take your little brother). Sought or not, joint interactions with members of the partner's network increase time with the partner.

Interaction with the partner's network was also related to other aspects of relational development, although not consistently. It was directly associated with adolescents' sense of closeness ($r = .26$, $p < .01$), but not their sense of commitment. Adolescents may make the romantic relationship more accessible to network members as it becomes closer (Baxter & Widenmann, 1993). At the same time, interacting more often with network members provides useful information about the partner, satisfies expectations, limits times for alternative activities and relationships, and enhances closeness in a variety of other ways.

Friends Versus Family in Adolescent Romantic Relationships.

Given shift in emphasis from family to peer relationships during adolescence, it is useful to explore whether family and friends play different roles in adolescent romantic relationships. Does each group, for instance, express different levels of support? Are the partner's friends liked more than the partner's family? Is there more contact with friends than with family? Do support, liking, and communication have a larger affect on relational development when they involve friends rather than family? The answers these questions are presented in Table 5.1. Other than a slight difference in the daily frequency of interaction with members of the partner's network, there were no differences. Adolescent romantic partners reported that they received similar levels of support from friends and family members. This was true for their partner's network as well as their own. At least at the level of the overall network, we found no evidence of "romantic reactivity," whereby adolescents underplayed support from family as a way to build closeness by creating an "us versus them" orientation. Indeed, the mean level of support across all sectors of

TABLE 5.1

Friend Versus Family Effects in Adolescent Romantic Relationships

Measure	Family Mean (SD)	Friends Mean (SD)	Difference
Support from own network (Scale: 2-10)	8.13 (1.57)	7.92 (1.43)	ns
Support from partner's network (Scale: 2-10)	7.28 (1.41)	7.09 (1.30)	ns
Liking for partner's network (Scale: 2-10)	5.99 (1.68)	5.82 (1.60)	ns
Communication with partner's network A (Scale: 0-14)	2.16 (2.52)	2.76 (2.82)	$p < .01$
Communication with partner's network B (Scale: 1-5)	1.87 (1.02)	1.99 (1.02)	ns

the network was relatively high. Liking was not. The average level of liking for members of the partner's network was slightly below the midpoint of the scale. So although adolescents didn't appear to greatly like either the partner's friends or family, they did not dislike one group more than the other. Moreover, aside from the small difference already alluded to, adolescents communicated about as frequently with their romantic partner's family as with his or her friends. This does not mean, however, that the relationships or the content of the communication were equivalent. Although relationships with the partner's siblings of similar age may be close, it is less likely that adolescent relationships with others in the partner's family will be as close as relationships with the partner's friends.

Although there were few differences between friends and family in the average levels of support, liking, and communication, there were substantial differences in their associations with the inner workings of the romantic relationship itself. This more general finding emerged from a large series of multiple regression analyses in which each of the five pairs of network indicators noted in Table 5.1 was correlated with each of the 11 individual indicators of relational development. This yielded 55 direct comparisons of friend versus family measures.

As should be expected, given the overall results, there were many cases (19 of 55) in which neither the family or friend measure was associated with a given developmental indicator. On the other hand, there were also no cases in which they were both related. This could imply that friends and family are not doing the same "work" in relational development. Support from friends, both one's own and the partner's, is more strongly associated with closeness, commitment, and communication between romantic partners than is support from family members. The pattern was less uniform for measures of liking

and communication, but measures based on friends were statistically significant over twice as often as those based on family members (26 vs. 10 significant
regression coefficients).

Thus, the development of romantic relationships among adolescents is
moderately, but firmly, intertwined with the dynamics of their surrounding
social networks. Within these networks, however, support, liking, and interaction involving friends not only appear to have greater impact on the developing relationship, but also are more affected by it. To determine whether
these findings can be generalized to a somewhat older age group, I now turn
to two studies of romantic relationships among young adults.

ROMANTIC RELATIONSHIP DEVELOPMENT IN EARLY ADULTHOOD

Studying the Development of Romantic Relationships in Early Adulthood: Study I

The next two studies shifted the focus from adolescents to young adults. The
first of these studies was a companion to the study of adolescent romantic relationships reported in the previous section. The same procedures and measures were used (see Appendix A). A sample of 245 participants was recruited
at the University of Washington. The sample was rather evenly split between
males and females (51% vs. 49%). Most subjects (95%) were between 18 and 23
years of age with the average age being just under 20. Most (73%) identified
themselves as European American. The two next largest ethnic groups, Chinese and Japanese, each made up just over 7% of the sample.

Participants reported on a current romantic relationship. Although the average person had been dating his or her partner for approximately 14 months,
relational duration ranged from less than 2 weeks to 6 years. About 30% had
been dating 4 months or less. Less than 10% had been dating for more than 3
years. How long people have been dating, however, is not a complete measure
of the duration of their relationship. Two thirds of the subjects (67.4%) had
known each other before they began dating. Although the length of acquaintance prior to dating was typically rather brief ($Mdn = 3$ months), some participants had rather long acquaintances that predated the current romantic
relationship. Just over 25% had known the prospective partner for over a year
before they began dating.

A Model of the Development of Romantic Relationships in Young Adulthood: Study I

The analysis followed the same plan used to derive the previous models—19
different measures of network and relational characteristics were organized
into underlying factors that were then related to each other using confirma-

tory factor analysis. Two somewhat different models emerged. They differed primarily in their handling of measures of communication with the partner's network. The first was similar to models emerging from the adolescent data sets: measures of frequency of communication and measures of the number of people known were assigned to a common factor. The second split them into separate factors. This was the model that emerged from the data on young adult friendships. Both models fit the data well and were conceptually sound. The second model was ultimately selected because it did a slightly better job of accounting for the variance in the indicators, fit the data somewhat better, and required fewer assumptions about correlated errors. Technical information about the final model may be found in Appendix B. The discussion here will focus on the correlations among the various relational and network factors. These are displayed in Fig. 5.2.

Associations Among Relational Factors.   The three relational development factors were tightly associated in this sample of young adults. Similar to what was observed in adolescent romantic relationships, young adults who

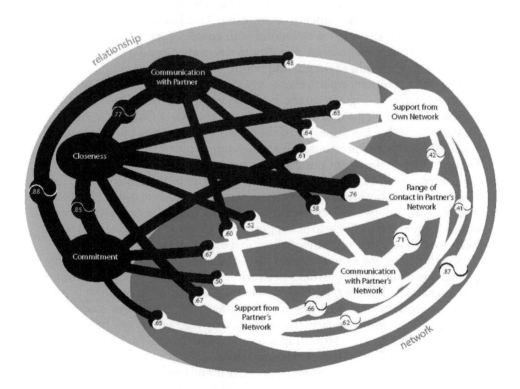

FIG. 5.2.   Young adult romantic relationships.

felt closer to their romantic partners also reported that they were more committed to the relationship ($r = .85$, $p < .0001$). The individual scales used to measure closeness predicted commitment in both the short and long term (being together for 3 months vs. someday getting married). The amount of communication with the romantic partner was much more closely linked to feelings of closeness and commitment among young adults than it was among adolescents (see Fig 5.1). Those who communicated more often with their partners also felt closer to them ($r = .77$, $p < .0001$) and were more committed to the relationship ($r = .88$, $p < .0001$). Communicating is probably both cause and consequence of closeness and commitment. Those who feel close and are committed to their partners communicate more often with them as well.

Associations Among Network Factors.   The four network factors were all positively and significantly related to each other. Support from members of the partner's network was linked to both the number of people met in the partner's network ($r = .62$, $p < .0001$) and the frequency of interaction with them ($r = .66$, $p < .0001$). Those who had met more of the romantic partner's friends and family and who interacted with them more often reported receiving more support for the romantic relationship. That last sentence could most likely be written the other way around with equal accuracy. When the network supports the relationship, romantic partners are more likely to meet and interact with each other's friends and family.

The support romantic partners perceived from their own network was tied in a particularly strong way to the level of support for the relationship they perceived from their partner's network ($r = .87$, $p < .0001$). Changes in support for the relationship from one side of the network appear to be mirrored on the other side. As I noted previously, this association could be the result of several factors. Individual perceptions could be biased toward consistency and this consistency could be further enhanced by the partners' information management strategies, both with each other and with network members. But it is also likely that network members really do take each other's views into account. They are more likely to be supportive if others are supportive and more likely to withhold support if they believe that others oppose the relationship.

Support from one's own network also appears to be related to how many people one meets in the partner's network ($r = .42$, $p < .0001$) and how often one interacts with them ($r = .41$, $p < .0001$). There are probably multiple processes at work here as well (see also Sprecher et al., 2002). For one thing, greater contact with the partner's network may lead one's own friends and family to infer that the relationship is accepted and thus merits their support. They may also infer that the relationship is more serious and feel compelled to be more supportive. Alternatively, supportive friends and family make it easier to spend time with the partner's network. They may reduce competing demands on time or may actively facilitate joint interactions with the partner's network. One partner's friends, for example, may invite the other's friends to a birthday party for one of the romantic pair.

Associations Between Relational and Network Factors.

The development of romantic relationships among young adults is strongly linked to the support they receive and the interaction they have with their friends and family. As Fig. 5.2 illustrates, every possible association between the relational and network factors examined in this study was positive and significant.

Romantic relationships blossom when they are supported by the partners' friends and families. And, romantic relationships that blossom are likely to be supported by the partners' friends and families. Young adults felt closer to their partners ($r = .63, p < .0001$), were more committed to their relationship ($r = .61, p < .0001$), and communicated more with each other when they perceived that their friends and family supported the relationship ($r = .48, p < .0001$). Similarly, support from the partner's friends and family was associated with greater closeness ($r = .67, p < .0001$), commitment ($r = .65, p < .0001$), and communication ($r = .60, p < .0001$). In addition to being robust, it appears that the links between support and relational development are rather uniform. Support from one's own network and support from the partner's network were correlated with closeness, commitment, and communication between the romantic partners in almost identical ways.

Contact with members of the partner's network was strongly associated with the status of young adults' romantic relationships. Those who had met a greater number of people in the partner's network reported that their romantic relationship was closer ($r = .76, p < .0001$), more committed ($r = .67, p < .0001$), and interacted more with their romantic partners ($r = .64, p < .0001$). Those who communicated more often with their partner's friends and family also reported that their romantic relationship was closer ($r = .52, p < .0001$), more committed ($r = .50, p < .0001$), and that they interacted more with their romantic partners ($r = .58, p < .0001$).

Meeting and interacting with the romantic partner's friends and family is undoubtedly linked to relational development in a mutually causal fashion. I will return to explore the nature of this reciprocal connection at the end of the chapter. Before that, however, it may be helpful to consider whether support and communication with family members functions in a different way than support and communication with friends.

Friends Versus Family in Young Adult Romantic Relationships.

The broad comparisons just mentioned may mask more particular differences between friends and family members. One group, for example, may be more supportive or their support may be more closely linked with what goes on inside the relationship. It is, after all, not just the amount of support, but also who provides it or fails to provide it that counts (Brock, I. Sarason, B. Sarason, & Pierce, 1996).

The first step was to determine whether perceptions of support, liking, and communication differed between friends and family in each person's core network. The results of those comparisons are provided in Table 5.2.

Family members were generally seen as more supportive or as supportive as friends. Romantic partners reported that they got more support for their romantic relationships from their families than from their friends, although both groups were generally seen as supportive. They also reported that they liked their partner's family members somewhat more than they liked their partner's friends. This was unexpected, though we should keep in mind that family members included not only parents and older relatives, but siblings and cousins who might be treated as peers. Indeed, these family members who are similar in age could very well serve important boundary-spanning functions between the partners' networks. Finally, as expected, romantic partners reported that they communicated more often with the partner's friends than with his or her family.

Differences in the average levels of support, liking, and communication do not, of course, automatically mean that the impact of friends and family on relational development differs (or that the developing relationship affects them differently). The next step was to determine whether support, liking, and communication were associated with relational development in different ways for friends and family. The strategy used in previous studies was also used with these analyses: each pair of indicators (family vs. friend) used to predict each of the 11 relational development indicators. Again, because

TABLE 5.2

Friend Versus Family Effects in Young Adult Romantic Relationships

Measure	Family Mean (SD)	Friends Mean (SD)	Difference
Support from own network (Scale: 2-10)	8.17 (1.43)	7.22 (1.50)	p < .0001
Support from partner's network (Scale: 2-10)	7.20 (1.58)	7.15 (1.29)	ns
Liking for partner's network (Scale: 2-10)	6.13 (1.63)	5.87 (1.34)	p < .01
Communication with partner's network A (Scale: 0-14)	1.46 (2.08)	2.03 (2.03)	p < .001
Communication with partner's network B (Scale: 1-5)	1.71 (1.01)	1.87 (.81)	p < .05

of the large number of tests involved (55 in all), I focus on the general patterns in the findings.

These analyses revealed that friends and family generally functioned in the same way. In nearly 75% of the tests, both friend and family measures were significantly correlated with the individual indicators of relational development. Support from one's own family and support from one's own friends were, for example, both strongly related to nearly all the individual indicators for closeness, commitment, and communication. The same general pattern held for comparisons between the partner's friends and family in terms of support, liking, and communication. In the remaining 25% of the tests, the measures directed at the partner's friends were significant predictors of development, but measures directly at the partner's family were not. These cases were centered on just three of the developmental indicators: perceived similarity, liking, and satisfaction with communication. These particular aspects of the romantic relationship were much more strongly related to the flow of support, attraction, and communication with the partner's friends than with the partner's family.

The studies presented so far in this chapter provide clear evidence linking the development of romantic relationships with how often the romantic partners interact with members of each other's network and with the extent to which network members are perceived to support the relationship. These links appear to be stronger and more extensive in the romantic relationships of young adults than in the romantic relationships of adolescents. Before examining those differences, however, I present a more detailed study of romantic relationships among young adults.

Studying the Development of Romantic Relationships in Early Adulthood: Study II

The four studies presented so far in this chapter and chapter 4 employed the same measures and differ only in the age of the sample (adolescent vs. young adult) or the target relationships (friendship vs. romantic relationship). I will take advantage of this in later chapters where I combine these subgroups for more general analyses. For now, however, I present a study that sought to address two of the shortcomings in the previous studies.

One of these shortcomings was a lack of ethnic and racial diversity in the sample. This is a common limitation in research on personal relationships. In our case, slightly over 75% of the total subjects in the first two studies reported in this chapter were European American. Although this was only somewhat above the proportion in the U.S. population as a whole (68% in 2003), the growing diversity of the U.S. population warrants a more diverse sample of young adults involved in romantic relationships. My colleague, April Trees, and I thus ran advertisements, spoke to classes, and contacted ethnic student groups in an effort to solicit greater numbers of non-White participants. Slightly less than half (47%) of the 232 participants in the final sample were European American. The majority represented 11 different ethnic or racial groups. The largest of these were Chinese/Chinese American (9%), Filipino (8%), Korean/Korean American (7%), Vietnamese/Vietnamese American (6%), African American (6%), and "Other" (7%). The final sample was evenly split between males and females. The typical participant was just over 20 years of age and had been dating his or her romantic partner for just over a year. Most subjects (66.8%) had known the dating partner before the beginning of the dating relationship. The median duration of previous acquaintance was 4 months.

We sought to extend the previous studies in a second way by exploring a more detailed set of relational and network factors. The previous studies had relied on a rather global relational factor ("closeness") and on measures of only a few of the network factors described in chapter 2. Whereas the previous studies examined only three relational development factors (global closeness, commitment, amount of communication), six factors were examined in this study. They were: synchrony of interaction, depth, commitment, code personalization, predictability/understanding, and amount of communication between the partners. The expanded set of network factors included: (a) support from the partner's network, (b) support from the subject's network, (c) network overlap, (d) the number of people the partners had met in each other's networks (*cross-network contact*), (e) how often the subject communicated with known members of the partner's network, and (f) estimates of how often members of the subject's and partner's networks communicated with each other (*cross-network density*).

Another Model of the Development of Romantic Relationships in Young adulthood: Study II

The six relational and the six network factors were measured using a series of 26 separate indicators and the associations among all 12 factors were estimated using confirmatory factor analysis. The measures are described more fully in Appendix A, and the analysis is summarized in Appendix B. Because of the greater number of factors, the final model is presented in three pieces, beginning with the associations among the relational factors and the associations among the network factors, and concluding with the associations between the relational and networks factors.

Associations Among Relational Factors.   Although I have chosen to focus on only a few associations in this section, all six factors were significantly correlated with one another, as shown in Fig. 5.3. In line with the results of the previous study, romantic partners expressed greater commitment when the depth dimension of the relationship was high ($r = .85$, $p < .0001$) and when they felt that they could understand and predict one another's behav-

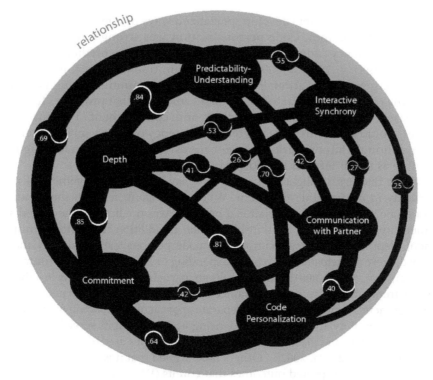

FIG. 5.3.   Young adult romantic relationships—sample 2 relational submodel.

ior ($r = .69$, $p < .0001$). The depth dimension as measured here included several items from Rubin's (1970) Love Scale and several self-disclosure items. The depth and predictability–understanding dimensions had been part of the global closeness dimension in the previous four studies. In all of those studies, they were positively associated with commitment.

This study included two aspects of relational development that have not received extensive attention in the previous literature. One was *interactive synchrony*, an aspect of conversational interdependence. Synchrony or smoothness of interaction involves both verbal and nonverbal behaviors and reflects an effortless and well-coordinated interaction (Altman & Taylor, 1973; Knapp, Ellis, & Williams, 1980). In this study, romantic partners who reported greater interactive synchrony also reported greater depth ($r = .53$, $p < .0001$) and predictability ($r = .55$, $p < .0001$) in the relationship. Or, put the other way, romantic partners who were more in love, who disclosed more intimately, and who felt that they understood one another also had greater synchrony in their interactions. Another less researched dimension of relational development is *code personalization*. This refers to the extent to which partners develop specialized ways of communicating (see chap. 2, this volume). Code personalization was strongly related to the depth or intimacy of interaction ($r = .81$, $p < .0001$), to predictability–understanding ($r = .70$, $p < .0001$), and to commitment ($r = .64$, $p < .0001$). The emergence of relationally distinct ways of communicating is likely both the result of these factors as well as something that promotes further increases in intimacy, understanding, and commitment. Personalized codes should also contribute to greater efficiency or synchrony of interaction, although the correlation between these factors, while certainly significant, was not as large as the others in the set ($r = .25$, $p < .01$).

These findings highlight the central role played by the management of uncertainty in relational development. When participants felt that they understood one another and that relational behavior was predictable, they rated all other dimensions of the relationship higher. In addition to greater commitment, depth, interactive synchrony, and code personalization, already mentioned, these participants also reported spending more time with their romantic partners ($r = .42$, $p < .0001$). These results are particularly noteworthy in light of recent trends favoring more fine-grained approaches to research on uncertainty management. Some have called for separate approaches depending on the topic of the uncertainty, the person experiencing it, the functions served by uncertainty reduction, and the information-seeking strategies used (e.g., Knobloch & Solomon, 1999, 2002a, 2002b). Others have argued that it is the interaction of uncertainty with expected outcomes that counts (W. A. Afifi & Weiner, 2004; Babrow, 2001; Brashers, 2001). That is, people may prefer to remain uncertain if reducing uncertainty is likely to reveal unpleasant information. All of these theoretic developments have merit and point in new directions that traditional uncertainty reduction theory did not. The results of this study remind us, however, that global perceptions of uncertainty, predictability, and understanding continue to play a major role in perceptions of relational development.

Finally, romantic partners who spent more time together also reported higher levels on all the other relational dimensions. The strongest associations were with commitment ($r = .42$, $p < .0001$), depth ($r = .41$, $p < .0001$), and predictability–understanding ($r = .42$, $p < .0001$). Although all these links were statistically significant, they were somewhat smaller than the remaining ones in the submodel. Here, as in the previous models of adolescent relationships, the amount of communication seemed to function somewhat more independently. This may reflect the effect of other obligations, as with the models of adolescent relationships, or it may be related in some way to the greater ethnic diversity of the sample for this study. The latter possibility will be explored in chapter 7.

Associations Among Network Factors.   The associations among the network factors are displayed in Fig. 5.4. The range of network factors examined

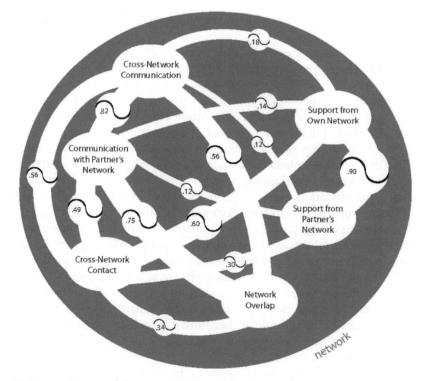

FIG. 5.4. Young adult romantic relationships—sample 2 network submodel.

in this study was more extensive than that generally considered in the literature on personal relationships and networks (For reviews, see Milardo &
Helms-Erikson, 2000; Sprecher et al., 2002). Because of that, it may be useful
to begin with a brief description of how the network factors were measured
(see Appendix A for additional information)

Participants were asked to list the 12 people with whom they had communicated most frequently in the previous 2 weeks. They were then instructed to
obtain a similar list from their romantic partner, to determine together how
many people their separate lists had in common, and to estimate how often
the people on the two lists communicated with each other. The number of
people common to both lists was our measure of *network overlap*, whereas the
estimated amount of communication between members of the partner's individual networks represented *cross-network density*. We also asked participants
to report how many people they had met in the partner's network and how
many the partner had met in theirs *(cross-network contact)*. They also reported
how often they had communicated in the previous two weeks with each person they knew on their partner's list *(communication with partner's network)*. Finally, they were asked to rate how much each member of their own network

and each known member of the partner's network supported or approved their dating relationship.

When there was greater contact between members of the partners' individual networks, romantic partners tended to have a larger mutual or overlapping network ($r = .56$, $p < .0001$). Greater contact among network members was also associated with meeting more people in the partner's network ($r = .56$, $p < .0001$) and with communicating with them more often ($r = .82$, $p < .0001$). Finally, when romantic partners communicated more frequently with members of their partner's network, they also reported that they had met more people in their partner's network ($r = .49$, $p < .0001$) and that they had a larger overlapping network ($r = .75$, $p < .0001$). Without further longitudinal data, we can not properly sort out the sequences by which these factors influence each other. For example, increases in communication between the networks, perhaps even before the partners even meet for the first time, may lead the individual to meet new people who happen to be part of the partner's network. Or, as partners introduce one another to the members of their networks (cross-network contact), and interact with them, the members of the networks themselves start interacting with each other. The telephone call between parents to discuss the romantic couple's plans for holiday visits is a good example of this. Both of these scenarios undoubtedly occur, as do other scenarios by which one might explain the associations between these network factors.

Several aspects of the findings involving network support for the relationship are noteworthy. First is the strong association between perceptions of support from one's own network and from the partner's network ($r = .90$, $p < .0001$). Just as in the previous study, differences in support for the relationship from one side of the network were mirrored on the other side. On the other hand, associations between the amount of communication with network members and support from either their partner's network ($r = .12$, $p < .05$) or their own network ($r = .14$, $p < .05$) were relatively weak.

The number of people one had met in the partner's network (cross-network contact) was a much better predictor of support for the relationship than how often one communicated with them. Meeting more people was associated with greater support both from the partner's network ($r = .30$, $p < .001$) and from one's own network ($r = .60$, $p < .0001$). Here again, multiple interpretations make sense. One is that members of the network are more likely to support the relationship when they see that the romantic partners are serious enough to put the relationship up for public view. Another is that the romantic partners infer that network members must support the relationship or they would not have been introduced to them. This is complicated by the fact that introductions may indeed be quite strategic—selecting only those most likely to support the relationship. From the other side, those who support the relationship may actively encourage further introductions—as in the case of the friend who hosts a party for one romantic partner where other friends can "meet the new boyfriend."

Associations Between Relational and Network Factors.

From the standpoint of relational development, our primary interest is in the associations between the network factors and the relational factors. These are displayed in Fig. 5.5. Rather than trying to discuss every linkage in such a complex model, I instead focus its most significant features. First, it is striking to note just how far network perceptions extend into the relationship. Every dimension of relationship development was significantly associated with at least two of the network factors. Moreover, the network touched aspects of romantic relationships that one would not typically consider—such as the synchrony or coordination of conversation between the partners. Yet romantic partners reported that their interactions were smoother and more coordinated when there was more support from their own network ($r = .36, p < .0001$) and from their partner's network ($r = .40, p < .0001$). It is not immediately clear why this should be so, al-

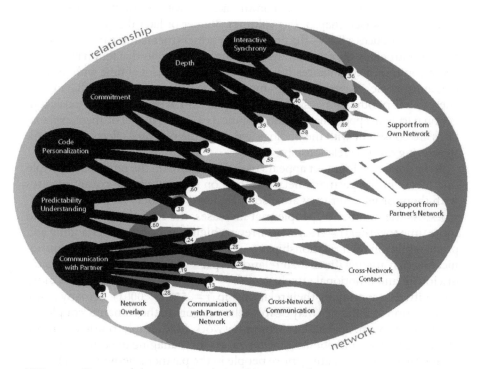

FIG. 5.5. Young adult romantic relationships—sample 2.

though it is likely that network members will be more supportive if they observe free flowing rather than awkward interactions between the partners.

The amount of communication between the romantic partners appears to be particularly sensitive to network factors. It was the only aspect of relationship development that was significantly associated with all six network factors. And it was the only dimension of development that was linked to cross-network communication ($r = .13, p < .05$), network overlap ($r = .21, p < .01$), and the amount of communication with members of the partner's network ($r = .28, p < .001$). Romantic partners spent more time together when members of their individual networks had greater contact with each other, when they had a larger overlapping or mutual network, and when they communicated more often with members of their partner's network. Sometimes, as I noted earlier, one has to spend time with the partner's network in order to spend more time with the partner. Conversely, as romantic partners begin spending more time together, network members begin paying more attention to the relationship. The relationship may become a topic of discussion among network members who know both parties. Those who do not know both members of the couple may expect introductions. Another plausible scenario begins even before the partners meet. Unknown to the partners, and for whatever reason, their social networks begin to slide together at some point and each prospective partner begins communicating with a few members of the other's network (see chap. 3, this volume). Sooner or later this primordial relational sea produces a flash—the prospective partners meet for the first time and a relationship begins. Shortly after that, they discover not only that they have a number of common acquaintances, but that they also spend a lot of time with some of the same people. These discoveries motivate further interaction and that in turn energizes all of other dimensions of development. This scenario is obviously longer on narrative appeal than it is on empirical evidence, but all of these explanations are consistent with the findings and show the potential effects of network structuring on close relationships.

Relational development appears to depend more on the number of people one meets in the partner's network than on how often one communicates with them or whether they are also considered members of one's own network. As the number of people met increases, the romantic partners spend more time together ($r = .19, p < .01$), report higher levels of understanding and predictability in their relationship ($r = .28, p < .001$), develop ways of communicating that are specific to their relationship ($r = .38, p < .0001$), report greater disclosure and emotional attachment ($r = .39, p < .0001$), and become more committed to continuing their relationship ($r = .55, p < .0001$). In many cases, the direction of influence may be from the network to the romantic couple. As one meets more people in the partners network, for example, one learns more about the partner and obtains new resources for managing uncertainty (Parks & Adelman, 1983). Meeting more people in the partner's network and knowing that he or she has met more in yours may enhance commitment by making the prospect of withdrawing from the relationship seem more difficult, but also by reinforcing the idea that the relationship fits into one's life more generally (Levinger, 1979; Parks, 2000). In other cases, relational development undoubtedly drives cross-network contact. As the couple finds that their relationship is deepening, becoming more committed, and so on, they are likely to begin introducing one another to more members of their network.

Finally, the results of this study provide further evidence of the connection between relationship development and approval from the other people with whom the participants interact most frequently. It did not seem to matter whether the support was perceived to come from one's own network or from the partner's network. Perceptions of support from one's own and the partner's network were very highly correlated, as I noted earlier, and there were no significant differences in how the two support measures correlated with each of the developmental dimensions. Most of the correlations between support from the partner's network and the developmental dimensions ranged from .40 to .60 ($ps < .0001$), except for the amount of communication with the partner ($r = .28$, $p < .001$). The correlations between support from the subject's own network and the development dimensions ranged from approximately .40 to .70, again except for the correlation with the amount of communication with the partner ($r = .24$, $p < .01$). Generally speaking, romantic partners who perceived greater levels of approval from network members also interacted with one another more easily or smoothly, adapted or personalized their verbal and nonverbal communication to the relationship, felt that they understood one another better, disclosed more intimately, were more emotionally attached, and were more committed to the relationship. Naturally, a relationship with these qualities is exactly the kind of couple that network members are most likely to support, so it is likely that the behavior of the couple also influences network members. In addition, we should remember that we are talking about the participants' perceptions of network members' views of their relationship—perceptions that may be subject to error, distortion, and strategic manipulation. Whatever their objective accuracy, however, it is these perceptions that appear to drive and be driven by relational development.

ROMANTIC RELATIONSHIPS IN SOCIAL CONTEXT

The three studies presented in this chapter all demonstrate the central role played by social network factors in the development of male-female romantic relationships. Furthermore, they illustrate the utility of relational sense-making and network structuring as explanatory tools for understanding why networks are so involved in the development of interpersonal relationships.

The amount of contact and communication romantic partners had with each other's networks was associated with measures of relational development across all three studies. In the adolescent sample, romantic partners who had more contact and communication with network members felt closer to one another and interacted with one another more often. In the two young adult samples, romantic partners who had met a greater number of those in their partner's network reported higher levels of development in all or nearly all of the aspects that we measured. Other researchers have also found that the number of people known in the partner's network was a significant predictor of relational development (e.g., H. J. Kim & Stiff, 1991). Romantic partners who interacted with the partner's network more often tended to interact with one another more often in these studies as well. Those who interacted more with the partner's network also felt closer and more committed to their romantic partner in the first of the young adult studies, but the amount of interaction with the partner's network was not significantly associated with other aspects of development in the second study. As I discuss later, this may reflect a difference in how network members were identified in the two studies.

Premarital romantic couples develop a larger overlapping or mutual network as their relationship develops (Agnew, Loving, & Drigotas, 2001; H. J. Kim & Stiff, 1991; Milardo, 1982; Milardo, Johnson, & Huston, 1983). Married couples also tend to be more satisfied, committed, and intimate when there is a larger shared network and when the overlapping members are drawn from each partner's individual networks more or less evenly (Julien & Markman, 1991; Kearns & Leonard, 2004; Stein, Bush, Ross, & Ward, 1992). Yet the association between relational development and network overlap may not be as straightforward as these results imply.

One study failed to find any increase in network overlap among premarital couples that were tracked over a 4-year period (Sprecher & Felmlee, 2000). Other studies have also suggested that having a common network may be more important in the early stages of marriage than once the marriage is more established (Julien, Chartrand, & Begin, 1999; Kearns & Leonard, 2004). Thus, network overlap may have a more powerful effect early in relationships and after major relational transitions such as marriage. It is also possible that network overlap increases to some desired point rather quickly in relationships and after major transitions and is then maintained. Alternatively, our findings imply that having common friends and other network members may not be as important as having broad contact with many people in the partner's network and interacting with at least some of them regularly. Network overlap itself was related to only one aspect of relationship development—romantic partners spent more time together if they shared a greater number of network members.

The remaining aspect of network structure considered in these studies was cross-network density. This represents the extent to which members of the partners' networks interacted with each other (i.e., do your friends talk to my friends?). It was related directly to only one aspect of relational development and that was how often the partners communicated with one another. However, it is probably indirectly related to several aspects of the relationship through its association with other network factors. Couples whose networks interacted more often tended to have more shared contacts and to meet and interact more with one another's networks.

As their relationship grows closer, romantic partners typically reprioritize their interactions with network members in order to make more time for each other. They typically spend less time and engage in fewer leisure activities with their friends and relatives (Huston, Surra, Fitzgerald, & Cate, 1981; M. P. Johnson & Leslie, 1982; Laursen & Williams, 1997; Milardo et al., 1983). This does not mean, however, that couples regress into a "world for two," as some have suggested (Slater, 1963). For one thing, the degree of withdrawal found in previous studies is usually not large in any absolute sense. Second, when it occurs at all, the withdrawal involves the members of the network to whom one is less attached. There is less withdrawal from relatives and close friends. Finally, as demonstrated in all three of the studies reported here, romantic partners typically spend more time with their partner's friends and family as their relationship develops. Thus, the overall process is not so much a process of withdrawal as a process of realignment and reprioritization.

There is no reason to believe that these realignments are permanent. Couples may withdraw for a period of time or even periodically, only to re-engage with network members at a later point. Moreover, there is no stable point of reference for judging withdrawal or engagement because relationships among all of the members of the larger network are continually in flux.

Researchers seeking to understand the role of network factors in relational development have focused their greatest attention on approval and support for the relationship. Nearly every previous study of premarital romantic relationships has linked higher levels of approval or support with greater development and stability (e.g., Lewis, 1973b; Parks et al., 1983; Sprecher, 1988; Sprecher & Felmlee, 2000). Married couples who perceive that their friends and extended families support their relationship are more likely to be satisfied and stay together, whereas divorce is more likely for those whose families disapprove of the marriage (e.g., Bryant & Conger, 1999; Cleek & Pearson, 1985; Thornes & Collard, 1979; Veroff, Douvan, & Hatchett, 1995).

Approval or support from network members for the romantic relationship was strongly associated with increases in relational development across all three studies reported here as well. Support from network members in these studies was linked to higher levels of commitment, understanding, disclosure, attachment, interactive synchrony, code personalization, and more frequent interaction. Furthermore, these studies suggest that the role of support is even more far-reaching than previously believed. For example, support from network members was linked to both the extent to which romantic partners were able to converse smoothly and employ specialized verbal and nonverbal expressions. Although they are observable to outside parties, these characteristics are also rather subtle aspects of the relationship. The fact that they were both correlated with support from network members could mean that romantic partners are extraordinarily sensitive to the level of approval or opposition from network members, that romantic partners with "finely tuned" interactions tend to assume that outsiders approve, or that network members take subtle features of the romantic partners' relationship into account, or all three.

Relationship development in these studies was closely associated with the perceived approval from both sides of the network. Support from one's own network and support from the partner's network were equally important. There was never a case in which support from one side of the network was associated with development but support from the other side was not. Nor were there any significant differences in the strength of these associations. These findings run counter to earlier work suggesting that support from one's own network may be more strongly associated with development than support from the partner's network (Parks & Adelman, 1983; Sprecher & Felmlee, 1992).

It did seem to matter, however, whether the approval was coming from friends or from family members. The approval of friends (one's own and one's partner's) was more strongly associated than the approval of family members with relational development among adolescents. Among young adults, on the other hand, approval from friends and approval from family were generally associated with relational development in similar ways.

In all of these studies, then, approval from network members goes hand in hand with relationship development, whereas disapproval or opposition is associated with their downfall. There could be exceptions to this broad trend, however. One of the more engaging exceptions comes from a study by Driscoll, Davis, and Lipetz (1972), who found that dating couples whose parents opposed the relationship were actually more in love than those whose parents were supportive or neutral. They dubbed this finding the "Romeo and Juliet Effect." It has never been replicated. One reason for this, Driscoll maintains, is that the effect only operates in a small window of opportunity. The romantic relationship must be new, but participants must have at least some commitment to it, and the parental interference cannot go on for too long (Driscoll's conjecture is cited in Sprecher et al., 2002).

If this is correct, parental interference should intensify feelings of love only at a very specific point in the relationship. The problem is in identifying exactly where "the window" occurs. The fact that most studies, including all three reported here, find that very few network members are actively opposed to the relationship suggests that the effect, if it occurs, probably occurs rarely. Nonetheless, opposition does occur and so it is entirely possible that Romeo and Juliet effects sometimes occur as well. That said, three more things should be added. First, in many cases, though presumably not with parents, romantic partners can simply drop or distance themselves from network members who express opposition. The effect should be less likely to occur or at least be small in these cases. Second, even with parents, it is unlikely that something like the Romeo and Juliet effect could occur if others in the network were opposed as well. Finally, because the image of young lovers battling against family or community is deeply ingrained in many cultures, we should distinguish between actual and romanticized opposition to the relationship. Romantic partners may sometimes distort the feedback they get from network members in a negative direction simply because it is romantic to do so.

Although the consistency in findings across the three studies bodes well for the social contextual approach to understanding personal relationships, there were obvious and not so obvious differences design and findings that warrant further attention. One is the difference in the way network members were identified in the last two studies. In the first study, subjects generated a "psychological network" based on who was important to them, whereas in the second, they generated an "interactive" network based on whom they communicated with most often. Although a great deal has been made of the difference between these two types of networks (e.g., Milardo, 1983, 1989; Surra & Milardo, 1991), it is not obvious that they play different roles in the process of relational development. In the present case, for example, we can ask if the correlations between variables common to the last two studies differed. Both studies included measures of support and commitment. Commitment was significantly associated with both support from the partner's network ($r = .65$, $p < .0001$), and support from the subject's own network ($r = .61$, $p < .0001$) in the first study. Commitment was also significantly associated with support from the partner's network ($r = .58$, $p < .0001$), and support from the subject's own network ($r = .69$, $p < .0001$), in the final study. There were no significant differences among these correlations. That is, perceptions of support from a network of significant others and perceptions of support from a network of frequent contacts seem be related to commitment in the same way. On the other hand, it is likely that a measures of network overlap or cross-network density based on people with whom both partners were close might have more impact than one based on people both partners simply interact with on a regular basis. Given that most people have regular contact and at least some level of acquaintance with literally hundreds of other people, we obviously need to know more about which subsets of the total network are most involved in the formation of a given close relationship.

Another obvious difference in design was the greater ethnic and racial diversity of people who participated in final study. Although nearly 75% of those who participated in the first of the two studies of young adult romantic relationships were European American, less than half of those in the final study were European American. The fact that social network factors and relational development were highly associated in both studies suggests that social contextual theory may have general application, but there is much more to explore. I consider the possible effects of racial and ethnic differences, as well as gender differences, in more detail in chapter 7. One of the major differences in the findings across the studies presented in the last two chapters is the fact that network factors and relational factors appear to be somewhat less tightly linked in the adolescent samples than in the young adult sample. I also explore this difference more systematically in chapter 6. The question of differences between male-female romantic relationships and same-sex friendships is also addressed in the next chapter.

Comparing Age Groups
and Relational Types

This chapter builds on chapters 4 and 5 by considering more general comparisons of different age groups and different types of relationships. Do social network factors function in the same way in relationships among young adults as they do in relationships among adolescents? Do they function in the same way in same-sex friendship as they do in male-female romantic relationships? Focusing on these more general effects helps us understand how relationships might compare across two pivotal periods in the passage to adulthood as well as how patterns of development play out in two different types of personal relationships. More importantly, these comparisons begin to inform us how generally the social contextual model of relationship development may be applied.

COMPARING RELATIONAL DEVELOPMENT
IN ADOLESCENCE AND EARLY ADULTHOOD

Social and developmental psychologists continue to debate what taking a social perspective on development might entail (Durkin, 1995). For some, the "social" in social development refers only to the effects of environment on development—a view that is often dismissed as ignoring the changes that are occurring inside the individual (e.g., M. H. Johnson & Morton, 1991). A truly social view on development would, it seems to me, acknowledge not only that environmental factors affect development, but also that the changes inside the individual affect the surrounding environment. Nowhere is this point more applicable than in the social development of adolescents and young adults.

The studies reported in this book offer a window on the social world of people between the ages of 14 and 26. We usually divide this period, somewhat arbitrarily, into two phases—adolescence and early adulthood. Although a distinct period of adolescence is widely recognized across cultures, we should keep in mind that it is both relatively recent historically and uncertain conceptually (Durkin, 1995). A distinct period of "early adulthood" is recognized in only about 20% of the world's cultures (Schlegel & Barry, 1991). In the majority of cultures, one steps from adolescence directly into adulthood in the late teens. This may change, of course, with increasing industrialization and globalization. Even when a distinct postadolescent period is recognized, there are wide differences in how it is categorized and discussed. Levinson (1978), for example described two postadolescent stages—"early adult transition" (17 to 22 years old) and "entering the adult world" (22 to 28 years old). In the first of these stages, the individual seeks to establish autonomy and engage a vision of his or her life in the future. In the second, the individual seeks to enter a job and to form a committed personal relationship. Other observers prefer the term *emerging adulthood* to describe the entire period from age 18 to 26. During this time, young people have a great deal of independence but have not yet taken on all of the responsibilities of adulthood (Arnett, 2000, 2001).

The period from age 14 to age 26 is inarguably one of great challenge, regardless of how it is categorized. Adolescents and young adults strive to accomplish a daunting series of social developmental tasks. They are commonly expected to establish an independent identity, learn to control their emotions and focus on others, live responsibly within cultural rule systems, advance and usually complete their education, establish financial independence, develop their own relational commitments, and perhaps take on family responsibilities of their own (e.g., Arnett, 2001, 2003; Facio & Mircocci, 2003; Mayseless & Scharf, 2003). Biological maturation is thus layered with cultural definitions about what it means to be an adult and what must be done in order to achieve adult status. Elias, Gara, and Ubriaco's (1985) description of the changes facing young people at the beginning of this period can easily be applied across the entire period. These include changes in expected behaviors and roles, changes in social networks, reorganization of support resources, restructuring attitudes and beliefs, and management of stress and uncertainty. Along with these changes, or in some cases perhaps because of them, risky behaviors such as binge drinking, drinking and driving, drug use, and unprotected sex rise through adolescence and peak in early adulthood (Arnett, 2000).

One of the more clearly defined markers near the middle of this period is the transition from high school to college. The proportion of secondary students attending college is rising worldwide and some sort of college experience has become the norm in the United States where over 60% of high school students go on to attend college (Arnett, 2000). Thus high school and college are not simply convenient sampling frames for adolescents and young adults, but also two of the primary social settings in which life changes unfold.

Major life changes do not occur in an isolated way, but are rather experienced and influenced by the individual's social network. Network members are often deeply involved in helping (and hindering) the individual making the transition from one phase to the next (Trickett & Buchanan, 2001). Moreover, many of the developmental tasks of adolescence and early adulthood are centered directly on the development of personal relationships. Two of the most important of these are same-sex friendships and cross-sex romantic relationships. Learning whether there are differences in the ways these relationships develop in high school and college will help us better understand the general pathways of social development. It may help identify the specific resources and skills that young people require, not only to assist them in developing social relationships, but also in drawing on those relationships to assist them with other tasks such as deciding where to live or finding a job. To determine what differences there might be, I conducted two different types of analyses. The first looked for differences in average values for each of the various developmental and network indicators discussed in the previous chapters. The second derived and compared models of the associations among developmental and network factors in the two age groups. These analyses and their results are described in the sections that follow.

Differences in Relational and Network Factors Between Adolescence and Early Adulthood

Do adolescents and young adults differ in the way they experience personal relationships or in the way they relate to their social networks? This is admittedly a very broad question, but we can at least cast some light on it by asking if there are important age group differences that occur across different types of personal relationships and that occur for both men and women. To address this question, I combined the separate samples described in earlier chapters into one larger sample that could be used to identify any general differences between high school and university students while using statistical procedures to control for any differences between relational types and genders. Although the larger sample size ($N = 858$) made it easier to sort out differences, it also allowed even very small differences to appear significant. In order to screen out substantively trivial, but statistically significant effects, the discussion that follows includes only those differences that exceeded a minimum effect size (partial $eta^2 \geq .02$).

High School Versus University Students' Perceptions of Relational Development. High school students and university students differed significantly on 4 of the 11 indicators of relational development (see Appendix A for a description of measures). Three of these differences occurred within the general cluster that we have been describing as *closeness*. High school students reported greater interpersonal solidarity, love, predictability, and understanding in their personal relationships than university-aged students.

The two age groups did not differ on the remaining indicators of closeness—liking, perceived similarity, and satisfaction with communication. High school and university students generally communicated with their relational partners with equivalent regularity and reported spending about the same amount of their free time with them.

The remaining significant difference in the relational indicators was found in one of the indicators of long-term commitment. High school students generally agreed more strongly with a statement that the relationship would go on forever (for friends) or lead to marriage (for dating partners). However, when asked to estimate the probability of these outcomes (0%–100%) in later questions, high school students and university students did not differ. Nor did they differ in their commitment to the relationship in the short term.

High School Versus University Students' Perceptions of Network Involvement.
There were even fewer differences in how high school and university aged students viewed social network involvement in their personal relationships. Each group reported similar and generally high levels of support for their relationship from members of their own network as well as their partner's network. This was true both for support from both family members and friends.

Although the two age groups did not differ overall in the number of people they had met face-to-face in their partner's network, there were significant differences when the type of relationship was taken into account. Regardless of whether they were reporting on a dating relationship or a same-sex friendship, people in high school had met an equal number of their partner's family. The same held true for meeting the partner's friends. In the young adult sample gathered at the university, however, people involved in dating relationships had met almost twice as many of their partner's family and friends as those involved in same-sex friendships.

How often respondents communicated with the people they had met in the partner's network differed between the two age groups in a more straightforward way. Adolescents reported that they communicated with the network members of their friends and dating partners significantly more often than young adults. There was also a significant interaction with relationship type. Young adults communicated more often with their romantic partner's friends and family, whereas adolescents communicated more often with their same-sex friend's friends and family.

Both young adults and adolescents liked their romantic partner's family more than the family members of their same-sex friends, but this difference was larger among young adults. There were no differences in how much adolescents and young adults liked their partners' friends. Respondents liked their partner's friends to the same degree, regardless of whether the respondent was an adolescent or a young adult, and regardless of whether the partner was a dating partner or a same-sex friend.

Comparing Relational Development Processes in Adolescence and Early Adulthood

Do personal relationships develop in the same general way for people at different points in their lives? Or does the process of relational development itself change as people move along their life paths? These are obviously larger questions than I can resolve here, but we can at least begin by asking if personal relationships develop in the same way for adolescents and young adults. Given the magnitude of the changes between age 14 and age 26, it would be surprising if the same model of relational development applied equally well for adolescents and young adults. And yet, some aspects of relationship formation may transcend setting and age group.

To find out, I aggregated the data on high school friendships and romantic relationships to create a data set covering both types of personal relationships in adolescence ($N = 339$). I did the same with the data from university samples to create a general data set on personal relationships in early adulthood ($N = 519$). Almost all (99%) of the subjects in the adolescent sample were between age 14 and age 18, whereas almost all (98%) of those in the young adult sample were between age 18 and age 26. Each sample included the 19 relational and network indicators used in the core studies described in chapters 4 and 5 and listed in Appendix A. These were grouped underlying factors that were then related to each other using confirmatory factor analysis.

The top layers of the final models for adolescent and young adult personal relationships are displayed in Fig. 6.1 and Fig. 6.2. These allow us to directly compare the associations among and between relational and network factors for each age group. Further technical information about the models may be found in Appendix B.

One may think of these models as aggregates of the more particular models of adolescent friendship and romantic relationship development presented in chapters 4 and 5. Because a more detailed commentary about the particular characteristics behind each model was provided there, the discussion here is focused on how they compare.

The most obvious difference is that communication with the partner's network is structured differently in the two models. In the adolescent sample, the number of people one has met in the partner's network and how often one interacts with them are much more closely associated than they are in the young adult sample. The more people one meets, the more often one communicates with the people one has met. Thus in adolescent relationships, the range of contact within the partner's network and the amount of communication tend to cluster together. In early adulthood, however, having met people does not so automatically imply that one will have ongoing contact with them. Although the range of contact (i.e., the number of people met) is positively associated with the amount of communication, the best fitting model is one in

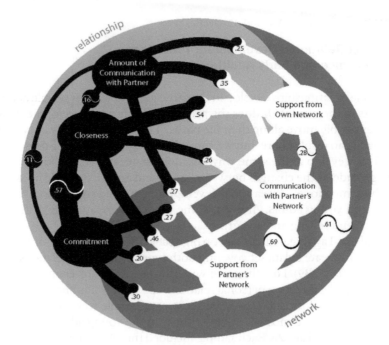

FIG. 6.1.   General model of adolescent personal relationships.

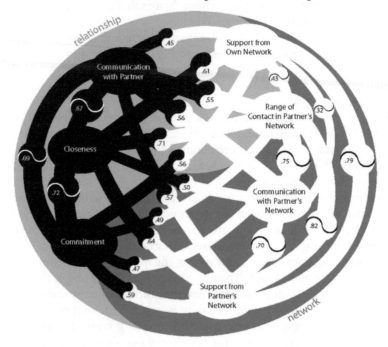

FIG. 6.2.   General model of young adult personal relationships.

which these two characteristics are treated as separate factors. Thus, the difference in social network factors that was first identified in friendships in chapter 4 appears to be a general difference in the personal relationships of adolescents and young adults. I speculated earlier that this structural difference might reflect the more bounded, closely controlled character of the high school environment. Before exploring that idea in greater detail, however, we should note several other ways in which the two models differ.

Another major difference in how relationships develop in adolescence and early adulthood may be found by looking at how tightly the relational factors are bound together. Commitment and closeness are positively related in the relationships of both adolescents ($r = .57, p < .0001$) and young adults ($r = .72, p < .0001$), although the correlation among young adults is significantly stronger than that among adolescents ($p < .001$). An even larger difference emerges when we compare how the amount of communication with the partner is related to commitment and closeness in the two age groups. Among adolescents, the amount of communication with the partner is only weakly associated with closeness ($r = .16, p < .05$) and unrelated to commitment ($r = .11, ns$). Among young adults, however, the amount of communication with the partner is strongly related to both closeness ($r = .67, p < .0001$) and commitment ($r = .69, p < .0001$). Both of these associations are significantly stronger ($ps < .0001$) among young adults than among adolescents.

A similar picture emerges when we inspect the associations among the network factors in Fig. 6.1 and Fig. 6.2. Although it is complicated by the difference in factor structure, it appears that the network factors are more strongly associated with each other in the personal relationships of young adults than in the personal relationships of adolescents. The correlations linking the support factors to the amount of communication with network members are generally larger in the young adult sample. And although support for the relationship from one's own network is strongly related to support from the partner's network in both adolescent relationships ($r = .61, p < .0001$) and young adult relationships ($r = .79, p < .0001$), the correlation is significantly larger among young adults ($p < .0001$).

The final overall difference of note is the generally stronger linkage between relational development and social network factors in the young adult sample. Of the six associations between relational and network factors that are common to both models, five are significantly stronger in relationships of young adults (p's $< .01$ to $< .0001$). Only the link between closeness and support for the relationship from the subject's own network fails to differ significantly between the models for adolescents ($r = .54, p < .0001$) and young adults ($r = .61, p < .0001$).

Before exploring how these differences might be explained, one larger similarity should be emphasized. Relational development and social network factors are deeply intertwined for both adolescents and young adults. Although the linkages are stronger in the case of young adult relationships, every possible association between relational and network factors is positive and statistically significant in both age groups. Regardless of age, communication, commitment, and closeness with a same-sex friend or romantic partner are uniformly linked with communication with and support from members of the partners' surrounding social network. Both models thus offer support for the social contextual perspective on personal relationships.

Understanding the Differences Between Adolescent and Young Adult Personal Relationships.   Adolescent and young adult personal relationships do appear to differ in several ways. Adolescents' personal relationships are somewhat closer, with greater feelings of love and solidarity, and perhaps slightly more committed (depending on the measure used to assess commitment). Adolescents and young adults have about the same amount of interaction with their relational partners, but in adolescent relationships, the amount of interaction with the partner is not connected with feelings of commitment or closeness. Adolescents communicate more often with members of their partner's network than young adults do. They regularly spend time with the people they meet, whereas young adults do not necessarily see the people they meet in their partner's network on a regular basis. However, the amount of contact, communication, and support from network members are less closely associated with relational development in adolescence than they are in early adulthood. Thus, it appears that personal relationships in adolescence may be experienced somewhat more intensely, but that the experience of closeness and commitment is less firmly tied to the amount of interaction relational partners have with one another or to their interactions with one another's surrounding social networks.

It is not immediately clear why this should be the case. There may be a sampling bias causing the two groups to differ in some subtle way. One possibility is that the relationships in the young adult sample could be of longer duration. In longer, more established relationships, for instance, there would presumably have been more time for the relational and network factors to come together. However, the duration of the relationships in the two groups did not differ significantly. Moreover, levels of development and social network involvement did not differ appreciably according to the length of the relationship.

It is more likely that these differences are trying to tell us something more fundamental about the transition from adolescence to adulthood. Like other life transitions, some aspects of this transition will involve changes in the material and institutional environment surrounding the individual, whereas others will occur internally in the subjective of experience of the individual (Wapner & Craig-Bray, 1992).

We might account for some of these differences by pointing to the changes in larger network structures or "affordances" that occur as people move from adolescence to adulthood. The typical American high school, for instance, is a far more contained setting that the typical large public university. Students are generally expected to stay within the school grounds during the day and often choose to return at other times for social and recreational activities. The result is that adolescents, especially in the United States, spend a great deal of their time with each other (Csikszentmihalyi & Larson, 1984; Csikszentmihalyi & Schneider, 2000). In addition, I am using the shift from high school to university to mark the boundary between adolescence and early adulthood. At least in these samples, this shift represented a transition from a smaller, more homogenous institutional setting to a larger, more diverse setting.

These changes, coupled with greater access to transportation and reduced parental control, give young adults greater choice in communication. They may meet members of the partner's network, but are less compelled by structural arrangements to interact with them regularly. High school students may have more interaction with members of their partner's network simply because they have to be around them. This lack of control might also diminish to value placed on interactions with the partner's network, thus accounting in part for why the network factors were less strongly related to relational development in the adolescent sample. Compared to young adults, adolescents probably also have less control over how much time they spend with their friends and romantic partners. Consequently, feelings of closeness or commitment may be separated from this less controllable aspect of the relationship.

Developmental changes in the individual may also help account for the differences in the way adolescents and young adults develop personal relationships. Although young people certainly arrive at adolescence with images of romantic relationships and close friendships already provided by cultural media, they do not necessary arrive with a clear sense of how to enact a specific relationship. I am reminded of Erikson's (1968) observation that adolescents often approach romantic relationships as an "attempt to arrive at a definition of one's identity by projecting one's diffused self-image on another and seeing it thus reflected and gradually clarified" (p. 132). In such circumstances, one's sense of what a romantic relationship is and how its pieces fit together should at first be somewhat fragmented and only become more coherent as one gains in experience from adolescence to early adulthood.

Several other developmental tasks facing adolescents have implications for how young people gain understanding of relationships. Adolescents often struggle to understand social cues and to differentiate their concerns and the concerns of others. Learning to take others into account and to take others' perspectives are among the more important social cognitive tasks of adolescence (e.g., Durkin, 1995; Elkind, 1967). In addition, young people must develop skills at reconciling and integrating contradictory experiences and feelings. This activity not only enhances skills for understanding and managing relationships, but also is thought to play an important role in the process of developing an independent identity (e.g., Kegan, 1982). The growing size and complexity of adolescents' social networks also fuel adolescents' attempts to develop more sophisticated cognitive and social skills (Bukowski, Newcomb, & Hoza, 1987). In addition to learning new forms of relationships, they must be able to distinguish among vaguely defined relational states such as "hanging out" and "dating."

If adolescents are still in the process of developing a coherent sense of how personal relationships function, then it should not be surprising to find that the cognitive, affective, behavioral, and social network components of relationships do not come together as tightly for them as for somewhat older people. With more experience, people learn, for example, that seeing one's romantic partner through the eyes of her best friend or her brother can provide valuable relational information. With more experience integrating relational events and perceptions, people should make more connections between actual interaction with a partner and the feelings of commitment or closeness one has for him or her.

Thus we might account for some of the differences in how adolescents and young adults go about relationships by pointing to *structural affordances* (e.g., institutional mechanisms, access to transportation) that give young adults greater control over their relationships and networks and by noting the social cognitive developments inside the individual that lead to greater sense of *relational coherence* and in turn to more complex expectations and behaviors for relationships. In exploring these conjectures, however, we should not lose sight of the fact that they were also striking similarities in the way adolescents and young adults developed personal relationships. In both groups, relational development—closeness, commitment, and communication—was closely associated with the partners' surrounding social networks of friends and family. Relationships in both groups were developed with active reference to what friends and family thought and to how the new relationship fit with existing relationships.

COMPARING MALE-FEMALE ROMANTIC RELATIONSHIPS AND SAME-SEX FRIENDSHIPS

One test of a theory of personal relationships is its ability to apply to different types of relationships. Friendship and male-female romantic relationships, including marriage, are the two primary voluntary human relationships. When asked to identify their "closest, deepest, most involved, and most intimate relationship," the young adults surveyed in one study overwhelmingly named romantic partners and same-sex friends (Berscheid, Snyder, & Omoto, 1989a). To be useful, a theory of interpersonal relationship development must have something to say about each and, to be powerful, it must offer a common way to understand each. The challenge facing the social contextual perspective is therefore to determine if it applies equally well to both types of relationships.

Distinguishing Friendships and Romantic Relationships

Social scientists have offered many different definitions for friendship (For a review, see Fehr, 1996). And they are not the only ones. Definitions of friendship may be found in the literary traditions of nearly every culture. For thousands of years, philosophers have offered their definitions as well (e.g., Aristotle, 1934; Emerson, 1939; Laurence, 1987). The literature on romantic love is even more voluminous (for social scientists' perspectives, see Hatfield & Rapson, 2002; S. Hendrick & C. Hendrick, 2000; Sternberg, 1998). One would expect, therefore, to find some general agreement in social scientific circles about what friendships and romantic relationships are and about how they might be distinguished. Unfortunately, this is not the case.

Our tendency to parse terms often adds to the confusion. The social scientific literature on friendship, for example, offers distinctions between different types of friendship, being *just friends* and *friends*, and between *friend, friendship*, and *friendliness* (e.g., Dykstra, 1987; Fehr, 1996; Kurth, 1970). In other cases, we use the same term to apply to different relationships. Thus it is commonplace for social scientists to talk about the friendship at the core of successful romantic relationships and for laypersons to describe their lover or spouse as also being their best friend (e.g., Driver, Tabares, Shapiro, Nahm, & Gottman, 2003; S. Hendrick & C. Hendrick, 1993).

Social scientists have made a number of attempts to compare the characteristics of friendship and romantic relationships. Some of these have provided finely grained analyses of specific linguistic and nonverbal behaviors. They show, for example, that romantic couples gaze at each other more, touch more often, sit closer, but are less fluent than pairs of same-sex friends (Guerrero, 1997). Other researchers have simply asked people to list the characteristics of an idealized friendship or romantic relationship. One difficulty with these "wish lists" is that they often fail to distinguish one type of relationship from another. Sapadin (1988), for instance, asked adults across the United States to list the characteristics of friendship. The most common responses were intimacy, trust, being dependable, sharing, acceptance, caring, and closeness. But certainly, most people want exactly the same things from a romantic relationship. Indeed, studies that explicitly compare descriptors for friendship and romantic relationships typically find that the majority of the terms apply to both kinds of relationships (e.g., K. E. Davis & Todd, 1982; Dykstra, 1987; Sprecher & Regan, 2002).

Nonetheless, distinctions do emerge. Although friendships and romantic relationships share qualities such as liking, enjoyment and comfort in shared activities, and to some extent, intimacy, romantic relationships are usually viewed as being energized by greater passion and a commitment to a long-term, exclusive relationship. These beliefs are common in the United States, Canada, and presumably in many other countries as well, and can be found among young people as early as ages 9 or 10 (Connolly, Craig, Goldberg, & Pepler, 1999; Hatfield, Schmitz, Cornelius, & Rapson, 1988; Sternberg, 1987; P. H. Wright, 1985).

As useful as comparisons of abstract or idealized descriptions of "friend" or "romantic partner" may be, it is not certain that they tell us much about the characteristics of lived relationships. At best they represent cognitive prototypes or "working models" of relationships (Fehr, 2004; Furman, Simon, Shaffer, & Bouchey, 2002). But even these may be quite malleable. I am persuaded by Swidler's (2001) observation that people actively rearrange or select their conception of relationships in order to make sense of the relational issues they are dealing with at the moment. Thus relational terms are not so much fixed templates or models as cognitive repertoires or toolkits that are selected, ignored, or altered as the situation demands.

In my view, it is far more useful to compare the characteristics of actual relationships. Instead of trying to define for people in advance what friendship and romance are, we should let them identify what they consider to be their friendships and romantic relationships and then try to determine if there are systematic differences in the two types of natively defined relationships. That is the approach followed here.

Differences in Relational and Network Factors Between Same-Sex Friendships and Romantic Relationships

The core sample of 858 subjects included reports on 478 same-sex friendships and 357 heterosexual romantic relationships. These were compared using statistical procedures that allowed us to identify the differences between friendships and romantic relationships while controlling for differences between age group and gender. The goal was to determine if there were systematic differences in any of the 21 specific indicators of relational development and social networks in the core studies. In order to filter out trivial differences, I again imposed a threshold minimum effect size (partial $eta^2 \geq .02$).

Perceptions of Relational Development in Friendships Versus Romantic Relationships.   Our respondents generally reported that they felt closer to their romantic partners than to their same-sex friends. Predictably, the largest difference was in Rubin's (1970) measure of romantic love. Respondents not only loved their romantic partners more than their same-sex friends, they also reported liking them more and feeling greater interpersonal solidarity with them. These differences occurred in both age groups and for both men and women. We obviously associate loving with romantic relationships, but the fact that liking and solidarity were also higher in romantic relationships was puzzling. Conceptually, they should apply as well or better to friendship. Perhaps this finding is explained by Sprecher and Regan's (2002) subtle observation that even when they want the same things in a romantic relationship and a friendship, people want more of them in their romantic relationships.

In spite of these differences, people reported being equally satisfied with their interactions in the two types of relationships. They also interacted with equal regularity. Participants in both romantic relationships and same-sex friendships had seen their partners, on average, 10 of the previous 14 days. However, people devoted a significantly greater percentage of their free time to their romantic partners than to any one of their same-sex friends (47% vs. 37%).

Our respondents generally perceived themselves to be moderately to highly similar to their relational partners. Perceived similarity scores were uniform across the sample and did not differ by relational type, age group, or sex. Our respondents also reported having similar levels of confidence in their ability to anticipate and understand each other's feelings and behavior. That is, there was no difference in the level of relational certainty or uncertainty people experienced in these friendships and dating relationships.

There were, however, significant differences on all of the indicators of commitment. Most people expected that their relationship would last for at least the next 3 months, but friends were more confident than romantic partners that it would. Friends rated the probability that they would be "friends forever" at an average of 68%. But romantic partners rated the probably that they would someday marry at only 42%. These judgments are not perfectly equivalent, but it does appear in fact that friends were more committed than romantic partners. This finding runs counter to the literature suggesting that people see romantic relationships as the more committed (e.g., Connolly et al., 1999; P. H. Wright, 1985). Of course, believing that romantic relationships ought to be more committed and being committed to a particular partner are two quite different things. Still, friendships were found to be more committed than romantic relationships in at least one other study using different measures of commitment (Winn, Crawford, & Fischer, 1991). Before we make too much of this difference, however, it would be useful to compare friendships and romantic relationships, especially marriage, in older samples. One would certainly like to think that people would rate their odds of staying married at something higher than 42%, but with the divorce rate the United States hovering around 50%, there may not be such a large difference after all.

Perceptions of Network Involvement in Friendships Versus Romantic Relationships. We used 10 different measures to determine how many people one had met in the partner's network, how often one communicated with them, how much they were liked, and how much they were perceived to support the relationship.

Network members generally supported friendships and romantic relationships to the same degree. No one sector of the partners' combined network was more supportive of any one type of relationship. One's own family and friends offered similar levels of support to both same-sex friendships and romantic relationships. Members of the partner's network were perceived to be just as supportive of romantic relationships as they were of same-sex friendships.

Participants in romantic relationships and participants in friendships had typically met the same number of people in their partners' networks of family and friends. However, as I noted in the discussion of age-group differences earlier in the chapter, the picture is complicated by interactions between relationship type and age group. Although adolescents in romantic relationships met about the same number of network members as adolescents involved in friendships, there was a sharp difference among young adults. Young adults in romantic relationships had met on average nearly twice as many of their partner's family members and friends as those involved in same-sex friendships.

Overall, the amount of communication with the partner's friends and family did not differ between romantic relationships and same-sex friendships. But the pattern differed for adolescents and young adults. Adolescents communicated more frequently with their friend's network, whereas young adults communicated more frequently with their romantic partner's network.

Although friends and romantic partners reported similar levels of liking for their partner's friends, there was a significant difference in liking for members of the partner's family. Romantic partners liked their partner's family more than same-sex friends liked the members of their partner's family. This difference held across both age groups, but was considerably greater among young adults than among adolescents.

Comparing Relational Development Processes in Same-Sex Friendships Versus Romantic Relationships

In order to determine if the various relational and network items clustered into factors and then covaried with each other in the same way, I conducted separate confirmatory factor analyses for same-sex friendships and romantic relationships. Although the models were developed independently, they drew on the same 19 measures of developmental and network factors used in the previous studies from the core data set (see Appendix A). The top layers of the final models for same-sex friendships and romantic relationships are displayed in Fig. 6.3 and Fig. 6.4.

Our interest at this point is in how the models for same-sex friendship and male-female romantic relationships compare. Further discussion associations between specific pairs of factors may be found in chapters 4 and 5. Both mod-

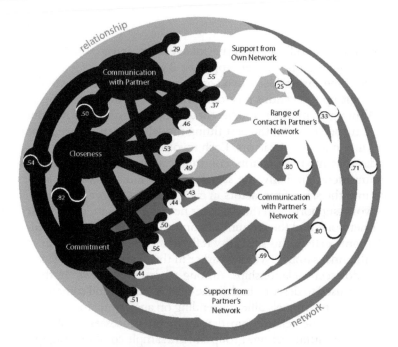

FIG. 6.3.   General model of friendships.

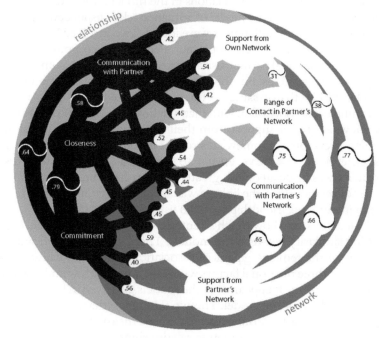

FIG. 6.4.   General model of romantic relationships.

els fit the data quite well and all of the linkages between factors in both models were statistically significant (see Appendix B).

The first thing to consider when comparing these models is whether it was possible to group the various relational and network indicators into the same factors. Although a number of different alternatives were explored during the analysis, it turned out that the best fitting model for each type of relationship had the same number of factors. Each involved grouping relational development indicators into three factors: communication with the partner, closeness, and commitment. Similarly, the social network indicators were successfully grouped into the same four factors in each model: support from the subject's own network, support from the partner's network, the range of contact in the partner's network, and the amount of communication with the partner's network. To some extent, this similarity reflects the greater proportion of young adults in the final sample. We saw earlier in the chapter that a 6-factor model better fit adolescent relationships. Among adolescents, however, this 6-factor model can be used to describe both same-sex friendships and romantic relationships. Although the models differ depending on age group, friendship development, and romantic relationship development, processes display the same factor structure within each age group and in a sample combining age groups.

The linkages among and between the relational and network factors may also be compared. Each of the 21 correlations in the model for friendship was compared to its counterpart in the model of romantic relationship development.

Only three significant differences were found. Two involved how often one communicated with the relational partner. People who communicated more often with their relational partner also reported higher levels of commitment in both types of relationships, but the association was somewhat stronger in romantic relationships than in same-sex friendships ($r = .64$ vs. $.54$, $p < .05$). People who communicated more often with their relational partner also tended to perceive somewhat greater support from their own friends and family, although again, this association was somewhat stronger in romantic relationships than in same-sex friendships ($r = .42$ vs. $.29$, $p < .05$). Finally, although greater cross-network contact was associated with greater support from network members in both types of relationships, the linkage was again stronger in romantic relationships than in same-sex friendships ($r = .80$ vs. $.66$, $p < .0001$).

It is difficult to know how much attention to give to these differences given the striking similarity between the models. There were no significant differences in any of the remaining pairs of associations. That is, the four network factors and the three relational factors were associated with a similar way in all of the remaining tests. It appears that the models displayed in Fig. 6.3 and Fig. 6.4 are essentially the same model. This would suggest that relational development processes, at least in so far as they have been measured here, are the same for same-sex friendships and romantic relationships.

AGE GROUPS AND RELATIONAL TYPES IN SOCIAL CONTEXT

The goal in this chapter was to consider how well the social contextual perspective could be applied to the development of personal relationships at different points in the lifespan of the individual and to different types of relationships. The effort was admittedly limited to only a small portion of the lifespan and restricted to just two types of personal relationships. Although the relationships of adolescence and early adulthood unquestionably form a foundation for relationships in later stages of adult life, later stages do not simply play out the social patterns established in adolescence and early adulthood. There are gaps even within the age-groups examined. In the late 1980s, the William T. Grant Foundation (1988) published a comprehensive study of the challenges facing *The Forgotten Half: Non-College Bound Youth in America*. Although the report centered on workforce issues, it was a striking reminder of how little research has been conducted on young adults who are not in college settings. In the time since the report was published, little has been done to correct this imbalance in the literature on personal relationships or in the social sciences more generally. Whether the model of relational development presented here would apply equally well to young adults who are outside the college setting remains an open question.

Same-sex friendships and premarital male-female romantic relationships are major types of personal relationships, but they are obviously not the only ones of interest. There is excellent work on social network factors in marriage, but it is often limited to associations between very global relational measures and a narrow range of network factors (For reviews, see Milardo & Allan, 1997; Sprecher et al., 2002). Personal relationship researchers have emphasized the importance of male-female friendships, but we still know relatively little about their patterns of development (e.g., Bleske-Rechek & Buss, 2001; Monsour, 2002). There is also a regrettably limited, but growing amount of research on gay and lesbian relationships (e.g., Kurdek, 1999; LaSala, 2002; Peplau & Spalding, 2003; Savin-Williams, 1996, 2003). These relationships often do not appear to differ from male-female relationships in terms of closeness, satisfaction, commitment, or the use of relational maintenance strategies (S. M. Duffy & Rusbult, 1986; Haas & Stafford, 1998; Peplau & Cochran, 1990). We do not yet, however, have a clear sense of the role played by social network factors in these relationships. Network support, for example, could function differently or be more or less important in these relationships. There may be critically important cross-network contacts or densities that arise in these relationships. Support from one's romantic partner or spouse may be crucial in cross-sex friendships, for example, and whether both gay and heterosexual members of the participants' network approve of the partner may be particularly important in gay and lesbian relationships.

The developmental course of two other relational types also merits additional attention. The first of these is between caregivers and recipients. We know, for instance, that those with AIDS or HIV cope with their disease more successfully when they have a closer relationship with volunteer caregivers. And we know that caregivers who feel closer and more committed to the recipient are more likely to continue to provide care as the recipient's condition worsens (Crain, Snyder, & Omoto, 2000; Omoto & Snyder, 2002). We know much less, however, about the broader developmental path that caregiver–recipient relationships follow or the linkages between caregivers and network resources. Finally, given that most adults spend a significant portion of their lives in the workplace, more attention should be given to how relationships with co-workers develop over time. Although the specific measures of some dimensions might change, the underlying dimensions of relational development and social network involvement should apply as well to workplace relationships as to friendships and romantic relationships outside the workplace.

In spite of their limited range, the studies to date provide consistent support for the social contextual perspective on relationship development. The central claim of this perspective is that any given relationship develops within the context of the participants' other relationships and both the relationship and the network are changed as contacts are made, information about the relationship is exchanged, and support or opposition is expressed. The studies reported here support this claim by showing that the core dimensions of relational development are in fact related to this interplay with the surrounding networks. In both age groups and in both same-sex friendships and romantic relationships, every social network factor was associated significantly with every dimension of the relational development.

This is not to say that the associations were the same in every case. The differences between adolescents and young adults were particularly striking. Adolescents not only felt closer to their partners, but their feelings of closeness and commitment were less dependent on the amount of interaction they had with their relational partners and to their interactions with network members. Although cultural media provide initial models, adolescents are largely left to figure out what close friendships and romantic relationships are like. There is no reason to assume that all the pieces come together at the same time. As a result, adolescents may be less likely to associate behavior in the network or even the amount of interaction they have with their partners with their inner experiences of commitment and closeness. Another way to approach these findings draws on the principle of *network structuring* discussed in chapter 2. This principle suggests that the amount and quality of interaction between relational partners will depend on the structural opportunities afforded by their networks. Compared to young adults attending college, adolescents are in the more bounded setting of high school, often have less access to transportation, and experience greater parental control over their comings and goings. The result is that they have less control over the people they see and how often they interact with them. And this in turn might loosen the connection between their assessment of the relationship and their level of interaction with the partner and network members. Such a conjecture is consistent with the results, but is still untested.

The comparison of adolescents and young adults also suggests several practical implications for parents and counselors working with teens. These findings remind us that how much time a teen spends with a friend or dating partner is not a reliable gauge of how serious the relationship is. Feeling close to the partner or being committed to maintaining the relationship does not depend on how much they interact. This also means that efforts to disrupt an undesirable relationship by preventing teens from seeing each other are not likely to have much effect. Relational feelings are more "in the head" for adolescents than they are for somewhat older people. What will have an effect, according to these studies, is expressing support or opposition for the relationship.

Popular parenting advice generally treats the Romeo and Juliet effect as a truism by warning parents that their opposition may make only make an undesirable relationship blossom. It would be better to encourage parents to express their opinions about boyfriends and girlfriends, but to do so in a way that affirms at least some aspect of the adolescent's judgment (e.g., Kastner & Wyatt, 2002). In addition, parents will be more effective if they encourage the adolescent to seek input from other members of the family as well as from their friends. I suspect that many perceptions of support, especially among adolescents, are relatively untested. By encouraging teens to test these perceptions for themselves, parents and counselors can help young people make more informed relational judgments, and at the same time help them to develop more general skills for managing social networks.

These studies also suggest, both to theorists and practitioners, that our various personal relationships are perhaps not as different from one another as we may imagine. Previous studies of social network factors in relational development have focused almost exclusively on premarital romantic relationships between men and women and marriage (e.g., Felmlee, 2001; M. P. Johnson & Milardo, 1984; Julien & Markman, 1991; Milardo, 1982; Milardo & Helms-Erikson, 2000; Sprecher & Felmlee, 2000). In addition to replicating many of the findings of these studies, the studies presented here demonstrate that social network factors are also deeply involved in the development of same-sex friendships. Indeed, it appears that social network factors are linked to relational development in almost identical ways in same-sex friendships and male-female romantic relationships. At a practical level this means that the skills, strategies, and resources used to develop a friendship can also be used to develop romantic relationships. Those who are able to make friends, but have difficulty with romantic relationships, may already have a model for success. At a theoretic level, the fact that same-sex friendship and male-female romantic relationships can be described with essentially the same model means that the social contextual perspective may have general application. There is obviously much more to do to test the generality of the social contextual perspective. That work begins in chapter 7, where I take up the question of how well the model can be applied across lines of gender and ethnicity.

CHAPTER SEVEN

Comparing Genders and Ethnicities

No contemporary discussion of personal relationships can be complete without a consideration of gender and ethnicity, and through them, a consideration of the role of culture. We should acknowledge at the outset that the concepts of *gender, sex, ethnicity,* and *culture* are themselves the object of important, often rancorous academic and public debate. The seemingly inexhaustible market for popular materials claiming huge gender differences, for example, has given a certain edge to academic exchanges about whether men and women's communication styles are so different as to constitute separate cultures (Canary, Emmers-Sommer, & Faulkner, 1997; F. L. Johnson, 2000; MacGeorge, Graves, Feng, Gillihan, & Burleson, 2004). The debate over the role of ethnicity and culture in personal relationships has also been joined on all sides. Researchers have tracked the magnitude of cultural differences, the extent to which interethnic relationships are socially accepted, and engaged the deeper question of "how culture means" in personal relationships (e.g., Gaines & Liu, 2000; Gudykunst, Ting-Toomey, & Nishida, 1996; Swidler, 2001).

These debates obviously extend far beyond the scope of the present chapter. My focus is on the effects of gender on relational development, social network involvement, and on the way they are associated. Following that, I turn to the question of whether personal relationships between people of different races and ethnicities develop in a different way than relationships between people of the same ethnicity. Here, too, I look both for differences in the relational and network factors as well for differences in the way they are associated. My concern throughout is with how generally the social contextual model may be applied and with how we might use it as a lens for examining questions of gender, ethnicity, and culture.

GENDER SIMILARITIES AND DIFFERENCES
IN RELATIONAL DEVELOPMENT

Those wishing to understand the role of gender in the development of personal relationships immediately encounter three problems with the previous literature. First, researchers have looked for sex or gender differences in only a few of the characteristics of personal relationships and their networks that change over time. Second, researchers have focused far more on whether males and females differ on select characteristics such as supportiveness than on the question of whether various characteristics are associated in different ways for males than for females. Finding that women typically express verbal support more often than males does not, for instance, imply that verbal support functions any differently for males and females. We must compare patterns of association and not merely average differences if we are to determine whether theoretic predictions about the process of relationship development hold equally for men and women. Finally, the terms *sex* and *gender* are often conflated. By convention, writers generally use the term, sex, to refer to biologically based characteristics and the term, gender, to refer to characteristics and behaviors that are acquired through cultural socialization. I have used *sex* when referring to specific, direct comparisons of male and female subjects and *gender* when referring to differences or similarities more generally. We should recognize, however, that nearly any distinction is arbitrary and misleading. As we come to understand more about the interplay of physiology and social experience, it becomes apparent that the biological and social can no longer be separated in a meaningful way. We know, for example, that differences in interaction with the physical and social environment lead to differences in the way genes are expressed, even in identical twins (Fraga et al., 2005).

Intimacy and supportiveness have been the dominant topics in research on sex in personal relationships. The most common conclusion reached in the studies and commentary on these topics is that women are more intimate, caring, and emotionally supportive than men (e.g., Bank & Hansford, 2000; Bascow & Rubenfeld, 2003; Fehr, 2004; Wood, 2000). It is also commonly argued that men and women specialize in different ways of expressing closeness or caring. Men, for example, tend toward doing favors, offering assistance, sharing activities, and other forms of behavioral or instrumental assistance as expressions of closeness; whereas women are more likely to judge how close a relationship is by its emotional expressiveness and level of personal disclosure (e.g., Maltz & Borker, 1982; Wood & Inman, 1993).

The emphasis on expressiveness and personal disclosure also emerges in studies of women's friendships (e.g., Aries & Johnson, 1983; Walker, 1994). Goodman and O'Brien (2000) gave this homage to talk when describing their longtime friendship: "We were friends; we had to talk. It was the single most important—and most obvious—connection. Talk is at the very heart of women's friendships, the core of the way women connect. It's the given, the absolute assumption of friendship" (pp. 34–35).

Whereas women's relationships emphasize closeness in talk, men's relationships emphasize "closeness in the doing" (Swain, 1989). Men express affection to their same-sex friends, but are likely to do it in more indirect ways (Floyd, 1995). The lower levels of intimacy and supportiveness assumed to characterize male relationships are usually viewed as the result of males being socialized to value emotional restraint and avoid behavior that might be viewed as a sign of homosexuality (Bank & Hansford, 2000).

The belief that men are less intimate or emotionally supportive than women has, however, come under intense criticism. Many of the most extreme claims in the popular press have been debunked (Goldsmith & Fulfs, 1999). The conclusions of several well-cited academic studies purporting to show sex differences have also been called into question (e.g., Kyratzis, 2001; MacGeorge et al., 2004). For example, common beliefs asserting that males are less supportive or that they express less concern for others have not withstood careful empirical test. Moreover, it appears that men and women have similar ideas of what being close is and that they rate the intimacy of a given interaction in the similar ways (Parks & Floyd, 1996b; Reis, Senchak, & Solomon, 1985). Differences in intimacy, closeness, support, and a variety of other personal relationship characteristics tend to be inconsistent and, when they appear at all, tend to be relatively small (Aries, 1996; Canary et al., 1997; Goldsmith & Dun, 1997; MacGeorge et al., 2004; P. H. Wright, 1982).

We are therefore left without a clear set of hypotheses about the role of gender in the social contextual model. The situation is made even difficult by the fact that there is almost no research on gender differences in the social network factors associated with relational development. We know that we need to look at gender differences and similarities, but we do not know how to place our bets.

Gender and sex differences in personal relationships may take two general forms. One is a difference between groups or means. Females may report, for example, they love their partners or interact with network members more or less, on average, than males. Gender differences could also appear in how these factors are correlated; that is, feelings of closeness and frequency of interaction with the partner's network might be much more strongly correlated for women than for men. These and other possibilities are examined in the three sections that follow.

Sex Differences in Relational and Network Factors

Males and females were compared on each of the relational and network indicators included in the core sample using statistical procedures that controlled for age group and relationship type. Because the literature on gender differences has been criticized for making too much of small differences (e.g.,

MacGeorge et al., 2004), I set a minimum effect size threshold regarding which effects would not be discussed (partial $eta^2 \geq .02$). This allowed us to filter out trivial differences that had become statistically significant by virtue of the large sample (357 males and 501 females).

Sex Differences in Relational Indicators.   Closeness, the amount of communication with the partner, and the level commitment were assessed with 11 different measures across the core studies. Six of these contributed to closeness. Of these, significant sex differences were observed on only two. Women reported greater satisfaction with their interactions than did men. Women also reported somewhat higher levels of interpersonal solidarity. Neither of these effects was particularly large, but the effect for communication satisfaction was the larger of the two ($eta^2 = .052$ vs. .022). There were no interaction effects, so these differences applied equally to same-sex friendships and romantic relationships as well as to adolescents and young adults. No other significant differences were observed among the remaining indicators of closeness. Women and men did not differ in how much they loved their partners, liked their partners, how similar they felt to their partners, or how uncertain they were about the relationship. Nor did any of these indicators interact with age or relational type. That is, men and women were similar across all groups.

Two measures were used to determine the amount of interaction between relational partners. One asked respondents to indicate how many days in the previous 2 weeks they had communicated with their partners, whereas the other asked respondents to estimate the percentage of their free time they had spent with the relational partner in the previous 2 weeks. There was no sex difference in the first of these. Women, however, reported spending 11% more of their free time (48% vs. 37%) with their partners than men reported spending with theirs.

The final set of relational indicators assessed commitment to the relationship. No significant differences were found in any of the three indicators. There were no significant interactions with age or relational type. Contrary to stereotype, men were just as committed to their personal relationships as women. This was true in both same-sex friendships and romantic relationships.

Sex Differences in Network Involvement.   The social contextual model contains several factors dealing the social network involvement. The first of these is support. The question that the social contextual model poses about support, however, is rather different from the one typically asked in the literature on sex and gender differences. Most researchers have been concerned with the support that network members provide for individuals. Here our concern is with whether the individual perceives that friends and family in the surrounding network approve or oppose the relationship. Individuals obviously cannot know for sure what network members really think. They may misjudge others' approval or opposition as well. Whatever the basis of the judgment, however, the women and men in our studies tended to report similar levels of support from network members. There was no difference in the level of support for the relationship that men and women perceived from members of their friends, their partner's friends, or their own family. Similar findings emerged in another study, although the men in that study reported that family members were more approving of their dating relationship (Sprecher & Felmlee, 2000). Interestingly, in our studies, women tended to believe that their partner's family members were somewhat more supportive. This was, however, a small difference. In general, men and women perceived similar levels of support across the network of friends and family. This was true for both adolescents and young adults and in both romantic relationships and same-sex friendships.

The next set of network factors dealt with how much contact people had with members of their partner's network. Once again, there were few sex differences. Men and women reported that they had met similar numbers of their partner's family and communicated with those whom they had met with equal regularity. Although women reported that they had met a slightly greater number of their partner's friends (5.0 vs. 4.2), there was no difference in how often they communicated with the ones they had met. These findings were consistent with previous investigations showing that men and women are equally likely to meet each other's networks, although women are somewhat more likely than men to tell friends or family about a date (Rose & Frieze, 1989, 1993). National survey data indicates that 70% to 80% of all adolescents in romantic relationships report having met their partner's parents. Females were slightly more likely to meet the partner's parents, to tell others that they were a couple, and to go out together as a couple in a group. Nonetheless, the majority of males and females engaged in these behaviors and the sex difference in the percentage of people doing each of these things is small, generally less than 10% (Carver et al., 2003).

The final pair of measures assessed the extent to which people liked the members of the partner's network. There was no difference in how much women and men liked the partner's family members. There was, however, a small difference in liking for the partner's friends. Women tended to like their partner's friends somewhat more. Although their study was limited to dating relationships, Sprecher and Felmlee (2000) also found that women expressed somewhat greater liking for their boyfriend's friends than men expressed for their girlfriend's friends.

In summary, significant sex differences were found on only 6 of the 21 measures of relational development and network involvement. Although women reported higher values on all six, the magnitude of differences was rather small (average $eta^2 = .027$). Moreover, there were no significant interactions with age or type of relationship observed in any of the analyses. Thus, both adolescent and young adult women and men reported similar levels of relational development and social network involvement in their same-sex friendships and romantic relationships.

Sex Similarities and Differences in Relational Development Processes

There may be sex differences in how the relational and network factors are related to each other even when there are no differences in the average values of those indicators. This possibility was tested with another series of confirmatory factor analyses. Separate models were derived for male and females in order to determine if there was a sex difference in how the various dimensions of relational development and social network involvement were associated with one another. These models were constructed using 19 measures of relational development and social network involvement (see Appendix A). The top layers of the final models for females and males are displayed in Fig. 7.1 and Fig. 7.2.

The discussion to follow focuses more on the comparison of the models than on the interpretation of any given association within a model. More on the latter may be found in chapters 4 and 5. Both models fit the data well and

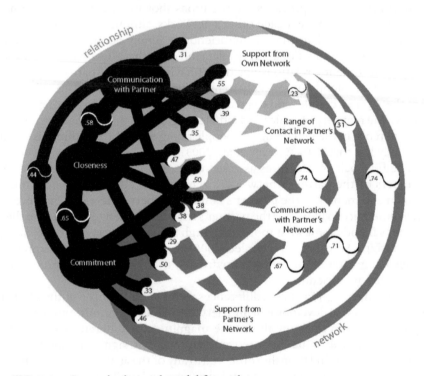

FIG. 7.1.   General relational model for males.

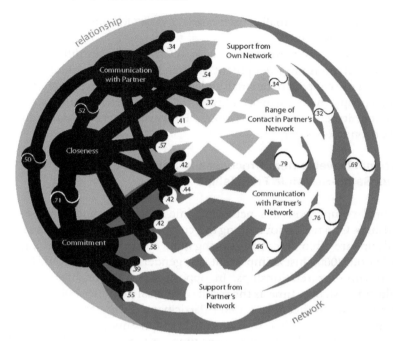

FIG. 7.2. General relational model for females.

all of the linkages between factors were statistically significant in both models (see Appendix B).

Several different models were examined during the analysis, but the best fitting models for male and female relationships—or more precisely, male and female perspectives on relationships—had very similar structures. Male and female scores on the 11 measures of relational development grouped into the same three factors described in previous chapters: *closeness, communication with the partner,* and *commitment.* Scores on the nine measures of social network involvement also grouped into the same four factors described previously: (a) support from the subject's own network, (b) support from the partner's network, (c) the range of contact in the partner's network, and (d) the amount of communication with the partner's network.

The next step was to compare each of the associations in the general model for males to its counterpart in the general model for females. These tests confirmed what is apparent from inspecting Fig. 7.1 and Fig. 7.2: The two models are remarkably similar. Indeed, even with a rather large sample size, a significant general difference was found in only 2 of the 21 associations in the model. The number of people met in the partner's network (range of contact) was significantly more strongly associated with commitment and closeness in women's relationships than in men's relationships. The difference in the associations was relatively small in each case (.57 vs. .47 for closeness, .42 vs. 29 for commitment, $ps < .05$).

These findings suggest that there are relatively few sex differences in the process of relationship development described by the social contextual model. Those that exist appear to be small and limited to the relatively greater impact meeting people in the partner's network has on women's feelings of closeness and commitment to their partners. However, there is one additional comparison to consider.

Relational Development Processes in Same-Sex Female Versus Same-Sex Male Friendships

The final comparison was between same-sex female and same-sex male friendships. One reason for making this comparison is that women's same-sex friendships are often described as being quite different than men's (e.g., Fehr, 1996; Wood, 2000). Just as important, any gender differences should be amplified in same-sex relationships. In opposite-sex relationships, differences should diminish over time as the result of mutual influence effects or accommodation (Burggraf & Sillars, 1987). Participants' attitudes and behaviors become more similar as their relationship developments and this in turn should reduce gender-based differences over time. In same-sex relationships, however, gender similarities should reinforce one another and thus result in a grater difference between male and female relationships.

To test this possibility, models for same-sex female ($N = 292$) and same-sex male friendships ($N = 186$) were constructed, using the same measures used in the previous section. The top layers of the final models for female same-sex friendships and male same-sex friendships are displayed in Fig. 7.3 and Fig. 7.4 (see Appendix B for additional technical information).

Like the general male and female models, the models for male and female same-sex relationships fit the data with a seven factor solution involving the same three relational development factors and four network involvement factors. Tests comparing each corresponding pair of associations in the two models identified significant differences in only 5 of the 21 tests.

How close one felt to his or her partner was more closely linked to the number of people he or she had met in the partner's network in female same-sex friendships than it was in male same-sex friendships. This was the largest difference between the two models ($rs = .56$ vs. .29, $p < .001$). The number of people met was also more strongly associated with commitment in female same-sex friendships than in male same-sex friendships ($rs = .50$ vs. .29, $p < .001$). These differences are the same ones observed in the general male and female models.

Three additional sex differences emerged in the models of same-sex friendship. Regardless of sex, friends who communicated more often also felt closer and more committed to the relationship. In female friendships, however, these link-

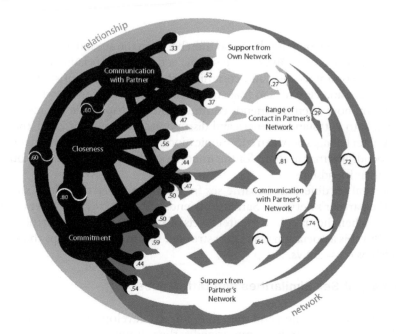

FIG. 7.3.   Same-sex female relationships.

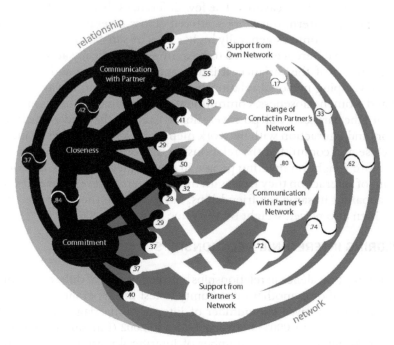

FIG. 7.4.   Same-sex male relationships.

ages were stronger, both for the association between the amount of communication and closeness (rs = .50 vs. .29, p < .001) and for the association between the amount of communication and commitment (rs = .50 vs. .29, p < .001). Thus commitment and closeness in male friendships appear to be somewhat less dependent on how often the friends communicate. Perhaps male friendships are better able to withstand absences and disruptions. On the other hand, the relatively tighter linkages between communication, closeness, and commitment in female friendships may account for the importance that women often attribute to talk in their friendships.

The final sex difference in same-sex friendship involved the role of support from the partner's network. Same-sex friends of both sexes felt closer to their partners when they received greater levels of support from their partner's network. But this association was again stronger in female friendships than male friendships (rs = .59 vs. .37, p < .01).

Summary of Sex Similarities and Differences

Comparisons of women and men in relational development and social network involvement can be summarized rather simply. There are a lot more similarities than differences. Men and women differed significantly on less than one third of the measures. The few differences that were observed did not fall into a pattern, but were scattered across several different factors. Aside from the women's generally higher level of satisfaction with their interactions, the differences tended to be quite small, typically accounting for only 2% to 3% of the variance. It is also appears that men and women go about developing personal relationships in much the same way. For both men and women, closeness, commitment, and the amount of communication with the partner are all positively linked to each other and to the level of support and interaction with network members. When it comes to judging how close and committed the relationship is, women appear to put somewhat more weight on meeting people in the partner's network and on the amount of interaction they have with their partners. These differences were most apparent in same-sex friendships, but even here they were relatively small. Men also placed weight on the same factors.

EXPLORING INTERETHNIC RELATIONSHIPS

The growing prevalence in relationships between people of different ethnic or racial groups affords another opportunity to test the generality of the social contextual perspective. The number of interracial marriages in the United States grew by over 1,000% between 1960 and 2002 (Bureau of the Census, 2002). Although the absolute number of interracial marriages is still small, more than one half of adults in the United States report having a family member or close friend who is involved in an interracial romantic relationship and, depending on the particular ethnic/racial combination, between one third and one half say they have dated outside their ethnic group themselves (Kaiser Family Foundation, 2001; Tucker & Mitchell-Kernan, 1995). Reliable figures are not available, but the proportion of people with interethnic friendships or workplace relationships is probably far higher.

In spite of their increasing prevalence, the mainstream literature on personal relationships has paid little attention to issues of multiethnic relationships, or to issues of culture and ethnicity in personal relationships more generally (Berscheid, 1999; Felmlee & Sprecher, 2000; Gaines & Liu, 2000). Researchers have traditionally focused on general attitudes toward interethnic relationships rather than on the relationships themselves (e.g., Fang, Sidanius, & Pratto, 1998; Todd, Mckinney, Harris, Chadderton, & Small, 1992). The literature at this writing contains only a handful of studies of relationship development between people of differing ethnicity or cultural background (e.g., Gaines et al., 1999; Gurung & Duong, 1999; Shibazaki & Brennan, 1998).

To overcome this limitation, I return to the study of dating relationships first described in chapter 5 (Study 2). Compared to our other studies, this study was intended to address a more detailed set of relational and network indicators and, most importantly, to draw a more diverse sample of young adult respondents. Just over half (51.4%) came from ethnic groups other than European American. Not counting European Americans, 11 different ethnic or racial groups were represented in the sample. Chinese/Chinese Americans, Filipinos, Korean/Korean Americans, Vietnamese/Vietnamese Americans, African Americans, and "Other" were the most common designations, each accounting for 5% or more of the sample.

Subjects who reported different ethnic backgrounds from their partners were classified as having an interethnic dating relationship. Subjects whose ethnic identification matched the ethnic identification obtained from the partner were classified as having a dating relationship within their ethnic group (intraethnic). A total of 82 relationships (38%) were classified as interethnic, while the remaining 136 relationships (62%) were classified as intraethnic. These groups were then compared, first in terms of mean differences on various indicators of relational development and network involvement, and then in terms of the associations between relational development and network factors.

Interethnic Versus Intraethnic Differences in Relational and Network Factors

The data set used for these comparisons contained 26 different measures that were grouped into the theoretic factors described in chapter 2. The six relational development factors included depth (intimacy), commitment, perceived interactive synchrony, personalized communication, predictability and understanding, and the amount of communication with the partner. The five network factors included the amount of overlap between the partner's networks, the number of people the subject had met in the partner's network, how often he or she communicated with them, the amount of contact between members of the two networks, and measures of support from the subject's own network as well as the partner's network. Differences that did not account for at least 2% of the variance (i.e., $eta^2 \geq .02$) are excluded from the discussion to follow.

Differences and Similarities in Measures of Relational Development.
Expectations for intimacy or depth of interaction in personal relationships vary considerably across cultural groups (Argyle, Henderson, Bond, Izuka, & Contarello, 1986; Gudykunst & Nishida, 1986; Ting-Toomey, 1991). Although love may be a cultural universal, its expression in specific relationships is nonetheless subject to substantial ethnic and cultural variation (S. Hendrick & C. Hendrick, 2000; Minatoya, 1988). Although these considerations suggest that depth and intimacy might be harder to obtain in interethnic relationships, we found no differences on our measures. Similar levels of self-disclosure, closeness, and love were reported in both types of relationships.

Those involved in interethnic and intraethnic relationships also displayed similar levels of commitment. Those in interethic relationships rated the probability (0% to 100%) of their relationship lasting in the short term (3 months) somewhat lower than those dating members of their own ethnic group (79% vs. 88%). Otherwise, there were no significant differences between the groups. Interethnic and intraethnic daters attributed similar importance to the relationship, expressed equal willingness to work to maintain it, and thought they were equally likely to get married at some point in the future. At least one other study has also failed to find differences in commitment in interethnic and intraethnic romantic relationships (Gurung & Duong, 1999).

Differences in ethnic background should make it more difficult for relational partners to understand and anticipate each others' responses. This belief has been supported in studies of interethnic acquaintance and friendship (Gudykunst, 1986; Gudykunst, Sodetani, & Sonoda, 1987). Studies of interethnic communication also point to differences in way that interaction is structured, regulated, and contextualized (Gumperz, 1982; Philips, 1983). These differences should make it more difficult for participants in interethnic relationships to coordinate or synchronize their interactions. When these ideas were put to the test, however, the results were mixed. Interethnic romantic partners expressed slightly more uncertainty about their relationship on a scale developed by Parks and Adelman (1983), but the two groups did not differ on a scale of attributional confidence developed by Gudykunst and Nishida (1986). The results for the measures of interactive synchrony were also mixed. Significant differences were found on two of the four items used to assess this dimension of interdependence. Interethnic re-lationships were characterized by more frequent awkward silences and the perception that it was not as easy to talk to the dating partner. On the other hand, participants in interethnic and intraethnic relationships did not differ with regard to perceptions of how smoothly conversation flowed or how much effort was needed to communicate.

There were no significant differences in the remaining measures of rela-tional development. Those involved in a romantic relationship with a person from a different ethnic group spent an almost identical proportion of their free time with their partners as those involved in a romantic relationship with someone from their own ethnic group (59% vs. 61%). Those involved in interethnic and intraethnic relationships also felt that their communication was personalized to the same degree. Participants in both types of relation-ships were equally likely to assign "special meanings" to words, to use distinc-tive nicknames or terms of endearment, to employ special looks or gestures, and to be able to communicate without having to be verbally explicit.

Differences and Similarities in Measures of Network Involvement.
Previous research provides little guidance to those embarking on a relation-ship outside their ethnic group regarding how others might react. It is com-monly assumed that interethnic couples will encounter hostile reactions from some, if not most, members of their social networks. To be sure, it depends on whether one is perceived as "dating up" or "dating down" in terms of social status. Nonetheless, multiracial couples often report that they are the recipi-ent of racist comments or behaviors (Rosenblatt, Karis, & Powell, 1995). Most observers believe that social network members place enormous stress on interethnic couples. The higher divorce rate among interracial marriages is sometimes attributed in part to lack of support from network members (Gaines & Brennan, 2001). Even when network members are supportive, geo-graphic and social segregation may make it more difficult for network mem-bers to come into contact with the partners or to provide support (Abrahamson, 1996; Tucker & Mitchell-Kernan, 1995).

Although these views might lead one that think that social network involve-ment would differ greatly for interethnic and intraethnic couples, we found lit-tle evidence that interethnic couples' social networks are structured differently or provide different levels of support. In purely structural terms, there were few differences in the level of network overlap, cross-network con-tact, or cross-network density. A significant difference was observed on only one of the seven measures of these dimensions. On average, participants in interethnic relationships had met about one fewer members in their partner's network of 12 frequent contacts. Interestingly, there was no difference in the number of people the partner had met in the subject's network. Generally, interethnic couples named a similar number of people as common members of their networks, had met the same or nearly the same number of people in each other's networks, and communicated with those people just as often. Moreover, there were similar levels of contact and communication between the members of the romantic couple's respective networks.

Participants reported similar levels of support for their romantic relationship from network members regardless of whether they were dating inside or outside of their own ethnic group. This was true both for one's own friends and family and for the partner's friends and family. Both sides of the network were equally supportive of both types of relationships. This is not to say, of course, that every individual in the network was equally supportive. But it does suggest that, at least within this group of young adults, embarking on a romantic relationship with a person outside of one's ethnic group did not provoke adverse reactions from network members as a group. As to individuals who may oppose the relationship, they are very likely to be managed in the same way in interethnic relationships that they are relationships between people of the same ethnic group. The management of oppositional or disliked network members is explored in chapter 8.

Relational Development Processes in Interethnic Versus Intraethnic Romantic Relationships

To determine if relational development and social network involvement were associated in the same way in interethnic relationships as they were in intraethnic relationships, separate models of each type of relationship were derived using confirmatory factor analysis and then compared. The overall model for this data set was presented in chapter 5. Because of the large number of factors, the final models are presented in three pieces, beginning with the submodel for the relational factors and the submodel for the network factors, and concluding with the submodel showing the linkages between the relational and network factors. Additional information about the individual measures beneath the top layer and the analysis may be found in Appendices A and B.

Associations Among Relational Factors. The associations between relational factors in interethnic and intraethnic relationships are displayed in Fig. 7.5 and Fig. 7.6, respectively. As these figures illustrate, the components of relational development are associated in similar ways for both types of relationships. In both cases the central aspect of relational development was *depth*, that is, the extent to which participants are willing to reveal personal information and the extent to which they feel the relationship is intimate. Depth was positively and significantly associated with all other aspects of relational development in both models, except among interethnic relationships, where the association between depth and synchrony fell just below the threshold for statistical significance ($r = .21$, $p < .07$). Although depth was more strongly associated

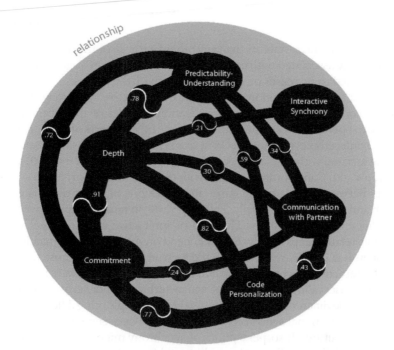

FIG. 7.5.   Interethnic romantic relationships–relational submodel.

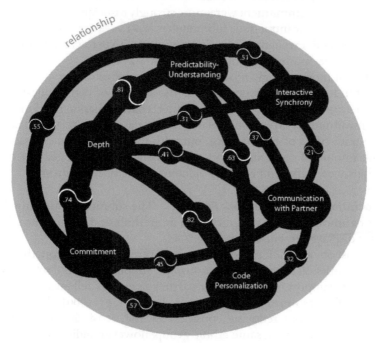

FIG. 7.6.   Intraethnic romantic relationships–relational submodel.

with the other relational factors than any other factor, all of the relational factors were generally associated with each other. Increases or decreases in any one factor were linked to increases or decreases in each of the others.

The most striking exception was the role of interactive synchrony. It was not related to commitment or code personalization in either of the submodels and appeared to operate almost independently of the other aspects of relational development in interethnic relationships. Whereas synchrony was positively and significantly associated with predictability and understanding ($r = .51, p < .0001$), depth ($r = .31, p < .001$), and communication with the partner ($r = .21, p < .05$) in relationships between people of the same ethnic group, synchrony was related only to depth and then only marginally ($r = .21, p < .07$) in relationships between people of different ethnic groups. The level of interactive synchrony achieved in interethnic relationships simply did not depend on other aspects of relational development. It is not clear why this should be true, especially because the overall levels of interactive synchrony in the two types of relationships were perceived to be similar. Observational measures of actual verbal and nonverbal synchronization might yield different results. It may also be that people bring different expectations for conversational synchrony to relationships between parties of differing ethnicities or cultures. If so, perceptions of synchrony might function in different ways or have different effects in interethnic and intraethnic relationships.

The remaining differences between the two submodels involved commitment. Depth and commitment were more strongly associated in the interethnic submodel than in the intraethnic submodel ($rs = .91$ vs. .74, $p < .0001$). Commitment was also somewhat more closely associated with predictability and understanding in the interethnic submodel ($rs = .72$ vs. .55, $p < .05$). Finally, commitment more strongly related to code personalization ($rs = .77$ vs. .57, $p < .01$), but less strongly associated with the amount of communication with the partner ($rs = .24$ vs. .45, $p < .05$) in interethnic romantic relationships. In sum, commitment was positively related to other aspects of relational development in both types of relationships, but with the exception of its association with the amount of communication, these linkages were stronger when the relationships were between people of different ethnic or racial groups.

Associations Among Network Factors.   The submodels showing the associations among the network factors in interethnic and intraethnic relationships are displayed in Fig. 7.7 and Fig. 7.8.

The most obvious difference is in the structure of support from the participants' networks. In interethnic relationships, support from the subject's own network and support from his or her partner's network fell into separate factors. These factors were strongly associated ($r = .71, p < .0001$), but could not be collapsed without reducing considerably the fit of the overall model. Among couples from the same ethnic group, however, indicators of support from the partner's network and support from the subject's own network were

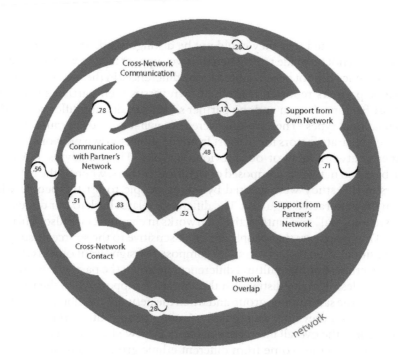

FIG. 7.7.   Interethnic romantic relationships–network submodel.

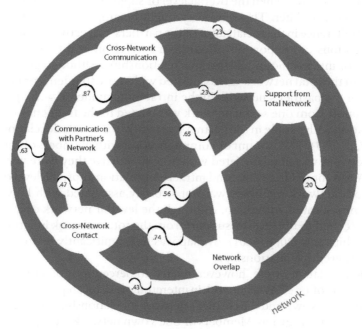

FIG. 7.8.   Intraethnic romantic relationships–network submodel.

so highly correlated that they could not be distinguished. Indeed the overall model could not be made to fit when the two support factors were separated. This difference cannot be accounted for by differences in the levels of support romantic partners reported from their own versus their partner's network. Support from one's own and the partner's network did not differ across the two relational types. These results were somewhat curious because we had obtained separate factors for support from the subject's own network and the partner's network in all of our previous analyses. These analyses, however, were based on networks composed of significant others, whereas the network rosters in this study were created by asking people to list the people with whom they interacted regularly. The difference relates back to our discussion of "psychological" and "interactive" networks in chapter 2 (see also, Milardo, 1992). Thus it appears that people are more sensitive to the source of support or opposition when the networks are composed of significant others or when there are ethnic or other cultural differences between the partners' networks. People are less likely to distinguish the source of support when the partners come from the same ethnic group and when the network members are all people with whom they interact regularly. Among young adults from the same ethnic group, the overall interactive network is viewed as relatively homogenous. But when they come from different ethnic groups, romantic partners tend to be more aware of "support from your network versus support from my network"—even when the overall level of support from the two network sectors may not differ. This sensitivity might be amplified when there is a marked difference in the social status of the partners' respective ethnic groups.

Perceptions of support also figured in several other differences in the models for interethnic and intraethnic relationships. Although greater support from the total network was associated with more frequent contact with people in the partner's network in the intraethnic model ($r = .23$, $p < .01$), only support from one's own network was related to the frequency of communication with people in the partner's network in interethnic relationships ($r = .17$, $p < .05$). The amount of communication with members of the partner's network was not associated with how supportive they were perceived to be. Across both interethnic and intraethnic relationships, the level of support from network members was not strongly associated with how often one communicated with them. Although the level of network overlap was slightly related to the level of support from the total network in intraethnic relationships ($r = .20$, $p < .01$), overlap was not significantly related to support in interethnic relationships.

Structural factors were, however, related to perceptions of support from the members of one's own network in interethnic relationships and to support from both one's own and the partner's network in relationships among people of the same ethnic group. Members of one's own network were perceived to be more supportive in interethnic relationships when the couple had met more people in one another's networks ($r = .52, p < .0001$) and when there was more contact and communication between members of the partner's separate networks ($r = .28, p < .01$). However, these factors were not related to how supportive the partner's network was perceived to be. In relationships between people of different ethnic groups, the perceived supportiveness of the partner's network did not appear to depend on the number of people one had met in the partner's network, how often one interacted with them, whether there was a larger or smaller shared network, or whether the members of the partners' separate networks interacted with one another regularly. In relationships between people of the same ethnic group, on the other hand, network members could not be differentiated, but in general they were seen to be more supportive when the partners had met more of them, communicated with them more often, when there was a larger overlapping network, and when nonoverlapping members of the partner's separate networks communicated with each other more often. In short, the distinction between "support from my network" and "support from your network" appeared to be more sharply drawn in romantic couples with different ethnic backgrounds.

Associations Between Relational Factors and Network Factors. The final set of submodels involved the links between the relational and network factors. These are displayed in Fig. 7.9 and Fig. 7.10.

In spite of the difference in how support indicators were grouped, the overall pattern of association between relational factors and network factors was remarkably similar in interethnic and intraethnic relationships. In both types of relationships, greater support from the network (either total support or support from the partner's separate networks) and meeting more people in the partner's network were associated with greater depth, commitment, predictability and understanding, use of personalized ways of communicating, and more frequent communication between the romantic partners. There were no significant differences in these associations when interethnic and intraethnic relationships were compared.

Interactive synchrony was the only relational factor that was not consistently associated with network factors in either model. It was not significantly related to any of the network factors in interethnic relationships and was related only marginally to network overlap ($r = .11, p < .08$) and total network support ($r = .28, p < .01$) in intraethnic relationships. These results paralleled those obtained for the entire sample in chapter 5, except that the association between synchrony and network support was somewhat stronger in the larger sample.

The only consistent difference between the way relational and network factors went together in the two types of relationships involved the role of communication with the partner. In relationships between people from the same ethnic group, romantic partners interacted with each other more often when they had more overlapping social networks ($r = .24, p < .01$) and when they had

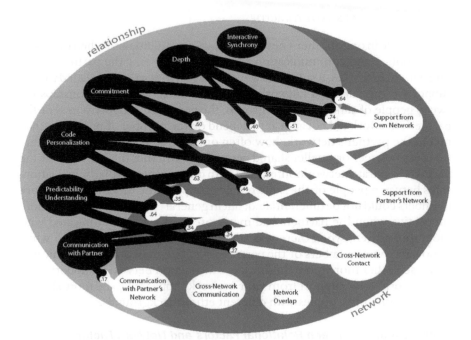

FIG. 7.9.   Interethnic romantic relationships.

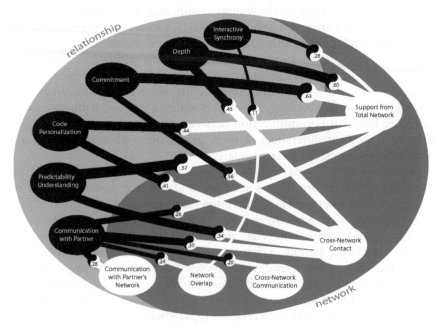

FIG. 7.10.   Intraethnic romantic relationships.

met a greater number of people in each other's network ($r = .30$, $p < .01$). Both of these correlations differed significantly from the corresponding correlations in interethnic relationships, where the amount of communication between the partners was not significantly related to either network overlap or the number of people met in the partner's networks.

GENDER AND ETHNICITY IN PERSPECTIVE

Gender and the degree of ethnic similarity appear to have relatively little impact on how personal relationships develop, on how relational partners relate to each other's social networks, or on how network factors are associated with the developmental pathways of romance and friendship. The young men and women we studied reported generally similar levels of intimacy, commitment, communication, contact with network members, and support from network members in their personal relationships. Support and communication with network members was related to perceptions of intimacy, commitment, and communication within the relationship in comparable ways for men and women. Similarly, within the limits of our sample, relationships between people of different ethnic groups were experienced in much the same way as relationships between people of the same ethnic group. There were few differences in measures of relational development, the structure of relational partners' social networks, or in the level of support they reported from network members.

This is not to say that there may not be important gender differences in other aspects of relational development or interpersonal behavior. However, rather than reinforcing the idea of difference by dwelling on the relatively minor differences, it may be more useful to ask why assumptions about gender and ethnicity play such a prominent role in the popular and academic literature on personal relationships. That is, why are we so eager to conclude that men and women experience relational life in dramatically different ways when the research shows that there are actually few differences of any magnitude? And if relationships between people of different ethnic groups develop and are experienced in the much same way as relationships between people of the same ethnic group, why do we place so much weight on ethnicity in personal relationships? Why do both lay observers and professional researchers persist in believing that gender and ethnicity will explain behavior in personal relationships when the evidence plainly suggests that they do not?

Part of the appeal of gender and ethnicity as explanations for interpersonal behavior is their visibility and simplicity. Except in rare cases, biological sex is readily discerned and almost instantly triggers a gender-based interpretative framework. Ethnic and racial differences are perhaps not so obvious, but are nonetheless more easily discerned than any number of other differences in socioeconomic background, personality, and communicative style. Because so little effort is needed to recognize these differences, we are likely to be biased in favor using them as a basis for explaining behavior. Put simply, we pay more attention to obvious factors than to more subtle factors that may take more effort to recognize (Zipf, 1949). This bias is reinforced by the fact that most people can readily identify examples that appear to confirm stereotyped differences. If one is looking for evidence, for example, that men are less committed than women to personal relationships, it is usually rather easy to think of a given male who is less committed than a given female within one's own circle of acquaintance. The fact that the overall distribution of commitment levels is generally very similar for males and females does not prevent people from selecting examples of less committed men and more committed women. Armed with an example that appears to confirm their initial stereotype, most people do not search their memories further for counterexamples or engage in more sophisticated cognitive evaluations.

Explanations based on gender and ethnicity are also appealing because of their simplicity. They each draw on straightforward binaries (female vs. male; same vs. different) that draw us into uncomplicated generalizations about human nature and human groups. They take advantage of the well-documented bias toward explaining others' behavior in terms of relatively stable characteristics and dispositions rather than in terms of less enduring, but often more relevant, interactive and situational factors (e.g., Ross & Nisbett, 1991). Once relational behavior is attributed to the actor's sex or ethnicity, it is no longer necessary to consider more complex situational or relational factors. Thus people frequently rely on gender and ethnicity to explain behavior because it is easy and simple to do so.

Unfortunately ease and simplicity do not always breed accuracy. The characteristics of the situation and the unfolding structure of the interaction itself are often more informative. Moreover, it may be misleading to attribute differences to sex or ethnicity even when they appear to make a difference. Differences that are assumed to be the result of sex, for example, have often been shown to be the result of underlying power differences (e.g, Molm, 1985; Scudder & Andrews, 1995).

In many parts of the world gender is still a critical feature in the organization and experience of personal relationships. In contemporary industrialized democracies like the United States, however, sex differences are becoming less pronounced. Ironically, this may be part of the reason we are so sensitive to them. As large differences disappear, small differences take on a greater perceptual importance. Thought about in this way, scholarly debate regarding whether *sex* or *gender* is the most appropriate term is in fact evidence that sex differences are attenuating. If biological sex differences were broadly predictive, it is doubtful that we would have as much need for the concept of *gender* in personal relations. Gender is, after all, an attempt to explain what cannot be explained by biological sex alone.

This is not to say that sex differences in personal relationships no longer exist or are unimportant. Important sex differences may exist in areas beyond those examined here. Some research, for example, suggests that young women may be more likely than men to attempt to alter their parents' views of their romantic partner or relationship (Leslie, Huston, & Johnson, 1986). This sort of finding begs additional research. Are women also more likely to try to influence their friends' views? Are they generally more successful at influencing network members? Are women and men equally able to ignore contrary views of network members?

Although ethnicity remains important, often to the point of bloodshed, in many parts of the world, ethnic differences are diminishing in many other areas. The young adults who participated in our research, for example, were all associated with a university in a rather diverse coastal North American city. They were therefore part of an institution that is more or less explicitly designed to bring differing ideas and people into amicable contact as well as residents of a city with numerous opportunities and mechanisms for bringing diverse people together. Moreover, young adults of diverse backgrounds often share elements of a common popular culture. Culturally diverse forms of music are, for instance, readily incorporated into popular music that is shared with an increasingly global audience.

This notion of shared culture is underscored by the fact that most (75%) of the participants in our study on ethnic differences had been born in the United States. One might argue that some shared version of "American culture" masked differences in ethnic background. A more complete examination of this hypothesis, as well as more detailed comparison of specific ethnic or racial groups, is beyond the scope of the present work. We did, however, compare subjects who were born in the United States to those who had not been born in the United States and found no consistent pattern of difference.

The similarities between relationships between people of the same and different ethnic groups also challenge our traditional conceptions of ethnicity and culture. The traditional approach to the concept of culture is to view it as a higher order social category that summarizes and controls all aspects of a more or less defined group of people. This is the view of culture as a shared set of beliefs, values, and ways of behaving. Within this perspective, any given behavior is explained by referring it to the common corpus of which it was a part. This is still a popular approach to understanding culture, including cultures of ethnicity and gender. Unfortunately, as the results in this chapter illustrate, it does not do a very good job of accounting for either the variation within cultural groups or the similarities across cultural groups. Nor is it the only way to view culture. By the 1970s, this traditional conceptualization of culture gave way, first, to views of culture as an historically transmitted symbol system by which people develop and express meanings for social life (e.g., Geertz, 1973), and then, to views of culture as a set of repertoires, tools, or resources that people draw on to make sense and solve the problems of daily life (Philipsen, 1992; Swidler, 2001). In the latter perspective, culture is not so much something one has as something one uses. It describes individual choices in interaction rather than consistent patterns of group difference. In sum, whether one looks to the growing cross-fertilization of cultural influences or follows recent trends in scholarly thought, it is apparent that differences in ethnicity and gender are diminishing.

In spite of this, explanations based on cultural stereotypes persist. They do so not only because they are easy, simple, and perhaps made more visible even as they grow smaller, but also because speculation about ethnic and gender differences frequently serves broader social agenda. Those wishing to advance the interests of minorities, for example, often take the position that members of the group speak "in a different voice" (Gilligan, 1982). The rhetoric of difference provides a basis for a common group identity and buttresses claims for enhanced status and more just treatment. In other cases the agenda is not so much political as it is commercial. Publishers and broadcasters find a ready and lucrative market for materials that play up differences in ethnicity and gender in personal relationships. These books and movies appear to offer some insight, but all too often simply recycle and reinforce existing stereotypes. They are successful, not because they challenge our existing views, but precisely because they give us comfort, making us feel that we understood all along.

The ultimate result of these discourses of difference is to encourage us to see large differences where there are small differences and to overlook underlying similarities in personal relationships across groups. In this chapter and in chapter 6, we have explored differences in age, relationship type, gender, and ethnic composition in personal relationships. Much remains to be done to test the generality of the theory, but it does appear that the social contextual approach can help us understand several different types of personal relationships. Although the results demonstrate that social network factors and relational factors are linked in similar ways across a variety of personal relationships, they have not adequately illuminated the more specific processes by which network and relational factors interact. The broad associations between network and relational factors examined thus far undoubtedly reflect the more particular ways in which people manage information and relationships from day to day and utterance to utterance. These more detailed processes are examined in chapter 8.

CHAPTER EIGHT

Managing Networks and Relational Boundaries

It is tempting to view the road connecting the social network with a personal relationship as a one-way street in which most of the traffic flows from the network to the relationship. Viewed this way, social networks operate as selection mechanisms determining which relationships survive in much the same way the environment functions in classic Darwinian natural selection. Network structure and interaction certainly do exert influence on personal relationships. But just as we are finding with theories of evolution, the interaction between personal relationships and their environment is much more complex than scholars at first believed. Although I have noted this complexity all along, I wish to explore the activity flowing back up the road from the relationship to the network in more detail in this chapter.

People actively manage their social networks. To understand how they do this in regard to the development, maintenance, and termination of their personal relationships, it is useful to ask two questions: First, how do people manage information about their personal relationships with other members of their network? That is, how do they "work the network" to obtain information, acquire support, and maintain the desired impression of their relationships? Second, how do people cope with unsupportive, disliked members of their partner's or their own social network? To set the stage for these questions, it is useful to first consider how we might approach the more general problem of relationships between relationships.

BOUNDARIES AND DIALECTIC TENSIONS IN NETWORKS

With few exceptions, the entire literature on personal relationships is focused either on how to manage a single relationship or on how to manage oneself within that relationship. In real life, however, relationships are often quite interconnected and as a result, individuals spend a good deal of their time managing not just relationships, but also relationships among relationships.

The complexity of imagining, let alone managing, a complex network of relationships can be illustrated by showing what happens when we move from the individual to the network level. Consider, for example, a scale developed by A. Aron, E. N. Aron, and Smollan (1992) to describe how the other becomes included in an expanding self as a relationship develops. The IOS—"inclusion of other in the self scale"—asks the individual to circle one of seven pictures that might describe his or her relationship with another person. Each picture offers two circles —one marked "self" and one marked "other." The level of overlap between the two circles increases from simply touching in the first picture to nearly complete overlap in the seventh picture. The diameter of the circles increases with overlap, reflecting the notion that including the other in the self functions to expand the self. The measure fails to capture the situational dynamics of relationships (i.e., two people may be closer in one context than another). Nonetheless, it is visually elegant (Fig. 8.1) and has proven to be predictive in a variety of studies (see Agnew, Loving, Le, & Goodfriend, 2004).

But now let's add some more people. Instead of one couple, imagine we have five people with varying relationships. Suppose we have Marta and John, a romantic couple, Marta's friend Alice, John's brother Ben, and Ben's wife Sharon. Alice and Sharon are also close friends, although not as close as Marta and Alice. Ben is close to Marta, but not so close to Alice. As Fig. 8.2 shows, we now have 10 relationships to consider even within this very small network.

If we try to visualize all these relationships together, it quickly becomes apparent that what was relatively straightforward at the level of a single relationship has become truly complex (see Fig. 8.3). Anyone who recalls blowing soap bubbles as a child will immediately appreciate how relationships become more intricately linked as we move to the network level. It is like blowing a sin-

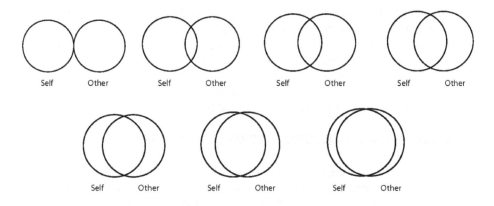

FIG. 8.1.   Inclusion of other in the self-scale (from Aron et al., 1992). Reprinted with permission from the author and the American Psychological Association.

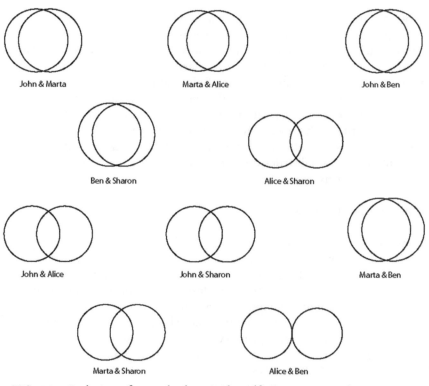

John & Marta

Marta & Alice

John & Ben

Ben & Sharon

Alice & Sharon

John & Alice

John & Sharon

Marta & Ben

Marta & Sharon

Alice & Ben

FIG. 8.2.   Inclusion of several others in the self.

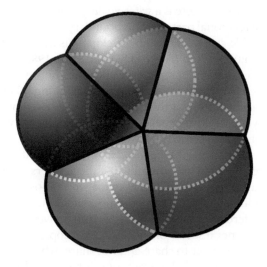

FIG. 8.3.   Interpreting selves in network space.

gle bubble, then catching it on the wand and blowing it into a multiple, then catching it again and blowing it into an even more complex structure. Like the bubbles, each self is shaped by all the others. The lines marking off relationships become more difficult to identify. Marta's decisions about her relationship with John are made in a complex field that involves other relationships and by a self that includes all of the other people to varying degrees. To make things even more complex, relational partners could well have different views of the extent to which they include each other in their self-images.

Two of the more useful starting points for understanding what goes on inside complex relational structures such as this are the concepts of *boundaries* and *dialectic tensions*.

Relational Boundaries

Boundaries are ubiquitous in social life. We define ourselves and fit into our social world by drawing lines around ourselves, our relationships, and the groups to which we belong. But boundaries are also inherently problematic. They must be managed. They are often difficult to identify. They overlap. People disagree about how and where they are drawn. They change over time and must often be transcended in order to achieve larger social goals, yet efforts to renegotiate boundaries are a primary source of misunderstanding, conflict, and miscommunication (Coupland, Wiemann, & Giles, 1991; Petronio, Ellemers, Giles, & Gallois, 1998).

We may identify three types of boundaries in interpersonal relationships. The first two of these are well recognized in the literature (e.g., Derlega & Chaikin, 1977). The first of these is a *self- boundary* that marks off what is and is not shared with the relational partner. This boundary is generally thought to become more permeable as a relationship develops—as the partner becomes included in one's definition of self (A. Aron & E. N. Aron, 1986; A. Aron, Mashek, & E. N. Aron, 2004). Even in a very close relationship, however, the self-boundary is never completely removed. René Magritte's painting, "The Kiss," offers a particularly striking illustration of this point. In it we see two lovers embraced in a passionate kiss, yet each lover's head is completely covered with a cloth and their lips touch only through the two layers separating them.

The second boundary is the *dyadic boundary* that marks off what is and is not shared about the relationship with members of the partners' surrounding social network. This boundary is quite actively managed in most personal relationships. Information shared with network members and sought from them varies over time, across different parts of the network, and between different individuals within the same general sector of the network. People regularly make complex decisions regarding what to share and not share, what to ask and not ask.

Yet in order to grasp the full dynamics of information flow within a set of relationships, I believe it is useful to consider a third type of boundary: the *network boundary*. This boundary marks the limits to which information is likely to be retransmitted once it has initially been transmitted across the dyadic boundary. It is the network boundary, for example, that a woman is thinking about when she worries that her mother might share her disclosure of marital problems with everybody in the family. Managing network boundaries is not merely about containment. Sometimes people want the information to be shared. As I noted in an earlier chapter, a person may deliberately tell a friend that he is attracted to one of their mutual acquaintances in hopes that she will relay the information to the acquaintance. Or, the woman in my previous example could have told her mother about her marital problems precisely because she knew her mother would save her the time and discomfort of having to tell other family members herself. Being concerned about network boundaries, in other words, is being concerned about other people's dyadic boundaries.

Self, dyadic, and network boundaries share a number of characteristics, although we should not presume they always function in identical ways. Four of the more common dimensions are control, ownership, levels, and permeability (Petronio, 2002). *Control* usually refers to how the boundary regulates the risk of disclosure, although I would broaden the notion to include regulating the risks of receiving information as well. Hearing a work associate constantly brag about how well his child is doing in school, for instance may increase one's anxiety about the troubles one's own child is having in school. Boundaries are also used to identify ownership of information. *Ownership* at the self-boundary marks the information that will not be disclosed to a particular person or perhaps generally. Family secrets fall into this category (T. D. Afifi & Olson, 2005; Vangelisti, Caughlin, & Timmerman, 2001). On a more positive note, one's hopes for the future of a budding romance may not be shared or, if shared, shared very selectively. Even then, ownership rules at the dyadic and network boundaries dictate that the information may not be retransmitted without permission from the original owner (e.g., "I can't tell you, you'll have to ask him."). Information and events in relationships are not always privately owned and so boundary structures often dictate levels of private and joint ownership. News of a son's impending marriage is a family as well as a personal item. Accordingly, boundary rules might dictate who is allowed to tell whom and in what order. The son, for example, may wish to inform the grandparents himself before they hear the good news from his mother. Finally, boundaries structures may be described in terms of their permeability. Boundaries have sometimes been cast as walls designed to screen out or perhaps even deny the existence of other relationships (M. M. McCall, 1970). More often, however, the permeability of boundaries varies across persons, topics, and occasions.

It is generally assumed that people rely on rule systems to control interpersonal boundaries and thus the tensions of being private or open, social or alone (Petronio, 1991, 2002). Some of these rules are based in culture; some are matters of personal habit, whereas others are triggered by a particular context or relationship. Rules for relational conduct, including boundary rules, are common topics of discussion in family and friendship networks. Baxter, Dun, and Sahlstein (2001), for example, asked 78 young adults to keep diaries of incidents in which they perceived that rules for romantic relationships were being communicated among the members of their social network. Over 600 incidents were reported over a 2-week period. At this rate, a person would have participated in a discussion of relationship rules on an average of once every other day. Rules were conveyed most often in the form of unsolicited advice. In fact, unsolicited advice was given about eight times more often than requested advice. Rules were also frequently inferred indirectly from the experiences of others or conveyed rather indirectly in the form of gossip about those not present in the discussion. Sometimes, although less often, the rule was conveyed through direct sanctioning as network members offered praise or criticism regarding the relational conduct of those present in the discussion.

Boundary rules are not just for scholars. People use them as a practical guide for addressing real situations. Negotiating rather explicit boundary rules may, for example, help family members manage information and interactions. This is particularly true during periods of "boundary turbulence," in which previous boundary expectations have been violated or network structure has suddenly changed and old rules no longer apply (Petronio, 2002). In stepfamilies, for example, it may be particularly adaptive to develop specific rules for disclosure and conflict management, both for those inside the family and those in the network (e.g., T. D. Afifi, 2003; Lofas, 1998).

Although it is frequently beneficial to articulate the rules, boundary management is a more complex process than can be captured in a given set of rules. It is often not apparent which rules apply. Typically we place people in social categories and then apply the rules that appear relevant to the people in that category. Unfortunately, as Petronio and her colleagues (1998) observed, people simultaneously belong to multiple categories and the participants in the interaction may not categorize each other in the same way. The classic example of this is the case in which one person defines the second as a potential romantic partner while the second categorizes the first as a platonic friend.

There are at least three other problems with rules as well. First, rules for close relationships often contradict one another. For example, people endorse the rule, "be completely open and honest with a romantic partner," as well as the rule "be discreet; even if your romantic partner wants to know, you shouldn't tell him/her everything" (Baxter et al., 2001, p. 192). Second, even when the rules do not contradict directly, contradictions may be created if the person trying to apply them has conflicting goals. A network member may be caught between the desire to be loyal to her friend and the desire to act on her attraction to her friend's former boyfriend. In cases such as these, little is gained by appealing to a rule for relational behavior. People do appeal to rules, but they often do so in a way that illustrates the third problem with rules-based approaches to relationships. They appropriate the rules for their own purposes. That is, they will appeal to the rule that best serves their goals in a given situation. In cases like these, rules become tools to justify action rather than guidelines or constraints on action. Relational rules, like the broader cultural repertoire of which they are a part, may be applied, modified, or ignored in any way that furthers one's goals in a specific situation (Swidler, 2001). It is not surprising, then, that most rules for close relationships do not have consistently high rates of compliance or strong perceived sanctions for violation (Baxter et al., 2001).

Relational Dialectics

While rules perspectives take a prescriptive approach to managing a network of relationships, dialectic approaches focus on the problems that the rules are trying to solve. Many of these problems revolve around conflicting relational goals or conditions. The contradictory aspects of social life have been the focus of a set of perspectives that are generally called *relational dialectics*. Intimacy and autonomy as well as several other mutually exclusive, yet essential, qualities of relationships have long been recognized (Altman et al., 1981; Guisinger & Blatt, 1994; Lawler, 1975; Parks, 1982; Prager & Roberts, 2004; Rawlins, 1992; Simmel, 1950).

The research program of Baxter and her colleagues provides one of the most comprehensive approaches to understanding the role of dialectics in managing relationships and relationships among relationships (e.g., Baxter, 1993; Baxter & Montgomery, 1996, 2000). This program centers on three core contradictions or dialectic tensions in relationships: integration–separation, stability–change, and expression–privacy (see Table 8.1). These contradictions manifest themselves, sometimes in different ways, both inside the relationship and in interactions between the relationship and its surrounding network. They are important here because they help us understand the problems that

TABLE 8.1

Dialectic Tensions in Personal Relationships (Adapted from Baxter, 1993)

	Dialectic Tensions		
Locus	Dialectic of integration– separation	Dialectic of stability–change	Dialectic of expression–privacy
Internal	Connection–autonomy	Predictability–novelty	Openness–closedness
External	Inclusion–seclusion	Conventionality–uniqueness	Revelation–concealment

relational partners and network members are trying to solve and to appreciate why they make some of the decisions they do.

The *integration–separation dialectic* represents conflicting desires for intimacy and autonomy inside the relationship and conflicting desires for inclusion and seclusion with respect to the surrounding network. The romantic couple deciding whether to spend the evening together or apart illustrates the interior of this dialectic; whereas the same couple deciding whether to stay home together or attend a family gathering together would illustrate its exterior. The inclusion-seclusion dialectic is an important one from the standpoint of relational development, maintenance, and dissolution. How the partners manage it will influence the level of information and support available to the relationship from network members.

The *stability–change dialectic* can also be seen inside a given relationship and in the way the relationship fits into its surrounding network. Inside, it is experienced as contradictory efforts to have both predictable and stable interactions and novel, fresh experiences. Outside, it is manifested by the tension between wanting one's relationship to be acceptable to others and yet wanting to be distinct in some way. How relational partners manage this tension between conventionality and uniqueness will obviously influence how much network members support the relationship and include its members in their activities.

The *expression–privacy dialectic* has perhaps received the greatest attention among researchers and is particularly relevant for understanding how development is influenced by the actions of relational participants and network members. Both inside and outside the relationship, this dialectic manifests itself as a conflict between withholding and disclosing information. We are most interested in the tensions at the dyadic and network boundaries—that is, the tensions regarding openness and privacy about the relationship with network members and the tensions regarding whether disclosures are retransmitted to other network members.

Although dialectic tensions are universal in human relationships, they are more obvious in some types of relationships than others. They are, for example, readily apparent in friendships that occur in work settings (Bridge & Baxter, 1992; Rawlins, 1992). The desire to support or be supported by a friend may, for instance, come into conflict with one's work obligation to be impartial or with one's knowledge of shortcomings in the friend's work. Differing positions in the organizational hierarchy may create difficulties for expectations of equality between friends. In addition, the overlap of work and private life may challenge the participants' need for time apart from each other. These same dilemmas might also be experienced by married couples who work in the same organization.

The dialectic contradictions and tensions that characterize marriage are often amplified in stepfamilies. Parents and children often feel caught in webs of conflicting loyalties as well as uncertainty about what should be revealed and to whom. These tensions extend to how the stepfamily deals with extended family, former spouses, and friends. For example, slightly over half of the stepfamilies interviewed in one study reported that children felt caught between custodial and noncustodial parents (T. D. Afifi, 2003). The feeling of being caught was created by inappropriate disclosures by former spouses to the children or by the former spouses to each other in front of the children. In some cases, these disclosures placed the child in the position of being a peer or counselor to a parent. In other cases, children were used as couriers and mediators between the former spouses. These cases illustrate that the way former spouses manage the relational dialectics of integration–separation and expression–privacy can have profound effects on their ability to develop a successful new family unit.

Before discussing the specific strategies people use to manage these dialectics, we should recognize that dialectic tensions are not always experienced in the same way across relationships. Some relationships may be structured to emphasize integration, whereas others may be constructed to achieve greater autonomy for the partners and separation from a joint network (M. A. Fitzpatrick, 1988). Moreover, even within the same relationship, dialectic tensions and the strategies for managing them can be expected to change over time—both in terms of the frequency or intensity with which a conflict may be experienced and in terms of the relational content that triggers it (Baxter, 1988).

MANAGING INFORMATION IN NETWORKS

People are, as I argued in the preceding section, not simply passive recipients of network influence. Instead, they actively "work the network" to obtain information and assistance in support of their relationship. They also continuously engage in problem solving to address the ongoing tensions between the relationship and the network. My goal in this section is to explore several of the major strategies used by relational partners to manage information in the network and thus to obtain what they want from the network at any one point. The six strategies presented both reflect and extend discussions of managing tensions around network boundaries (e.g., Baxter & Montgomery, 1996; Baxter & Widenmann, 1993; Goldsmith, 1988; Goldsmith & Parks, 1990). These strategies are disclosure and access, withdrawal and withholding, selective access and disclosure, equivocation, relational tests, and participation in boundary rituals.

Disclosure and Access

Prospective relational partners often enlist the help of network members in starting their relationship (see chap. 3, this volume). After that, their next move toward the network is probably to inform those that do not already know of the relationship's existence. Informing others is an explicit bid for recognition and support and often elicits responses that assist the relational participants in evaluating their relationship (Baxter & Widenmann, 1993). "Going public" may take the form of an announcement and can be seen as a turning point in the development of a relationship (Baxter & Bullis, 1986). However, the direct strategy may not be the strategy of choice, especially if the partners are uncertain about their relationship or weigh privacy concerns heavily (Krain, 1977). In cases like these, participants may seek to manage dialectic tensions through less direct revelations. Allowing network members to see the partners together in a social setting is one of the most common of these strategies (Baxter & Widenmann, 1993). All this presumes that it is possible to go public. Extramarital affairs or relationships that are likely to prove socially unacceptable for other reasons must naturally manage disclosure in the other direction—particularly in their early stages.

Beyond disclosure of its existence, relational partners may reveal information about the relationship in order to accomplish a variety of other goals. One of the most common is to engage in sense-making about events that are causing them uncertainty about the relationship (Goldsmith, 1988). In one study of such events, for instance, subjects reported that they had discussed the uncertainty increasing event with one or more network members in about 75% of the cases (Planalp, Rutherford, & Honeycutt, 1988). Network members may offer distinct or particularly useful perspectives on relational problems (Agnew et al., 2001). Disclosure of otherwise private information about a romantic partner or relationship to network members may also be a way to gain social support, to obtain direct assistance, or to promote a positive impression of the self among network members (Goldsmith, 1988).

Sharing relational concerns or problems with network members is also one of the more reliable strategies for finding out what they really think. As a rule, network members do not generally tell the relational partners what concerns them about the relationship (Blumberg, 1972; L. L. Wilson, Roloff, & Carey, 1998). When they do, it is usually because the relational partner has raised the issue first—often following a fight or other incident inside the relationship. Unless the issue involves the network member or is deemed to be extremely serious, feedback is generally withheld until a disclosure by the relational partner opens the door for further discussion. Network members may, of course, already be discussing the problem among themselves. Indeed, people are more likely to complain to network members about a friend's negative behavior than they are to confront the friend directly (Blumberg, 1972). The consequences of this discussion are largely unknown, although it is possible that discussion among network members could encourage someone to step forward individually or set the stage for a more organized group intervention in the case of serious problems (L. L. Wilson et al., 1998).

Finally, it is worth noting that people sometimes disclose information about a relationship, not for the sake of that relationship, but rather to maintain or enhance their relationship with a network member or to assist the network member in some other way (Goldsmith, 1988). These may be positive disclosures intended to create a favorable impression, but information revealed need not always be positive. Revealing relational troubles or a partner's odd personal habits may be done in order to empathize with the other person. Sharing previously withheld information, regardless of whether it is positive or negative, lets the recipient in on a secret and thus sends a powerful relational signal (e.g., "I didn't want to tell you this until I knew I could trust you, but I'm thinking of proposing to Jennifer"). Even when the intent is not to enhance the relationship with the network member, people may disclose both positive and negative information about one of their relationships as a way of helping the network member in one of his or her other relationships.

Revelations to and among network members can serve either altruistic or self-oriented goals. One might, for example, brief a family member who is about to meet the romantic partner for the first time. This is particularly true if there is concern that the family member and the partner may not get along. Or one may disclose to a network member in order to work the relational boundaries. One of Goldsmith's (1988) respondents, for example, told her that he had disclosed information to his romantic partner's sister because he worried that the parents might not approve of the relationship and he wanted to get the sister on his side. Although people do not always seek to manipulate the network so overtly, this incident underscores the fact that actions within a network can not always be deconstructed to separate dyads or triads.

Indeed the decision to disclose something to one person might involve a complex social calculation involving several different individuals and relationships. Consider, for example, the thought process that the woman in the following example goes through as she tries to decide what to reveal to her friend Suzy (suggested by D. J. Goldsmith, Personal communication. June 1, 2005):

> It might help Suzy to hear that my marriage isn't perfect and I don't mind her knowing, but that's not fair to my husband. Suzy is pretty good friends with my sister, too. While I don't care what my sister thinks, she already finds it hard to be around my husband and all this could make family gatherings uncomfortable. I don't want Mom to have to suffer through that. My sister would also probably tell my brother and really I hate it when he gets a chance to feel superior. Plus, Suzy's husband works in the same company as my husband and I don't think it is appropriate for him to know personal information about a co-worker.

Withdrawal and Withholding

The second major strategy for managing information and access about a relationship is the opposite of the first. Instead of displaying the relationship and disclosing information, relational partners attempt to promote their relationship by denying access and withholding disclosure. The fact that people withhold information from network members should not imply that the information is always disclosed inside the relationship. Certain topics, such as the state of the relationship, are typically avoided inside the relationship, particularly if discussion of them is likely to increase uncertainty (Baxter & Wilmot, 1985; Knobloch & Carpenter-Theune, 2004; Roloff & Cloven, 1990).

Avoidance and withholding can promote the relationship in a variety of ways. They are used to maintain control over sensitive information, to foster intimacy with the romantic partner by helping relational partners manage their uncertainty about the relationship, to avoid loyalty conflicts among network members, and to maintain a positive impression of the self among network members (Goldsmith, 1988; Parks, 1982).

As one would expect, given the dialectic tensions associated with these functions, many of the reasons to withhold information are the same as the reasons to disclose it. In some cases, the valence of the information may tip the balance one way or the other. We are more likely to disclose the good news of a partner's latest achievement than a violent or abusive incident. Managing dialectic tensions, however, does not come down to any simple rule such as "disclose the positive, withhold the negative." One may disclose the partner's abusive behavior in an attempt to obtain social support, but withhold her or his latest achievement so as to not appear to be bragging at the expense of less successful network members.

In many cases, the decision to avoid contact or withhold information has less to do with the valence of the information than with one's concern about the loss of control that might result if the information were known (Goldsmith, 1988). For example, telling a network member about a problem in a romantic relationship can result in the problem getting blown out of proportion and becoming a bigger topic of discussion than the discloser wishes. It might also result in interference by the network member. Even when interference is not a concern, individuals may choose to withhold information because they do not want the network member to seek additional information. A young man might not, for example, want to tell his mother about his romantic relationship at the present time because he knows that she would want to know all about it.

Concerns about the loss of control frequently overlap with the desire to protect relational boundaries. Information was often withheld by the people interviewed by Goldsmith (1988) because they believed that disclosure would violate a relational rule regarding privacy. Sometimes they decided this independently and sometimes their partner had expressly requested that the matter not be discussed outside the relationship. Even without this prohibition, however, people may not disclose to network members if they believe that the disclosure is likely to get back to the partner. Boundary concerns may also be expressed in an ethic of relational fairness. It is not fair to the partner, for example, to complain to network members about something if one has not first approached the partner with the complaint. Regardless of the specific circumstances, honoring the relational expectation that information not be shared outside the relationship is intended to maintain and enhance the relationship.

Whether avoidance and withholding actually have their intended effect is not always clear. In many situations, overly vigilant attempts to protect relational boundaries work to the detriment of all involved. I noted earlier that friends may not feel free to comment on the problems they see in others' relationships until one of the relational participants raises the issue (L. L. Wilson et al., 1998). If so, unwillingness to disclose to network members serves to trap the relational partners with their problems and prevent network members from providing assistance. Avoiding contact with network members may place other relational participants in a bind if they want to maintain contact with the excluded parties. Sour relationships between avoidant former spouses, for instance, model dysfunctional coping and create discomfort among their children.

Individuals frequently withhold information about a relationship from network members in order to manage uncertainty. One of Goldsmith's (1988) respondents explained her decision to withhold information about her romantic relationship from a friend in this way: "It gave me a chance to sort it out for myself. Because sometimes if you just get the other person's opinion, you don't really know how you're feeling and you hear an idea from them and that sounds good" (p. 54).

People also withhold information because they believe, usually in hindsight, that revealing it would have created even more confusion and uncertainty than they were already experiencing (Goldsmith, 1988). In some cases, such as those involving financial difficulties or a partner's drinking, it appeared that the individual was not ready to confront the issue themselves. For better or for worse, this kind of denial is a form of sense-making that functions to protect and maintain the relationship.

Finally, relational partners withhold information in order to protect their relationships with network members (Goldsmith, 1988; Goldsmith & Parks, 1990). The topic may simply be inappropriate for particular network members (e.g., children, co-workers). Parents and their young adult children, for instance, may implicitly agree to a code of silence regarding the young person's sexual activity. Even when disclosure is appropriate, however, information may be withheld because disclosing it might have a negative impact on the relationship with the network member. The disclosure might unduly impose on the network member, put her or him in an awkward position, create conflict, or cause the network member to think less of the discloser.

Selective Disclosure and Access

Participants have other options besides full disclosure or complete avoidance as they seek to manage information about their relationship. Although disclosure and access are probably always selective in some sense, *selectivity* is itself a strategy. Selectivity as a strategy may be manifested in three broad dimensions of interaction with network members. One is the *topic*—one may disclose more or less about an issue or handle an issue in a selective way. Another is the *target*—one may make a disclosure to some network members rather than others, or in some ways, to some network members, and in different ways, to others. Finally, *time*—one may disclose at one time but not another. The overall willingness to disclose and allow access may change over time as well.

Topics. Perhaps the most direct way relational participants manage topics is by *omission*. They disclose about some aspects of a topic, but avoid others. For example, although adolescents will generally reveal aspects of their romantic relationships to their parents, they are quite selective in doing so—revealing only those aspects that are likely to elicit parental approval (Leslie et al., 1986). When potentially negative topics arise, relational partners may omit details or key pieces of information. When pressed, attempts may be made to create an explicit rule regarding how far discussion is expected to go along a topical line.

Topics may also be regulated through *summarization*. This tactic involves synthesizing a large, potentially problematic body of information into a less problematic summary that emphasizes what is deemed to be appropriate or necessary for a given network member (Huber & Daft, 1987). When done well, a summary not only emphasizes the information that the individual is willing to share, but also, by virtue of being a summary of the whole story, discourages attempts to find out more. Summarization is used to manage both dyadic and network boundaries. One may, for example, provide a fellow co-worker with only a summary of the troubles one has had with a new employee. Or, the co-worker might get the full story, but be assisted in developing a summary that can be shared with the supervisor.

A third way to manage a topic is through *enrichment*. Enrichment allows the speaker to resolve the conflicting goals he or she may have in a given situation. It is similar to some of the more sophisticated strategies for managing dialectic tensions more generally (see Baxter, 1993). Consider, for example, the following statement to a close friend who is concerned about being supplanted by one's new romantic partner: "Don't worry, I'll always feel close to you even if we don't see each other as much as I'd like." This statement artfully reinforces the friendship while simultaneously suggesting that the friendship can be maintained successfully with less interaction than it once had. Or consider this statement as a response to a friend who has hinted that he wants to know more than you are willing to tell: "One of the best things about our friendship is that we respect each other's privacy." Enrichment tactics are difficult to classify because they may involve a mix of omission, summarization, and selection. They may also add new elements that shift the way the listener frames what is heard. Ultimately, however, they function to allow selective disclosure to occur.

Targets.   Sometimes it is not the topic that is managed, but rather the choice of targets, that is, the choice of network members who are given access or with whom a given topic is discussed. This approach is sometimes called *message routing* in the literature on organizations and *segmentation* in the literature on dialectics in interpersonal relationships (Baxter & Montgomery, 1996; Huber & Daft, 1987). It is the most common choice for people who want to discuss a relational problem, but are worried that seeking support might make them vulnerable (Goldsmith & Parks, 1990). They select the network member whom they expect both to be very supportive and to do a good job of protecting their information.

The concern with protecting a disclosure may prompt linguistic strategies (e.g., "don't tell anybody but …") that are intended to discourage retransmission of the information. Whether these are effective is largely unknown, though exploratory research suggests people often pass along information to other network members in spite of their promises not to do so. At best, the effort to limit retransmission may only encourage the listeners to be more selective about the persons with whom information is shared (Petronio & Bantz, 1991).

This brings us to an issue that appears to have been completely overlooked in the study of personal relationships: reputation. Relational partners will consider whether a particular network member has generally been supportive and maintained confidentiality in the past. Confidence is increased when judgments can be based on more than the individual's own direct experience with the potential target. This means there must be a "reputation system" for sharing information among network members. Although they are rarely appreciated as such, gossip, storytelling, and "bull sessions" among network members function as just such a system, calibrating and recalibrating network members' estimates of each others' expertise, trustworthiness, tact, and supportiveness. Reputation systems help identify network members who may have the knowledge or experience to be helpful. Even when they are talking about others, those participating in the reputation system are acting in ways that reveal their own suitability for disclosure. The gossip who sympathetically shares the problems of others will be remembered far differently than the gossip who appears to delight in others' troubles. Regardless of the outcome, the benefits of the reputation system are available only to those who participate. Those who avoid gossip, storytelling, and other such discussions may not be as adept at selecting network members when the need for support arises.

Timing.   Relational partners also exercise selectivity with respect to the timing of disclosures to network members. They disclose to a given network member on some occasions, but not others. Researchers have given a number of different names to variations on this general strategy: alternation, temporal separation, spiraling inversion (Baxter & Montgomery, 1996; Goldsmith & Parks, 1990). By disclosing at some times and withholding or avoiding at other times, the individual is able over time to honor both the desire to reveal and the desire to conceal. The decision to alternate periods of openness and avoidance reflects the individual's own motivations as well as estimates of the target's ability to tolerate further disclosure or to offer further support. One of the respondents in Goldsmith's (1988) study, for example, reported that she had stopped telling a friend about her husband's drinking problems because the friend had loaned them money and helped get her husband into a treatment program in the past. The woman said, "I just figured he had certainly done his duties" (p. 49).

The decision to reveal or withhold information often depends on the progression of events associated with the issue or topic itself. Couples may not widely discuss a pregnancy until after the first trimester when the greatest risk of miscarriage has passed. Law school applicants may not be eager to discuss acceptances or rejections until they receive a decision from their most favored choice. In these examples, as well as many others, the changes in what is known about the topic or issue help dictate periods of disclosure and withholding.

The tendency to disclose or withhold information may also change more generally as a relationship develops. Some have argued that disclosure to network members decreases with development, whereas others have found no relationship between how close the relationship was and the tendency to reveal or conceal information from network members (Baxter & Widenmann, 1993; M. P. Johnson & Leslie, 1982). My suspicion is that it depends greatly on the type of relationship. One might expect same-sex friendships, opposite-sex friendships, dating relationships, and marital relationships to differ. More importantly, it is likely that revelation and concealment ebb and flow over time, not only with events inside the relationship, but with events in the network as well. A divorce elsewhere in the network may, for example, cause couples to either increase or decrease their disclosure about how well they are doing in their own relationship.

Changes might also occur in how romantic couples manage the inclusion–seclusion dialectic over time. Couples generally need time alone in order to solidify their relationship, but they also need time with network members in order to gain support and recognition (e.g., Krain, 1977; Lewis, 1973b). How couples manage this tension probably varies as their relationship develops. Surra (1985), for example, found that couples generally decreased the number of leisure activities with network members and increased leisure activities with each other as their relationship deepened. On the other hand,

Baxter and Simon (1993) reported that married couples were more likely to worry that they were spending too much time together and not enough with friends and family. This may help explain why married couples are more likely than dating couples to view spending time with friends and family as a relationship maintenance strategy (Stafford & Canary, 1991).

Equivocation

Equivocation offers another option for managing information about the relationship in complex situations in which open disclosure and complete avoidance are unacceptable choices. Equivocation in the name of politeness is universal (Brown & Levenson, 1978). We use it in situations where we do not wish to lie, but in which telling the truth might lead to negative consequences. But equivocal communication is used for more than simply maintaining social order. It is also a communicative strategy by which individuals pursue their goals in situations that contain contradictory demands or a great deal of uncertainty (J. B. Bavelas, Black, Chovil, & Mullett, 1990). As Chovil (1994) observed, "equivocation is a solution to [a] difficult social dilemma; it is a way of avoiding any of the direct alternatives while at the same time enabling the speaker to respond in the situation" (p. 115).

Equivocation enables relational participants to respond to network members who expect opposite replies (Chovil, 1994). It may be used to facilitate change or enhance relationships in other ways as well. An ambiguous or equivocal message, for example, leaves network members greater freedom to interpret the message in a way that is consistent with their own beliefs, thus encouraging listeners to perceive greater similarity than may actually exist with the beliefs of the speaker (Eisenberg, 1984).

Perhaps the most comprehensive approach to understanding equivocation as a message strategy is the one developed by Bavelas and her colleagues (J. B. Bavelas et al., 1990). Building on previous work by Haley (1959), this group suggested that a message could become equivocal in any one of four ways: (a) if its content is ambiguous or contradictory, (b) if it is not clear that the opinions being expressed are those of the speaker, (c) if it is not clear that the message is intended for the listener, and (d) if the message and its context are incongruent. Examples of the latter include indirect answers and topic changes.

One would not have to look far to find examples of each of these forms of equivocation in relational participants' communication with network members. Unwanted questions about the state of one's relationship, for instance, might be given ambiguous responses like "better than okay" or "basically fine." Or, the relational participant may respond by saying something like "most people would be pleased to be doing as well as we are," a message that equivocates with regard to what its source's own opinion is. Alternatively, the relational participant may give a verbal response while simultaneously avoiding eye contact or engaging in other behaviors that make it unclear that the response was really directed at the person asking the question. Or, one could equivocate by offering a response that is not precisely on topic. Asked how he was getting on with his wife, for example, a man might say "Well, we're going to Hawaii together for vacation after Christmas." Although this response conveys some relational information, it does not provide a direct answer to the question being asked.

Equivocation is generally viewed as a strategy for parrying direct requests for information. At the boundary between one relationship and another, however, participants on both sides may conspire to maintain ambiguity by asking indirect questions that leave the other person a great deal of latitude in response. A husband may, for example, show interest by asking his wife what she and her friends talked about on their night out, but ask in such an equivocal or noncommittal way that she is freed to respond with an equal level of equivocality. Ambiguous as it is, the exchange functions to reinforce their overall relationship while simultaneously obscuring the fact that the wife really doesn't want to share all of the information she discussed with her friends. Mutual equivocation is thus a tool by which people can simultaneously manage otherwise conflicting relational demands in the network.

Relational Tests

Because of the risks associated with revealing relational information to network members as well as with asking network members for their opinions directly, relational partners may opt for indirect ways to gauge their responses. The goal of these tests is to obtain information in an implicit fashion. People regularly compare their relationships to the relationships of others (Titus, 1980), but relational testing goes beyond simple social comparison. It is more deliberate, more strategic.

In the early 1980s, Baxter and Wilmot (1984) used the phrase, "secret tests," to describe a set of indirect strategies that relational partners might use to find out what each other really thought about their relationship. They called these "secret tests" in recognition of that fact that they did not involve straightforward talk about the state of the relationship. Indeed direct talk about the status of the relationship is often avoided between relational partners, especially when uncertainty about the relationship is high (e.g., Baxter & Wilmot, 1985; Knobloch & Carpenter-Theune, 2004).

Relational participants frequently involve network members in their tests. In the "asking third parties test," for instance, the relational partner goes directly to people in the other partner's network for information. One person reported: "I asked my girlfriend's sister to tell me anything she could about how my girlfriend felt about me and our future" (Baxter & Wilmot, 1984, p. 182). In the "public presentation test," one relational partner places the other in a social setting to see how he or she will react to others viewing their relationship. One young man who found himself the object of such a test commented (Baxter & Wilmot, 1984):

> At the time, I didn't know it was a test, but it was. She invited me to her family's home for a week. They started to talk to me in terms of being just like a son, how much they hoped we wanted kids someday, etc. She ... wanted to see if I would get scared by hearing her parents talk like that. (p. 184)

Network members are often unwitting participants in what Baxter and Wilmot (1984) called "triangle tests." These tests usually involve exposing the current partner to a former or alternative partner to gauge loyalty or commitment. The young woman who arranged for her current boyfriend to see her talking to her former boyfriend was, for example, hoping that the current boyfriend would become upset and thus reveal how much he cared for her. The young man who left his girlfriend alone with one of his attractive male friends was interested in knowing whether she would react to the friend in a way that would question her loyalty. Regardless of how these tests are judged, they illustrate the lengths to which people will go to manage their relational uncertainty and the extent to which they will involve third parties in the process. Half of the subjects in Baxter and Wilmot's (1984) study reported that they had involved network members in their efforts to test their romantic partner's feelings.

Although Baxter and Wilmot focused on tests of the relational partner, we could just as well focus on tests of network members. One network member may be quizzed about what another thinks of the relationship. "Public presentations" not only test the relational partner, but also the network members. The trial weekend with the girlfriend's family, for example, tests both the boyfriend and the family. And triangle tests, in which participants' interests are pitted against each other, have a way of testing all of the players. The young woman in my example just cited, for instance, may discover that her former boyfriend is more interested than her current boyfriend. In short, the boundaries between the relationships within a network create an arena for indirect tests and informal social experiments that all parties can use to evaluate each other's feelings and intentions. Calling them "secret tests" may be something of a misnomer; however, because I suspect that the participants are usually much more aware than they let on. As I noted in chapter 3, network members may sometimes be active collaborators in these tests.

Participation in Boundary Rituals

A final, often underappreciated, way in which relational participants manage boundaries and the demands of multiple relationships is through social rituals. Celebrations and rituals not only provide mechanisms for working through conflicting obligations and expectations, but also contribute directly to relational development by highlighting the relationship in general and special events in its history in particular (Werner, Altman, Brown, & Ginat, 1993).

Wolin and Bennett (1984) identified three types of family rituals: (a) *celebrations*, such as Christmas or *Cinco de Mayo*, that are shared widely within a culture, (b) *family traditions* that are not prescribed by the larger society but may occur as part of a cultural celebration (e.g., traditions regarding how a holiday or birthday is to be spent), and (c) *patterned routines* that are recurrent, but smaller scale activities such as particular interaction patterns among friends or family members (e.g., "You can depend on Uncle Frank to flirt with each of the wives at family gatherings"). Although much of the research on rituals in close relationships has focused on families, it can be usefully applied to other interpersonal relationships such as friendships, childless couples, and work groups.

Rituals provide readymade roles and scripts that honor, yet contain, potentially difficult interactions with and among network members. Weddings are perhaps the prime example. Factions and individuals who are likely to be disruptive can be assigned tasks and roles that include and honor them, yet limit their ability to stir up mischief. The scripted character of weddings, for example, allows the divorced parents of the bride or groom to get through an otherwise awkward event. The divorced parents can each be given a clearly defined set of activities that will minimize interaction between them, yet give each a more or less equal role to play. One writer referred to this characteristic of rituals as "socially controlled civility" (C. L. Johnson, 1988).

Stepfamilies often develop traditions and rituals to regulate the tensions that arise as the newly created family tries to organize itself and avoid disruptive alliances (Lofas, 1998). The creation of traditions and rituals unique to the group may be particularly useful when larger societal models are lacking. Research on the polygamous families of Utah, for example, points to how family traditions are used to manage events that might otherwise produce conflict, such as the birthday of each wife, or gift giving between children of different wives (Werner et al., 1993).

Rituals also provide tools for managing the conventionality–uniqueness dialectic—that is, the tension between wanting the relationship to fit in, to be socially acceptable, on one hand, and to be socially distinctive on the other. Couples may, for example, develop a distinctive contribution to extended family gatherings—as in the case of the couple that can be depended upon to bring a certain food to family events. Relational partners may celebrate an unusual holiday or celebrate a common holiday in an unusual way. In all of these examples, relational partners are using rituals in ways that honor their social commitments to network members, while simultaneously distinguishing and reinforcing a separate relational identity.

Competing demands from network members can often be handled within the frameworks afforded by rituals. Married couples, for instance, may decide to alternate which holidays they spend with their families—Christmas day with his and New Years with hers this year, Christmas day with hers and New Years with his next year. Ritual holidays are easily counted, but are also both memorable and bounded. This combination of qualities makes rituals valuable tools for meeting the conflicting expectations of network members.

Ritual holidays offer another benefit to network members. They allow network members to remain in contact and express generalized support for relational participants without necessarily endorsing the specific features of their relationship. Family members who are uncomfortable with a gay or lesbian couple in their midst may nonetheless be comfortable participating in holidays with the couple. Holiday rituals provide scripts for comfortable interactions in uncomfortable circumstances. (When they go wrong, of course, the resulting conflict can be severe because there are few other social buffers to ensure civility.)

Finally, ritualized gatherings of network members extend the range of potential supporters and implicitly reinforce their readiness to support relational participants. This benefit can be seen most readily in gatherings that include a broad range of network members. By participating in neighborhood celebrations and traditions, for example, people not only maintain contact with those with whom they have relatively weaker relationships, but also create a reservoir of potential help that is more easily drawn upon when the need arises (Werner et al., 1993).

Thus, rituals act as vehicles for managing the conflicting tensions that are often found at the boundaries between relationships. Along with other information management strategies such as disclosure and avoidance, selectivity, equivocation, and testing, rituals are tools for handling the often complex tasks that come with managing relationships among relationships.

MANAGING PROBLEMATIC RELATIONSHIPS IN NETWORKS

The fabric of social life is rarely woven smoothly. Although we may desire social networks in which everyone feels positively toward one another, most of our social circles contain both people we like and people we dislike. Disliked parties may not be easily avoided or dropped. They may be the close friends of our close friends. They may be part of the family or they may be related to close friends. The challenges posed by the disliked associates of liked persons go beyond the management of information. The information management strategies described in the previous section certainly apply, but it is likely that additional, more general strategies must be utilized as well.

Unfortunately, two biases in the literature on personal relationships have limited our understanding of how people manage networks containing mixes of liked and disliked individuals. The first is the now familiar tendency to focus on individual and dyadic factors to the exclusion of network factors.

This is important because it is only at the network level that the complexities of relational ecology become visible. The second is the widespread tendency to focus on positive social relationships to the exclusion of negative ones. Thus we have more studies of liking than disliking, more studies of friends than of enemies. Although this bias has been noted for some time (e.g., Parks, 1982), there is still almost no research on how people cope with the disliked associates of liked persons. Negative relational states have been given greater attention in the last decade (e.g., Arriaga & Oskamp, 1999; Cupach & Spitzberg, 1994; Spitzberg & Cupach, 1998), but again, most of that attention has focused on single relationships rather than on the challenges of multiple relationships within a network.

Traditional principles of balance and transitivity in interpersonal relations imply that disliking the close friend of a close friend should be a relatively uncommon state of affairs. Transitivity in liking should be the norm: If A likes B and B likes C, then A will like or will come to like C (e.g., Hallinan, 1974; Heider, 1946; Newcomb, 1953). When an imbalance occurs, the discomfort and dissonance it produces should motivate members to restore balance either by liking the disliked person more or by liking the liked person less. However, there are a number of difficulties with this explanation. Foremost is our very human capacity to ignore inconsistencies in our thoughts and actions. Even when people gravitate toward balanced relationships over time, there may be considerable imbalance across the network at any one point in time. Moreover, balance is not the only consideration in a network of relationships. Some imbalanced relationships may be quite acceptable if they fit into a larger set of associations or a more general situation that the individual finds pleasant (Jordan, 1953). Imbalanced relationships may act as stabilizers and bridges that mediate conflict among the various individuals and groups with whom a person is forced to deal (Granovetter, 1979).

Prevalence of Imbalanced Relationships

Because most of the research on relational balance and transitivity has been conducted in highly structured laboratory settings, the first question to ask is simply how often people actually experience significant imbalances in their personal networks. More particularly, how often do people have close friends who have close friends that the first person dislikes? To address this question, my student, Lisa Riveland, and I conducted a survey of 137 high school and university students. Slightly over half (55%) were female. They ranged in age from 13 to 30, but most were between the ages of 14 and 19 ($M = 16.84$, $SD = 2.57$).

We began by asking study participants to list up to 10 close friends. We then asked them to consider the close friends of their close friends. Among the 137 participants, 82% reported that they did indeed have at least one close friend who had a close friend who was "moderately or strongly" disliked by the subject. That is, fewer than one in five persons had the sort of fully positive friendship networks envisioned by the traditional transitivity assumption. Disliked friends of friends were also common within the average person's network. Among the close friends listed, nearly 30% were identified as having close friends that the subject disliked.

It is often not possible to avoid the disliked friends of friends. When we asked our subjects to report on the person they disliked the most, for example, they reported that they had known the disliked individual for nearly 3 years and had communicated with him or her an average of three times in the preceding 2 weeks. The prevalence of disliked parties in the friendship network or the level of contact with them did not differ by sex or age.

Strategies for Managing the Disliked Friends of Friends

It therefore appears common for us to have close friends who are closely linked to people we dislike. So how do people manage interactions with the disliked parties when avoidance is impossible? Traditional balance theories offer just two options: One can reduce liking and contact with the close friend, or one can increase liking and contact with the disliked party. Both options presume that individuals make cognitive or communicative adjustments aimed at resolving the imbalance.

We wanted to see how these options were enacted, but we also wanted to determine what else people might do if their goal was to cope with the imbalance rather than to change it. Riveland and I began by combing the traditional literature for specific strategies used to resolve imbalanced interpersonal situations (e.g., Heider, 1946; Horowitz, Lyons, & Perlmutter, 1951; Newcomb, 1953). We then conducted a series of preliminary interviews in which adolescents and young adults were asked to comment on our initial list of strategies and to suggest alternatives that they had used or observed. Over a number of iterations, the list of strategy choices was winnowed to a final set of 33 described in Table 8.2. Participants in the primary study were then asked to rate how often they had used each of the various strategies in dealing with the person they disliked the most among their close friends' friends. Responses were recorded on 5-point scales anchored by the phrases "never" and "very often."

The frequency with which each of these strategies was actually used for managing imbalanced friendship networks is displayed in Table 8.2. Two larger patterns are worth noting in the findings. First, people generally did little to alter the relational imbalances. Only five of the 33 strategies were scored above the midpoint of the scale measuring usage—suggesting that the remaining strategies were used infrequently. It might be that there are wide variations in preference for strategies. If so, those who never use a given strategy would lower the average. But if this were true, we would expect to see larger

TABLE 8.2
Strategies for Managing Disliked Friends of Friends

Strategy Description	Frequency of Use (1-5)	
	Mean	SD
I am polite to the disliked person (DP).	4.05	1.22
I try not to think about my feelings for the disliked person.	3.45	1.24
I am annoyed when I must spend time with the disliked person.	3.28	1.38
I hint to my close friend (CF) about my dislike for the disliked person.	3.03	1.44
I tell my close friend about the disliked characteristics of DP.	3.01	1.42
I respond positively to my CF's talk about time spent with DP.	2.98	1.37
I try to see some good qualities in the disliked person (DP)	2.94	1.25
I tell my CF I would rather not spend time with the DP.	2.84	1.55
My close friend and I talk openly about my feelings for DP.	2.79	1.42
I tell others about disliked qualities of the DP.	2.75	1.43
When I am with the disliked person, I ignore him/her.	2.73	1.39
I ask myself what my close friend sees in the disliked person.	2.69	1.35
I am supportive of my close friend's relationship with DP.	2.69	1.21
I think my CF is blind to the disliked person's true qualities.	2.69	1.39
I think that the relationship between CF and DP won't last.	2.66	1.24
When I go out with my CF, I ask that the DP not be invited.	2.48	1.48
I welcome the chance to know the disliked person (DP) better.	2.46	1.20
I see that my CF has some qualities that I dislike in DP.	2.41	1.21
I feel less close to my CF since the DP has been around.	2.28	1.42
I ask my close friend (CF) what he or she sees in the DP.	2.23	1.33
I am only nice to the DP when my close friend is around.	2.17	1.21
The disliked person and I often argue when we are together.	2.17	1.46
I tell my close friend that the DP is a bad influence.	2.13	1.45
I am unfriendly to the disliked person.	2.10	1.34
If my close friend asks, I avoid telling my feelings for DP.	2.05	1.15
If my close friend asks, I say I like the disliked person.	1.94	1.20
I avoid going to the same social event as the disliked person.	1.83	1.24
I ask others for advice about my situation.	1.80	1.18
My close friend and I argue about my feelings for the DP	1.72	1.02
I tell the disliked person what I dislike about her/him	1.67	1.21
I ask the disliked person why we don't get along	1.28	0.77
I ask another friend to tell my close friend about my feelings for the disliked person.	1.28	0.85
I ask my close friend to make a choice between the disliked person and me.	1.26	0.87

variances in the ratings themselves. It seems more likely that people simply do little or use few strategies in response to disliked friends of friends.

Cognitive strategies were used somewhat more often than behavioral strategies. The three most frequently used strategies, for example, imply cognitive and emotional coping (trying not to think about the disliked person, feeling annoyed) or at least behavioral acceptance of the situation (i.e., being polite to the disliked person). Some of these may alter the imbalance in time—such as looking for good qualities in the disliked person or feeling less close to the close friend. However, the preferred cognitive strategies as a group are aimed at tolerating rather than changing the interpersonal situation. Thus, people try to ignore or not think about the disliked person or they hope that the relationship between their friend and the disliked person will not last.

Finally, positive or "prosocial" strategies were clearly favored over negative or confrontational strategies. The two most common strategies, being polite and trying not to think about feelings for the disliked person, are certainly nonconfrontational. The next most common response, being annoyed at having to spend time with the disliked person, is negative, but is cognitive rather than behavioral. It is also less confrontational than overt efforts to avoid the other person. After this, the next most frequently used responses involved hinting to or directly telling the close friend what is disliked about the other person. These are certainly more direct strategies, but again they are comparatively less negative and confrontational than many less frequently used alternatives such as asking the close friend to justify the relationship or choose between the two parties. These findings are consistent with the literature on interpersonal influence and impression management, which generally documents a preference for positive strategies that avoid negative emotional states and confrontation (e.g., Boucher & Osgood, 1969; G. R. Miller, Boster, Roloff, & Seibold, 1977). When it comes to managing the disliked friends of friends, then, it appears that most people opt to cope with the existing relational configuration rather than to pursue "interventionist" strategies designed to make significant alterations in their networks.

Correlates of Strategy Use

The final question was whether there were any individual or situational differences that might account for variations in how people dealt with the disliked friends of friends. Specifically, we asked whether strategy choices depended on the subject's sex, the amount of interaction, or the degree of liking (or disliking) among the parties.

Significant sex differences were found in the use of 12 of the 33 strategies. Overall, males were considerably more open, direct, and confrontational than females in the way they responded to disliked friends of friends. They were more likely to tell or at least hint to the close friend what they disliked about the other person. They were more likely to tell the close friend that the other was a bad influence and to complain about the disliked person to others in the network. They were more likely to argue, to be unfriendly, and to tell the disliked person what they disliked. Females, on the other hand, were more likely to rely on politeness strategies, to hide their true feelings from the close friend, and to try to be supportive of the close friend's relationship with the disliked person. Almost all the sex differences in strategy use, however, occurred at low frequencies. The largest difference, for example, involved arguing with the disliked person. Males ($M = 3.02$, $SD = 1.60$) did this significantly more often than females ($M = 1.54$, $SD = .95$), but the frequency for males was barely above the midpoint of the scale ($p < .0001$). Thus all of the sex differences involved males occasionally using strategies that females used quite rarely.

To determine if strategies for managing disliked friends of friends were affected by the amount of contact the parties had, we asked subjects to rate how frequently the relevant parties had communicated in the last 2 weeks. It turned out, however, that the frequency of communication between the subject and his or her close friend was completely unrelated to strategy choices. The frequency of communication between the subject and the disliked person was a stronger correlate of strategy choice, but was only significantly related to the use of 4 of the 33 strategies. Those who communicated more often with the disliked person were less likely to ignore the disliked person, less likely to withhold their feelings regarding the disliked person from their close friend, more interested in getting to know the disliked person, and more likely to ask other network members for advice on dealing with the situation.

The subject's estimate, accurate or inaccurate, of how often the close friend communicated with the disliked person was a more potent predictor of strategy use. When the friend and the disliked person were thought to communicate regularly, subjects were less likely to reveal their negative feelings to their friend. Although subjects as a group preferred positive strategies, this tendency was more pronounced when the friend and the disliked person were perceived to interact frequently. Subjects in these cases were less likely to avoid or confront the disliked person and more likely to be polite, try to see his or her good qualities, and to try to get to know him or her better.

A similar pattern emerged when we considered how much people making up the friendship triangles liked or disliked each other. Participants' attraction to their close friends and to the disliked person was assessed using Rubin's (1970) liking scale; their estimate of the attraction between their friend and the disliked person was assessed with four items, focusing on how close these two people were and how much they liked each other. Generally speaking, people tended to act more benevolently toward the disliked person when that person was the friend of a very close friend rather than the friend of a less close friend. Attraction to close friend was significantly related to the use of 10 of the 33 strategies. The strongest of these associations suggested that subjects who liked their friend more were more polite to the disliked person, less annoyed at having to spend time with him or her, and less likely to ask third parties to convey their complaints back to their close friend.

Friends of friends can obviously be disliked in varying degrees. Subjects who strongly disliked their friend's friend tended to prefer different strategies than those who only moderately disliked the friend's friend. The degree of disliking was associated with preferences for 22 of the 33 strategies. Those who strongly disliked their friend's friend were less supportive and more likely to confront their close friend. They were more likely to bring up the disliked person with the close friend, to tell him or her that the other person was a bad influence, and to ask the friend to justify his or her relationship with the disliked person. As one would expect, friends of friends who were more intensely disliked received poorer treatment. Subjects were less polite, less friendly, less interested in, and more likely to avoid or ignore the more intensely disliked person.

Finally, the strategy choices were mediated by the extent to which one's friend liked the disliked person. Perceived attraction in this relationship was associated with 22 of the 33 strategies. Subjects who thought, rightly or wrongly, that their friends were strongly attracted to the disliked person were generally more likely to avoid discussion of the disliked person, but also more likely to respond supportively and positively when the topic was raised. They made a greater effort to get to know the disliked person, but they also reported feeling less close to their friend.

In summary, it is clear that network members carefully calibrate their reactions to their friends and to their friends' friends. Although most of the strategies they use suggest that they accept or at least tolerate imbalances, it is also clear that strategy choices are influenced by relatively stable factors like sex as well as factors that are in more or less constant flux, such as contact and liking among network members.

INFORMATION AND NETWORK MANAGEMENT IN PERSPECTIVE

Most efforts to understand social networks have followed a structuralist tradition in which individuals and individual relationships are viewed as products of larger social forces and structures (see chap. 2, this volume). Yet as I have demonstrated in this chapter, individuals approach their networks actively, even strategically. They are not simply influenced by others or controlled by social structure. They are influenced, of course, but they also actively manage information and relationships within their networks. Throughout the chapter, I have talked about "managing" information and networks, but the process is so varied that many other terms could be equally descriptive. People arrange, create, conduct, contrive, plan, and plot. They accomplish, they adapt. They tolerate, cope, endure, and survive their networks. It is in this give and take among network members that social identities, relationships, and social structures are forged.

Sometimes it is possible to express a rule that seems to summarize what people are trying to do as they manage relationships among relationships. Indeed everyday discourse among network members is filled with relational rules and expectations (Baxter et al., 2001). Such discourse socializes relational novices, offers a forum in which participants can judge one another, and can provide tools that help people cope with difficult or turbulent relationships (e.g., stepfamilies).

Yet relational rules only hint at the strategies people utilize as they manage complex, inherently contradictory interpersonal situations. The ecology of networks involves multiple participants linked in multiple ways and having multiple goals. No rule or set of rules is likely to capture the ongoing problem solving that is demanded. Instead, we can articulate the basic dimensions of the problems to be solved—particularly the dialectic tensions between integration and separation, stability and change, and expression and privacy.

We can also identify several of the most common strategies for managing information in a complex relational field. Six of these general strategies were discussed in this chapter: (a) granting access and making disclosures, (b) withdrawing and withholding, (c) selective access and disclosure, (d) equivocation, (e) relational tests, and (f) participating in boundary rituals. These strategies can be put to a variety of purposes, as we have seen, but among the most central are to obtain information from network members that helps relational participants feel supported and make sense of their relationship.

Using these strategies does not guarantee smooth sailing in the network. It is common, indeed the norm, for networks to contain disliked people. Moreover, the disliked people are seen frequently and cannot be easily dropped, given that they have often have close relationships with other network members in whose good graces we wish to remain. It was surprising, given traditional theories about social transitivity and psychological balance, to see just how tolerant most people were of these negative relationships. They generally behaved in ways that conveyed acceptance. Even when they tried to influence others to change their opinions of the disliked person, they opted for more positive, less confrontational strategies. Their coping strategies in most cases were cognitive rather than behavioral—that is, they sought to change their own views of the disliked person rather than avoiding him or her and rather than trying to change other's views of the disliked person. These findings do not imply that people are passive, but instead illustrate that people take relatively complex social calculations into account when figuring out how to respond to network members.

Knowing how people cope with the disliked friends of friends may give us an added glimpse into what network members may be thinking about us as relational participants. Those who dislike us will generally avoid confrontation except in the most serious circumstances. They generally try to tolerate us. As a result, we are likely to overestimate how much network members support our relationship or like us personally. This might account for the relatively high levels of approval perceived by relational participants (see chaps. 4 & 5, this volume). More important, it may be precisely this level of overestimation and tolerance that allows groups of people who do not all like one another to maintain relatively harmonious relationships over time.

Our understanding of how people manage information and relationships is still limited in many ways. The strategies discussed in this chapter undoubtedly represent only a partial listing and we know relatively little about the basic dimensions along which strategies might vary. Perhaps the most obvious limitation, however, is that we still know very little about how a given relationship changes over time and how these changes might be linked to changes in the broader social networks of the participants. These issues are addressed in chapter 9.

CHAPTER NINE

Following Personal Relationships to Their End and Beyond

It seems that nearly everyone has a theory about why personal relationships succeed or fail. Lay observers often focus on the personal flaws of individuals, mismatches of personalities, or "incompatibility" as reasons why relationships end. Social scientific theory is naturally expected to go beyond everyday observation and, in many cases, it does. But in other cases, academic theorizing adds little to what is already obvious to the everyday observer. Take, for example, the research on marital satisfaction, perhaps the most widely studied predictor of divorce (Gottman & Levenson, 2000; Karney & Bradbury, 1995). Discovering that people who are unhappy with their marriage are more likely to get divorced does not deepen our understanding to any great extent. Measures such as satisfaction and commitment are certainly useful, but they pose deeper questions about what causes people to become unhappy or less committed and about how relationships deteriorate over time. They leave us to search for more subtle or distal predictors that might be more informative. My goal in this chapter, as elsewhere in the book, is to suggest that some of those more subtle or underappreciated factors may be found in the social networks that surround relationships.

Before exploring the role of social network factors in the deterioration of personal relationships, we should note several additional limitations of the previous literature. First, most of what we know about how personal relationships come apart is based on participants' memories of past relationships or on cross-sectional studies in which troubled or terminated relationships are compared to more satisfied, intact relationships. Longitudinal studies, in which relationships are followed over time, are less common. Nonetheless, longitudinal studies will be given special weight in this chapter because they allow for sustained observation and hence offer a better opportunity to understand the actual process of relational change.

Another shortcoming is that nearly everything we know about changes in personal relationships over time comes from studies of heterosexual romantic relationships. There are relatively few longitudinal studies of gay and lesbian relationships (for a notable exception, see Kurdek, 1998, 2000). There is almost no research that tracks changes in friendships or business relationships over time (for exceptions, see Burt, 2000; Gibbons & Olk, 2003; Salzinger, 1982). We cannot assume that the same factors that cause romantic relationships to deteriorate are also responsible for the deterioration of other types of personal relationships or, if they are, that they function in the same way across different types of relationships.

In spite of these shortcomings, previous research has identified a wide range of factors that may cause relationships to end. Some are relatively straightforward. Among the very elderly, for example, close friendships are often lost simply because one person has become too ill, too needy, or has passed away (Wenger & Jerrome, 1999). Research on divorce has identified two general classes of factors. One set of factors involves the broad social and economic conditions that affect marital stability. Studies in this line generally show that divorce is more common among groups with less income, less education, more children, unfair divisions of family labor, and a lower social standing within the community. Another set of factors involves the spouses' personalities, relational histories, and attitudes toward marriage as well as they way they manage critical types of interaction, particularly those involving intimacy and conflict. Studies in this line indicate that people are more likely to divorce when they are dissatisfied with their partners, do not feel that their needs are being met, express more negative than positive feelings to their partners, regret having married, have insecure or avoidant attachment styles, and conduct conflict in harmful ways (for reviews, see Gottman, 1994; Karney & Bradbury, 1995; Lowenstein, 2005; Orbuch, Veroff, Hassan, & Horrocks, 2002).

Missing from this picture is a thoughtful analysis of the role of social context in the fate of relationships. Although there is a good deal of research on social factors like race, income, and education, these are usually conceived in fixed, opaque terms rather than in terms of the process by which they might directly influence a given relationship. Most researchers have simply ignored the social context in which personal relationships are embedded. In their review of 115 studies longitudinal studies of marital quality and stability conducted since 1938, for example, Karney and Bradbury (1995) did not find a single study that appeared to include any extensive analysis of social network factors. Nor did they call for additional studies on social network influences in their recommendations for future research. The situation has not changed greatly in the decade following their review. When social contextual factors are considered at all, the focus is usually restricted to assessments of whether network members put pressure on relational participants or whether the participants believe they have viable alternatives to the present relationship (e.g., Impett, Beals, & Peplau, 2002; Kurdek, 1998). Thus, only a few studies have actively followed personal relationships over time to determine what processes might be involved in relationship survival. Of these, only a tiny handful have looked beyond the relationship's interior to consider what social network factors might be at work when relationships end. Yet the findings from these few studies point in tantalizing directions and provide the foundation for this chapter. I begin by outlining the broader aspects of what these findings imply and then turn to a closer examination of the role of particular network factors in relational deterioration.

RELATIONAL TERMINATION IN EVERYDAY LIFE

Most Relationships End

Most personal relationships are fleeting. This fact is usually obscured by our tendency to focus only on the most stable, highly developed personal relationships. Nonetheless, very few personal relationships ever reach high levels of development. We take comparatively little notice of the continual turnover in our less developed relationships with acquaintances, causal friends, co-workers, neighbors, salespeople, church members, club members, and so on. In one study, college students reported that they had stayed in touch with only a little more than half (54%) of those whom they had described as contacts just 6 months earlier (Feld, 1997). In general, the less highly developed a relationship is, the more likely it is to dissolve over a given period of time (Burt, 2000). Some less developed relationships are surely lasting, but most are temporary arrangements that do not survive changes in jobs, schools, residences, work assignments, personal interests, or patterns of shopping and commuting.

More highly developed personal relationships also demonstrate high rates of instability. This appears to be the case across every type of relationship that has been examined to date. Burt (2000), for instance, found that 92% of the close business associates of a group of people working in the financial industry were no longer identified as close associates 3 years later. Almost half (46%) of the people that recent widows identified as having a significant emotional impact on their lives were not named again a year later (Morgan, Neal, & Carder, 1997). When Suitor and Keeton (1997) examined who was important to adult women returning to college, they found that one third of those named as important sources of emotional support were not named again a year later and almost two thirds of those with whom the women had regularly socialized were not named again a year later. After 10 years, the attrition rate had risen to approximately 80% for emotional supporters and social contacts. In another study, in which people had been asked to name intimate ties in their community, 73% of those initially named were not named again in a follow-up 10 years later (Wellman, Wong, Tindall, & Nazer, 1997).

The fragile state of personal relationships is particularly apparent when we examine romantic relationships. Although the picture must be pieced together, most romantic relationships appear to end, and the less developed they are, the more likely they are to terminate. In one study, approximately 65% of couples who had just started dating ended their relationship within 4 months (Berg & McQuinn, 1986). Put another way, the termination rate averaged just over 16% per month during the first 4 months. The average termination rate falls to 3% to 6% per month for couples who have been dating between 1 and 2 years (see Agnew et al., 2001; J. Fitzpatrick & Sollie, 1999). Half of the couples who had broken up in one study had done so within the first 16 months (Hill, Rubin, & Peplau, 1976). Even successful dating relationships rarely continue unchanged for long periods of time. Only 13% of the couples who had been dating when Sprecher and Felmlee (2000) began their study were still dating 5 years later. The remaining couples had either broken up (59%) or were married or cohabitating (28%). It has been estimated that approximately 40% of couples who cohabitate break up without marrying (Amato, 1999). Although only about 5% of all first marriages ended in divorce in the United States when divorce statistics first became reliable in the 1870s, approximately 60% of first marriages in the United States now end in divorce or permanent separation and about one third do so within the first 5 years (Bumpass, 1990; Preston & McDonald, 1979). The divorce rate for second marriages is even higher than that for first marriages and it appears that nearly 20% of adults will experience two or more divorces (Cherlin, 1992).

Or Do They?

When we look closely at the ends of relationships, however, the picture becomes considerably more complicated (and interesting). In a strict sense a relationship ends only when the partners no longer have any contact and no longer influence one another in any way. Yet many breakups, terminations, and divorces fail to pass this test. In some cases, it is simply a matter of perspective. Dating partners, for example, typically have quite different views of what happens when their relationship "breaks up." They often disagree about how long the breakup had been coming, about when it started, who started it, and, most importantly, even about whether the relationship has truly ended (Berg & McQuinn, 1986; Hill et al., 1976).

Even when the participants agree that their relationship is over, they may continue to interact, to influence each other, and to engage each other both cognitively and emotionally. They clearly still have a relationship. These endings are not endings at all, but rather transformations of the relationship. One need not look far to find examples of such transformations. In one study of divorced couples, for instance, approximately 28% of the ex-spouses agreed that they were currently on friendly or sometimes friendly terms, another 25%

agreed that their current relationship was currently distant or unfriendly. Only 27% agreed that they had no current relationship (Ambert, 1989). The remaining 20% had differing views of their postmarital relationships, although in most cases, the difference in perspective was small. In short, the majority of these couples continued to have a relationship of some sort even after their divorce. It may have been friendly or unfriendly, but it was a relationship nonetheless. As I observed in an earlier chapter, we should not assume that hostile relationships are any less developed than more positive relationships. Indeed former spouses locked in conflict may be highly interdependent, engage in conflicts with remarkable levels of breadth and depth, and be committed to causing each other as much misery as possible.

Efforts by one party to end a relationship may only intensify the other's attempts to pursue it. Sometimes the first party is merely testing the other's commitment (see chap. 8, this volume). More often, however, the pursuit is genuinely unwelcome. According to at least one study, pursuit incidents are common and, disturbingly, more common in romantic relationships with a history of violence (Langhinrichsen-Rohling, Palarea, Cohen, & Rohling, 2000).

Not all "nonendings" have such a dark side. Dating relationships or marriages may transform themselves in friendships. Close working relationships may attenuate once a project is completed, but be maintained at a lower level of development. Those who were once "best friends" may remain good friends as their lives continue to unfold. These examples point to a bias in the way we view transformations from one type of relationship to another. When an acquaintance or work relationship blossoms into friendship or romance, we generally view the change as growth or development rather than as the end of one type of relationship and the beginning of another. On the other hand, when a romantic relationship changes into a friendship or postmarital parenting relationship, we usually say that something ended and something else began.

Sometimes the relationship is not really over when it is over. This admittedly nonsensical statement begins to make some sense when we step into a network perspective that includes indirect as well as direct contacts. Long after former partners discontinue direct contact with one another, there may be residual interdependence mediated by third parties. Children may act as information relays for divorced parents who no longer speak to one another. Former dating partners may quiz mutual friends about one another's new love lives. Former friends and work associates may "keep tabs" on each other through network members. In each of these instances, former relational partners continue to exert influence on each other, perhaps unwittingly, even though they no longer have direct contact. Thus, although most relationships end, many events that we label as *endings* are actually transformations rather than terminations, and even after contact ends, former relational partners are often still indirectly linked through their social network.

NETWORKS AT THE END OF RELATIONSHIPS AND BEYOND

The implications of a network perspective for understanding how relationships deteriorate are so varied that it is useful to focus on the role of specific network characteristics. The six characteristics described in chapter 2 provide a starting point. These are network distance, overlap, cross-network contact, cross-network density, attraction to members of the partner's network, and support for the relationship from network members. Changes in each of these network factors, I argue, help account for why some personal relationships deteriorate and for how people move from one personal relationship to another.

Network Distance and Relational Deterioration

Network distance refers to the number of people necessary to link two people in a network. The study of network distances has broad application (for overview, see Watts, 2003), but two types of network distances are particularly relevant if we are trying to understand relational endings and their aftermath. These are the distance from alternative partners and, following termination, the distance from the ex-partner.

Before exploring these characteristics, however, it is helpful to think about how the overall structure of networks changes over time. The findings presented thus far, as well as others' findings, provide ample evidence that the relational choices individuals make at one point in time influence their later relational choices (Carley, 1999; Carley & Krackhardt, 1996; Gibbons & Olk, 2003). Thus the implications of ending any one relationship depend on when that change occurs within a larger set of changes in the network. The effect of a divorce on friendship networks, for example, may differ depending on when it occurs in the course of the marriage. Generally speaking, the number of close friends steadily declines from dating to marriage, with the arrival of children, as the children grow, and after the children leave home (Kalmijn, 2003). Thus, whether divorced people have more or fewer friends than when they were married depends in part on what stage the marriage was in. Women and men also appear to differ. Women may experience a dramatic loss of network members after the divorce and then rebuild over time. Men, on the other hand, are more likely to experience longer term losses (Terhell, Broese van Groenou, & Van Tilburg, 2004).

Distance From Alternative Partners. Relational commitment depends in part on the belief that one's current partner is the best available partner. This belief is facilitated by cognitive processes that lead people to devalue the attractiveness of alternative partners as a way to enhance commitment to the current partner (D. J. Johnson & Rusbult, 1989). But this cognitive strategy only appears to work for people who are already highly committed to their relationship. When people are less committed, the availability of alternative partners becomes a more powerful factor. That is, when the distance from an alternative partner shrinks, the relationship becomes less stable. Thus, couples who have been dating nonexclusively are significantly more likely to terminate their relationship than couples who are dating exclusively (Hill et al., 1976). People who believe that the opportunities for remarriage are better are more likely to divorce than those who believe that their chances for remarriage are not so good (Udry, 1981).

In some cases, contact with the alternative partner begins while the original relationship is still in place, while in other cases, it begins once the relationship encounters difficulty. In her survey of divorced couples who had remarried Ambert (1989) found that 11% of the new relationships had started while the original couple was still living together. That is, the new marriage started as an extramarital affair during the first marriage. In another 34% of the cases, the new relationship had started while the original couple was separated but the divorce was not yet final. Although these figures suggest that the new partner was frequently a part of the couple's social network before their marriage ended, they probably underestimate the distance between the spouse and his or her new partner. After all, one need not have started dating the future partner in order for him or her to already be a part of the network.

The observation that decreasing distance from an alternative partner is linked to the demise of current relationships and the creation of new ones brings us full circle back to the social proximity hypothesis advanced in chapter 3. There I argued that the probability of any two people meeting increased as the number of links separating them in the network decreased. Evidence of social proximity effects came from our studies in which two thirds of dating partners and friends claimed that at least one member of their network had known the future partner before they themselves had met that person for the first time. Findings indicating that nearly half of married and cohabiting couples had friends in common before they met are also consistent with the social proximity hypothesis (Kalmijn & Flap, 2001). If we think of these new relationships as replacements for previous ones, it becomes clear that the new partner was on a shortening path toward the individual even when the individual may still have been involved in another relationship.

Friends appear to play a particularly important role in linking individuals to new partners. Married couples are far more likely to have known each other's friends prior to meeting than they were to have known members of each other's families (Kalmijn & Flap, 2001). After divorce, friends are more likely than family members to assist people in meeting new partners (Spanier & Thompson, 1984). It takes some time following the divorce, however, before the friendship network is sufficiently rebuilt to perform this linking role. Although some gain friends immediately following divorce, the majority sustain losses that are only slowly, if ever, replaced (Terhell et al., 2004). Based on their longitudinal study of divorced mothers, for example, Albeck and Kaydar (2002) concluded that it may take up to 4 years for women to reorganize their friendship networks following divorce. The primary transition is the addition of single friends, both female and male, to what had previously been a network dominated by couples. As the network is restructured and rebuilt, the distance between the divorced person and potential new romantic partners is greatly reduced and the chance for a new relationship increases.

   Distance From the Former Partner.   Although we commonly think of divorcing couples making a "clean break" from one another, family scholars are coming to appreciate that long-term marriages, like other types of long-term relationships, merge human and material capital in ways that are not easily divided when the relationship ends (R. A. Thompson & Wyatt, 1999). This is particularly true when children are involved, as Ambert (1989) found when she tracked approximately 50 couples for several years after they had separated or divorced. Between 40% and 50% reported seeing their ex-spouse in person once a month or more when children were involved. However, less than 6% of the ex-spouses who had not had children together saw each other once a month or more, while 88% said they saw each other less than once a year or never. Former partners may judge the distance separating them in either positively or negatively, but they rarely judge it in neutral terms. Divorced parents, for instance, may want either more or less contact with each other. Usually the issue revolves around the level of contact a noncustodial father has with his children. Nearly one third of divorced fathers surveyed in one study, for example, had seen their children only once or not at all during the previous year (Seltzer, 1991).

   Individuals sometimes use relationships with members of a former partner's network as a way to monitor the activities of the former partner. This has a dark side, as I have already noted. But even when they do not seek to restart the old relationship, former partners may still wish to know how the other is doing. As the former partner moves further away in network distance, they may attempt to find individuals who are familiar with the former partner's activities. Former partners may also take advantage of the Internet to locate and check up on each other (for a first-person account, see Pollitt, 2004). When part of one's identity exists on the Internet, the network distance between the individual and any former friend, business associate, or romantic partner is effectively brought to zero.

Network Overlap, Cross-Network Contact, and Relational Deterioration

Reductions in the partners' shared network are both cause and consequence of relational deterioration. Networks may be shared in several different ways and we would expect all of them to be related to the fate of relationships. One is network overlap—the number or proportion of network members that the relational participants name in common. Another is cross-network contact or communication—the number of people each person knows in the partner's network and how often he or she communicates with them. Although these are two rather different measures (see chap. 2, this volume), researchers typically combine elements of both into a more general assessment that is described in broad terms as *network sharing, embeddedness,* or *interdependence.*

Relationships in which the participants share a common network should, all things considered, be more stable than relationships in which the participants are not so embedded in a common network. Researchers in one study, for example, found that premarital couples whose friendship networks contained a greater proportion of people with whom they both interacted also tended to be more committed to their relationship, more satisfied, more invested, to feel closer, to say that alternative relationships would not fulfill their intimacy needs as well, and to still be together 6 to 7 months later (Agnew et al., 2001). Other studies have also shown that dating couples with more overlapping networks and with more frequent communication with members of the partner's network are less likely to break up (Milardo, 1982; Parks & Adelman, 1983). In a study that tracked 347 couples during the first 2 years of marriage, Kearns and Leonard (2004) found that couples with higher levels of network overlap and cross-network communication were more satisfied, better adjusted, and more intimate. The strength of the association between marital quality and network sharing increased over the first year of marriage and remained strong at the end of the second year of marriage. Results from several other studies also support the linkage between network overlap and marital satisfaction and stability (e.g., Cotton, Cunningham, & Antill, 1993; Hansen, Fallon, & Novotny, 1991). Finally, although we know less about the stability of relationships in the workplace, it appears that people will be less likely to end work relationships or leave their jobs when their networks are more highly linked and when they are connected with a larger number of people in the organization (Burt, 2000; Feeley, 2000).

It follows from these findings that relationships should deteriorate when participants' networks begin to diverge. Put simply, when the shared network begins to tear apart, so too does the relationship. But why? One reason is that relational sense-making is disrupted and uncertainty becomes more difficult to manage. When relational participants have contact with those in their partner's network, they feel they know more about their relational partners and understand them better. Cross-network communication yields not only specific information about the partner, but also provides a frame of reference for interpreting the partner's actions (see chap. 2, this volume). Indeed, in one of our early studies (Parks & Adelman, 1983), we found that how often romantic couples communicated with the partner's network was a better predictor of their uncertainty about their relationship than how often the dating partners directly communicated with one another. Being part of a shared network should help reduce uncertainty in other ways as well. Among other things, it confirms that others whom you value have made the same relational choice you have. When the network begins to come apart, uncertainty about the partner and the relationship rises as these vital tools become less available and less effective.

The concept of *network structuring* also helps explain why relationships should come apart when networks come apart. When the network is highly overlapping, participants have to worry that ending the relationship will cost them not only a partner, but many friends and perhaps a broader social status as well (Kalmijn, 2003; Milardo, 1987). This barrier to dissolution no longer functions as effectively once the shared network begins to pull apart. Alternative partners and activities become more available and attractive as the shared network comes apart.

The deterioration of the relationship itself leads to still further reductions, often quite dramatic ones, in the level of network overlap and the amount of contact partners have with the members of each other's network. Over a 3-month period, for example, dating couples whose relationship deteriorated showed a marked decrease in network overlap (Milardo, 1982). Following divorce, the network of shared friends shrinks significantly, sometimes by as much as 40% for women, according to some estimates (M. Duffy, 1993; Hughes, Good, & Candell, 1993). Even when predivorce relationships are maintained, the level of contact with friends and other relatives by marriage is usually far lower than it was prior to the divorce (Albeck & Kaydar, 2002; Ambert, 1988). There is some evidence to suggest that similar reductions occur following the termination of gay and lesbian relationships as well (Lannutti & Cameron, 2002).

Thus divorce and other breakups bring changes in patterns of contact that ultimately restructure the individual's network and move him or her away from previous friendship patterns. This occurs, not only with the former partner's friends, but also with one's own friends. Some friends may draw closer following divorce, but a significant number of people (25% to 50%) report that they received less support from their friends and that their friends initiated contact with them less often following divorce (Huddleston & Hawkings, 1993; Spanier & Thompson, 1984). The divorced or soon-to-be divorced person may feel shunned by network members, as in the case of Becky, a 57-year-old women who was divorcing her husband of 32 years (Schneller & Arditti, 2004):

> Because I didn't want people talking about this behind my back, I went around to all my neighbors and I told them that I was getting a divorce. And I called all my friends and all my relatives .... I thought they would be sympathetic or at least "that's really too bad," and life would go on. But I

found that ... a lot of people just walked to the other side of the street and just turned their head away ... That was the end of a lot of friendships and relationships ... (p. 8)

Understanding the social terrain of the postrelational setting is a daunting task. The network after divorce contains ex-spouses, new spouses of ex-spouses, ex-spouses of new partners of ex-spouses, former-in laws, new in-laws of ex-spouses, and so on. Even well-intentioned people can make mistakes as they try to chart their path through these new and uncertain social categories. Our language has not yet caught up with changing postmarital relations (Ambert, 1989). Sometimes people just confuse categories. In a popular tribute to their friendship, for example, Ellen Goodman and Pat O'Brien (2000) tell the story of how Pat, following her divorce, was "mysteriously" left off the invitation list to the block party in her neighborhood. In spite of the fact that she had known her neighbors for years and had not moved, the divorce somehow removed her status as "neighbor."

Understanding how the importance of having a shared network changes over time is another major challenge. There is some evidence, as we noted in chapter 5, that the degree of overlap and the amount of communication with those in the partner's network have a greater influence in the early stages of relationships. It could be that these characteristics signal acceptance of a new relationship or a relational status (i.e., following marriage), but become less important once the signal has been received. Perhaps the information network members provide about the partner is more important early in relationships when less is known. There may be an upper limit to the level of overlap and cross-network communication that is structurally possible in a given setting. Perhaps something near the maximum is reached relatively early in the relationship. All this has profound implications for identifying when changes in network structure will adversely affect the relationship. We do not yet have a good understanding of why some relationships are more resilient than others when the network around them unravels.

Cross-Network Density and Relational Deterioration

Cross-network density represents the extent to which members of the relational partners' networks know and communicate with each other on a regular basis. At first consideration, it is not immediately obvious that changes in cross-network density should be associated with the deterioration in personal relationships. Yet I have included it in this discussion precisely because it may cast light on how changes further out in the network affect and are affected by changes inside a particular relationship. To my knowledge, the first study of cross-network density was the study of premarital romantic relationships presented earlier in this volume (chap. 5). Although quite limited, the findings from that study allow us to begin thinking about how communication between network members might be linked to the fate of relationships.

Communication between network members appears to influence relationships primarily through its effect on other network factors rather than on the relationship directly. We found, for example, that cross-network density was associated directly with only one aspect of the relationship between romantic partners. When network members communicated with each other more often, romantic partners also tended to communicate with each other slightly more often. Cross-network density was not directly related to intimacy, understanding, commitment, or any of the other relational dimensions we examined. Several other findings, however, suggest that reductions in contact between the partners' networks may have a significant, but indirect effect. Cross-network density was strongly associated with both the number of people that the romantic partners had met in each other's network and how often they communicated with them. These factors, in turn, were linked with many aspects of the relationship, including how often the partners interacted, how well they felt they understood each other, how intimate they were, and how committed they were to maintaining the relationship. Over time, then, reductions in the amount of communication between the partners' networks might indirectly produce a wide range of negative effects inside the relationship.

High cross-network density, on the other hand, can be thought of as a barrier to dissolving the relationship. It limits access to alternative partners. It suggests that the costs of termination will be high because there are more connections to broken or at least considered. Network members who value their relationships with those on the other side might conspire to put pressure on the couple to stay together. Like other barriers, these factors probably have greater impact when the relationship is highly developed and well established. Moreover, the impact of network barriers may depend on participants' commitment and satisfaction. If highly satisfied, external network constraints may not have much impact or they may be redefined as further positive indicators of commitment (Kurdek, 2000; Murray, Holmes, & Griffin, 1996). This last point deserves emphasis. The fact that people in happy relationships do not focus on the constraints or barriers does not mean that the barriers are absent or that the barriers have no impact. Many of them are simply redefined so that they become attractions to the relationship (e.g., being part of a large shared network in which everybody knows everybody else). These redefinitions are important. Spouses who can only name a set of barriers to divorce as the source of cohesion in their marriage are far more likely to divorce than those who can describe attractions or who have interpreted the barriers in positive terms (Previti & Amato, 2003).

Reductions in the amount of contact between members of partners' networks work their way into the interior of the relationship in many ways. But troubles inside the relationship can also work their way out to reduce cross-network density. Married couples whose relationship is beginning to flounder, for example, often avoid socializing together (Vaughan, 1986). As social events that brought network members into contact become less frequent, network members now have less opportunity to interact with each other. One spouse may also actively discourage network members from socializing with those in the other spouse's network. Even when they do not, network members often take sides and reduce contact as a way of expressing loyalty. As the relationship deteriorates, partners frequently reveal negative information about one another in a bid for support from friends and family. This in turn may spoil relations with those in the partner's network (e.g., "Why would I talk to someone whose son treated my daughter so badly?"). The cumulative effect of these actions is to drive the participants' networks apart. Relationships between in-laws, for example, rarely survive following divorce (Ambert, 1988; Finch & Mason, 1990).

The loosening of network connections that occurs as relationships come apart is usually cast in a negative light. In many cases, however, the reduction in density gives relief from enmeshed, even dysfunctional, relationships and opens up new possibilities for network members and relational participants alike. This may be true of groups more generally, as Fuchs (2001) points out:

> As coupling loosens, density declines, and outside contacts increase, more contingency and alternative possibilities flow into the world. The group increases its tolerance for deviance and dissent. Some nonconformity is rewarded as innovation. Some facts become ambiguous, some universals turn out to be historical individuals, and some moral certainties become less sure of themselves. Criticism emerges and no longer indicates moral failure and irresponsibility. The future becomes more uncertain, not just an extension of the good traditions. Instead the open future promises more innovations and discoveries; it is a future that needs to be made, and might be made in different ways. (p. 61)

Attraction to Network Members and Relational Deterioration

Networks are structured, not only by the linkages of individuals, but also by the content that flows through them. Feelings of liking are one such content. Patterns of attraction among network members have been of enduring interest to sociologists (e.g., Cartwright & Harary, 1956; Hallinan, 1974). For our purposes, the most important issue is whether relational partners like the members of each other's networks. Studies comparing relationships at different stages indicate that people in more developed relationships generally like the members of their partner's network more than those in less developed or failing relationships. Across our studies of friendship and romantic relationships, for example, we consistently found that people who liked those in the partner's network also reported closer, more committed relationships. Predictably, we also found that people generally liked network members more when the network members were perceived to be supportive. These associations very likely represent influence, not only from relationship to network, but from network to relationship. The more you like network members, the more developed your relationship becomes; and the more developed your relationship becomes, the more they like you. By the same token, if you dislike your partner's friends and family, your relationship is likely to have difficulties; and if your relationship is having difficulties, then people in your partner's network are probably going to dislike you.

After following romantic couples for 5 years, however, Sprecher and Felmlee (2000) found those who broke up did not like their partner's friends and family any less than those who had stayed together. Perhaps how much one likes those in the partner's network does not ultimately matter all that much. As we saw in chapter 8, people employ a wide range of cognitive and behavioral strategies to cope with disliked network members. These strategies may prevent or at least significantly reduce the impact of disliked persons on the relationship. However, researchers may also be underestimating the significance of attraction to network members because of the way they have constructed their measures. Participants in our studies were asked to indicate how much they liked or disliked each person they had met in the partner's network. These scores were then averaged into summary scores for the partner's friends and family as groups. Sprecher and Felmlee (2000) used single items asking how much individuals liked their partner's family as a group and their partner's friends as a group. I suspect that these averaged or group-level measures do not reveal the full story.

From the individual's perspective, it is probably less important that the average level of liking is high than it is that he or she finds a few likable people in the partner's network. If there is at least one such person, then it becomes easier to tolerate the rest using the various cognitive and behavioral strategies discussed earlier. If no such person can be found, then I predict that the relationship will suffer a swift demise. Moreover, in the partner's eyes, it may more important to like some network members more than others. It may be acceptable to dislike the odd sister, but not the beloved brother. A relational partner may joke about the foibles of one network member, but brook no criticism of another. What counts, then, is not whether one likes everyone in the partner's network, but whether one likes the people the partner thinks must be liked. Finally, it is probably more essential that one like, or at least not strongly dislike, the network members with whom one has regular contact. The most positive and preferred strategies for dealing with disliked friends of friends (e.g., being polite, trying not to think about the disliked person) are difficult to sustain when one is forced to deal with a strongly disliked person on a regular basis. When that happens, our research suggests that people will be more likely to complain to partners and confront the disliked network member directly (see chap. 8, this volume). This in turn may adversely affect the relationship with the partner.

How much one likes or has contact with a given person fluctuates over time. Personal networks are in perpetual realignment. As relational partners forge a shared network, new friends will be added and some old ones will become more distant. One may find it inconvenient to see a friend as often if he or she does not get along with one's partner. All of these considerations imply that the average level of attraction to those in the partner's network may not be very informative. The vital questions may be whether there is at least one person to like, whether one likes those the partner sees as important to like, and whether one can minimize interaction with those one strongly dislikes. If these conditions are not met, we would expect the relationship either not to develop very far or, if already established, to deteriorate rapidly.

These effects should flow both ways. Troubles inside the relationship may lead to negative feelings toward members of the partner's network. This can happen in a number of ways. When the relationship is in trouble, information shared with members of one's own network is usually biased toward blaming the other partner (Gray & Silver, 1990). These people may alter their behavior toward the blamed partner and, in turn, their increasingly negative response may cause him or her to dislike the network members in question. Unfortunately, these may be the very people whom it is most critical to like. As the relationship deteriorates further, individuals may assume that negative accounts have become widely known in the partner's network and this may cause the average or overall level of attraction to network members to drop. Much of this is conjecture, but we do know that couples who break up typically report decreased liking for their former partner's family and friends. Sprecher and Felmlee (2000) found that both men and women liked their former partner's family less after the breakup. Although the change was smaller for men, both women and men reported liking their former partner's friends less as well.

Social Support and Relational Deterioration

Support for the relationship from network members acts as a barrier to ending the relationship, but makes a more positive contribution to the relationship as well. Couples who believe that friends and family members want them to stay together tend to be more committed to their relationship, regardless of how satisfied they are, how much time and energy partners feel they have invested in the relationship, and whether they believe that they have viable alternatives to the relationship (Cox, Wexler, Rusbult, & Gaines, 1997). Couples who end their relationship generally feel that their friends and family approved of the breakup (Sprecher & Felmlee, 2000). Thus, support from friends and family plays a critical role both in the decision to stay together and the decision to end a relationship.

The significance of support from network members has been widely documented in studies on the stability of both premarital and marital romantic relationships. Researchers have generally found that the less support for their relationship dating couples perceive from the partner's family and friends, the more likely they are to end their relationship within the following year (e.g., Felmlee & Greenberg, 1999; M. P. Johnson & Milardo, 1984; Lewis, 1973a; Parks & Adelman, 1983). Other researchers have questioned the value of support from network members, however, by pointing to studies in which support failed to make a unique contribution to relational stability or commitment after other variables such as satisfaction, time and energy invested in the relationship, and the quality of alternatives had been factored out (e.g., Lin & Rusbult, 1995; Sprecher, 1988). But the strategy of statistically controlling these other factors may be misleading. First, at least one study has demonstrated that support from network members continues to make a significant contribution to commitment even after other influences have been statistically controlled (Cox et al., 1997). More to the point, support probably influences stability and commitment indirectly by enhancing relational satisfaction, encouraging greater investment in the relationship, and making it less likely that one will be exposed to alternate relational partners. Analysis strategies that statistically remove all these potential indirect influences are therefore likely to underestimate the effects of support.

The association between support and relational development emerges most clearly in studies that have used either concurrent measures or have tracked relationships over relatively short periods of time. Studies that have followed relationships over a longer period of time have found significant sex differences as well differences the impact of support from different sectors of network (Sprecher & Felmlee, 1992, 2000). In the longest running of these studies, Sprecher and Felmlee (2000) found that couples who had stayed together over a 5-year period reported increases in approval for the relationship from network members. Men reported increased approval from their friends, their family, and the partner's friends, and the partner's family. Women reported high, but not increasing, levels of approval from their friends and family. However, they reported that approval from their partner's friends and family had increased over time. Women who had became engaged and married reported additional increases in approval from the male partner's friends. Support from friends and family when the study began did not, however, predict whether the couple would break up over time. Only the woman's perception of approval from her friends and her liking for her partner's family were related to the stability of the relationship. Men's perceptions of approval were not related to stability. The authors explain these sex differences by suggesting that women's networks may be more active in their attempts to influence the relationships of their members. They also speculate that women's networks may be better at predicting relational outcomes—a speculation that I explore in more detail later in this section.

Research on marriage and divorce has also confirmed that support from network members plays a critical role in marital stability. Greeff (2000), for example, created a general index of family functioning based on satisfaction, quality of life, family cohesion and adaptability, and marital and family strengths. Families that scored higher on this index also reported, among other things, that they had more positive relationships with family and friends. Spouses who believe that their network supports their marriage, as opposed to those who believe that friends and family are unsupportive, are less likely to consider separating or divorcing (Bryant & Conger, 1999). When asked why their marriage ended, people typically identify opposition from network members, especially in-laws, as one of the major causes of the divorce (e.g., Cleek & Pearson, 1985).

The importance of relationships with in-laws was underscored by the results of a 4-year study of couples who had been married an average of nearly 20 years (Bryant, Conger, & Meehan, 2001). For both husbands and wives, greater tension and conflict with their mother-in-law was linked to lower levels of marital satisfaction, commitment, and stability a year later. The same pattern emerged for relationships with fathers-in-law, although not as consistently for the husbands as for the wives. The causal pattern was also somewhat different for husbands and wives. For wives, conflict with in-laws spoiled the marriage, but there was no evidence that it worked the other way around. The quality of the marriage at one point in time was not related to the level of conflict with in-laws a year later. For husbands, conflict with in-laws and relational deterioration appeared to drive each other; greater conflict with in-laws reduced marital quality, and reduced marital quality resulted in more conflict with the in-laws.

This last finding reminds us that that the association between relational deterioration and support from network members is often a two-way street. A lack of support from network members can have deleterious effects on the quality of the marriage or dating relationship. By the same token, as the relationship deteriorates, network members may reevaluate their previous positions and shift to supporting the end rather than the continuance of the relationship. Recently divorced people typically report that network members approved of the divorce (Huddleston & Hawkings, 1993; Spanier & Thompson, 1984; Sprecher & Felmlee, 2000). These perceptions undoubtedly reflect protective cognitive biases as well as the results of the strategic management of information about the failing relationship by the divorced individual (see chap. 8, this volume). But in many cases, if not most, these perceptions also reflect real changes in the views of network members.

Disapproval for the relationship is expressed most powerfully through explicit criticisms of the relationship or the relational partner and attempts to interfere with the relationship. Relationships are less likely to survive when network members are perceived to be actively interfering or opposing the relationship (M. P. Johnson & Milardo, 1984). But seemingly innocuous criticism can also have profound effects over time. To appreciate why, we need to understand the social character of a cognitive phenomenon called *sentiment override*. Sentiment overrides occur when relational partners interpret each other's behavior on the basis of a more global image of that person rather than on the actual behavior at hand (Weiss, 1980). They perceive only the behavior that matches their preexisting views of the partner. Distressed couples, for example, tend to overlook positive behaviors and focus instead on negative events that reinforce their overall view of the relationship as an unhappy one (Notarius, Benson, Sloane, Vanzetti, & Hornyak, 1989). The cumulative impact of this negative outlook can spell disaster for the relationship. For instance, recently married couples who described their relationship history in more disappointed and negative terms were far more likely to divorce over the next 10 years than those who had a more positive outlook on their relational history (Carrère, Buehlman, Gottman, Coan, & Ruckstuhl, 2000).

Negative sentiment overrides may, in part, result from the memories prompted by network members. Consider the mother who repeatedly reminds her daughter that her daughter's husband drove recklessly when they were dating. The mother's fearful reminders, although seemingly minor, cannot help but register over time. Without overstating my example, it is fair to say that interactions with network members hold the potential to prime attention, memory, and judgments about the relationship. This is an important point from a therapeutic standpoint. The marital therapist working to help couples overcome destructive cognitive patterns may be helpless in the face of a network that continually reinforces the status quo.

When one spouse withdraws in response to other's attempt to confide about a problem, the problem is perceived to be more intense (Roberts, 2000). One can easily imagine this happening at the level of the network as well. When a network member avoids discussion of problems within the relationship, relational partners are left to struggle without support, thus intensifying the impact of whatever relational problem they are experiencing. This occurs even if the network member has been so tactful or so subtle that the person with the problem never notices the avoidance. Thus, network members have a variety of options for registering their lack of confidence in the relationship, ranging from explicit interference attempts to seemingly minor or even unnoticed actions that quietly undermine the relationship.

The judgments of friends and family clearly have a tremendous potential to help or hurt relationships. But how much do network members really know about the relationship? Do they perceive it accurately? To address these questions, Agnew, Loving, and Drigotas (2001) compared romantic partners' and network members' perceptions of a number of common relational characteristics. They found that network members' perceptions of a couple's commitment, satisfaction, and investment in the relationship were strongly correlated with the couple's own evaluations. There are two important caveats in these findings, however. First, couples tended to rate their relationship more positively than did network members. Also, the correlation depended on which sector of the couple's network was being examined. The correlation between network member perceptions and couple perceptions was strongest among friends the female interacted with more than the male ("her friends"). The perceptions of friends with whom both interacted were positively correlated with the couple's own perception of commitment and relational investment, but not satisfaction. And the perceptions of those the male interacted with more than the female ("his friends") were associated only with the couples own perception of commitment. Moreover, "her friends" were generally better able to predict whether or not the relationship would breakup 6 to 7 months later. Agnew and colleagues explained these differences by suggesting that women disclose more to their friends, share more intimate information when they do disclose, and are more likely to attend to relational information.

The apparent predictive superiority of women's friends may provide an alternative explanation for another common finding. Over the years, numerous studies have documented that women are more likely than men to initiate the breakup of romantic relationships. This is usually explained by suggesting either that women are more relationally sensitive and hence are more aware of problems in the relationship, or that women's relatively greater economic dependency on men makes them more practical about getting out of relationships that lack long-term potential (Hill et al., 1976). Without debating the merit of these explanations, the findings on the accuracy of network members imply that women may simply get better feedback and advice about their romantic relationships than men get from theirs.

TO THE END AND NEW BEGINNINGS

I began this chapter by offering the social network as one place to look for the more subtle factors that help explain why personal relationships succeed and fail. My goal was to extend the work presented in the previous chapters by emphasizing findings from research that has tracked relationships over time and by exploring the role of networks as relationships deteriorate.

Longitudinal studies confirm that personal relationships flourish when the partners meet and interact with each other's friends and family, when they develop a shared network, and when network members are perceived as supporting the relationship. When relational partners have little contact with one another's friends and family, when they lack a common network, and when they are met with opposition by network members, their relationship is likely to deteriorate, perhaps to the point of termination.

The longitudinal work also raises several questions and challenges regarding previous research. It challenges, for example, whether the overall level of liking one has for another person's friends and family has much impact on the relationship with that person. It will probably be more useful to look first at whether you like at least one person in the partner's network, and then how much you like the people you cannot avoid as well as the people your partner wants you to like.

Longitudinal research has also pointed to sex differences at the end of heterosexual romantic relationships. Conflict with in-laws diminishes the quality of the marriage for both men and women, but women appear to be more successful than men at not letting disruptions or problems in the marriage affect relationships with the in-laws (Bryant et al., 2001). Although women's perceptions of support are related to the stability of the relationship over time, men's perceptions of support do not appear to be related to the stability of the relationship (Sprecher & Felmlee, 2000). Network members who interact predominantly with the female seem to do better at predicting relational stability than network members who interact more with the male partner. Finally, both sexes decreased liking for members of the partner's network after the relationship ended, but the change was less for men than it was for women (Sprecher & Felmlee, 2000). There is still much we do not know about why these differences occur. Nor do we know if they occur in nonromantic heterosexual relationships. Perhaps the greatest gap in research on relational deterioration is that there is so little attention paid to how friendships, work relationships, civic associations, and other kinds of personal relationships come apart.

We also have much to learn about the aftermath of relational endings. In many cases, the end is more of a transformation of a relationship than a true ending. Former partners may still continue to have considerable contact, particularly when they continue to have significant relationships in common. Even when former partners no longer have direct contact, they may continue to take an interest and be influenced by one another through indirect network linkages. The dynamics of these "postrelational relationships" represent uncharted territory for personal relationship researchers.

As we learn more about how relationships come apart and what happens in their aftermath, we find ourselves once again at the beginning. Some network members will be dropped or become more distant and others will move closer to us in social space. At some point, some of the people in the newly aligned network may decide or be recruited to assist in the initiation of a new relationship. And thus, with the close of this chapter, we have come full circle back to the role of networks in the formation of personal relationships.

Prospects
for the Social Contextual Perspective

In the past 35 years researchers have charted a new understanding of personal relationships, exploring the reasons why some are close, committed, and satisfying, and others are not. The largest group of researchers followed the path inward to examine the interior of relationships and the psychology of interpersonal interactions. To choose a particularly influential instance, John Gottman and his colleagues have shown that satisfaction and stability in personal relationships rest in large part on the interplay of verbal and nonverbal interaction with physiological arousal (e.g., Gottman, 1994; Gottman & Levenson, 2000). This inward path, and ones like it, ultimately leads us into the biological realm. And, as I described in chapter 1, the state of our personal relationships has indeed been linked to many aspects of our health and physiological well-being.

Another, smaller group has followed a different path to look outward. We have sought to demonstrate that the quality and stability of personal relationships also depends on how participants interact within larger social networks. Along with a number of other researchers, I have endeavored to articulate a perspective that locates individual choice and action in relationships within a social network composed of other relationships. The fundamental assumption of the social contextual perspective, as I have envisioned it, is that interpersonal relationships and broader social structures are communication patterns. They have no existence apart from the communication practices in which they are continuously made, unmade, and remade.

Although the process of relating is fluid and emergent, we can identify the fundamental dimensions along which change occurs and determine their value at any one point in time. Much can, and has, been learned both by comparing assessments taken in one relationship to those taken in another relationship and by comparing assessments of the same relationship at different points in time. I have argued that the state of a relationship at any one time can be described in terms of seven dimensions. These include (a) the frequency of interaction between the participants, (b) their level of interdependence, (c) the depth or intimacy of their interaction, (d) the breadth or variety of their interaction, (e) the extent to which their past interactions have resulted in a desire to continue the relationship, (f) the extent to which their past interactions have resulted in feelings of understanding and predictability, and, finally (g), the extent to which interaction between the participants takes on distinctive qualities. Changes in these dimensions mark the pathways along which relationships develop, are maintained or restored, and deteriorate.

What we call social structure is enacted through communication as well. There are no fixed entities—groups, organizations, and cultures—all exist in the social networks defined by the interactions among a particular set of people (see chap. 2, this volume; see also Fuchs, 2001; White, 1992). Like relationships, social networks are in constant flux. And like relationships, the dimensions along which social networks change can also be described. For our purposes, the social network of greatest interest is the one composed of the friends and families of the people whose relationship we want to understand. The dimensions of greatest interest are (a) the social distance between network members, (b) the degree to which relational participants' networks overlap, (c) the degree to which each participant interacts with the friends and family of the other, (d) the degree to which each participant likes the people he or she meets in the partner's network, (e) the degree to which he or she feels they support the relationship, and (f) the degree to which the members of the two participants' network interact with each other.

My goal in this volume has been to link these dimensions of social networks to the relational dimensions in a way that accounts for the development and deterioration of personal relationships. The major findings are summarized in the next section, while broader applications and implications of the social contextual perspective are explored in the closing sections.

LINKING RELATIONSHIPS AND NETWORKS: WHAT WE HAVE LEARNED

Because the detailed findings are described in preceding chapters, I will focus here on the broader aspects of what we learned and what remains to be learned. I begin with brief summaries of what we have learned about the initiation, development, and deterioration of personal relationships using the social contextual perspective. I then consider how we might understand these findings both from the perspective of relational participants and the perspective of the network.

Initiating Relationships

The social contextual perspective enriches our understanding of how relationships begin in at least two ways. First, it gives us a useful way to think about a fundamental, but seldom addressed, question in the study of personal relationships: Why do particular people meet in the first place?

The standard answer to this question for the last 70 years has been that people who live or work in close physical proximity are more likely to meet than those whose homes or workplaces are separated by greater distances. Indeed, this has been the accepted answer for so long that research has moved onto other topics and the original studies are rarely read anymore. When I started rereading them, however, two problems became immediately apparent. First, much of the original research was badly flawed. As I noted in chapter 3, in calculating how far apart men and women lived at the time they applied for marriage licenses, one researcher simply threw out the 35% of the sample who lived in different cities. No wonder it appeared that most people lived relatively close. Even if it had been based on better science, however, the physical proximity explanation would still have another serious shortcoming. It cannot account for why certain people within a given geographic radius meet and others within that same radius do not.

By defining proximity in terms of social space rather than physical or geographic space, the social contextual perspective offers another way to think about why people meet. Two thirds of the people in our core studies reported that they had known at least one, often more than one, person in their partner's network prior to meeting their partner for the first time. In a large survey in the Netherlands, nearly half of the people men and women who were married or living together reported having mutual friends before they met (Kalmijn & Flap, 2001). These findings suggest that previously unacquainted people become more likely to meet as their proximity in the social network increases.

A true test of the social proximity hypothesis would require that we follow relatively large, unbounded networks over time to see if meetings were truly predicted by social distance in the network. That test awaits future research as does an explanation for why those who start romantic relationships appear to have more friends in common at the time they meet than those who start same-sex friendships.

The social contextual perspective also enriches our understanding of how relationships begin by underscoring the active role played by network members. We found that the first meeting between prospective romantic partners had frequently been arranged by a network member. In addition to making direct introductions, network members organized joint activities or simply arranged for the prospective partners to be in the same place at the same time. Here is the idea of physical proximity, but not in its traditional role as a passive background factor. Now it becomes an active strategy wielded by network members deliberately seeking to bring people together.

Network members were actively involved in the initiation and early development of romantic relationships in many other ways as well. They frequently said or did things designed to boost the attractiveness or credibility of one person in the eyes of the other. They frequently went a step further to enlist other network members in this effort. They also provided coaching, relayed information, or did other things to facilitate prospective partners to contact each other or to get off to a good start. Overall, more than half of the people we sampled reported that they had been helped by third parties at the beginning of their relationship. Although our research on third party helpers focused on the initiation of romantic relationships, we can easily imagine that network members play similar roles in the initiation of friendships and business relationships.

Help from network members often comes unbidden, but in nearly half of the cases we examined, helpers reported that their assistance had been directly requested by one or both prospective romantic partners. Nearly two thirds of the cases helpers felt that they had received hints or other indirect requests for assistance. Whether help was requested or not, those who received assistance from network members tended to have significantly more active social lives than those who worked alone. Thus the initiation of personal relationships is most often a broadly social accomplishment that involves changes in the structure of the network surrounding the individual as well as the active involvement of network members.

Developing Relationships

Network members remain keenly involved in the development of personal relationships long after initiation. The studies presented in this volume demonstrated that, as personal relationships develop, they become even more intertwined with the participants' networks of friends and family. Perhaps the best way to convey the major themes across these studies is to present one final model—a general model of relational development combining all the data from the core studies presented in chapters 4 through 7. This model is based reports on same-sex friendships and premarital romantic relationships from nearly 860 adolescents and young adults.

As Fig. 10.1 illustrates, how often relational participants communicate with each other, how close they feel, and how committed they are to maintaining their relationship are consistently associated with the structure and content of their social networks. Those who meet more people in their partner's network, who communicate with them more often, and who believe that friends and family support their relationship also report higher levels of commitment, closeness, and communication with their partners. This overall finding strongly supports the social contextual perspective on personal relationships.

Similar findings emerged in nearly every analysis we conducted. In nearly every case, closeness, commitment, and communication inside the relationship were positively and significantly related to perceived support from net-

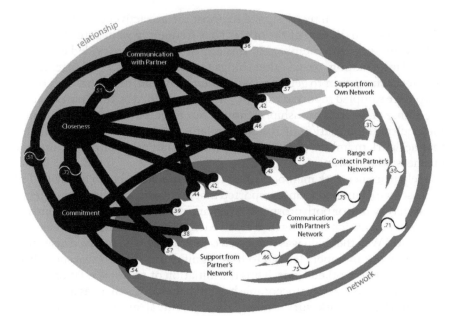

FIG. 10.1.   General model of personal relationships.

work members and the amount of contact one had with network members. This was true for men and women, adolescents and young adults, and in friendships and romantic relationships. Much work remains to be done, of course, but it appears that the social contextual perspective has potential as a general theory of relationship development.

Differences in the results most often reflected differences in how well a particular measure performed across settings or modest differences in the strength of association between factors. Relational development and network involvement were, for instance, somewhat less tightly linked in adolescence than in young adulthood (compare Fig. 6.1 and Fig. 6.2). Although all of the associations are slightly weaker, those involving the amount of communication between the relational partners themselves are notably weaker in the adolescent models and almost completely drop out in adolescent romantic relationships (see Fig. 4.1 and Fig. 5.1). In adolescent relationships then, especially romantic relationships, feelings of closeness and commitment do not depend to a great degree on how much the participants interact with one another. Nor is the amount of communication between the partners as strongly linked to the network factors in adolescent relationships as it is in young adult relationships. Two possibilities might help us make sense of these findings. One is the principle of network structuring, which suggests that the amount of interaction between partners will depend on the structural opportunities afforded by their networks. Compared to young adults, adolescents may have less control over the people they see and how much time they spend with them as the result of being in a structured school setting, less access to transportation, and greater parental oversight. If so, the connection between how often they communicate and how they view their relationship and the network might be weakened. Another possibility is that adolescents' understanding of relationships, especially romantic relationships, is still in a formative stage in which the various elements of the relational world do not yet have a coherent organization. If so, adolescents may be less likely to associate the amount of interaction with their partner with the reactions of network members or their own feelings of closeness and commitment to the partner. Whether the reason is structural, cognitive, a combination of the two, or the result of some as yet unrecognized factor, has practical implications for parents as well as for those designing interventions aimed at reducing the spread of sexually transmitted disease among adolescents. Although social network factors played a strong role in both adolescent and young adult relationships, the differences remind us that the role of personal networks is not fixed. Rather, it varies with age and network structure beyond the participants' immediate social circle.

Deteriorating Relationships

High levels of turnover are the norm in personal relationships. The less developed the relationship, the more vulnerable it is; but high divorce rates testify that even highly developed relationships can flounder. Unfortunately, there are relatively few studies that have followed relationships over time and even fewer that have also included measures of social network characteristics. Nonetheless, it appears that social network factors come into play both as relationships come apart and as people navigate their way through postrelational settings.

Research on marital and premarital relationships demonstrates that relationships are more stable when the participants have a larger overlapping network and when they communicate more often with each other's friends and family. Having a shared network helps the participants manage uncertainty about the relationship, provides access to information and resources, and restricts access to alternative partners. The importance of this last point is underscored by research showing that people who have or think that they will have access to relational alternatives are more likely to end their relationship over time.

As a relationship begins to deteriorate, the shared network is pushed or pulled apart. Contact with members of the partner's network is reduced and the size of the overlapping network decreases. The impact of these changes is probably greatest in relationships that are less developed and still have a relatively small shared network.

We found that dating partners communicated more regularly both with each other and with the members of each other's networks when the members of those networks had direct contact with each other. These findings were suggestive and there is as yet no longitudinal research on the role played by cross-network density. It is reasonable to assume, however, that this higher level joining of networks functions to limit access to alternative partners and to reinforce the relationship. Once the relationship begins to dissolve, we would expect contact between the partner's networks to decrease as the number of joint gatherings declines and network members choose sides.

Relationships are less likely to dissolve if participants feel that network members support them. Although there is some question how far the effects of support at one point in time extend into the future, researchers have consistently found that support from network members is linked with greater stability and satisfaction during the year that follows. Conversely, former relational partners often cite opposition from network members as one of the reasons their relationship ended.

The research described in chapter 8 suggests that relational partners carefully manage revelations of relational problems in terms of both what is revealed and to whom it is shared. They also employ a variety of strategies to blunt the effects of unsupportive network members. At some point, however, as the relationship deteriorates, even those who were once supportive may become opposed. This change may be the result of what they have observed or they may have been recruited as supporters in an effort, not to save the relationship, but rather to end it.

The network that partners once shared continues to be pushed and pulled apart after the relationship ends. At least in divorce, contact with the former partner goes first. Researchers have found that contact between former spouses is usually minimal unless children are involved. Even then, contact typically occurs at very low rates. The research also points to significant decreases in the frequency on contact with shared network members following divorce. This decline includes ex-spouse's friends, but is particularly dramatic for the ex-spouse's relatives with whom contact is maintained only in rare cases. Although network members often approve of the breakup, a significant number of divorced people complain that their friends and family offer less support and make fewer attempts to contact them after the divorce. The period immediately following divorce is therefore marked by reductions in the size of ex-spouses' networks. It may take a substantial period of time for old connections to be reestablished and for new members to be added (Albeck & Kaydar, 2002; Terhell et al., 2004). The network that emerges out of this period will be more diverse and will, in many cases, contain new partners or at least people who are linked more directly to prospective new partners.

What Drives Relational Change?

Is relational change driven by the choices and behavior of the relational participants themselves or is it driven primarily by the changes occurring in the social networks surrounding the relationship? The social contextual model yields coherent accounts of relational development regardless of whether the relationship or the network is placed at center stage. To illustrate this point, I now briefly resummarize the primary findings from the research in this volume, first from a perspective that emphasizes the choices of relational partners and then from a perspective that emphasizes the influence of the network factors.

Placing the Relational Participants at Center Stage.   Individuals who are interested in developing a relationship scan their social environment for opportunities. Sometimes they also ask their friends to help locate potential partners. They join in groups and activities where they think the opportunities will be greater. Once a prospective partner is identified, individuals often ask network members to help them meet that person and then to help them get the prospective partner to think positively of them. After the relationship begins, individuals introduce the new partner to each other's friends and family. Interaction with network members generates a great deal of information about the partner that is then used to determine how close or committed one wants the relationship to become. Socializing jointly with network members and developing common friends also helps relational partners manage competing demands on their time.

Individuals also pay close attention to whether network members support the relationship. Support from network members reassures them that they have made a good choice. Support is not just something to be obtained; it is something to be made. Relational partners actively manage information about the relationship in order to gain and maintain the support of network members. When network members are unsupportive, the individual may attempt to bring them around by presenting only positive information about the relationship. Sometimes the individual has to make a difficult choice between the new partner and an existing network member. Whether by attrition or as the result of the active efforts of the partners, the network will become more supportive over time. As it does, the individual feels more comfortable with the partner's friends and family and spends even more time with them. Partners thus develop a shared network that enhances the value of their relationship, thus encouraging them to become even closer and more committed.

Network members may also be enlisted to provide support when problems arise in the relationship. Individuals will manage the information given to network members in order to protect their self-esteem and achieve their relational goals.

If there is too much opposition, especially from one's own friends and family, individuals begin to question their own judgment and reconsider their loyalties. They may decide that they no longer wish to maintain their current level of involvement with the partner. As they reduce involvement with the partner, they also begin to reduce contact with the partner's friends and family and the shared network shrinks. They may also begin to scan their social environment for alternative partners. This process continues after the relationship ends. Network members who were perceived as unsupportive will be dropped and room is made for new network members, some of whom may be future partners or may be enlisted in the search for a new partner.

Placing the Network at Center Stage.

We can also locate the driving force in the network rather than in the decisions of individuals. If we tell the story of the findings this way, we would begin by observing that individuals move closer or further apart in a social network as larger patterns of human contact and cooperation change. The number of links separating any two people shrinks or grows with these realignments. At some point, the network may bring our future partners into a position where they are separated from each other by only one link. They now have at least one social contact in common. Having one or more contacts in common greatly increases the probability that the two will meet.

Once they meet, the individuals are likely to spend more time together if they already have more contacts in common. Moreover, the creation of the new relationship represents a microrealignment of the network that increases the probability that the members of the partner's once-separate networks will meet. This makes it easier for the partners to spend time together. As the partners spend more time together, their interaction becomes more predictable and moves into new areas. This encourages feelings of closeness and commitment. The increasing local density of the network around the couple also increases commitment to by limiting access to alternative partners and by increasing the costs of ending the relationship. Commitment in this view is not so much an active choice as the recognition that one has become embedded in a set of circumstances. By the same token, as network members spend more time with the partners, interaction with them also becomes more predictable and moves into new areas. This encourages network members to continue interaction and that in turn is perceived as support by the relational partners. Network members whose relationship with the partners does not become more established are seen as unsupportive. With only a weak link holding them in position, these people are likely to move away as the network continues to realign.

The shared network surrounding the now well-developed relationship continues to realign over time. As changes occur further out in the network, the shared network sometimes begins to unravel. Members of the shared network are now pulled in other directions, causing reductions in the amount of contact with the relational partners. The partners perceive this as a loss of support for their relationship and interaction within the relationship becomes less predictable. Feelings of closeness and commitment attenuate and interaction with the partner is reduced. Further realignments result in contact being first with network members and ultimately with the partner. With the end of the relationship, new relationships are established, either with new partners or with those who are, as at the beginning, only one link away from a prospective new partner.

Several points should be made about these starkly contrasting accounts of the relational life cycle. First, both are consistent with the results of the research presented in this volume. Second, both accounts are generic and could be used describe change in a wide range of personal relationships. Third, the central explanatory devices of the social contextual model—relational sense-making and network structure—figure prominently in both accounts. Finally, both stories are true, but more significantly, they are ultimately the *same* story. Structural changes are, as I argued at length in chapter 2, enacted in the actions and communication of individuals within a network. Changes in network structure may seem impersonal to those whose own choices are affected, but they are born in the communicative choices and actions of other individuals in the network.

APPLICATIONS OF THE SOCIAL CONTEXTUAL PERSPECTIVE

Research on the development, maintenance, and deterioration of personal relationships in a network context is still in its infancy. As it advances, researchers will inevitably turn to the unfinished work of providing more detailed descriptions of both relationships and networks, to tracking relationships over time, and to examining a wider range of subject populations and relationships. Attention should also turn to the practical applications of the social contextual perspective for individuals and groups. Although hardly a complete list, several of these applications are discussed in the paragraphs that follow.

The Diagnostic and Information Value of Networks

Although people go to great lengths to manage and defend the public face of their personal relationships, sometimes it is better just to listen to what network members have to say. Consider the following letter written to advice columnist Carolyn Hax (2004):

Dear Carolyn:

My parents think my boyfriend, "Johnny," isn't good enough for me. They don't see the incredibly devoted side of him. I'm 23 and a recent college graduate. I'm back at home. Johnny is completing his undergraduate work at the university I attended, 375 miles away. My parents get this impression of him just because, for example, Johnny doesn't like it when I talk to male friends from high school I see in line at the grocery store. He says the only reason men talk to women is to, well, you know. Since he avoids the opposite sex, I think this is fair, so I don't go out with my girlfriends any more when they go clubbing and stuff. He also doesn't like my talking with my parents about us, because he is a very private person. I respect that. Also, my parents think it is strange that even though his parents live close to school, I have never met them.

I think he may be the one for me. Other than these things, he has always been there for me. How do I get my parents off my back?—Out West

To her credit, Carolyn Hax sides with the parents and goes on to call the young woman's attention to abusive nature of her boyfriend's jealous and controlling behavior. One immediate practical benefit of taking a network perspective is that network members now become valuable sources of information. They may be canaries in the relational coalmine, seeing trouble long before we see it or admit it to ourselves. Beyond this, the more we know about an individual's behavior toward others in the network, the more we know about how he or she will treat us. Network members may be particularly useful in recognizing the signs of abusive relationships (Arriaga & Oskamp, 1999).

Taking a network perspective also helps us appreciate larger patterns of interaction that exist beyond the view of any one individual and his or her immediate contacts. This was illustrated in a particularly striking way in a recent study of sexual activity among students at a high school located in a midsized town in the midwestern United States (Bearman, Moody, & Stovel, 2004). Nearly 70% of the 832 students who completed the study were sexually active over the 18-month period of the study. Of these, approximately 22% were involved in fully monogamous sexual relationships—that is, they had sex with each other but with no one else. However, most students—just over 50% of those who were sexually active and over 25% of the total school population—were connected in a single large sexual network. Although 113 of the 288 people in this network reported having had sex with just one other person, each of them was linked with everyone one else because their partner had not been monogamous (see Fig. 10.2). Structures like this have broad implications for the spread of sexually transmitted disease, but also testify to the more general value of looking beyond the perspectives of individuals and small groups.

Improving Network Skills

The therapist–client relationship is sometimes viewed as a platform for the development of social skills that can then be transferred to the client's other relationships (e.g., Mallinckrodt, 2001). Alternatively, we could think of therapy as a place to enhance the client's network resources and skills. Clients who have difficulty initiating social relationships might, for example, be better served if

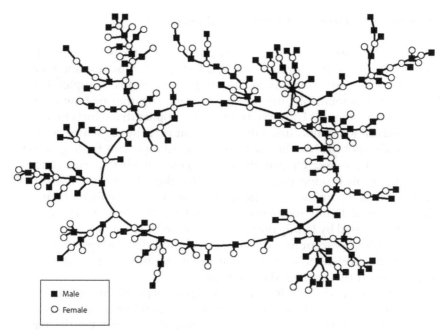

FIG. 10.2.   The sexual network at "Jefferson High School" (Adapted from Bearman et al., 2004).

the therapist assisted them in recognizing the value of third parties in identifying and contacting potential relational partners. The findings and strategies described in chapter 3 are one starting point. In other cases, clients may benefit from recognizing that they already have the skills they need. We found, for instance, that the process of developing romantic relationships was very similar to the process of developing friendships (see chap. 6, this volume). This implies that those who have difficulty with romantic relationships, but healthy friendships, already have models for success.

The social contextual perspective also implies that therapy and other skill building programs that focus on self-management or the management of a single relationship may be missing an entire category of vital social skills. Even if one is successful at managing oneself in a relationship, or managing a single relationship, she or he may not possess the skills needed to manage relationships among relationships. And yet managing relationships among relationships is an unrelenting demand of social life. Skills at recognizing and negotiating relational boundaries, in managing the spread of information in a network, in network rituals, as well as the other tactics and strategies identified in chapter 8, contribute not only to the management of complex sets of relationships in a network, but also to the integrity of the self.

Network Knowledge for Parents of Adolescents

Several findings from our research have direct applications for the parents of adolescents. We found, for instance, that feelings of closeness and commitment in adolescents' romantic relationships were almost completely unaffected by the amount of time the couple spent together or how regularly they saw each other. As I observed earlier, this implies that efforts to discourage serious attachments during the adolescent years by regulating peer contacts are also not likely to be successful. According to our findings and the findings of other research, parents are much more likely to have an effect by expressing explicit opposition or support for the relationship. Predictably, we found that the opinions of friends weighed more heavily on teens than the opinions of family members. Nonetheless, the level of opposition or support expressed by family members was linked to closeness and commitment in both adolescent friendship and romantic relationships. Contrary to much of the received wisdom in the popular literature on parenting, these results suggest that parents should speak up.

Parents may also benefit from developing contact with the parents of their adolescents' friends and romantic partners. Parent-to-parent contacts create an accountability mechanism. They also provide support for the parents themselves (J. Elium & D. Elium, 1999).

In their popular advice book for parents, Kastner and Wyatt (2002) argue that by late adolescence, parents should be moving away from an "authoritative model" to a more "relational approach," in which parents talk about "their own feelings and needs relative to their child's behavior" (p. 94). They add that this approach "banks on the young adult's need for less parental authority and on the child-parent relationship as a valued resource" (p. 94). The effectiveness of the "relational approach" to parenting, it seems to me, is greatly enhanced when parents take an active interest in their adolescent's social network and, just as important, share their own network contacts and experiences. This will undoubtedly strike many parents, including this one, as a tall order, but even so, it is difficult to achieve a more collaborative relationship with offspring if the networks in which parents and adolescents are invested remain unknown and undiscussed.

Networks in Therapeutic and Protective Interventions

Friends, family members, and other network members can be enlisted as therapeutic or protective agents. Existing relationships in the network will typically provide more meaningful and influential social support than relationships that are "grafted" into the individual's network during the course of therapy (Heller & Rook, 2001). Support groups created as part of smoking cessation programs, for example, have generally proven less effective in promoting behavior change than support from the individual's own close relationships (Cohen et al., 1988). In another case, researchers found that adolescents who had reciprocated friendships at school were less likely to be the object of bullying over the course of the school year (Boulton et al., 1999). More generally, research on support processes following natural disasters shows that people consistently receive the greatest portion of support from family members and friends. Compared to community and professional resources, personal networks are more readily available, less stigmatizing, and less costly (Kaniasty & Norris, 2001).

Indeed the decision to mobilize community and professional supports should be based on an assessment of the support currently available in existing relationships. Without such an assessment, service providers run the risk of wasting valuable resources by merely duplicating support that is already available. Divorce support groups, for example, appear to have less value to those who are well integrated into an existing network and have already found a new partner (Øygard, 2004). Resources may also be misdirected if community and professional support is at odds with the prevailing sentiment of the existing network.

Therapists have for many years recognized the value of expanding individual therapy to include the entire family system (e.g., Satir, 1964). Some have also advocated involving more than one family in support and therapeutic activities (e.g., Asen, 2002; O'Shea & Phelps, 1985). These traditions point toward a broader engagement of social networks as tools or objects of therapy and support. Efforts along this line go by a variety of names, including network therapy, informal social support intervention, and social network intervention. Applications are even more varied. One line of work has demonstrated that enlisting friends and family members enhances the effectiveness of programs designed to reduce substance abuse (e.g., Copello, Orford, Hodgson, Tober, & Barrett, 2002; Galanter et al., 2004; Glazer, Galanter, Megwinoff, Dermatis, & Keller, 2003). Other lines of research have demonstrated the value of involving network members to assist in the management of chronic diseases such as rheumatoid arthritis (Fyrand, Moum, Finset, & Glennås, 2003). And, naturally there is a long tradition of involving family members or friends as informal patient advocates during hospital stays or visits to the physician. All of these opportunities can be utilized more effectively if healthcare providers, therapists, and social workers develop greater skill in evaluating and drawing on resources in their clients' existing networks. When they do, however, they will also need to develop additional sensitivities to the dilemmas of confidentiality and privacy that arise when network members are included (see chap. 8, this volume, as well as Petronio, Sargent, Andea, Reganis, & Cichocki, 2004).

Although friends and family often provide the most effective support, there are many situations in which they will not be able to provide adequate assis-

tance. Heller and Rook (2001) identified several limitations of naturally occurring personal relationships as sources of support in times of distress. Other
network members may also be struggling with the stressor themselves, as in
the case of an entire community devastated by a hurricane, and not be capable
of providing support. Network members may lack experience or expertise, as
in the case of an uncommon disease. They may have little more to offer than
good intentions. In other cases, network members may hold unhelpful stereotypes about how to be supportive. Even if they know what to do, network
members' support efforts may become overly invasive, thus backfiring and
further reducing the distressed person's sense of control over the situation.
People may seek support groups and professional helpers to overcome these
limitations, but face-to-face support groups also have shortcomings. People
worry about privacy, about how to present themselves, and face-to-face support groups are not always available. In the past several years, researchers have
found that people are making use increasingly of online support groups in order to overcome the shortcomings of both their existing networks and of
face-to-face groups (Walther & Boyd, 2002).

The idea that support and other therapeutic goals can be enhanced by graft-
ing new members into networks is appealing. Yet we should not expect that programs aimed at adding new contacts will generate immediate benefits (Heller &
Rook, 2001). Instead, the benefits of such programs will accrue slowly because
new friends and supporters must be integrated into the individual's existing network. The social contextual perspective helps us understand why this process
will take less time in some cases than in others. New people who are already
linked to existing network members should be integrated more rapidly than
those who are not. Whenever possible, then, therapeutic interventions aimed at
expanding the individual's network should first reach out to those who are only
two or three links away in the current network.

Networking in Business and Civic Life

Deliberate efforts to enhance the size and reach of one's network are often
essential to success in business and civic life. Yet because of the rather merce-
nary way in which these efforts are so often made, the term *networking* car-
ries negative connotations for many people. Indeed the relationships
conjured up by most networking events are abysmally shallow and usually
discarded with the next clearing of the Rolodex™. There is "no there, there."
One currently popular event, for example, features "5-minute networking,"
in which participants are shuffled from table to table for brief meetings with
potential customers, suppliers, and strategic allies. Although chance dictates
that some of these contacts will prove to be useful, the vast majority will not.
Ironically, an event touted as an efficient way to meet people ultimately
proves to be incredibly inefficient.

There are better ways to do this. The social contextual perspective would suggest that the best new contacts are made through existing contacts. The first step toward successful networking would therefore be a thoughtful assessment of one's current network with an eye toward how one may already be indirectly linked with the kind of people one wishes to meet. As we found in the study of third parties in the initiation of romantic relationships (chap. 3, this volume), current network members can often be recruited to assist with introductions and credibility enhancement. Working through existing network members not only expands the range of contact available, but also has to the potential to reduce anxieties about "cold calling" strangers.

Effective networking is ultimately about the art of cultivating less developed relationships without attempting to turn them into close relationships. Researchers have long emphasized the value of "weak ties" in finding employment and in gaining access to new information and opportunities (Granovetter, 1973). The role of civic and business associations in this process is less appreciated. Yet participation in churches, clubs, business political, and civic associations brings people into contact with strangers who already share a common geographic locale and at least some common interests. These institutions act as mechanisms for the creation of new social contacts that can then be extended in other ways beyond the group. Perhaps one reason people are drawn to contrived "networking events" is that participation in civic and political associations has fallen dramatically in the United States over the past 50 years (Putnam, 2000).

The Internet provides powerful tools for matching those with common interests, but it is too soon to tell what role it can play in providing substitutes for more geographically placed associations. Using technology to identify common interests is probably not enough. The most promising applications, it seems to me, are those that not only help people identify those with common interests, but then provide a mechanism for organizing face-to-face meetings for those who live in close proximity. A site called "meetup.com" offered this combination of services during the 2004 U.S. elections and played a significant role in rallying grassroots support for at least two candidates during the early campaign.

Improving Relations Between Groups

It would be difficult to understate to damage done by prejudice and hostility between groups, regardless of whether those groups are identified on the basis of politics, sexual orientation, religion, or ethnicity. One of the most enduring proposals for reducing tensions between groups is based on what Allport (1954) called the *contact hypothesis*. Allport reasoned that prejudice is usually caused by a lack of knowledge about other groups that leads people to make hasty generalizations. By increasing contact between the groups, prejudice should be reduced as individuals fill in gaps in their knowledge and correct errors in their assumptions.

This reasoning has led to social programs that attempt to reduce prejudice by increasing direct contact between the members of disaffiliated groups. These range from national experiments, such as the Truth and Reconciliation Commission in South Africa between 1996 and 1998, to a variety of more specific interventions intended to increase tolerance for cultural diversity in classrooms and workplaces in the United States. The results of these efforts have been mixed. Although the Truth and Reconciliation Commission effectively revealed the suffering of apartheid, it was much less successful as a vehicle for racial reconciliation (J. A. Vora & E. Vora, 2004). Similarly, intergroup dialogue methods often do not result in the hoped for increases in tolerance and understanding among students from diverse backgrounds (e.g., Nagda & Zúñiga, 2003). This should not surprise us. Nearly 50 years ago, in their classic field experiment at a boys camp, M. Sherif, Harvey, White, Hood, and C. W. Sherif (1961) demonstrated that contact and communication were not sufficient to reduce tensions between groups. Tensions were reduced only when groups were required to work together toward a common, mutually valued goal. In other words, unless there is truly some basis for interdependence, efforts to graft members of a distrusted group into an individual's network are likely to fail.

Prejudice is more likely to be reduced when individuals from different groups find a basis for developing a relationship. People who do find a basis for friendship with those in an opposing group are generally less prejudiced (e.g., Paolini, Hewstone, Cairns, & Voci, 2004; Pettigrew, 1997). Interestingly, these cross-group friendships do not appear to be maintained by avoiding discussion of the differences that separate the participants. There is some evidence, in fact, that areas of difference are more actively discussed in cross-group friendships than in friendships with members of one's own group (D. Taylor, Dubé, & Bellerose, 1986). If so, cross-group friendship may provide a unique forum for productively addressing prejudice and tension between groups. Moreover, the societal benefits of cross-group friendship may be quite long-lasting. During World War II, for example, individuals who risked their lives to save Jews recalled having had more friendships with Jews and members of other minority groups as children than those who did not make rescue attempts (S. P. Oliner & P. M. Oliner, 1988).

Indirect contacts also play an important role in reducing tensions between groups. Individuals from different groups are more likely to strike up a relationship if they are already indirectly linked (e.g., have friends in common). Just discovering that that one's friends have friends in the disliked group may by itself reduce prejudice. It is thought to reduce the cognitive separation between self and other, making the disliked group more similar to or a part of oneself (A. Aron et al., 2004; S. C. Wright, A. Aron, McLaughlin-Volpe, & Ropp, 1997). Regardless of how these network effects are explained, there is a growing body of experimental and field research demonstrating that those who are aware of linkages between their friends and the members of other groups are generally less prejudiced toward those groups (Paolini et al., 2004; S. C. Wright et al., 1997).

These findings suggest that network knowledge might play a particularly important role in efforts to improve relations between groups. Instead of forcing direct contact, it might be more productive to help people recognize and use the indirect contacts they already have in their own networks. In many cases individuals may not even be aware of the range of contacts maintained by their friends. Programs might be designed, for example, that begin with practical exercises to trace linkages to members of other groups and then go on to use those shared contacts to facilitate direct interaction between members of different groups. These efforts might be augmented by media presentations portraying members of other groups in a positive light or portraying cross-group friendships in a positive light. Both types of media portrayals have been shown to reduce negative attitudes toward the members of other groups (e.g., Liebkind & McAlister, 1999; Schiappa, Greg, & Hewes, 2005).

PROSPECTS FOR THE SOCIAL CONTEXTUAL PERSPECTIVE

The belief that social relations were once closer and more integrated into communities than they are today is probably as old as nostalgia itself. There is wide agreement that the structure of social relations, including personal relations, has been transformed over the past 250 years by industrialization, transportation, communication technology, and the changing role of women (e.g., Allan, 1998; Heller, 1989; Levinger, 1994; Masiglio & Scanzoni, 1995). Fear that these changes are disrupting our communities and distorting our personal relationships has roots as deep as the changes themselves (e.g., Tönnies, 1887/1957; Wellman, 1979; Wirth, 1938). It has particular currency in an era that is defined by globalizing technologies and values. We have, it is often said, become self-absorbed, disconnected from our past, our local communities, our leaders, and from a social world that is experienced primarily in mediated form.

But perhaps we are more connected to the world than we think. In this volume, I have endeavored to show that our inner experience of our most private relationships is in fact deeply interwoven with other relationships, which are themselves interwoven with still other relationships. I have argued that the social contextual perspective can yield insights as well as practical guidance on a variety of social problems. But I also intend the perspective to be a more general way of placing ourselves in the world—as a means of connecting ourselves to others in time and space.

Cultivating a network perspective begins with deliberate efforts to understand how we are linked to others, both directly and indirectly. And we are linked, even to groups and individuals who seem distant and hostile. Often we are linked far more directly than we imagine. Paolini and her colleagues

(2004), for example, found that Catholics and Protestants in conflict-torn Northern Ireland were usually linked by both direct and indirect friendships. Nearly 90% had at least a few friends in the other group and over 90% could think of friends who had friends in the other group (S. Paolini, personal communication, May 5, 2005). If groups with such a history of strife are linked, how might each of us be linked to those whose views seem alien to us or whose lifestyles seem abhorrent? Much has been made of the idea that we are all connected by just a few "degrees of separation" in a network. But how could we use this knowledge to create a sense of community and a sense of personal connection to events and people that are far away or that we know only through mediated images? On a personal level, when a great or terrible event occurs in the world, we might gather our friends and family together to discuss whether we know people who were there, who were affected. We could reach out to gather and compare similar reports from those who lie just beyond our immediate social circle.

Within our communities, taking a network perspective means that we look for opportunities to make visible the too often invisible connections between groups as well as between the present and the past. This happened recently in my own town of Seattle when Julie Otsuka was invited to read from *When the Emperor Was Divine* (2002), her emotionally moving novel of Japanese American internment during World War II. The reading took place in a civic book club at a local branch library (Marshall, 2005). On this evening, the normally small audience swelled to over 130. After Ms. Otsuka had finished her reading and answered a few questions, the moderator thought to ask if there were any former internees in the audience. Silently, they began to rise to their feet. First a few in the front, then others scattered throughout the audience, sometimes in small groups, sometimes in pairs, sometimes alone; until 30 people were standing in silence. And in this moment of recognition, the audience of strangers broke into an applause that both honored the internees and ratified the common bonds of community.

Beyond a way of placing ourselves in the world, the social contextual perspective gives us a new appreciation for the power of personal choice and action. What we say and do flows out into the social world like ripples from a pebble cast into a pond. Others are changed in this widening arc of consequence. Our choices and actions become the context to which others respond. They reverberate in social networks in places far beyond our recognition. Sometimes they even come back to change us. In this way the effects of what we say and do go on for a very long time. Maybe they go on forever.

Measures of Relationship Development and Networks

This appendix contains descriptions of the measures used to derive most of the original models and tests presented in the preceding chapters. Four of the data sets used common measures and differed from each other only in terms of whether they were focused on same-sex friendships or romantic relationships and whether the sample was composed of adolescents or young adults. The measures used in these core studies are now described, followed by a description of the measures utilized in a more detailed study of romantic relationships. Additional notes on the specific analyses used to derive the models presented in chapters 4 through 7 may be found in Appendix B.

CORE STUDIES OF RELATIONAL AND NETWORK FACTORS

The four primary data sets used in this book (see Table A.1) were drawn from two high schools located in the suburbs of Seattle, Washington and from students at the University of Washington. These data sets were used for the analysis of relationship initiation in chapter 3, for the analyses of same-sex friendships in chapter 4, romantic relationships in chapter 5, for the comparisons of relational types and age groups in chapter 6, for the exploration of sexual differences and similarities in chapter 7, and for the general model presented in chapter 10.

Measures of Relational Development

The studies presented in chapters 4 and 5 addressed three broad aspects of relational development: closeness, commitment, and the amount of communication with the partner. Each of these factors was based on a series of more specific measures, now described.

TABLE A.1

Design of Four Core Studies

Relationship Type	Age Group	
	Adolescent	Young Adult
Same-sex friendships	Study 1	Study 2
	$N = 204$	$N = 274$
Heterosexual romantic relationships	Study 3	Study 4
	$N = 135$	$N = 245$

Closeness.   A general factor assessing intimacy or closeness between relational partners was derived from six measures:

1. *Love.*   Responses to Rubin's (1970) 13-item love scale assessing the degree of emotional attachment were recorded on 5-point scales and summed to yield a total score.
2. *Liking.*   Responses to Rubin's (1970) 13-item measure of liking were recorded on 5-point scales and summed to yield a total score.
3. *Perceived Similarity.*   Subjects responded to five items assessing the degree to which they felt that the relational partner was generally similar, liked the same things, had similar attitudes, values, and a similar outlook on life. Subjects recorded their level of agreement or disagreement with each item on 5-point scales, which were then summed.
4. *Solidarity.*   This general measure of intimacy was developed by Wheeless (1976) and consists of 10 items assessing interdependence, trust, attraction, and disclosure. Responses were recorded on 5-point scales and summed.
5. *Uncertainty.*   An 8-item measure (Parks et al., 1983) was used to assess the extent to which subjects felt that they knew and could predict and explain their relational partner's feelings, attitudes, and behaviors. Items were summed to produce a total score. Higher values were indicative of greater uncertainty about the partner and the relationship.
6. *Communication Satisfaction.*   A 19-item measure developed by Hecht (1978) was used to evaluate the level of enjoyment, ease, understanding, and satisfaction that subjects experienced in interactions with their partners. Items were assessed using 5-point scales and summed.

Commitment.   A factor assessing commitment to the relationship created from responses to these three measures:

1. *Relational Commitment.*   Subjects reporting on a romantic relationship were asked to rate their level of agreement with the statement, "I think that the two of us will get married someday." Those reporting on same-sex friendships were responded to the statement, "I think that the two of us will be friends forever." Responses were recorded on a 5-point scale.
2. *Short-term commitment.*   Subjects were asked to rate the probability (0 to 100%) that they would still be with their current friend or romantic partner in 3 months.
3. *Long-term commitment.*   Subjects were asked to rate the probability (0 to 100%) that they would, depending on the type of relationship, get married someday or be friends forever.

Amount of Communication With the Partner.   The amount of interaction with the relational partner (same-sex friend or romantic partner) was assessed in these studies with two items:

1. *Frequency of interaction.*   Subjects reported the number of days in the previous 2 weeks (0 to 14) in which they had any face-to-face communication with their partner.
2. *Time.*   Subjects were asked to estimate what percentage (0 to 100%) of their free time in the previous 2 weeks that they had spent with their relational partner.

Measures of Network Factors

The first step in measuring the social network factors assessed in these studies was to create rosters both for the subject's own network and for the partner's network. Subjects were first asked to list the four family members or relatives to whom they felt the closest and the eight nonkin to whom they felt the closest. They were then asked to obtain a similar list from their relational partner (dating partner or same-sex friend). This resulted in a total network roster of 24 persons—12 from the subject's network and 12 from the partner's network (see chap. 2, this volume, for a discussion of approaches to generating network rosters).

Once the rosters were generated, subjects were asked several additional questions about each person in the total network.

1. *Range of contact in the partner's network.*   Subjects indicated whether or not they had ever met each person in the partner's network face to face. Separate counts were made for the number of the partner's relatives (0 to 4) and nonrelatives (0 to 8) that the subject had actually met.

2. *Prior contact.*   Subjects indicated whether they had known each member of their own network and each member of the partner's network prior to meeting the relational partner for the first time. Responses were summed to produce separate totals (0 to 12) measuring the degree of prior contact with the members of their own network and with he members of the partner's network.

3. *Frequency of communication with the partner's network.*   Subjects responded to two items about the frequency of communication for each person in the partner's network whom they had met. In the first item, they reported the number of days in the previous two weeks (0 to 14) in which they had communicated with the network member. They also rated their level of agreement or disagreement, using a 5-point scale, with a statement asserting that they communicated "very often" with the network member. Scores on each of these scales were averaged across known network members to yield two separate indicators.

4. *Liking for the partner's network.*   Subjects rated how much they disliked or liked each known member of the partner's network on a 5-point scale. Responses were averaged so as to yield measures of attraction to the partner's relatives and to the partner's friends.

5. *Support.*   Subjects evaluated network members' support for the relationship by indicating how much they disagreed or agreed, using 5-point scales, with two statements, one asserting that the network member approved of the relationship and another asserting that the network often expressed support or approval for the relationship. Responses were summed and then averaged to yield support scores for each network sector (family and friends) as well as for the total network. These measures were obtained both for the members of the subject's own network and for the known members of the partner's network.

AN ELABORATED STUDY OF RELATIONAL AND NETWORK FACTORS

Compared to the others, the final primary data set centered on a richer, more specific set of relational and network factors in young adult romantic relationships. The primary analysis of this data set was presented in chapter 5 and secondary analysis of gender and ethnic differences was presented in chapter 7.

Measures of Relational Factors

Six dimensions of relationship change were examined: the amount of interaction, depth of interaction, interactive synchrony (conversational interdependence), commitment, predictability, and code personalization. Each of these factors was based on a series of more specific measures, now described.

Amount of Communication With the Partner.   Subjects were asked to estimate what percentage (0 to 100%) of their free time in the last 2 weeks they had spent with their relational partner.

Depth of Interaction.   Two scales were used to measure the overall intimacy or depth of interaction between the relational partners:

1. *Love.*   Responses to Rubin's (1970) 13-item love scale assessing the degree of emotional attachment were recorded on 7-point scales and summed to yield a total score.
2. *Intimacy.*   Three items dealing with the disclosure of intimate personal information were adapted from Wheeless' (1978) global self-disclosure and combined with three original items to yield a measure of the overall intimacy of the relationship. The original items assessed perceptions of closeness, love, and openness. These six items were rated on 7-point scales and summed to produce a total score.

Interactive Synchrony.   Subjects responded to four items regarding the extent to which conversations with the partner were perceived as containing awkward silences (reversed), taking a lot of effort (reversed), easy, or smooth and free-flowing. These items were rated on 7-point scales and summed to yield a total score.

Commitment.   Three types of items were used to measure the subject's commitment to his or her romantic relationship:

1. *Short-term commitment.*   Subjects were asked to rate the probability (0 to 100%) that they would still be with their romantic partner in 3 months.
2. *Long-term commitment.*   Subjects were asked to rate the probability (0 to 100%) that they would get married someday.
3. *General commitment.*   Subjects completed a five-item global commitment scale, focusing on the extent to which the subject felt the relationship was important, was committed to maintaining it, and would work to maintain it. Items were rated on 7-point scales and summed.

Predictability (Uncertainty).   The degree to which respondents felt able to reduce uncertainty about the partner's behavior and about the relationship was assessed with two separate measures:

1. *Uncertainty.*   Responses to an eight-item uncertainty scale developed by Parks and Adelman (1983) were scored on 7-point scales and summed.
2. *Attributional confidence.*   Responses to an eight-item measure of respondents' confidence in their understanding of their relational partner's mo-

tives and actions (Gudykunst & Nishida, 1986) were assessed on 100-point scales and averaged to yield a total score between zero and 100.

Code Personalization. Three items were used to evaluate the extent to which participants assigned "special meanings" to their words, used special nicknames or terms of endearment, and relied on private gestures or looks that communicated relationally specific meanings. These items were rated on 7-point scales and summed.

Measures of Network Factors

Participants in the study were asked to list the names of the 12 people with whom they had communicated most often in the previous 2 weeks. The communication could include conversations, phone calls, and other forms of contact, but subjects were told to exclude people with whom the communication was primarily one-way (e.g., sitting in a lecture listening to a teacher). Subjects were instructed not to list their romantic partner, but they were instructed to obtain a similar list from their romantic partner. This yielded a total network roster containing the subject's 12 most frequent contacts and the partner's 12 most frequent contacts. Additional questions regarding these contacts and the relationships between them provided measures of the six network factors now described.

Network Overlap. The number of matches between people listed by the subject and those listed by his or her partner yielded a measure of network overlap. Although it was possible for subjects to have completely overlapping networks, in practice, most subjects reported between two and four overlapping network members ($M = 2.63$, $SD = 2.24$).

Cross-Network Contact. Two measures were used to assess the participants' range of contact in each other's networks:

1. *Range 1* - The number of people the partner had met in the respondent's network (0 to 12).
2. *Range2* - The number of people the respondent had met in the partner's network (0 to 12).

Cross-Network Density. Cross-network density represents the extent to which the members of one partner's network communicate with the members of the other partner's network. It is a measure of network-to-network communication quite apart from how often the partners communicate with each other or with network members themselves. The number of the potential cross-network linkages for a given couple may be calculated using the following formula:

$$\text{Cross-network links} = \frac{(N)(N-1)-(X)(X-1)-(Y)(Y-1)}{2}$$

Where:

X = The total number of people in Partner A's network, not counting either relational partner.

Y = The total number of people in Partner B's network, not counting either relational partner.

N = The total number of people in the combined network, not counting either relational partner.

In our case, we asked each partner to his or her 12 most frequent contacts. Thus there were 12 in Partner A's network (X), 12 in Partner B's network (Y), and a total of 24, not counting the partners themselves. There are 276 possible linkages among members of the total network, but 66 are within Partner A's network and 66 are within Partner B's network, so that leaves the total number of potential cross-network contacts to be 144. These were explored by asking respondents to rate how often the numbers of each other's network had communicated with each other on a scale ranging from zero to four (with zero being that they didn't know each other and four representing a common or overlapping member). Two measures were derived:

1. *Net 1* - The number of actual links between members of the subject's network and members of the partner's network that were reported out of the possible total of 144 (i.e., nonzero entries).
2. *Net 2* - The total frequency of cross-network communication, measured as the sum of all cross-network communication scores (0 to 4) minus the total for any shared or overlapping members.

Frequency of Communication With Partner's Network.   Respondents reported the number of days (0 to 14) they had communicated with each known member of the partner's network during the previous 2 weeks. They were instructed to include telephone as well as face-to-face contacts. The partner's 12-person roster was randomly split into two equal groups and frequency scores within each group were averaged. This provided two indicators for the amount of communication with the partner's network.

Support From Network Members.   Respondents rated support or approval for the dating relationship from each known member of the partner's network as well as from each member of their own network. Responses were registered on 9-point scales bounded by the phrases, "strong disapproval" and "strong approval." Subjects were instructed to use the median value when they thought the network member was neutral or when they felt they could not guess how the person actually felt. The partner's 12-person roster was randomly split into to equal groups and scores with each group were averaged. The respondent's own 12-person roster was split similarly. The result was four indicators for network support—two assessing support from the partner's network and two assessing support from the subject's own network.

Technical Notes on the Models

DEVELOPING AND FITTING THE MODELS

Structural equation modeling techniques were used to derive the primary models presented in this volume. This approach allowed us to manage multiple indicators or measures of theoretic concepts and to evaluate how the more general theoretic concepts or factors were associated with each other. This was accomplished by means of a series of confirmatory factor analyses using AMOS 4.0 (Arbuckle & Wothke, 1999). Developing these models entailed first assigning specific measures or indicators to a series of underlying theoretic factors and then specifying the predicted relationships among the theoretic factors. From a substantive standpoint, our greatest interest is in the associations among the theoretic factors, and these have been presented in the figures accompanying chapters 4, 5, 6, 7, and 10. In this Appendix, additional information is presented regarding the technical features of these models and their derivation.

One of these features is the "loading" of individual indicators on the underlying theoretical factors. In a well-formed model, all of the indicators should load at least moderately on a single factor (standardized coefficient $\geq .50$). The component of observed variance not due to an indicator's loading on its assigned factors was specified as *error variance*. In some cases these errors may be correlated with each other. For example, survey items that have similar formats may elicit responses associated not with the content of the questions, but with their format. That is, the errors represent variance due to a common method rather than the content of the items. Items that are physically close together in a survey may generate correlated errors even if their content differs. Correlated errors were allowed in the models presented in this volume in cases where a sound rationale could be constructed for their inclusion.

Fitting the Models

Models were developed through an iterative process in which an initial model was tested, revised, and retested. This continued until further changes in the model failed to significantly improve the overall fit between the model and the data (using a 1-degree of freedom Chi-square test). Goodness of fit or the overall quality of each model was evaluated using several criteria:

1. *Significance of parameters.* The extent to which the parameters predicted to be significant in the model were actually statistically significant (e.g., factor loadings, correlated errors, correlations between factors).
2. *Chi-square test for discrepancy.* A nonsignificant probability ($p > .05$) value for this test indicates that there is not a large discrepancy between the model being tested and the data in the population (Arbuckle & Wothke, 1999).
3. *CFI.* The comparative fit ratio represents a ratio of the discrepancy between the fit of the model being tested to the data, on one hand, and the discrepancy between the fit of an independence model in which all observed variables are assumed to be uncorrelated and the data, on the other hand. CFI values approaching 1.0 are considered evident of a good fit, while values greater than .90 are considered evidence of an acceptable fit (Arbuckle & Wothke, 1999; Bentler, 1990).
4. *RFI.* Although it is a more conservative measure than the comparative fit index, the relative fit index is evaluated in the same way—a good fit is indicated by values close to 1.0 and values greater than .90 and considered evidence of an acceptable fit (Arbuckle & Wothke, 1999; Bollen, 1986).
5. *RMSEA.* A model is generally considered a close fit when the value of the root mean square error of approximation is .05 or less (Browne & Cudeck, 1993).

In general, then, an acceptable model would be one in which all of the predicted parameters were statistically significant, the overall chi-square was not significant, the CFI and RFI were greater than .90, and the RMSEA was less than .05 (see also, B. M. Byrne, 2001; Hu & Bentler, 1995).

Analysis Notes

The most important substantive features of the models presented in this volume—particularly the associations between and among the various relational and network factors—are described in the text of chapters 4, 5, 6, 7, and 10. Additional technical information about the quality and fit of the models is now provided. It is keyed to the figures in which the models are described in these chapters.

Figure 4.1—Adolescent Friendships.   The model was based on observations gathered from 204 adolescents. All 19 indicators loaded significantly on their assigned factors and all but two loaded (standardized regression weights) at greater than .50 (uncertainty and commitment to continuing the relationship for 3 more months). Predicted correlations between factors were statistically significant, except the correlation between communication and commitment ($r = .11$, ns). Goodness of fit: $\chi^2 = (df\ 120) = 140.33$, $p = .10$; CFI = .998; RFI = .982, RMSEA = .029.

Figure 4.2—Young Adult Friendships.   The model was based on observations gathered from 274 young adults. Loadings for all 19 indicators were statistically significant and greater than .50. All predicted correlations between factors were statistically significant. Goodness of fit: $\chi^2 = (df\ 113) = 157.24$, $p = .004$; CFI = .997; RFI = .984, RMSEA = .038.

Figure 5.1—Adolescent Romantic Relationships.   Observations on 19 indicators from 135 adolescents in opposite-sex romantic relationships were used to develop this model. All indicators loaded significantly on their assigned factors. With the exception of an indicator measuring support from the subject's own family, which loaded at .49, all loaded at .50 or above. Figure 5.1 illustrates the linkages between factors that were statistically significant. Goodness of fit: $\chi^2 = (df\ 135) = 160.65$, $p = .065$; CFI = .997; RFI = .971, RMSEA = .038.

Figure 5.2—Young Adult Romantic Relationships I.   This model was derived from observations gathered from 245 young adults involved in opposite-sex romantic relationships. The indicators all loaded significantly on their assigned factors. All but two of the 19 loaded at .50 or above. The exceptions were indicators of liking and perceived similarity, which loaded at .43 and .49, respectively on the closeness factor. All correlations between and among the relational and network factors were statistically significant ($p < .0001$). Goodness of fit: $\chi^2 = (df\ 116) = 146.19$, $p = .030$; CFI = .998; RFI = .983, RMSEA = .033.

Figures 5.3 to 5.5—Young Adult Romantic Relationships II.   Observations on 26 indicators were gathered from 232 young adults. Indicators were assigned to six relational and six network factors. Two of the factors, *network overlap* and the *amount of communication with the partner*, were estimated with single indicators whose loading was fixed at 1.0. The remaining 24 indicators all loaded significantly and above .60, except for the indicator of synchrony that assessed the incidence of awkward silence in conversations with the partner. It loaded at .44 on the *synchrony* factor. Correlations among the relational factors are given in Fig. 5.3, while the correlations among the network factors are given in Fig. 5.4. The correlations between relational and network factors are provided in Fig. 5.5. Goodness of fit: $\chi^2 = (df\ 247) = 282.06$, $p = .062$; CFI = .998; RFI = .979, RMSEA = .025.

Figure 6.1—Adolescent Personal Relationships.   This model was derived by combining the samples for adolescent friendships and adolescent romantic relationships into a single dataset ($N = 339$). In the final model, all 19 indicators were associated significantly and at .45 or greater with the six factors to which they had been assigned. As discussed in text, all six factors were significantly associated. Goodness of fit: $\chi^2 = (df\ 112) = 137.93$, $p = .049$; CFI = .999; RFI = .988, RMSEA = .026.

Figure 6.2—Young Adult Personal Relationships.   The friendship and romantic relationship samples for young adults were combined to yield a larger sample of young adult personal relationships ($N = 519$). All 19 indicators loaded at $\geq .58$ ($ps < .0001$) on the relational and network factors to which they had been assigned. Factors were significantly associated in the manner portrayed in Fig. 6.2. Goodness of fit: $\chi^2 = (df\ 106) = 175.27$, $p < .001$; CFI = .998; RFI = .990, RMSEA = .036.

Figure 6.3—General Model of Friendships.   This model was derived from surveys of same-sex friendships in both age groups ($N = 478$). Indicators loaded at $\geq .55$ ($ps < .0001$) on the relational and network factors to which they had been assigned. Factors were associated as portrayed in Fig. 6.3. Goodness of fit: $\chi^2 = (df\ 97) = 136.27$, $p = .005$; CFI = .999; RFI = .991, RMSEA = .029.

Figure 6.4—General Model of Romantic Relationships.   This model was derived from surveys of opposite-sex romantic relationships in both age groups ($N = 390$). Indicators loaded at $\geq .55$ ($ps < .0001$) on the relational and network factors to which they had been assigned. Factors were associated as portrayed in Fig. 6.4. Goodness of fit: $\chi^2 = (df\ 109) = 132.61$, $p = .062$; CFI = .999; RFI = .989, RMSEA = .024.

Figure 7.1—General Relational Model for Males.   The 357 males in both age groups who participated in our core studies of friendship and romantic relationships were brought together into a single sample. The final model arrayed 19 indicators on three relational and four network factors. All indicators loaded on their assigned factors at $\geq .51$ (p's $< .0001$). Correlations among and between the network and relational factors were statistically significant ($ps < .001$). Goodness of fit: $\chi^2 = (df\ 107) = 155.30$, $p = .002$; CFI = .998; RFI = .986, RMSEA = .036.

Figure 7.2—General Relational Model for Females. The 501 females in both age groups who participated in our core studies of friendship and romantic relationships were brought together into a single sample. The final model arrayed 19 indicators on three relational and four network factors. All indicators loaded on their assigned factors at $\geq .51$ ($ps < .0001$). Correlations among and between the network and relational factors were statistically significant ($ps < .0001$). Goodness of fit: $\chi^2 = (df\ 104) = 137.50$, $p = .016$; CFI $= .999$; RFI $= .991$, RMSEA $= .025$.

Figure 7.3—Same-Sex Female Relationships. In the samples of adolescent and young adult friendships, a total of 292 represented friendships between females. A model was derived for this group. The 18 of the 19 indicators loaded at $\geq .58$. Rubin's liking scale loaded on the closeness factor at .49. All indicators loaded significantly on their assigned factors ($ps < .0001$) and each factor was significantly correlated with all of the other factors ($ps < .0001$). Goodness of fit: $\chi^2 = (df\ 112) = 132.54$, $p = .090$; CFI $= .999$; RFI $= .987$, RMSEA $= .025$.

Figure 7.4—Same-Sex Male Relationships. The core samples of adolescents and young adults contained 186 males who had reported on a same-sex friendship. Loadings for the 19 indicators all loaded $\geq .55$, except for a measure of the likelihood of remaining friends for the next 3 months. This indicator loaded at .45. All 19 indicators loaded significantly on their assigned factors ($ps < .0001$), however, and each factor was associated significantly with each of the others ($ps < .05$). Goodness of fit: $\chi^2 = (df\ 112) = 158.61$, $p = .002$; CFI $= .996$; RFI $= .975$, RMSEA $= .047$.

Figures 7.5, 7.7, 7.9—Interethnic Romantic Relationships.
The larger sample of young adult romantic relationships in Study II was split into two groups. One group contained 82 relationships between people of different ethnic groups. The model derived for this group included 26 indicators that had been assigned to six relational and six network factors. Two of the factors, network overlap and the amount of communication with the partner, were estimated with single indicators whose loading was fixed at 1.0. The remaining indicators loaded at $\geq .56$, except for an item regarding the prevalence of awkward silences in conversation that loaded at .35 on the synchrony factor. All nonfixed loadings were significant ($ps < .01$). Correlations among the factors are presented in the figures and discussed in text. All of these correlations were significant with the exception of a marginal association between the depth and synchrony factors ($p < .07$). Goodness of fit: $\chi^2 = (df\ 257) = 288.03$, $p = .089$; CFI $= .995$; RFI $= .941$, RMSEA $= .039$.

Figures 7.6, 7.8, 7.10—Intraethnic Romantic Relationships.   A model of 136 romantic relationships between people of the same ethnic group was derived from a study of young adult romantic relationships (Study II). This model was based on 26 indicators arrayed across six relational and five network factors. Two indicators were fixed as already noted, but the remaining 24 indicators all loaded $\geq .61$ on their assigned factors ($ps < .0001$). All of the correlations among factors included in the final model were significant (p < .05) with the exception of the association between synchrony and network overlap ($r = .11, p < .08$). Goodness of fit: $\chi^2 = (df\,255) = 288.64, p = .072$; CFI = .997; RFI = .965, RMSEA = .031.

Figure 10.1—General Model of Personal Relationships.   The 858 subjects in the core studies of friendship and romantic relationships among adolescents and young adults were brought together into a single sample. A general model of personal relationships was derived from 19 indicators arrayed across three relational factors and four network factors. All indicators loaded on their respective factors $\geq .55$ ($ps < .0001$). As noted in Fig. 10.1, each factor was significantly correlated with each other factor. Goodness of fit: $\chi^2 = (df\,96) = 176.11, p < .001$; CFI = .998; RFI = .993, RMSEA = .031.

References

Abbey, E. (1988). *The fool's progress: An honest novel.* New York: Holt.

Abrahamson, M. (1996). *Urban enclaves: Identity and place in America.* New York: St. Martin's Press.

Acitelli, L. K. (2001). Maintaining and enhancing a relationship by attending to it. In J. H. Harvey & A. Wenzel (Eds.), *Close romantic relationships: Maintenance and enhancement* (pp. 153–167). Mahwah, NJ: Lawrence Erlbaum Associates.

Adams, J. M., & Jones, W. H. (1997). The conceptualization of marital commitment: An integrative analysis. *Journal of Personality and Social Psychology, 69,* 1177–1196.

Adelman, M. B., & Siemon, M. (1986). Communicating the relational shift: Separation among adult twins. *American Journal of Psychotherapy, 40,* 96–109.

Adolescent unintended pregnancy: The scope of the problem. (1994). *Contraception Reports, 5*(2), 4–5.

Adolph, C., Ramos, D. E., Linton, K. L., & Grimes, D. A. (1995). Pregnancy among Hispanic teenagers: Is good parental communication a deterrent? *Contraception, 51*(5), 303–306.

Afifi, T. D. (2003). "Feeling caught" in stepfamilies: Managing boundary turbulence through appropriate communication privacy rules. *Journal of Social and Personal Relationships, 20,* 729–755.

Afifi, T. D., & Olson, L. (2005). The chilling effect in families and the pressure to conceal secrets. *Communication Monographs, 72,* 192–216.

Afifi, W. A., & Weiner, J. L. (2004). Toward a theory of motivated information management. *Communication Theory, 14,* 167–190.

Agnew, C. R., Loving, T. J., & Drigotas, S. M. (2001). Substituting the forest for the trees: Social networks and the prediction of romantic relationship state and fate. *Journal of Personality and Social Psychology, 81,* 1042–1057.

Agnew, C. R., Loving, T. J., Le, B., & Goodfriend, W. (2004). Thinking close: Measuring relational closeness a perceived self-other inclusion. In D. J. Mashek & A. Aron (Eds.), *Handbook of closeness and intimacy* (pp. 103–115). Mahwah, NJ: Lawrence Erlbaum Associates.

Albeck, S., & Kaydar, D. (2002). Divorced mothers: Their network of friends pre- and post-divorce. *Journal of Divorce and Remarriage, 36*(3–4), 111–138.

Albrecht, T. L., & Adelman, M. B. (1987). Communicating social support: A theoretical perspective. In T. L. Albrecht & M. B. Adelman (Eds.), *Communicating social support* (pp. 18–39). Newbury Park, CA: Sage.

Albrecht, T. L., & Hall, B. J. (1991a). Facilitating talk about new ideas: The role of personal relationships in organizational innovation. *Communication Monographs, 58,* 273–288.

Albrecht, T. L., & Hall, B. J. (1991b). Relational and content differences between elites and outsiders in innovation networks. *Human Communication Research, 17,* 535–561.

Albrecht, T. L., & Ropp, V. A. (1984). Communicating about innovation in networks of three U.S. organizations. *Journal of Communication, 34,* 78–91.

Alexander, F. (1950). *Psychosomatic medicine.* New York: Norton.

Allan, G. (1998). Friendship, sociology and social structure. *Journal of Social and Personal Relationships, 15,* 685–702.

Allison, P. D., & Furstenberg, F. F. (1989). How marital dissolution affects children: Variations by age and sex. *Developmental Psychology, 25,* 540–549.

Allport, F. (1924). *Social psychology.* Boston: Houghton Mifflin.

Allport, G. W. (1954). *The nature of prejudice.* Cambridge, MA: Perseus Books.

Altman, I., & Haythorn, W. W. (1965). Interpersonal exchange in isolation. *Sociometry, 28,* 411–426.

Altman, I., & Taylor, D. (1973). *Social penetration: The development of interpersonal relationships.* New York: Holt, Rinehart, & Winston.

Altman, I., Vinsel, A., & Brown, B. B. (1981). Dialectic conceptions in social psychology: An application to social penetration and privacy regulation. In L. Berkowitz (Ed.), *Advances in experimental social psychology* (Vol. 14, pp. 107–160). New York: Academic Press.

Amato, P. R. (1999). The postdivorce society: How divorce is shaping the family and other forms of social organization. In R. A. Thompson & P. R. Amato (Eds.), *The postdivorce family: Children, parenting, and society* (pp. 161–190). Thousand Oaks, CA: Sage.

Ambert, A. (1988). Relationships with former in-laws: A research note. *Journal of Marriage and the Family, 50,* 679–686.

Ambert, A. (1989). *Ex-spouses and new spouses: A study of relationships.* Greenwich, CT: JAI Press.

Appleyard, M. (1996). How does knowledge flow? Interfirm patterns in the semiconductor industry. *Strategic Management Journal, 17,* 137–154.

Arbuckle, J. L., & Wothke, W. (1999). *Amos 4.0 User's Guide.* Chicago: SmallWaters Corporation.

Argyle, M. (1969). *Social interaction.* New York: Atherton.

Argyle, M., Henderson, M., Bond, M., Izuka, Y., & Contarello, A. (1986). Cross-cultural variations in relationship rules. *International Journal of Psychology, 21,* 287–315.

Aries, E. J. (1996). *Men and women in interaction: Reconsidering the differences.* New York: Oxford University Press.

Aries, E. J., & Johnson, F. L. (1983). Close friendship in adulthood: Conversational content between same-sex friends. *Sex Roles, 9,* 1183–1196.

Aristotle. (1934). *Nicomachean ethics* (H. Rackham, Trans.). Cambridge, MA: Harvard University Press.

Aristotle. (1954). *Rhetoric* (W. Roberts, Trans.). New York: Random House.

Arnett, J. J. (2000). Emerging adulthood: A theory of development from the late teens through the twenties. *American Psychologist, 55,* 469–480.

Arnett, J. J. (2001). Conceptions of the transition to adulthood: Perspectives from adolescence through midlife. *Journal of Adult Development, 8,* 133–143.

Arnett, J. J. (2003). Conceptions of the transition to adulthood among emerging adults in American ethnic groups. In J. J. Arnett & N. L. Galambos (Eds.), *Exploring cultural conceptions of the transition to adulthood: New directions for child and adolescent development* (pp. 63–75). San Francisco: Jossey-Bass.

Aron, A., & Aron, E. N. (1986). *Love as the expansion of self: Understanding attraction and satisfaction.* New York: Hemisphere.

Aron, A., Aron, E. N., & Smollan, D. (1992). Inclusion of other in the self scale and the structure of interpersonal closeness. *Journal of Personality and Social Psychology, 63,* 596–612.

Aron, A., Mashek, D. J., & Aron, E. N. (2004). Closeness as including other in the self. In D. J. Mashek & A. Aron (Eds.), *Handbook of closeness and intimacy* (pp. 27–41). Mahwah, NJ: Lawrence Erlbaum Associates.

Aron, A., Norman, C. C., & Aron, E. N. (2001). Shared self-expanding activities as a means of maintaining and enhancing close romantic relationships. In J. H. Harvey & A. Wenzel (Eds.), *Close romantic relationships: Maintenance and enhancement* (pp. 47–66). Mahwah, NJ: Lawrence Erlbaum Associates.

Arriaga, X. B., & Foshee, V. A. (2004). Adolescent dating violence: Do adolescents follow in their friends', or their parents', footsteps? *Journal of Interpersonal Violence, 19*, 162–184.

Arriaga, X. B., & Oskamp, S. (Eds.). (1999). *Violence in intimate relationships.* Thousand Oaks, CA: Sage.

Asen, E. (2002). Multiple family therapy: An overview. *Journal of Family Therapy, 24*(1), 3–16.

Augustyn, M., & Simons-Morton, B. G. (1995). Adolescent drinking and driving: Etiology and interpretation. *Journal of Drug Education, 25*, 41–59.

Babrow, A. S. (2001). Uncertainty, value, communication and problematic integration. *Journal of Communication, 51*, 553–573.

Backman, C. W. (1980). The premature abandonment of promising research. In R. Gilmour & S. W. Duck (Eds.), *The development of social psychology* (pp. 163–179). New York: Academic Associates.

Ballard-Reisch, D. S., & Weigel, D. J. (1999). Communication processes in marital commitment. In J. M. Adams & W. H. Jones (Eds.), *Handbook of interpersonal commitment and relationship stability* (pp. 407–424). New York: Kluwer Adademic/Plenum Publishers.

Bank, B. J., & Hansford, S. L. (2000). Gender and friendship: Why are men's best same-sex friendships less intimate and supportive? *Personal Relationships, 7*, 63–78.

Barnes, J. A. (1954). Class and committees in a Norwegian island parish. *Human Relations, 7*, 39–58.

Barnes, J. A. (1969a). Graph theory and social networks: A technical comment on connectedness and connectivity. *Sociology, 3*, 215–232.

Barnes, J. A. (1969b). Networks and political process. In J. C. Mitchell (Ed.), *Social networks in urban situations: Analyses of personal relationships in Central African towns* (pp. 51–76). Manchester, England: Manchester University Press.

Barzun, J. (2000). *From dawn to decadence: 500 years of Western cultural life.* New York: HarperCollins.

Bascow, S. A., & Rubenfeld, K. (2003). "Troubles talk": Effects of gender and gender-typing. *Sex Roles, 48*, 183–187.

Basu, M. (2005, February 7). In India, no expense is spared on weddings. *Seattle Post-Intelligencer,* p. A4.

Bateson, G. (1958). *Naven* (2nd ed.). Stanford: Stanford University Press.

Bavelas, A. (1948). A mathematical model for group structures. *Applied Anthropology, 7*, 16–30.

Bavelas, J. B., Black, A., Chovil, N., & Mullett, J. (1990). *Equivocal communication.* Newbury Park, CA: Sage.

Baxter, L. A. (1987). Symbols of relationship identity in relationship cultures. *Journal of Social and Personal Relationships, 4*, 261–280.

Baxter, L. A. (1988). A dialectical perspective on communication strategies in relationship development. In S. Duck (Ed.), *Handbook of personal relationships* (pp. 257–273). New York: Wiley.

Baxter, L. A. (1992). Root metaphors in accounts of developing romantic relationships. *Journal of Social and Personal Relationships, 9*, 253–275.

Baxter, L. A. (1993). The social side of personal relationships: A dialectical perspective. In S. Duck (Ed.), *Social context and relationships* (pp. 139–165). Newbury Park, CA: Sage.

Baxter, L. A., & Bullis, C. (1986). Turning points in developing romantic relationships. *Human Communication Research, 12*, 469–493.

Baxter, L. A., Dun, T., & Sahlstein, E. (2001). Rules for relating communicated among social network members. *Journal of Social and Personal Relationships, 18*(2), 173–199.

Baxter, L. A., & Montgomery, B. M. (1996). *Relating: Dialogues and dialectics*. New York: Guilford.

Baxter, L. A., & Montgomery, B. M. (2000). Rethinking communication in personal relationships from a dialectical perspective. In K. Dindia & S. Duck (Eds.), *Communication and personal relationships* (pp. 31–53). New York: Wiley.

Baxter, L. A., & Pittman, G. (2001). Communicatively remembering turning points of relational development in heterosexual romantic relationships. *Communication Reports, 14*(1), 1–17.

Baxter, L. A., & Simon, E. P. (1993). Relationship maintenance strategies and dialectical contradictions in personal relationships. *Journal of Social and Personal Relationships, 10*, 225–242.

Baxter, L. A., & Widenmann, S. (1993). Revealing and not revealing the status of romantic relationships to social networks. *Journal of Social and Personal Relationships, 10*, 321–337.

Baxter, L. A., & Wilmot, W. W. (1984). "Secret tests": Social strategies for acquiring information about the state of the relationship. *Human Communication Research, 11*, 171–202.

Baxter, L. A., & Wilmot, W. W. (1985). Taboo topics in close relationships. *Journal of Social and Personal Relationships, 2*, 253–296.

Bearman, P. S., Moody, J., & Stovel, K. (2004). Chains of affection: The structure of adolescent romantic and sexual networks. *American Journal of Sociology, 110*, 44–91.

Beautrais, A. L., Joyce, P. R., & Mulder, R. T. (1996). Risk factors for serious suicide attempts among youths aged 13 through 24 years. *Journal of the American Academy of Child and Adolescent Psychiatry, 35*, 1174–1182.

Bell, R. A., & Buerkel-Rothfuss, N. L. (1990). S(he) loves me, s(he) loves me not: Predictors of relational information-seeking in courtship and beyond. *Communication Quarterly, 38*, 64–82.

Bell, R. A., Buerkel-Rothfuss, N. L., & Gore, K. E. (1987). "Did you bring the yarmulke for the cabbage patch kid?" The idiomatic communication of young lovers. *Human Communication Research, 14*, 47–67.

Bell, R. A., & Healey, J. G. (1992). Idiomatic communication and interpersonal solidarity in friends' relational cultures. *Human Communication Research, 18*, 307–335.

Bentler, P. M. (1990). Comparative fit indexes in structural models. *Psychological Bulletin, 107*, 238–246.

Berg, J. H., & McQuinn, R. D. (1986). Attraction and exchange in continuing and noncontinuing dating relationships. *Journal of Personality and Social Psychology, 50*, 942–952.

Berg, J. H., Piner, K. E., & Frank, S. M. (1993). Resource theory and close relationships. In U. G. Foa, P. E. Converse & K. Y. Tornblom (Eds.), *Resource theory: Explorations and applications* (pp. 169–196). San Diego, CA: Academic Press.

Berger, C. R. (1979). Beyond initial interaction: Uncertainty, understanding, and the development of interpersonal relationships. In H. Giles & R. St. Clair (Eds.), *Language and social psychology* (pp. 122–144). Oxford: Basil Blackwood.

Berger, C. R., & Calabrese, R. J. (1975). Some explorations in initial interaction and beyond: Toward a developmental theory of interpersonal communication. *Human Communication Research, 1*, 99–112.

Bergler, E. (1948). *Divorce won't help*. New York: Harper.

Bergman, B., & Brismar, B. (1993). Assailants and victims: A comparative study of male wife-beaters and battered males. *Journal of Addictive Diseases, 12*(4), 1–10.

Berkowitz, S. D. (1982). *An introduction to structural analysis*. Toronto: Butterworth & Co.

Bernard, J. (1934). Factors in the distribution of success in marriage. *American Journal of Sociology, 40*, 49–60.

Bernstein, B. (1964). Elaborated and restricted codes: Their social origins and some consequences. *American Anthropologist, 66*(2), 55–69.

Berscheid, E. (1999). The greening of relationship science. *American Psychologist, 54*, 260–266.

Berscheid, E., Snyder, M., & Omoto, A. M. (1989a). Issues in studying close relationships: Conceptualizing and measuring closeness. In C. Hendrick (Ed.), *Close relationships* (pp. 63–91). Newbury Park, CA: Sage.

Berscheid, E., Snyder, M., & Omoto, A. M. (1989b). The relationship closeness inventory: Assessing the closeness of interpersonal relationships. *Journal of Personality and Social Psychology, 57,* 792–807.

Berscheid, E., Snyder, M., & Omoto, A. M. (2004). Measuring closeness: The relationship closeness inventory (RCI) revisited. In D. J. Mashek & A. Aron (Eds.), *Handbook of closeness and intimacy* (pp. 81–101). Mahwah, NJ: Lawrence Erlbaum Associates.

Berscheid, E., & Walster, E. H. (1978). *Interpersonal attraction* (2nd ed.). Reading, MA: Addison-Wesley.

Bigelow, B. J., & LaGaipa, J. J. (1980). The development of friendship values and choice. In H. C. Foot, A. J. Chapman & J. R. Smith (Eds.), *Friendship and social relations in children* (pp. 15–44). New York: John Wiley.

Bijur, P. E., Kurzon, M., Overpeck, M. D., & Scheidt, P. C. (1992). Parental alcohol use, problem drinking, and children's injuries. *Journal of the American Medical Association, 267,* 3166–3171.

Billingham, R. E., & Notebaert, N. L. (1993). Divorce and dating violence revisited: Multivariate analyses using Straus's conflict tactics subscores. *Psychological Reports, 73,* 679–684.

Blau, P. M. (1977a). *Inequality and heterogeneity: A primitive theory of social structure.* New York: Free Press.

Blau, P. M. (1977b). A macrosociological theory of social structure. *American Journal of Sociology, 83,* 26–54.

Bleske-Rechek, A. L., & Buss, D. M. (2001). Opposite-sex friendship: Sex differences and similarities in initiation, selection, and dissolution. *Personality and Social Psychology Bulletin, 27,* 1310–1323.

Blumberg, H. H. (1972). Communication of interpersonal evaluations. *Journal of Personality and Social Psychology, 23,* 157–162.

Blumer, H. (1969). *Symbolic interactionism: Perspective and method.* Englewood Cliffs, NJ: Prentice-Hall.

Blyth, D. A., & Traeger, C. (1988). Adolescent self-esteem and perceived relationships with parents and peers. In S. Salzinger, J. Antrobus, & M. Hammer (Eds.), *Social networks of children, adolescents, and college students* (pp. 171–194). Hillsdale, NJ: Lawrence Erlbaum Associates.

Bochner, A. P., Ellis, C., & Tillmann-Healy, L. M. (1997). Relationships as stories. In S. Duck (Ed.), *Handbook of personal relationships* (2nd ed., pp. 307–324). Chichester, England: Wiley.

Bollen, K. A. (1986). Sample size and Bentler and Bonett's nonnormed fit index. *Psychometrika, 51,* 375–377.

Bossard, J. H. S. (1932). Residential propinquity in marriage selection. *American Journal of Sociology, 38,* 219–224.

Bott, E. (1971). *Family and social network* (2nd ed.). New York: Free Press.

Boucher, J., & Osgood, C. (1969). The pollyanna hypothesis. *Journal of Verbal Learning and Verbal Behavior, 8,* 1–8.

Boulton, M. J., Trueman, M., Chau, C., Whitehand, C., & Amatya, K. (1999). Concurrent and longitudinal links between friendship and peer victimization: Implications for befriending interventions. *Journal of Adolescence, 22,* 461–466.

Brashers, D. E. (2001). Communication and uncertainty management. *Journal of Communication, 51,* 477–497.

Bridge, K., & Baxter, L. A. (1992). Blended friendships: Friends as work associates. *Western Journal of Communication, 56,* 200–225.

Brock, D., Sarason, I., Sarason, B., & Pierce, G. (1996). Simultaneous assessment of perceived global and relationship-specific support. *Journal of Social and Personal Relationships, 13,* 143–152.

Brouilette, S., Singh, R. K., Thompson, J. R., Goodall, A. H., & Samani, N. J. (2003). White cell telomere length and risk of premature myocardial infarction. *Arteriosclerosis, Thrombosis, and Vascular Biology, 23,* 842–846.

Brown, P., & Levenson, S. (1978). Universals in language usage: Politeness phenomena. In E. Goody (Ed.), *Questions and politeness* (pp. 56–310). Cambridge, England: Cambridge University Press.

Browne, M. W., & Cudeck, R. (1993). Alternative ways of assessing model fit. In K. A. Bollen & J. S. Long (Eds.), *Testing structural equation models* (pp. 136–162). Newbury Park, CA: Sage.

Bruess, C. J. S., & Pearson, J. C. (1993). 'Sweet pea' and 'pussy cat': An examination of idiom use and marital satisfaction over the life cycle. *Journal of Social and Personal Relationships, 10,* 609–615.

Bryant, C., & Conger, R. (1999). Marital success and domains of social support in long-term relationships: Does the influence of network members never end? *Journal of Marriage and the Family, 61,* 437–450.

Bryant, C., Conger, R., & Meehan, J. M. (2001). The influence of in-laws on change in marital success. *Journal of Marriage and the Family, 63,* 614–626.

Buckley, W. (1967). *Sociology and moderns systems theory.* Englewood Cliffs, NJ: Prentice-Hall.

Bui, K.-V., Peplau, L. A., & Hill, C. T. (1996). Testing the Rusbult model of relationship commitment and stability in a 15–year study of heterosexual couples. *Personality and Social Psychology Bulletin, 22,* 1244–1257.

Bukowski, W. M., Newcomb, A. F., & Hoza, B. (1987). Friendship conceptions among early adolescents: A longitudinal study of stability and change. *Journal of Early Adolescence, 7,* 143–152.

Bumpass, L. L. (1990). What's happening to the family? Interactions between demographic and institutional change. *Demography, 27,* 483–498.

Bureau of the Census. (2002). *Interracial married couples.* Retrieved January 25, 2003, from http://landview.census.gov/population/socdemo/ms-la/tabms-3.txt and http://landview.census.gov/population/socdemo/hh-fam/tabMS-3.txt

Burgess, E. W., & Cottrell, L. S. (1939). *Predicting success or failure in marriage.* New York: Prentice-Hall.

Burggraf, C. S., & Sillars, A. L. (1987). A critical examination of sex differences in communication. *Communication Monographs, 54,* 276–294.

Burt, R. S. (1983). Distinguishing relational contents. In R. S. Burt & M. J. Minor (Eds.), *Applied network analysis: A methodological introduction* (pp. 35–74). Beverly Hills, CA: Sage.

Burt, R. S. (2000). Decay functions. *Social Networks, 22,* 1–28.

Butterfield, F. (1990, June 2). Family first, Mrs. Bush tells friend and foe at Wellesley. *New York Times,* pp. 1, 5.

Bygrave, W. D. (2003, April 29). *Financing entrepreneurs and their businesses.* Paper presented at the The Entrepreneurial Advantage of Nations: First Annual Global Entrepreneurship Symposium, New York.

Byrne, B. M. (2001). *Structural equation modeling with AMOS: Basic concepts, applications, and programming.* Mahwah, NJ: Lawrence Erlbaum Associates.

Byrne, D. (1961). Interpersonal attraction and attitude similarity. *Journal of Abnormal and Social Psychology, 62,* 713–715.

Byrne, D. (1971). *The attraction paradigm.* New York: Academic Press.

Byrne, D. (1992). The transition from controlled laboratory experimentation to less controlled settings: Surprise! Additional variables are operative. *Communication Monographs, 59*(2), 190–198.

Byrne, D., & Nelson, D. (1965). Attraction as a linear function of proportion of positive reinforcements. *Journal of Personality and Social Psychology, 1,* 659–663.

Canary, D. J., & Dainton, M. (2003). *Maintaining relationships through communication: Relational, contextual, and cultural variations.* Mahwah, NJ: Lawrence Erlbaum Associates.

Canary, D. J., Emmers-Sommer, T. M., & Faulkner, S. (1997). *Sex and gender differences in personal relationships.* New York: Guilford Press.

Canary, D. J., & Stafford, L. (2001). Equity in the preservation of personal relationships. In J. H. Harvey & A. Wenzel (Eds.), *Close romantic relationships: Maintenance and enhancement* (pp. 133–151). Mahwah, NJ: Lawrence Erlbaum Associates.

Caplow, T., & Forman, R. (1950). Neighborhood interaction in a homogeneous community. *American Sociological Review, 15,* 357–366.

Carley, K. M. (1999). On the evolution of social and organizational networks. *Research in the Sociology of Organizations, 16,* 3–30.

Carley, K. M., & Krackhardt, D. (1996). Cognitive inconsistencies and non-symmetric friendship. *Social Networks, 18,* 1–27.

Carrère, S., Buehlman, K. T., Gottman, J. M., Coan, J. A., & Ruckstuhl, L. (2000). Predicting marital stability and divorce in newlywed couples. *Journal of Family Psychology, 14,* 42–58.

Carson, R. C. (1969). *Interaction concepts of personality.* Chicago: Aldine.

Cartwright, D., & Harary, F. (1956). Structural balance: A generalization of Heider's theory. *Psychological Review, 63,* 277–293.

Carver, K., Joyner, K., & Udry, J. R. (2003). National estimates of adolescent romantic relationships. In P. Florsheim (Ed.), *Adolescent romantic relations and sexual behavior: Theory, research, and practical implications* (pp. 23–56). Mahwah, NJ: Lawrence Erlbaum Associates.

Chambers, V. J., Christiansen, J. R., & Kunz, P. R. (1983). Physiognomic homogamy: A test of physical similarity as a factor in the mate selection process. *Social Biology, 30,* 151–157.

Chang, J. (1991). *Wild swans : Three daughters of China.* New York: Simon & Schuster.

Chapple, N. L., & Badger, M. (1989). Social isolation and well-being. *Journal of Gerontology, 44(5),* S169–S176.

Cherlin, A. J. (1992). *Marriage, divorce, remarriage.* Cambridge, MA: Harvard University Press.

Chesson, H. W., Blandford, J. M., Gift, T. L., Tao, G., & Irwin, K. L. (2004). The estimated direct medical cost of sexually transmitted diseases among American youth, 2000. *Perspectives on Sexual and Reproductive Health, 36,* 11–19.

Chovil, N. (1994). Equivocation as an interactional event. In W. R. Cupach & B. H. Spitzberg (Eds.), *The dark side of interpersonal communication* (pp. 105–123). Hillsdale, NJ: Lawrence Erlbaum Associates.

Clark, M. S., & Reis, H. T. (1988). Interpersonal processes in close relationships. *Annual Review of Psychology, 39,* 609–672.

Clarke, A. C. (1952). An examination of the operation of residential propinquity as a factor in mate selection. *American Sociological Review, 17,* 17–22.

Cleek, M., & Pearson, T. A. (1985). Perceived causes of divorce: An analysis of interrelationships. *Journal of Marriage and the Family, 47,* 179–191.

Clergy not a big help. (1989, April 14). *Seattle Times,* p. 3.

Cohen, S., Lichtenstein, E., Mermelstein, R., Kingsolver, K., Baer, J. S., & Kamarck, T. W. (1988). Social support interventions for smoking cessation. In B. H. Gottlieb (Ed.), *Marshalling social support: Formats, processes, and effects* (pp. 211–240). Newbury Park, CA: Sage.

Cohn, J. F., Campbell, S. B., Matias, R., & Hopkins, J. (1990). Face-to-face interactions of postpartum depressed and nondepressed mother-infant pairs at 2 months. *Developmental Psychology, 26,* 15–23.

Coleman, J. S., Katz, E., & Menzel, H. (1957). The diffusion of an innovation among physicians. *Sociometry, 20,* 253–270.

Coley, R. L., & Chase-Lansdale, P. L. (1998). Adolescent pregnancy and parenthood: Recent evidence and future directions. *American Psychologist, 53,* 152–166.

Collins, R. (1998). *The sociology of philosophies: A global theory of intellectual change.* Cambridge, MA: Harvard University Press.

Collins, R. (2003). A network-location theory of culture. *Sociological Theory, 21,* 69–73.

Collins, R. (2004). *Interaction ritual chains.* Princeton, NJ: Princeton University Press.

Connolly, J. A., Craig, W., Goldberg, A., & Pepler, D. (1999). Conceptions of cross-sex friendships and romantic relationships in early adolescence. *Journal of Youth and Adolescence, 28,* 481–494.

Connolly, J. A., Furman, W., & Konarski, R. (2000). The role of peers in the emergence of heterosexual romantic relationships in adolescence. *Child Development, 71,* 1395–1408.

Connolly, J. A., & Johnson, A. M. (1996). Adolescents' romantic relationships and the structure and quality of their close interpersonal ties. *Personal Relationships, 3,* 185–195.

Cooley, C. H. (1902). *Human nature and the social order.* New York: C. Scribner's Sons.

Copello, A., Orford, J., Hodgson, R., Tober, G., & Barrett, C. (2002). Social behaviour and network therapy: Basic principles and early experiences. *Addictive Behaviors, 27,* 346–366.

Cotton, S., Cunningham, J., & Antill, J. (1993). Network structure, network support and the marital satisfaction of husbands and wives. *Australian Journal of Psychology, 45,* 176–181.

Coupland, N., Wiemann, J. M., & Giles, H. (1991). Talk as "problem" and communication as "miscommunication": An integrative analysis. In N. Coupland, J. M. Wiemann, & H. Giles (Eds.), *"Miscommunication" and problematic talk* (pp. 1–17). Newbury Park, CA: Sage.

Cox, C. L., Wexler, M. O., Rusbult, C. E., & Gaines, S. O., Jr. (1997). Prescriptive support and commitment processes in close relationships. *Social Psychology Quarterly, 60,* 79–90.

Coyne, J. C. (1999). Thinking interactionally about depression: A radical restatement. In T. Joiner & J. C. Coyne (Eds.), *The interactional nature of depression* (pp. 365–392). Washington, DC: American Psychological Association.

Crain, A. L., Snyder, M., & Omoto, A. M. (May, 2000). *Volunteers make a difference: Relationship quality, active coping, and functioning among PWAs with volunteer buddies.* Paper presented at the Midwestern Psychological Association, Chicago, Illinois.

Croog, S. H., & Levine, S. (1977). *The heart patient recovers: Social and psychological factors.* New York: Human Sciences Press.

Cross, R., Rice, R. E., & Parker, A. (2001). Information seeking in social context: Structural influences and receipt of information benefits. *IEEE Transactions on Systems, Man, and Cybernetics, 31*(4), 438–448.

Csikszentmihalyi, M., & Larson, R. (1984). *Being adolescent.* New York: Basic Books.

Csikszentmihalyi, M., & Schneider, B. (2000). *Becoming adult: How teenagers prepare for the world of work.* New York: Basic Books.

Cupach, W. R., & Spitzberg, B. H. (Eds.). (1994). *The dark side of interpersonal communication.* Hillsdale, NJ: Lawrence Erlbaum Associates.

Davis, J. A. (1970). Clustering and hierarchy in interpersonal relations: Test two graph theoretical models on 742 sociomatrices. *American Sociological Review, 35,* 843–851.

Davis, K. E., & Todd, M. J. (1982). Friendship and love relationships. In K. E. Davis & T. Mitchell (Eds.), *Advances in descriptive psychology* (Vol. 2, pp. 79–122). Greenwich, CT: JAI.

Davis, M. S. (1973). *Intimate relations.* New York: Free Press.

Derlega, V. J., & Chaikin, A. L. (1977). Privacy and self-disclosure in social relationships. *Journal of Social Issues, 33,* 102–115.

Derlega, V. J., Metts, S., Petronio, S., & Margulis, S. T. (1993). *Self-disclosure.* Newbury Park, CA: Sage.

Desowitz, R. S. (1987). *The thorn in the starfish: How the human immune system works.* New York: Norton.

Dindia, K. (1997). Self-disclosure, self-identity, and relationship development: A transactional/dialectical perspective. In S. Duck (Ed.), *Handbook of personal relationships* (2nd ed., pp. 411–426). Chichester, England: Wiley.

Dindia, K. (2002). Self-disclosure research: Knowledge through meta-analysis. In M. Allen, R. W. Preiss, B. M. Gayle, & N. A. Burrell (Eds.), *Interpersonal communication research: Advances through meta-analysis.* (pp. 169–185). Mahwah, NJ: Lawrence Erlbaum Associates.

Dinwiddie, S. H., Heath, A. C., Dunne, M. P., Bucholz, K. K., Madden, P. A. F., Slutske, W. S., et al. (2000). Early sexual abuse and lifetime psychopathology: A co-twin-control study. *Psychological Medicine, 30,* 41–52.

Dodds, P. S., Muhamad, R., & Watts, D. J. (2003). An experimental study of search in global social networks. *Science, 301,* 827–829.

Donn, J. E., & Sherman, R. C. (2002). Attitudes and practices regarding the formation of romantic relationships on the Internet. *Cyberpsychology & Behavior, 5(2),* 107–123.

Driscoll, R., Davis, K. E., & Lipetz, M. E. (1972). Parental interference and romantic love: The Romeo and Juliet effect. *Journal of Personality and Social Psychology, 24,* 1–10.

Driver, J., Tabares, A., Shapiro, A., Nahm, E. Y., & Gottman, J. M. (2003). Interactional patterns in marital success and failure: Gottman laboratory studies. In F. Walsh (Ed.), *Normal family processes: Growing diversity and complexity* (3rd ed., pp. 493–513). New York: Guilford.

Duck, S. W. (1994). *Meaningful relationships: Talking, sense, and relating.* Thousand Oaks, CA: Sage.

Duck, S. W., & Barnes, M. K. (1992). Disagreeing about agreement: Reconciling differences about similarity. *Communication Monographs, 59(2),* 199–208.

Duck, S. W., & Sants, H. (1983). On the origin of the specious: Are personal relationships really interpersonal states? *Journal of Social & Clinical Psychology, 1,* 27–41.

Duffy, M. (1993). Social networks and social support of recently divorced women. *Public Health Nursing, 10(1),* 19–24.

Duffy, S. M., & Rusbult, C. E. (1986). Satisfaction and commitment in homosexual and heterosexual relationships. *Journal of Homosexuality, 12,* 1–23.

Dunphy, D. C. (1963). The social structure of urban adolescent peer groups. *Sociometry, 26,* 230–246.

Durkheim, E. (1951). *Suicide.* New York: Free Press. (Original work published 1897)

Durkin, K. (1995). *Developmental social psychology: From infancy to old age.* Cambridge, MA: Blackwell.

Dutton, D., & Aron, A. (1974). Some evidence for heightened sexual attraction under conditions of high anxiety. *Journal of Personality and Social Psychology, 30,* 510–517.

Dykstra, P. (1987). Vrienden en vriendinnen. Anders dan andere persoonlijke relaties? [Friends. Different than other personal relationships?]. *Mens en Maatschappij [People and Society], 62(2),* 257–269.

Dymond, R. (1954). Interpersonal perception and marital happiness. *Canadian Journal of Psychology, 8,* 164–171.

Ebrahim, S., Wannamethee, G., McCallum, A., Walker, M., & Shaper, A. G. (1995). Marital status, change in marital status, and mortality in middle-aged British men. *American Journal of Epidemiology, 142,* 834–842.

Eggert, L. L., & Parks, M. R. (1987). Communication network involvement in adolescents' friendships and romantic relationships. In M. L. McLaughlin (Ed.), *Communication yearbook 10* (pp. 283–322). Newbury Park, CA: Sage.

Eggert, L. L., Thompson, E. A., Herting, J. R., Nicholas, L. J., & Dicker, B. G. (1994). Preventing adolescent drug abuse and high school dropout through an intensive school-based social network development program. *American Journal of Health Promotion, 8,* 202–215.

Eisenberg, E. M. (1984). Ambiguity as strategy in organizational communication. *Communication Monographs, 51,* 227–242.

Elias, M. J., Gara, M., & Ubriaco, M. (1985). Sources of stress and support in children's transition to middle school. *Journal of Clinical Child Psychology, 14,* 112–118.

Elium, J., & Elium, D. (1999). *Raising a teenager: Parents and the nurturing of a responsible teen.* Berkeley, CA: Celestial Arts.

Elkind, D. (1967). Egocentrism in adolescence. *Child Development, 38,* 1025–1034.

Elms, A. C. (1975). The crisis of confidence in social psychology. *American Psychologist, 30,* 967–976.

Emerson, R. W. (1939). *Friendship.* Worcester, MA: Achille J. St. Onge.

Emirbayer, M., & Mische, A. (1998). What is agency? *American Journal of Sociology, 103,* 962–1023.

Epel, E. E., Blackburn, E. H., Lin, J., Dhabhar, F. S., Adler, N. E., Morrow, J. D., et al. (2004). Accelerated telomere shortening in response to life stress. *Proceedings of the National Academy of Sciences, 101*(49), 17312–17315.

Erikson, E. H. (1968). *Identity, youth, and crisis.* New York: Norton.

Evans, K. (1996, March). The price of marriage. *Middle East, 254,* 38.

Evans, M. D. R., Kelley, J., & Wanner, R. A. (2001). Educational attainment of the children of divorce: Australia, 1940–1990. *Journal of Sociology, 37,* 275–297.

Evers, A., Kraaimaat, F. W., Geene, R., Jacobs, J., & Bijlsma, J. (2003). Pain coping and social support as predictors of long-term functional disability and pain in early rheumatoid arthritis. *Behaviour Research & Therapy, 41,* 1295–1310.

Facio, A., & Mircocci, F. (2003). Emerging adulthood in Argentina. In J. J. Arnett & N. L. Galambos (Eds.), *Exploring cultural conceptions of the transition to adulthood: New directions for child and adolescent development* (pp. 21–31). San Francisco: Jossey-Bass.

Fang, C. Y., Sidanius, J., & Pratto, F. (1998). Romance across the social status continuum: Interracial marriage and the ideological asymmetry effect. *Journal of Cross-Cultural Psychology, 29,* 290–305.

Fararo, T. J. (1989). *The meaning of general theoretical sociology: Tradition and formalization.* New York: Cambridge University Press.

Feeley, T. H. (2000). Testing a communication network model of employee turnover based on centrality. *Journal of Applied Communication Research, 28,* 262–278.

Fehr, B. A. (1996). *Friendship processes.* Thousand Oaks, CA: Sage.

Fehr, B. A. (2000). The life cycle of friendship. In C. Hendrick & S. Hendrick (Eds.), *Close relationships: A sourcebook* (pp. 71–82). Thousand Oaks, CA: Sage.

Fehr, B. A. (2004). A prototype model of intimacy interactions in same-sex friendships. In D. J. Mashek & A. Aron (Eds.), *Handbook of closeness and intimacy* (pp. 9–26). Mahwah, NJ: Lawrence Erlbaum Associates.

Feiring, C. (1996). Concept of romance in 15–year-old adolescents. *Journal of Research on Adolescence, 6,* 181–200.

Feiring, C. (1999). Other-sex friendship networks and the development of romantic relationships in adolescence. *Journal of Youth and Adolescence, 28,* 495–512.

Feiring, C., & Lewis, M. (1988). The child's social network from three to six years: The effects of age, sex, and socioeconomic status. In S. Salzinger, J. Antrobus & M. Hammer (Eds.), *Social networks of children, adolescents, and college students* (pp. 93–112). Hillsdale, NJ: Lawrence Erlbaum Associates.

Feld, S. L. (1997). Structural embeddedness and the stability of interpersonal relations. *Social Networks, 19,* 91–95.

Felmlee, D. (2001). No couple is an island: A social network perspective on dyadic stability. *Social Forces, 79,* 1259–1287.

Felmlee, D., & Greenberg, S. (1999). A dynamic systems model of dyadic interaction. *Journal of Mathematical Sociology, 23,* 155–180.

Felmlee, D., & Sprecher, S. (2000). Close relationships and social psychology: Intersections and future paths. *Social Psychology Quarterly, 63,* 365–376.

Fessler, K. B. (2003). Social outcomes of early childbearing: Important considerations for the provision of clinical care. *Journal of Midwifery and Women's Health, 48,* 178–185.

Festinger, L., Schachter, S., & Back, K. W. (1963). *Social pressures in informal groups: A study of human factors in housing.* Stanford, CA: Stanford University Press.

Fielding, N. G. (1988). Between micro and macro. In N. G. Fielding (Ed.), *Actions and structures: Research methods and social theory* (pp. 1–19). Beverly Hills, CA: Sage.

Finch, J., & Mason, J. (1990). Divorce, remarriage and family obligations. *The Sociological Review, 38*(2), 219–246.

Fischer, C. S. (1977). *Networks and places: Social relations in the urban setting.* New York: Free Press.

Fischer, C. S. (1982). *To dwell among friends: Personal networks in town and city.* Chicago: University of Chicago Press.

Fitzpatrick, J., & Sollie, D. L. (1999). Influence of individual and interpersonal factors on satisfaction and stability in romantic relationships. *Personal Relationships, 6,* 337–350.

Fitzpatrick, M. A. (1988). *Between husbands and wives: Communication in marriage.* Newbury Park, CA: Sage.

Fleshner, M., & Laudenslager, M. L. (2004). Psychoneuroimmunology: Then and now. *Behavioral & Cognitive Neuroscience Reviews, 3*(2), 114–130.

Flewelling, R. L., & Bauman, K. E. (1990). Family structure as a predictor of initial substance use and sexual intercourse in early adolescence. *Journal of Marriage and the Family, 52,* 171–181.

Flora, J., & Segrin, C. (2003). Relational well-being and perceptions of relational history in married and dating couples. *Journal of Social and Personal Relationships, 20,* 515–536.

Floyd, K. (1995). Gender and closeness among friends and siblings. *Journal of Psychology: Interdisciplinary and Applied, 129,* 193–202.

Fortes, M. (Ed.). (1949). *The web of kinship among the Tallensi.* London: Oxford University Press.

Fraga, M. F., Ballestar, E., Paz, M. F., Ropero, S., Setien, F., Ballestar, M. L., et al. (2005). Epigenetic differences arise during the lifetime of monozygotic twins. *Proceedings of the National Academy of Sciences, 102,* 10604–10609.

Freeman, L. (1996). Some antecedents of social network analysis. *Connections, 19, 39–42.*

Fuchs, S. (2001). *Against essentialism: A theory of culture and society.* Cambridge, MA: Harvard University Press.

Furman, W., & Buhrmester, D. (1992). Age and sex differences in perceptions of networks of personal relationships. *Child Development, 63,* 103–115.

Furman, W., & Shaffer, L. (2003). The role of romantic relationships in adolescent development. In P. Florsheim (Ed.), *Adolescent romantic relations and sexual behavior: Theory, research, and practical implications* (pp. 3–22). Mahwah, NJ: Lawrence Erlbaum Associates.

Furman, W., Simon, V. A., Shaffer, L., & Bouchey, H. A. (2002). Adolescents' working models and styles for relationships with parents, friends, and romantic partners. *Child Development, 75,* 241–255.

Fyrand, L., Moum, T., Finset, A., & Glennås, A. (2003). The effect of social network intervention for women with rheumatoid arthritis. *Family Process, 42,* 71–89.

Gadlin, H. (1977). Private lives and public order: A critical view of the history of intimate relations in the United States. In G. Levinger & H. L. Raush (Eds.), *Close relationships: Perspectives on the meaning of intimacy* (pp. 33–72). Amherst, MA: University of Massachusetts Press.

Gaines, S. O., Jr. (1995). Relationships between members of cultural minorities. In J. T. Wood & S. Duck (Eds.), *Under-studied relationships: Off the beaten track* (pp. 51–88). Thousand Oaks, CA: Sage.

Gaines, S. O., Jr., & Brennan, K. A. (2001). Establishing and maintaining satisfaction in multicultural relationships. In J. H. Harvey & A. Wenzel (Eds.), *Close romantic relationships: Maintenance and enhancement* (pp. 237–253). Mahwah, NJ: Lawrence Erlbaum Associates.

Gaines, S. O., Jr., Granrose, C. S., Rios, D. I., Garcia, B. F., Youn, M. S. P., Farris, K. R., et al. (1999). Patterns of attachment and responses to accommodative dilemmas among interethnic/interracial couples. *Journal of Social and Personal Relationships, 16*(2), 275–285.

Gaines, S. O., Jr., & Liu, J. H. (2000). Multicultural/multiracial relationships. In C. Hendrick & S. Hendrick (Eds.), *Close relationships: A sourcebook* (pp. 97–108). Thousand Oaks, CA: Sage.

Galanter, M., Dermatis, H., Glickman, L., Maslansky, R., Sellers, M. B., Neumann, E., et al. (2004). Network therapy: Decreased secondary opioid use during buprenorphine maintenance. *Journal of Substance Abuse Treatment, 26,* 313–318.

Geertz, C. (1973). *The interpretation of cultures.* New York: Basic Books.

Gergen, K. J. (1973). Social psychology as history. *Journal of Personality and Social Psychology, 26,* 309–320.

Geronimus, A. T. (2003). Damned if you do: Culture, identity, privilege, and teenage childbearing in the United States. *Social Science and Medicine, 57,* 881–893.

Gibbons, D., & Olk, P. (2003). Individual and structural origins of friendship and social position among professionals. *Journal of Personality and Social Psychology, 84,* 340–351.

Giddens, A. (1976). *New rules of sociological method.* New York: Basic Books.

Giddens, A. (1984). *The constitution of society.* Berkeley, CA: University of California Press.

Gilligan, C. (1982). *In a different voice: Psychological theory and women's development.* Cambridge, MA: Harvard University Press.

Gillis, J. S., & Avis, W. E. (1980). The male-taller norm in mate selection. *Personality and Social Psychology Bulletin, 6,* 396–401.

Glass, N., Fredland, N., Campbell, J., Yonas, M., Sharps, P., & Kub, J. (2003). Adolescent dating violence: Prevalence, risk factors, health outcomes, and implications for clinical practice. *Journal of Obstetric, Gynecologic, and Neonatal Nursing, 32*(2), 227–238.

Glazer, S. S., Galanter, M., Megwinoff, O., Dermatis, H., & Keller, D. S. (2003). The role of therapeutic alliance in network therapy: A family and peer support-based treatment for cocaine abuse. *Substance Abuse, 24,* 93–100.

Goethe, J. W. (1971). *The sorrows of young Werther.* New York: Random House. (Original work published 1774).

Goffman, E. (1959). *The presentation of self in everyday life.* Garden City, NY: Doubleday Anchor.

Goffman, E. (1967). *Interaction ritual.* Garden City, NY: Doubleday Anchor.

Goldsmith, D. J. (1988). *To talk or not to talk: The flow of information between romantic dyads and members of their communication networks.* Unpublished Mater's thesis, University of Washington, Seattle.

Goldsmith, D. J. (2001). A normative approach to the study of uncertainty and communication. *Journal of Communication, 51,* 514–533.

Goldsmith, D. J., & Baxter, L. A. (1996). Constituting relationships in talk: A taxonomy of speech events in social and personal relationships. *Human Communication Research, 23,* 87–114.

Goldsmith, D. J., & Dun, S. A. (1997). Sex differences and similarities in the communication of social support. *Journal of Social and Personal Relationships, 14,* 317–337.

Goldsmith, D. J., & Fulfs, P. A. (1999). "You just don't have the evidence": An analysis of claims and evidence in Deborah Tannen's *You Just Don't Understand.* In M. E. Roloff (Ed.), *Communication yearbook 22* (pp. 1–49). Thousand Oaks, CA: Sage.

Goldsmith, D. J., & Parks, M. R. (1990). Communicative strategies for managing the risks of seeking social support. In S. Duck & R. C. Silver (Eds.), *Personal relationships and social support* (pp. 104–121). Newbury Park, CA: Sage.

Goldstein, S. E., Davis-Kean, P. E., & Eccles, J. S. (2005). Parents, peers, and problem behavior: A longitudinal investigation of the impact of relationship perceptions and characteristics on the development of adolescent problem behavior. *Developmental Psychology, 41,* 401–413.

Golembiewski, R. T. (1962). *The small group.* Chicago: University of Chicago Press.

Goode, W. J. (1982). *The family* (2nd ed.). Englewood Cliffs, NJ: Prentice-Hall.

Goodman, E., & O'Brien, P. (2000). *I know just what you mean: The power of friendship in women's lives.* New York: Simon & Schuster.

Gorin, A., Phelan, S., Tate, D., Sherwood, N., Jeffery, R., & Wing, R. (2005). Involving support partners in obesity treatment. *Journal of Consulting and Clinical Psychology, 73,* 341–343.

Gottlieb, B. H. (1983). *Social support strategies: Guidelines for mental health practice.* Beverly Hills, CA: Sage.

Gottman, J. M. (1994). *What predicts divorce? The relationship between marital processes and marital outcomes.* Hillsdale, NJ: Lawrence Erlbaum Associates.

Gottman, J. M., & Levenson, R. W. (2000). The timing of divorce: Predicting when a couple will divorce over a 14–year period. *Journal of Marriage and the Family, 62,* 737–745.

Granovetter, M. S. (1973). The strength of weak ties. *American Journal of Sociology, 78,* 1361–1380.

Granovetter, M. S. (1979). The theory-gap in social network analysis. In P. Holland & L. Leinhardt (Eds.), *Perspectives on social network research* (pp. 501–518). New York: Academic Press.

Gray, J. D., & Silver, R. C. (1990). Opposite sides of the same coin: Former spouses' divergent perspectives in coping with their divorce. *Journal of Personality and Social Psychology, 59,* 1180–1191.

Greeff, A. P. (2000). Characteristics of families that function well. *Journal of Family Issues, 21,* 948–962.

Green, S. K., Buchanan, D. R., & Heuer, S. K. (1984). Winners, losers, and choosers: A field investigation of dating initiation. *Personality and Social Psychology Bulletin, 10,* 502–511.

Gudykunst, W. B. (1986). Ethnicity, type of relationship, and intraethnic and interethnic uncertainty reduction. In Y. Kim (Ed.), *Interethnic communication* (pp. 201–224). Beverly Hills, CA: Sage.

Gudykunst, W. B., & Nishida, T. (1986). The influence of cultural variability on perceptions of communication behavior associated with relationship terms. *Human Communication Research, 13*(147–166).

Gudykunst, W. B., Sodetani, L. L., & Sonoda, K. T. (1987). Uncertainty reduction in Japanese-American/Caucasian Relationships in Hawaii. *The Western Journal of Speech Communication, 51,* 256–278.

Gudykunst, W. B., Ting-Toomey, S., & Nishida, T. (Eds.). (1996). *Communication in personal relationships across cultures.* Thousand Oaks, CA: Sage.

Guerrero, L. K. (1997). Nonverbal involvement across interactions with same-sex friends, opposite-sex friends and romantic partners: Consistency or change. *Journal of Social and Personal Relationships, 14,* 31–58.

Guisinger, S., & Blatt, S. J. (1994). Individuality and relatedness: Evolution of a fundamental dialectic. *American Psychologist, 49,* 104–111.

Gumperz, J. J. (1982). *Discourse strategies.* Cambridge, England: Cambridge University Press.

Gurung, R. A. R., & Duong, T. (1999). Mixing and matching: Assessing the concomitants of mixed-ethnic relationships. *Journal of Social and Personal Relationships, 16,* 639–657.

Guttmann, J. (1987). Test anxiety and performance of adolescent children of divorced parents. *Educational Psychology, 7,* 225–229.

Guttmann, J., Amir, T., & Katz, M. (1987). Threshold of withdrawal from schoolwork among children of divorced parents. *Educational Psychology, 7,* 295–302.

Guttmann, J., Geva, N., & Gefen, S. (1988). Teachers' and school children's stereotypic perception of "the child of divorce." *American Educational Research Journal, 25,* 555–571.

Haas, S. M., & Stafford, L. (1998). An initial examination of maintenance behavior in gay and lesbian relationships. *Journal of Social and Personal Relationships, 15,* 846–855.

Hagenbaugh, B. (2003, February 13). Valentine's chocolate could cost far more next year. *USA Today,* p. B3.

Hahn, J., & Blass, T. (1997). Dating partner preferences: A function of similarity of love styles. *Journal of Social Behavior & Personality, 12,* 595–610.

Haley, J. (1959). An interactional description of schizophrenia. *Psychiatry, 22*(321–332).

Hallinan, M. T. (1974). *The structure of positive sentiment.* New York: Elsevier.

Hallinan, M. T. (1980). Patterns of cliquing among youth. In H. C. Foot, A. J. Chapman, & J. R. Smith (Eds.), *Friendship and social relations in children* (pp. 321–342). New York: Wiley.

Ham, B. D. (2004). The effects of divorce and remarriage on the academic achievement of high school seniors. *Journal of Divorce and Remarriage, 42*(1–2), 159–178.

Hammer, M. (1980). Predictability of social connections over time. *Social Networks, 2,* 165–180.

Hansen, F. J., Fallon, A. E., & Novotny, S. L. (1991). The relationship between social network structure and marital satisfaction in distressed and nondistressed couples: A pilot study. *Family Therapy, 18,* 101–114.

Hanson, C. L., De Guire, M. J., Schinkel, A. M., & Kolterman, O. G. (1995). Empirical validation for a family-centered model of care. *Diabetes Care, 18*(10), 1347–1356.

Harary, F., Norman, R. Z., & Cartwright, D. (1965). *Structural models: An introduction to the theory of directed graphs.* New York: Wiley.

Harvey, J. H., Orbuch, T. L., & Weber, A. L. (1992). The convergence of the attribution and accounts concepts in the study of close relationships. In J. H. Harvey, T. L. Orbuch & A. L. Weber (Eds.), *Attributions, accounts and close relationships* (pp. 1–18). New York: Springer.

Harvey, J. H., & Weber, A. L. (2002). *Odyssey of the heart: Close relationships in the 21st century* (2nd ed.). Mahwah, NJ: Lawrence Erlbaum Associates.

Harvey, J. H., & Wenzel, A. (Eds.). (2001). *Close romantic relationships: Maintenance and enhancement.* Mahwah, NJ: Lawrence Erlbaum Associates.

Hatfield, E., & Rapson, R. L. (2002). Passionate love and sexual desire: Cultural and historical perspectives. In A. L. Vangelisti, H. T. Reis & M. A. Fitzpatrick (Eds.), *Stability and change in relationships* (pp. 306–324). New York: Cambridge University Press.

Hatfield, E., Schmitz, E., Cornelius, J., & Rapson, R. L. (1988). Passionate love: How early does it begin? *Journal of Psychology & Human Sexuality, 1*(1), 35–51.

Hax, C. (2004, April 9). Tell Me About It: 'Devotion' and secrecy signal abusiveness. *Seattle Post Intelligencer,* p. E2.

Hayes, B. C., & Jones, F. L. (1991). Education and marriage patterns in Australia. *The International Journal of Sociology and Social Policy, 11*(4), 1–16.

Hays, R. B. (1984). The development and maintenance of friendship. *Journal of Social and Personal Relationships, 1,* 75–98.

Hecht, M. L. (1978). The conceptualization and measurement of interpersonal communication satisfaction. *Human Communication Research, 4,* 253–264.

Heider, F. (1946). Attitudes and cognitive organization. *Journal of Psychology, 21,* 107–112.

Heider, F. (1958). *The psychology of interpersonal relations.* New York: Wiley.

Heller, K. (1989). The return to community. *American Journal of Community, 17,* 1–15.

Heller, K., & Rook, K. S. (2001). Distinguishing the theoretical functions of social ties: Implications for support interventions. In B. Sarason & S. Duck (Eds.), *Personal relationships: Implications for clinical and community psychology* (pp. 119–139). Chichester, England: Wiley.

Hendrick, S., & Hendrick, C. (1993). Lovers as friends. *Journal of Social and Personal Relationships, 10,* 459–466.

Hendrick, S., & Hendrick, C. (2000). Romantic love. In C. Hendrick & S. Hendrick (Eds.), *Close relationships: A sourcebook* (pp. 203–215). Thousand Oaks, CA: Sage.

Hill, C. T., Rubin, Z., & Peplau, L. A. (1976). Breakups before marriage: The end of 103 affairs. *Journal of Social Issues, 32*(1), 147–168.

Hinde, R. A. (1987). *Individuals, relationships, and culture.* Cambridge, England: Cambridge University Press.

Hintikka, J., Koskela, T., Kuntula, O., Koskela, K., & Viinamäki, H. (2000). Men, women and friends—are there differences in relation to mental well-being? *Quality of Life Research, 9,* 841–845.

Hobfoll, S. E. (1988). *The ecology of stress.* Washington, DC: Hemisphere.

Hochschild, A. R. (2003). *The commercialization of intimate life: Notes from home and work*. Berkeley: University of California Press.

Hoffmann, J. P. (2003). A contextual analysis of differential association, social control, and strain theories of delinquency. *Social Forces, 81*, 753–785.

Holland, P. W., & Leinhardt, L. (1977a). Social structure as a network process. *Zeitschrift fur Soziologie [Magazine for sociology], 6*(4), 386–402.

Holland, P. W., & Leinhardt, S. (1977b). Transitivity in structural models of small groups. In L. Leinhardt (Ed.), *Social networks: A developing paradigm* (pp. 49–66). New York: Academic Press.

Holtzman, S., Newth, S., & Delongis, A. (2004). The role of social support in coping with daily pain among patients with rheumatoid arthritis. *Journal of Health Psychology, 9*, 677–695.

Homans, G. C. (1961). *Social behavior: Its elementary forms*. New York: Harcourt.

Hopper, R., Knapp, M. L., & Scott, L. (1981). Couples' personal idioms: Exploring intimate talk. *Journal of Communication, 31*, 23–33.

Horney, K. (1937). *The neurotic personality of our time*. New York: Norton.

Horney, K. (1942). *Self analysis*. New York: Norton.

Hornstein, G. A. (1985). Intimacy in conversational style as a function of the degree of closeness between members of a dyad. *Journal of Personality and Social Psychology, 49*, 671–681.

Horowitz, M., Lyons, J., & Perlmutter, H. (1951). Induction of forces in discussion groups. *Human Relations, 4*, 57–76.

House, J. (1977). The three faces of social psychology. *Sociometry, 40*, 161–177.

House, J., Landis, K., & Umberson, D. (1988). Social relationships and health. *Science, 241*(4865), 540–545.

Hu, L. T., & Bentler, P. M. (1995). Evaluating model fit. In R. H. Hoyle (Ed.), *Structural equation modeling: Concepts, issues, and applications* (pp. 76–99). Thousand Oaks, CA: Sage.

Huber, G. P., & Daft, R. L. (1987). The information environment of organizations. In F. M. Jablin, L. L. Putnam, K. H. Roberts & L. W. Porter (Eds.), *Handbook of organizational communication: An interdisciplinary perspective* (pp. 130–164). Newbury Park, CA: Sage.

Huddleston, R. J., & Hawkings, L. (1993). The reaction of friends and family to divorce. *Journal of Divorce and Remarriage, 19*(1–2), 195–207.

Hudson, J. L., & Rapee, R. M. (2000). The origins of social phobia. *Behavior Modification, 24*(1), 102–129.

Hughes, R., Good, E., & Candell, K. (1993). A longitudinal study of the effects of social support on the psychological adjustment of the divorced mothers. *Journal of Divorce and Remarriage, 19*(1–2), 37–56.

Huston, T. L., & Burgess, R. L. (1979). Social exchange in developing relationships: An overview. In R. L. Burgess & T. L. Huston (Eds.), *Social exchange in developing relationships* (pp. 3–28). New York: Academic Press.

Huston, T. L., Surra, C. A., Fitzgerald, N., & Cate, R. (1981). From courtship to marriage: Mate selection as an interpersonal process. In S. Duck & R. Gilmour (Eds.), *Personal relationships* (Vol. 2, pp. 53–88). London: Academic Press.

Ickes, W., & Simpson, J. A. (1997). Managing empathic accuracy in close relationships. In W. Ickes (Ed.), *Empathic accuracy* (pp. 218–250). New York: Guilford.

Impett, E. A., Beals, K. P., & Peplau, L. A. (2002). Testing the investment model of relationship commitment and stability in a longitudinal study of married couples. *Current Psychology: Developmental, Learning, Personality, Social, 20*(4), 312–326.

Jahn, G. (2003, June 29). In the new Romania, some old ways survive. *Seattle Times*, p. 16.

Jeynes, W. H. (2001). The effects of recent parental divorce on their children's consumption of marijuana and cocaine. *Journal of Divorce and Remarriage, 35*(3–4), 43–65.

Johnson, C. L. (1988). Socially controlled civility. *American Behavioral Scientist, 31*, 685–701.

Johnson, D. J., & Rusbult, C. E. (1989). Resisting temptation: Devaluation of alternative partners as a means of maintaining commitment in close relationships. *Journal of Personality and Social Psychology, 57,* 967–980.

Johnson, F. L. (2000). *Speaking culturally: Language diversity in the United States.* Thousand Oaks, CA: Sage.

Johnson, M. H., & Morton, J. (1991). *Biology and cognitive development: The case of face recognition.* Oxford: Blackwell.

Johnson, M. P., Caughlin, J. P., & Huston, T. L. (1999). The tripartite nature of marital commitment: Personal, moral, and structural reasons to stay married. *Journal of Marriage and the Family, 61,* 160–177.

Johnson, M. P., & Leslie, L. (1982). Couple involvement and network structure: A test of the dyadic withdrawal hypothesis. *Social Psychology Quarterly, 45,* 34–43.

Johnson, M. P., & Milardo, R. M. (1984). Network interference in pair relationships: A social psychological recasting of Slater's theory of social regression. *Journal of Marriage and the Family, 46,* 893–899.

Jones, L. Y. (1980). *Great expectations: America and the baby boom generation.* New York: Ballantine.

Jordan, N. (1953). Behavioral forces that are a function of attitudes and of cognitive organization. *Human Relations, 6,* 273–287.

Jourard, S. M. (1971). *Self-disclosure: An experimental analysis of the transparent self.* New York: Wiley.

Joyner, K., & Kao, G. (2000). School racial composition and adolescent racial homophily. *Social Science Quarterly, 81,* 810–825.

Julien, D., Brault, M., Chartrand, E., & Begin, J. (2000). Immediacy behaviours and synchrony in satisfied and dissatisfied couples. *Canadian Journal of Behavioural Science, 32,* 84–90.

Julien, D., Chartrand, E., & Begin, J. (1999). Social networks, structural interdependence, and conjugal adjustment in heterosexual, gay, and lesbian couples. *Journal of Marriage & the Family, 61,* 516–530.

Julien, D., & Markman, H. J. (1991). Social support and social networks as determinants of individual and marital outcomes. *Journal of Social and Personal Relationships, 8,* 549–568.

Kaiser Family Foundation. (2001). *Race and ethnicity in 2001: Attitudes, perceptions and experiences.* Retrieved January 25, 2003, from http://www.kff.org/content/2001/3143/

Kalmijn, M. (1991). Status homogamy in the United States. *American Journal of Sociology, 97,* 496–523.

Kalmijn, M. (1993). Spouse selection among the children of European immigrants: A comparison of marriage cohorts in the 1960 Census. *International Migration Review, 27,* 51–78.

Kalmijn, M. (1994). Assortative mating by cultural and economic occupational status. *American Journal of Sociology, 100,* 422–452.

Kalmijn, M. (1998). Intermarriage and homogamy: Causes, patterns, trends. *Annual Review of Sociology, 24,* 395–421.

Kalmijn, M. (2002). Sex segregation of friendship networks: Individual and structural determinants of having cross-sex friends. *European Sociological Review, 18,* 101–117.

Kalmijn, M. (2003). Shared friendship networks and the life course: An analysis of survey data on married and cohabiting couples. *Social Networks, 25,* 231–249.

Kalmijn, M., & Flap, H. (2001). Assortative meeting and mating: Unintended consequences of organized settings for partner choices. *Social Forces, 79,* 1289–1312.

Kaniasty, K., & Norris, F. H. (2001). Social support dynamics in adjustment to disasters. In B. Sarason & S. Duck (Eds.), *Personal relationships: Implications for clinical and community psychology* (pp. 201–224). Chichester, England: Wiley.

Kaplan, H. B. (1991). Social psychology of the immune system: A conceptual framework and review of the literature. *Social Science and Medicine, 33,* 909–923.

Karney, B. R., & Bradbury, T. N. (1995). The longitudinal course of marital quality and stability: A review of theory, methods, and research. *Psychological Bulletin, 118*(1), 3–34.

Kastner, L., & Wyatt, J. (2002). *Launching years: Strategies for parenting from senior year to college life.* New York: Three Rivers Press.

Katz, J., Arias, I., Beach, S. R., Brody, G., & Roman, P. (1995). Excuses, excuses: Accounting for the effects of partner violence on marital satisfaction and stability. *Violence and Victims, 10,* 315–326.

Katz, P. P. (1995). The impact of rheumatoid arthritis on life activities. *Arthritis Care and Research, 8,* 272–278.

Kaye, S. H. (1988). The impact of divorce on children's academic performance. *Journal of Divorce, 12,* 283–298.

Kearns, J. N., & Leonard, K. E. (2004). Social networks, structural interdependence, and marital quality over the transition to marriage: A prospective analysis. *Journal of Family Psychology, 18,* 383–395.

Kegan, R. (1982). *The evolving self.* Cambridge, MA: Harvard University Press.

Keller, R. T. (1983). Predicting absenteeism from prior absenteeism, attitudinal factors, and nonattitudinal factors. *Journal of Applied Psychology, 68,* 536–540.

Kelley, D. L., & Burgoon, J. K. (1991). Understanding marital satisfaction and couple type as functions of relational expectations. *Human Communication Research, 18,* 40–69.

Kelley, H. H., Berscheid, E., Christensen, A., Harvey, J. H., Huston, T. L., Levinger, G., et al. (1983). *Close relationships.* New York: W. H. Freeman.

Kelley, H. H., & Thibaut, J. W. (1978). *Interpersonal relations: A theory of interdependence.* New York: Wiley.

Kennedy, R. J. R. (1943). Premarital residential propinquity and ethnic endogamy. *American Journal of Sociology, 48,* 580–584.

Kerckhoff, A. C. (1974). The social context of interpersonal attraction. In T. L. Huston (Ed.), *Foundations of interpersonal attraction* (pp. 61–78). New York: Academic Press.

Killworth, P. D., Bernard, H. R., & McCarty, C. (1984). Measuring patterns of acquaintanceship. *Current Anthropology, 25,* 381–397.

Kim, H. J., & Stiff, J. B. (1991). Social networks and the development of close relationships. *Human Communication Research, 18,* 70–91.

Kim, K. J., Conger, R., Lorenz, F. O., & Elder, G. H. (2001). Parent-adolescent reciprocity in negative affect and its relation to early adult social development. *Developmental Psychology, 37,* 775–790.

King, L. A., Mattimore, L. K., King, D. W., & Adams, G. A. (1995). Family support inventory for workers: A new measure of perceived social support from family members. *Journal of Organizational Behavior, 16,* 235–258.

Kinsella, B. (1996, March 18). Second only to Christmas; in springtime, books are rapidly becoming the gifts of choice for moms, dads and grads. *Publishers Weekly, 243,* 37.

Kivimäki, M., Länsisalmi, H., Elovainio, M., Heikkilä, A., Lindström, K., Harisalo, R., et al. (2000). Communication as a determinant of organizational innovation. *R&D Management, 30*(1), 33–42.

Knapp, M. L., Ellis, D. G., & Williams, B. A. (1980). Perceptions of communication behavior associated with relationship terms. *Communication Monographs, 47*(262–278).

Knapp, M. L., & Taylor, E. H. (1994). Commitment and its communication in romantic relationships. In A. L. Weber & J. H. Harvey (Eds.), *Perspectives on close relationships* (pp. 153–175). Boston: Allyn & Bacon.

Knapp, M. L., & Vangelisti, A. L. (1999). *Interpersonal communication and human relationships* (4th ed.). Boston: Allyn & Bacon.

Knight, J. (1995). Municipal matchmaking in rural Japan. *Anthropology Today, 11*(2), 9–17.

Knobloch, L. K., & Carpenter-Theune, K. E. (2004). Topic avoidance in developing romantic relationships: Associations with intimacy and relational uncertainty. *Communication Research, 31*, 173–205.

Knobloch, L. K., & Solomon, D. H. (1999). Measuring the sources and content of relational uncertainty. *Communication Studies, 50*, 261–278.

Knobloch, L. K., & Solomon, D. H. (2002a). Information seeking beyond initial interaction: Negotiating relational uncertainty within close relationships. *Human Communication Research, 28*, 243–257.

Knobloch, L. K., & Solomon, D. H. (2002b). Intimacy and the magnitude and experience of episodic relational uncertainty within romantic relationships. *Personal Relationships, 9*, 457–478.

Komarovsky, M. (1971). *The unemployed man and his family.* New York: Octagon.

Konstan, D. (1997). *Friendship in the classical world.* Cambridge, England: Cambridge University Press.

Kop, W. J., Krantz, D. S., Howell, R. H., Ferguson, M. A., Papademetriou, V., Lu, D., et al. (2001). Effects of mental stress on coronary epicardial vasomotion and flow velocity in coronary artery disease: Relationship with hemodynamic stress responses. *Journal of the American College of Cardiology, 37*, 1359–1366.

Krafft, S. (1994). Love, love me doo. *American Demographics, 16*(6), 15.

Krain, M. (1977). A definition of dyadic boundaries and an empirical study of boundary establishment in courtship. *International Journal of Sociology of the Family, 7*, 107–123.

Krokoff, L. J. (1991). Job distress is no laughing matter in marriage, or is it? *Journal of Social and Personal Relationships, 8*, 5–25.

Krulewitch, C. J., Roberts, D. W., & Thompson, L. S. (2003). Adolescent pregnancy and homicide: Findings from the Maryland Office of the Chief Medical Examiner, 1994–1998. *Child Maltreatment, 8*(2), 122–128.

Kundera, M. (1984). *The unbearable lightness of being.* New York: Harper Collins.

Kundera, M. (1996). *The book of laughter and forgetting* (Rev. ed.). New York: Harper Collins.

Kurdek, L. A. (1998). Relationship outcomes and their predictors: Longitudinal evidence from heterosexual married, gay cohabitating, and lesbian cohabiting couples. *Journal of Marriage and the Family, 60*, 553–568.

Kurdek, L. A. (1999). Relationship outcomes and their predictors: Longitudinal evidence from heterosexual married, gay cohabitating, and lesbian cohabiting couples. *Journal of Marriage and the Family, 60*, 553–568.

Kurdek, L. A. (2000). Attractions and constraints as determinants of relationships commitment: Longitudinal evidence from gay, lesbian, and heterosexual couples. *Personal Relationships, 7*, 245–262.

Kurth, S. B. (1970). Friendships and friendly relations. In G. J. McCall, M. M. McCall, N. K. Denzin, G. D. Suttles & S. B. Kurth (Eds.), *Social relationships* (pp. 136–170). Chicago: Aldine.

Kyratzis, A. (2001). Children's gender indexing in language: From the separate worlds hypothesis to considerations of culture, context, and power. *Research on Language and Social Interaction, 34*, 1–13.

Lagarde, E., Chastang, J. F., Gueguen, A., Coeuret-Pellicer, M., Chiron, M., & Lafont, S. (2004). Emotional stress and traffic accidents: The impact of separation and divorce. *Epidemiology, 15*, 762–766.

Lance, L. M. (1998). Gender differences in heterosexual dating: A content analysis of personal ads. *Journal of Men's Studies, 6*(3), 297–305.

Landers, A. (1996, October 13). Happy marriages began as cases of being in right place at right time. *Seattle Post Intelligencer,* p. 3.

Langhinrichsen-Rohling, J., Palarea, R. E., Cohen, J., & Rohling, M. L. (2000). Breaking up is hard to do: Unwanted pursuit behaviors following the dissolution of a romantic relationship. *Violence and Victims, 15*, 73–90.

Lannutti, P. J., & Cameron, K. A. (2002). Beyond the breakup. *Communication Quarterly, 50*, 153–170.

LaRocco, J. M., House, J. S., & French, J. R., Jr. (1980). Social support, occupational stress, and health. *Journal of Health and Social Behavior, 21*, 202–218.

LaSala, M. (2002). Walls and bridges: How coupled gay men and lesbians manage their intergenerational relationships. *Journal of Marital and Family Therapy, 28*(3), 327–339.

Latman, N. S., & Walls, R. (1996). Personality and stress: An exploratory comparison of rheumatoid arthritis and osteoarthritis. *Archives of Physical and Medical Rehabilitation, 77*, 796–800.

Laumann, E. O. (1973). *Bonds of pluralism: The form and substance of urban social networks.* New York: Wiley.

Laumann, E. O., Gagnon, J. H., Michael, R. T., & Michaels, S. (1994). *The social organization of sexuality: Sexual practices in the United States.* Chicago: University of Chicago Press.

Laurence, T. (1987). Friendship. *Synthese, 72*(2), 217–236.

Laurenceau, J.-P., Rivera, L. M., Schaffer, A., & Pietromonaco, P. R. (2004). Intimacy as an interpersonal process: Current status and future directions. In D. J. Mashek & A. Aron (Eds.), *Handbook of closeness and intimacy* (pp. 61–78). Mahwah, NJ: Lawrence Erlbaum Associates.

Laursen, B., & Williams, V. A. (1997). Perceptions of interdependence and closeness in family and peer relationships among adolescents with and without romantic partners. In S. Shulman & W. A. Collins (Eds.), *Romantic relationships in adolescence: New directions for child development* (Vol. 78, pp. 3–20). San Francisco: Jossey-Bass.

Lawler, J. (1975). Dialectic philosophy and developmental psychology: Hegel and Piaget on contradiction. *Human Development, 18*, 1–17.

Lederer, W. J., & Jackson, D. D. (1968). *The mirages of marriage.* New York: Norton.

Leslie, L. A., Huston, T. L., & Johnson, M. P. (1986). Parental reactions to dating relationships: Do they make a difference? *Journal of Marriage and the Family, 48*, 57–66.

Levinger, G. (1979). A social exchange view of the dissolution of pair relationships. In R. L. Burgess & T. L. Huston (Eds.), *Social exchange in developing relationships* (pp. 169–193). New York: Academic Press.

Levinger, G. (1991). Commitment vs. cohesiveness: Two complementary perspectives. In W. H. Jones & D. W. Perlman (Eds.), *Advances in personal relationships* (Vol. 3, pp. 145–150). London: Jessica Kingsley.

Levinger, G. (1994). Figure versus ground: Micro- and macroperspectives on the social psychology of personal relationships. In R. Erber & R. Gilmour (Eds.), *Theoretical frameworks for personal relationships* (pp. 1–28). Hillsdale, NJ: Lawrence Erlbaum Associates.

Levinger, G., & Snoek, D. J. (1972). *Attraction in relationship: A new look at interpersonal attraction.* Morristown, NJ: General Learning Press.

Levinson, D. J. (1978). *The seasons of a man's life.* New York:: Ballentine.

Lewin, K. (1948). *Resolving social conflicts, selected papers on group dynamics [1935–1946]* (G. W. Lewin, Ed.). New York: Harper.

Lewin, K. (1952). *Field theory in social science.* London: Tavistock.

Lewin, K. (1948). Social psychological differences between the United States and Germany. In G. W. Lewin (Ed.), *Resolving social conflicts, selected papers on group dynamics [1935–1946]* (pp. 3–33). New York: Harper.

Lewin, K., Adams, D. K., & Zener, K. E. (1935). *A dynamic theory of personality.* New York: McGraw-Hill.

Lewis, R. A. (1973a). A longitudinal test of a developmental framework for premarital dyadic formation. *Journal of Marriage and the Family, 35*(1), 16–25.

Lewis, R. A. (1973b). Social reaction and the formation of dyads: An interactionist approach to mate selection. *Sociometry, 36*(3), 409–418.

Lewthwaite, J., Owen, N., Coates, A., Henderson, B., & Steptoe, A. (2002). Circulating human heat shock protein 60 in the plasma of British civil servants: Relationship to physiological and psychosocial stress. *Circulation, 106,* 196–201.

Liebkind, K., & McAlister, A. L. (1999). Extended contact through peer modelling to promote tolerance in Finland. *European Journal of Social Psychology, 29,* 765–780.

Lin, Y. W., & Rusbult, C. E. (1995). Commitment to dating relationships and cross-sex friendships in America and China. *Journal of Social and Personal Relationships, 12,* 7–26.

Loether, H. J. (1960). Propinquity and homogeneity as factors in the choice of best buddies in the Air Force. *Pacific Sociological Review, 3,* 8–22.

Lofas, J. (1998). *Family rules: Helping stepfamilies and single parents build happy homes.* New York: Kensington Books.

Long, J. D., Anderson, J., & Williams, R. L. (1990). Life reflections by older kinsmen about critical life issues. *Educational Gerontology, 16,* 61–71.

Louch, H. (2000). Personal network integration: Transitivity and homophily in strong-tie networks. *Social Networks, 22,* 45–64.

Lowenstein, L. F. (2005). Causes and associated features of divorce as seen by recent research. *Journal of Divorce and Remarriage, 2005(3–4),* 153–171.

Lowrey, T. M., Otnes, C. C., & Ruth, J. A. (2004). Social influences on dyadic giving over time: A taxonomy from the giver's perspective. *Journal of Consumer Research, 30,* 547–558.

Lynch, J. J. (1977). *The broken heart: The medical consequences of loneliness.* New York: Basic Books.

Lynch, J. J. (1985). *The language of the heart.* New York: Basic Books.

MacGeorge, E. L., Graves, A. R., Feng, B., Gillihan, S. J., & Burleson, B. R. (2004). The myth of gender cultures: Similarities outweigh differences in men's and women's provision of and responses to supportive communication. *Sex Roles, 50,* 143–175.

Maconachie, M. (1988). Bound by language: Homogamous marriages among a sample of White South Africans. *Suid-Afrikaanse Tydskrif vir Sosiologie [The South African Journal of Sociology], 19(1),* 34–41.

Magnusson, D., & Endler, N. S. (1977). Interactional psychology: Present status and future prospects. In D. Magnusson & N. S. Endler (Eds.), *Personality at the crossroads: Current issues in interactional psychology* (pp. 3–31). Hillsdale, NJ: Lawrence Erlbaum Associates.

Mahlstedt, D., & Keeny, L. (1993). Female survivors of dating violence and their social networks. *Feminism & Psychology, 3,* 319–333.

Mallinckrodt, B. (2001). Interpersonal processes, attachment, and development of social competencies in individual and group psychotherapy. In B. Sarason & S. Duck (Eds.), *Personal relationships: Implications for clinical and community psychology* (pp. 89–117). Chichester, England: Wiley.

Mallinckrodt, B., McCreary, B. A., & Robertson, A. K. (1995). Co-occurrence of eating disorders and incest: The role of attachment, family environment, and social competencies. *Journal of Counseling Psychology, 42,* 178–186.

Maltz, D. N., & Borker, R. A. (1982). A cultural approach to male–female miscommunication. In J. J. Gumperz (Ed.), *Language and social identity* (pp. 196–216). Cambridge, England: Cambridge University Press.

Marsden, P. V. (1987). Core discussion networks of Americans. *American Sociological Review, 52,* 122–131.

Marshall, J. (2005, May 7). Onetime internees move author and audiences. *Seattle Post-Intelligencer,* pp. C1, C3.

Marston, C., & Cleland, J. (2003). Do unintended pregnancies carried to term lead to adverse outcomes for mother and child? An assessment in five developing countries. *Population Studies, 57,* 77–93.

Marx, K. (1963). *The eighteenth Brumaire of Louis Bonaparte.* New York: International Publishers.

Masiglio, W., & Scanzoni, J. (1995). *Families and friendships.* New York: Harper.

Matter, D. E., & Matter, R. M. (1984). Suicide among elementary school children: A serious concern for counselors. *Elementary School Guidance and Counseling, 18,* 260–267.

Mayseless, O., & Scharf, M. (2003). What does it mean to be an adult? The Israeli experience. In J. J. Arnett & N. L. Galambos (Eds.), *Exploring cultural conceptions of the transition to adulthood: New directions for child and adolescent development* (pp. 5–20). San Francisco: Jossey-Bass.

McCall, G. J., & Simmons, J. L. (1966). *Identities and interactions.* New York: Free Press.

McCall, M. M. (1970). Boundary rules in relationships and encounters. In G. J. McCall, M. M. McCall, N. K. Denzin, G. D. Suttles & S. B. Kurth (Eds.), *Social relationships* (pp. 35–61). Chicago: Aldine.

McMurdy, D. (2003, February 13). Canadian businesses love Valentine's Day. *Ottawa Citizen,* p. 4.

McPherson, M., Smith-Lovin, L., & Cook, J. M. (2001). Birds of a feather: Homophily in social networks. *Annual Review of Sociology, 27,* 415–444.

Mead, G. H. (1934). *Mind, self, and society.* Chicago: University of Chicago Press.

Medalie, J. H., & Goldbourt, U. (1976). Angina pectoris among 10,000 men. II. Psychosocial and other risk factors as evidenced by a multivariate analysis of a five-year incidence study. *American Journal of Medicine, 60,* 910–921.

Mednick, B., Baker, R. L., Reznick, C., & Hocevar, D. (1990). Long-term effects of divorce on adolescent academic achievement. *Journal of Divorce,* 69–88.

Meyer, R. J., & Haggerty, R. J. (1962). Streptococcal infections in families. Factors altering individual susceptibility. *Pediatrics, 29,* 539–549.

Milardo, R. M. (1982). Friendship networks in developing relationships: Converging and diverging social environments. *Social Psychology Quarterly, 45,* 162–172.

Milardo, R. M. (1983). Social networks and pair relationships: A review of substantive and measurement issues. *Sociology and Social Research, 68,* 1–18.

Milardo, R. M. (1987). Changes in social networks of women and men following divorce. *Journal of Family Issues, 8,* 78–96.

Milardo, R. M. (1989). Theoretical and methodological issues in the identification of the social networks of spouses. *Journal of Marriage and the Family, 51,* 165–174.

Milardo, R. M. (1992). Comparative methods for delineating social networks. *Journal of Social and Personal Relationships, 9,* 447–461.

Milardo, R. M., & Allan, G. (1997). Social networks and marital relationships. In S. Duck (Ed.), *Handbook of personal relationships* (2nd ed., pp. 505–522). Chichester, England: Wiley.

Milardo, R. M., & Helms-Erikson, H. (2000). Network overlap and third-party influence in close relationships. In C. Hendrick & S. Hendrick (Eds.), *Close relationships: A sourcebook* (pp. 33–45). Thousand Oaks, CA: Sage.

Milardo, R. M., Johnson, M. P., & Huston, T. L. (1983). Developing close relationships: Changing patterns of interaction between pair members and social networks. *Journal of Personality and Social Psychology, 44,* 964–976.

Milgram, S. (1967). The small-world problem. *Psychology Today, 1*(1), 60–67.

Milgram, S. (1977). *The individual in a social world: Essays and experiments.* Reading, MA: Addison-Wesley.

Miller, G. R., Boster, F., Roloff, M. E., & Seibold, D. (1977). Compliance-gaining message strategies: A typology and some findings concerning effects of situational differences. *Communication Monographs, 44,* 37–51.

Miller, G. R., & Steinberg, M. (1975). *Between people : A new analysis of interpersonal communication.* Chicago: Science Research Associates.

Miller, J. B., & Stubblefield, A. (1993). Parental disclosure from the perspective of late adolescents. *Journal of Adolescence, 16,* 439–455.

Minatoya, L. Y. (1988). Women's attitudes and behaviors in American, Japanese, and cross-national marriages. *Journal of Multicultural Counseling and Development, 16,* 45–62.

Mitchell, J. C. (1969). The concept and use of social networks. In J. C. Mitchell (Ed.), *Social networks in urban situations: Analyses of personal relationships in central African towns* (pp. 1–50). Manchester, England: Manchester University Press.

Mitchell, J. C. (1979). Networks, algorithms and analysis. In P. W. Holland & S. Leinhardt (Eds.), *Perspectives on social network research* (pp. 425–451). New York: Academic Press.

Molm, D. (1985). Gender and power use: An experimental analysis of behavior and perceptions. *Social Psychology Quarterly, 48,* 285–300.

Monge, P. R., & Contractor, N. S. (2003). *Theories of communication network.* New York: Oxford.

Monsour, M. (2002). *Women and men as friends: Relationships across the life span in the 21st century.* Mahwah, NJ: Lawrence. Erlbaum Associates.

Moody, J. (2001). Race, school integration, and friendship segregation in America. *American Journal of Sociology, 107,* 679–716.

Moore, D. W. (2003, January 3). Family, health most important aspects of life. *Gallup Pool Tuesday Briefing,* pp. 19–20.

Moreno, J. L. (1953). *Who shall survive? Foundations of sociometry, group psychotherapy and sociodrama.* Beacon, New York: Beacon House.

Morgan, D. L., Neal, M. B., & Carder, P. (1997). The stability of core and peripheral networks over time. *Social Networks, 19,* 9–25.

Murray, S. L., Holmes, J. G., & Griffin, D. W. (1996). The benefits of positive illusions: Idealization and the construction of satisfaction in close relationships. *Journal of Personality and Social Psychology, 71,* 1155–1180.

Murstein, B. I. (1970). Stimulus—value—role: A theory of marital choice. *Journal of Marriage and the Family, 32,* 465–481.

Nagda, B. A., & Zúñiga, X. (2003). Fostering meaningful racial engagement through intergroup dialogues. *Group Processes and Intergroup Relations, 6*(1), 115–132.

Nahemow, L., & Lawton, M. P. (1975). Similarity and propinquity in friendship formation. *Journal of Personality and Social Psychology, 32,* 205–213.

National Clearinghouse of Plastic Surgery Statistics. (2001). Retrieved September 30, 2005, from http://www.plasticsurgery.org/public_education/expanded_2001_statistics.cfm

Needle, R. H., Su, S. S., & Doherty, W. J. (1990). Divorce, remarriage, and adolescent substance use: A prospective longitudinal study. *Journal of Marriage and the Family, 52,* 157–169.

Newcomb, T. M. (1953). An approach to the study of communicative acts. *Psychological Review, 60,* 391–404.

Newcomb, T. M. (1961). *The acquaintance process.* New York: Holt.

Newman, P. J., Jr., & Nelson, M. R. (1996). Mainstream legitimization of homosexual men through Valentine's Day gift-giving and consumption rituals. *Journal of Homosexuality, 31*(1–2), 57–69.

Nielsen, L. (1993). Students from divorced and blended families. *Educational Psychology Review, 5,* 177–199.

Notarius, C. I., Benson, P. R., Sloane, D., Vanzetti, N. A., & Hornyak, L. M. (1989). Exploring the interface between perception and behavior: An analysis of marital interaction in distressed and nondistressed couples. *Behavioral Assessment, 11,* 39–64.

Oliner, S. P., & Oliner, P. M. (1988). *The altruistic personality: Rescuers of Jews in Nazi Europe.* New York: Free Press.

Olk, P., & Elvira, M. (2001). Friends and strategic agents: The role of friendship and discretion in negotiating strategic alliances. *Group & Organization Management, 26*(2), 124–164.

Omoto, A. M., & Snyder, M. (2002). Considerations of community: The context and process of volunterism. *American Behavioral Scientist, 45,* 846–867.

Orbuch, T. L., Veroff, J., Hassan, H., & Horrocks, J. (2002). Who will divorce: A 14–year longitudinal study of Black couples and White couples. *Journal of Social and Personal Relationships, 19,* 179–202.

Oring, E. (1984). Dyadic traditions. *Journal of Folklore Research, 21,* 19–28.

Orth-Gomer, K., Wamala, S. P., Horsten, M., Schenck-Gustafsson, K., Schneiderman, N., & Mittleman, M. A. (2000). Marital stress worsens prognosis in women with coronary heart disease: The Stockholm Female Coronary Risk Study. *Journal of the American Medical Association, 284,* 3008–3014.

O'Shea, M. D., & Phelps, R. (1985). Multiple family therapy: Current status and critical appraisal. *Family Process, 24,* 555–582.

Otsuka, J. (2002). *When the emperor was divine.* New York: Alfred A. Knopf.

Øygard, L. (2004). Divorce support groups: What is the role of the participants' personal capital regarding adjustment to divorce? *Journal of Divorce and Remarriage, 40(3–4),* 103–119.

Paolini, S., Hewstone, M., Cairns, E., & Voci, A. (2004). Effects of direct and indirect cross-group friendships on judgments of Catholics and Protestants in Northern Ireland: The mediating role of an anxiety-reduction mechanism. *Personality and Social Psychology Bulletin, 30,* 770–786.

Parker, P. A., & Kulik, J. A. (1995). Burnout, self- and supervisor-related job performance, and absenteeism among nurses. *Journal of Behavioral Medicine, 18,* 581–599.

Parks, M. R. (1976). *Communication and relational change processes: Conceptualization and findings.* Unpublished dissertation, Michigan State University, East Lansing, Michigan.

Parks, M. R. (1980). A test of the cross-situational consistency of communication apprehension. *Communication Monographs, 47,* 220–232.

Parks, M. R. (1982). Ideology in interpersonal communication: Off the couch and into the world. In M. Burgoon (Ed.), *Communication yearbook 5* (pp. 79–108). New Brunswick, NJ: Transaction.

Parks, M. R. (1995). Webs of influence in interpersonal relationships. In C. R. Burger & M. E. Burgoon (Eds.), *Communication and social influence processes* (pp. 155–178). East Lansing: Michigan State University Press.

Parks, M. R. (2000). Communication networks and relationship life cycles. In K. Dindia & S. Duck (Eds.), *Communication and personal relationships* (pp. 55–75). Chichester, England: Wiley.

Parks, M. R., & Adelman, M. B. (1983). Communication networks and the development of romantic relationships: An expansion of uncertainty reduction theory. *Human Communication Research, 10,* 55–79.

Parks, M. R., & Eggert, L. L. (1991). The role of social context in the dynamics of personal relationships. In W. H. Jones & D. Perlman (Eds.), *Advances in personal relationships* (Vol. 2, pp. 1–34). London: Jessica Kingsley.

Parks, M. R., & Floyd, K. (1996a). Making friends in cyberspace. *Journal of Communication, 46(1),* 80–97.

Parks, M. R., & Floyd, K. (1996b). Meanings for closeness and intimacy in friendship. *Journal of Social and Personal Relationships, 13,* 85–107.

Parks, M. R., & Roberts, L. D. (1998). "Making MOOsic": The development of personal relationships online and a comparison to their off-line counterparts. *Journal of Social and Personal Relationships, 15,* 517–537.

Parks, M. R., Stan, C. M., & Eggert, L. L. (1983). Romantic involvement and social network involvement. *Social Psychology Quarterly, 46(2),* 116–131.

Parsons, T. (1937). *The structure of social action: A study in social theory with special reference to a group of recent European writers.* New York: McGraw-Hill.

Pasternak, B. L. (1958). *Doctor Zhivago.* New York: Pantheon.

Pattison, P. (1993). *Algebraic models for social networks.* New York: Cambridge University Press.

Paul, E., & Brier, S. (2001). Friendsickness in the transition to college: Precollege predictors and college adjustment correlates. *Journal of Counseling & Development, 70,* 77–89.

Peplau, L. A., & Cochran, S. D. (1990). A relationship perspective on homosexuality. In D. P. McWhirter, S. A. Sanders & J. M. Reinsch (Eds.), *Homosexuality/heterosexuality: Concepts of sexual orientation* (pp. 321–349). New York: Oxford.

Peplau, L. A., & Spalding, L. R. (2003). The close relationships of lesbians, gay men, and bisexuals. In L. D. Garnets & D. C. Kimmel (Eds.), *Psychological perspectives on lesbian, gay, and bisexual experiences* (2nd. ed., pp. 449–474). New York: Columbia University Press.

Personal care: The market, competitors & trends. (2001). Retrieved December 10, 2002, from http://www.unitymarketingonline.com/reports2/personal_care/

Petronio, S. (1991). Communication boundary management: A theoretical model of managing disclosure of private information between marital couples. *Communication Theory, 1,* 311–335.

Petronio, S. (2002). *Boundaries of private disclosures.* New York: SUNY Press.

Petronio, S., & Bantz, C. (1991). Controlling the ramifications of disclosure: "Don't tell anybody but ..." *Journal of Language and Social Psychology, 10,* 263–269.

Petronio, S., Ellemers, N., Giles, H., & Gallois, C. (1998). (Mis)communicating across boundaries. *Communication Research, 25,* 571–595.

Petronio, S., Sargent, J., Andea, L., Reganis, P., & Cichocki, D. (2004). Family and friends as healthcare advocates: Dilemmas of confidentiality and privacy. *Journal of Social and Personal Relationships, 21,* 33–52.

Pettigrew, T. F. (1997). Generalized intergroup contact effects on prejudice. *Personality & Social Psychology Bulletin, 23,* 173–185.

Philips, S. U. (1983). *The invisible culture: Communication in classroom and community on the Warm Springs Indian Reservation.* New York: Longman.

Philipsen, G. (1992). *Speaking culturally: Explorations in social communication.* Albany: SUNY Press.

Picking physicians. (1986, June 24). *Wall Street Journal,* p. 31.

Planalp, S., & Garvin-Doxas, K. (1994). Using mutual knowledge in conversation: Friends as experts in each other. In S. Duck (Ed.), *Dynamics of interactions* (pp. 1–26). Thousand Oaks, CA: Sage.

Planalp, S., & Honeycutt, J. M. (1985). Events that increase uncertainty in personal relationships. *Human Communication Research, 11,* 593–604.

Planalp, S., Rutherford, D. K., & Honeycutt, J. M. (1988). Events that increase uncertainty in personal relationships: II. Replication and extension. *Human Communication Research, 14,* 516–547.

Plaut, S. M., & Friedman, S. B. (1981). Psychosocial factors in infectious disease. In R. Ader (Ed.), *Psychoneuroimmunology* (pp. 3–30). New York: Academic Press.

Pollitt, K. (2004, January 19). Webstalker: When it's time to stop checking on your ex. *The New Yorker, 409,* 38–42.

Prager, K. J., & Roberts, L. J. (2004). Deep intimate connection: Self and intimacy in couple relationships. In D. J. Mashek & A. Aron (Eds.), *Handbook of closeness and intimacy* (pp. 43–60). Mahwah, NJ: Lawrence Erlbaum Associates.

Preston, S. H., & McDonald, J. (1979). The incidence of divorce within cohorts of American marriages contracted since the Civil War. *Demography, 16,* 1–26.

Previti, D., & Amato, P. R. (2003). Why stay married? Rewards, barriers, and marital stability. *Journal of Marriage and the Family, 65,* 561–573.

Putnam, R. D. (2000). *Bowling alone: The collapse and revival of American community.* New York: Simon & Schuster.

Radcliffe-Brown, A. R. (1952). *Structure and function in primitive society, essays and addresses.* London: Cohen & West.

Rapoport, A. (1956). The diffusion problem in mass behavior. *General Systems, 1,* 48–55.

Rawlins, W. K. (1992). *Friendship matters: Communication, dialectics, and the life course.* New York: Aldine de Gruyter.

Reid, K. (1984). Some social, psychological and educational aspects related to persistent school absenteeism. *Research in Education, 31,* 63–82.

Reifman, A., Villa, L. C., Amans, J. A., Rethinam, V., & Telesca, T. Y. (2001). Children of divorce in the 1990s: A meta-analysis. *Journal of Divorce and Remarriage, 36*(1–2), 27–36.

Reis, H. T., Senchak, M., & Solomon, B. (1985). Sex differences in the intimacy of social interaction: Further examination of the potential explanations. *Journal of Personality and Social Psychology, 48,* 1204–1217.

Reis, H. T., & Shaver, P. (1988). Intimacy as an interpersonal process. In S. Duck (Ed.), *Handbook of personal relationships* (pp. 367–389). Chichester, England: Wiley.

Ridley, C. A., & Avery, A. W. (1979). Social network influence on the dyadic relationship. In R. L. Burgess & T. L. Huston (Eds.), *Social exchange in developing relationships* (pp. 223–246). New York: Academic Press.

Riesch, S. K., Jacobson, G. A., & Tosi, C. B. (1994). Young adolescents' identification of difficult life events. *Clinical Nursing Research, 3,* 393–413.

Risser, D., Bonsch, A., & Schneider, B. (1996). Family background of drug-related deaths: A descriptive study based on interviews with relatives of deceased drug users. *Journal of Forensic Science, 41,* 960–962.

Ritzer, G., & Goodman, D. J. (2004). *Classical sociological theory* (4th ed.). Boston: McGraw-Hill.

Roberts, L. J. (2000). Fire and ice in marital communication: Hostile and distancing behaviors as predictors of marital distress. *Journal of Marriage and the Family, 62,* 693–707.

Rockman, H. (1994). Matchmaker matchmaker make me a match: The art and conventions of Jewish arranged marriages. *Sexual and Marital Therapy, 9,* 277–284.

Rogers, E. M. (2003). *Diffusion of innovations* (5th ed.). New York: Free Press.

Rogers, S. J., & May, D. C. (2003). Spillover between marital quality and job satisfaction: Long-term patterns and gender differences. *Journal of Marriage and the Family, 65,* 482–495.

Rollie, S. S., & Duck, S. (in press). Stage theories of marital breakdown. In J. H. Harvey & M. A. Fine (Eds.), *Handbook of divorce and dissolution of romantic relationships.* Mahwah, NJ: Lawrence Erlbaum Associates.

Roloff, M. E., & Cloven, D. H. (1990). The chilling effect in interpersonal relationships: The reluctance to speak one's mind. In D. D. Cahn (Ed.), *Intimates in conflict* (pp. 49–76). Hillsdale, NJ: Lawrence Erlbaum Associates.

Rose, S., & Frieze, I. H. (1989). Young singles' scripts for a first date. *Gender and Society, 3,* 258–268.

Rose, S., & Frieze, I. H. (1993). Young singles' contemporary dating scripts. *Sex Roles, 28,* 499–509.

Rosenblatt, P. C., Karis, T. A., & Powell, R. D. (1995). *Multiracial couples: Black and White voices.* Thousand Oaks, CA: Sage.

Rosengren, A., Hawken, S., Ôunpuu, S., Silwa, K., Zubain, M., Almahmeed, W. A., et al. (2004). Association of psychosocial risk factors with risk of acute myocardial infarction in 11,119 cases and 13,648 controls from 52 countries (the Interheart Study): Case-control study. *Lancet, 364,* 953–962.

Ross, L., & Nisbett, R. E. (1991). *The person and the situation: Perspectives of social psychology.* Philadelphia: Temple University Press.

Roxburgh, S. (1999). Exploring the work and family relationship. *Journal of Family Issues, 20,* 771–788.

Rubin, Z. (1970). Measurement of romantic love. *Journal of Personality and Social Psychology, 16,* 265–273.

Ruesch, J., & Bateson, G. (1951). *Communication, the social matrix of psychiatry.* New York: Norton.

Rusbult, C. E. (1980). Commitment and satisfaction in romantic associations: A test of the investment model. *Journal of Experimental Social Psychology, 16,* 172–186.

Rusbult, C. E. (1983). A longitudinal test of the investment model: The development (and deterioration) of satisfaction and commitment in heterosexual involvements. *Journal of Personality and Social Psychology, 45,* 101–117.

Rusbult, C. E., Kumashir, M., Coolsen, M. K., & Kirchner, J. L. (2004). Interdependence, closeness, and relationships. In D. J. Mashek & A. Aron (Eds.), *Handbook of closeness and intimacy* (pp. 137–161). Mahwah, NJ: Lawrence Erlbaum Associates.

Sahlstein, E., & Baxter, L. A. (2001). Improvising commitment in close relationships: A relational dialectics perspective. In J. H. Harvey & A. Wenzel (Eds.), *Close romantic relationships: Maintenance and enhancement* (pp. 115–132). Mahwah, NJ: Lawrence Erlbaum Associates.

Salzinger, L. L. (1982). The ties that bind: The effect of clustering on dyadic relationships. *Social Networks, 4,* 117–145.

Sapadin, L. A. (1988). Friendship and gender: Perspectives of professional men and women. *Journal of Social and Personal Relationships, 5,* 387–403.

Satir, V. M. (1964). *Conjoint family therapy: A guide to theory and technique.* Palo Alto, CA: Science & Behavior Books.

Savin-Williams, R. C. (1996). Dating and romantic relationships among gay, lesbian, and bisexual youths. In R. C. Savin-Williams & K. M. Cohen (Eds.), *The lives of lesbians, gays, and bisexuals: Children to adults* (pp. 166–180). Fort Worth, TX: Harcourt Brace.

Savin-Williams, R. C. (2003). Lesbian, gay, and bisexual youths' relationships with their parents. In L. D. Garnets & D. C. Kimmel (Eds.), *Psychological perspectives on lesbian, gay, and bisexual experiences* (2nd ed., pp. 299–326). New York: Columbia University Press.

Schachter, S. (1959). *The psychology of affiliation: Experimental studies of the sources of gregariousness.* Stanford, CA: Stanford University Press.

Schafer, R. B., & Keith, P. M. (1990). Matching by weight in married couples: A life cycle perspective. *Journal of Social Psychology, 130,* 657–664.

Scharlott, B. W., & Christ, W. G. (1995). Overcoming relationship-initiation barriers: The impact of a computer-dating system on sex role, shyness, and appearance inhibitions. *Computers in Human Behavior, 11*(2), 191–204.

Schiappa, E., Greg, P. B., & Hewes, D. E. (2005). The parasocial contact hypothesis. *Communication Monographs, 72,* 92–115.

Schlegel, A., & Barry, H. (1991). *Adolescence: An anthropological inquiry.* New York: Free Press.

Schneller, D. P., & Arditti, J. A. (2004). After the breakup: Interpreting divorce and rethinking intimacy. *Journal of Divorce and Remarriage, 42*(1–2), 1–37.

Schultz, J. B., & Henderson, C. (1985). Family satisfaction and job performance: Implications for career development. *Journal of Career Development, 12,* 33–47.

Scott, J. (2000). *Social network analysis: A handbook* (2nd ed.). Thousand Oaks, CA: Sage.

Scudder, J. N., & Andrews, P. H. (1995). A comparison of two alternative models of powerful speech: The impact of power and gender upon the use of threats. *Communication Research Reports, 12,* 25–33.

Searle, J. R. (1969). *Speech acts: An essay in the philosophy of language.* Cambridge, England: Cambridge University Press.

Segerstrom, S. C., & Miller, G. E. (2004). Psychological stress and the human immune system: A meta-analytic study of 30 years of inquiry. *Psychological Bulletin, 130,* 601–630.

Segrin, C. (2001). *Interpersonal processes in psychological problems.* New York: Guilford Press.

Selman, R. L., Watts, C. L., & Schultz, L. H. (Eds.). (1997). *Fostering friendship: Pair therapy for treatment and prevention.* New York: Aldine De Gruyter.

Seltzer, J. A. (1991). Relationships between fathers and children who live apart: The father's role after separation. *Journal of Marriage and the Family, 53,* 79–101.

Sherif, M., Harvey, O. J., White, B. J., Hood, W. R., & Sherif, C. W. (1961). *Intergroup conflict and cooperation: The robbers cave experiment.* Norman, OK: University Book Exchange.

Shibazaki, K., & Brennan, K. A. (1998). When birds of different feathers flock together: A preliminary comparison of intra-ethnic and inter-ethnic dating relationships. *Journal of Social and Personal Relationships, 15,* 248–256.

Shulman, S., Collins, W. A., & Knafo, D. (1997). Afterword: Romantic relationships in adolescence—more than casual dating. *New Directions for Child Development, 78,* 105–110.

Shulman, S., Laursen, B., Kalman, Z., & Karpovsky, S. (1997). Adolescent intimacy revisited. *Journal of Youth & Adolescence, 26,* 597–617.

Silva, M., & Ross, I. (2002). Association of perceived parental attitudes towards premarital sex with initiation of sexual intercourse in adolescence. *Psychological Reports, 91(3,Pt. 1),* 781–784.

Simmel, G. (1950). *The sociology of Georg Simmel* (K. H. Wolff, Trans.). Glencoe, IL: Free Press.

Simmel, G. (1922). *Conflict and the web of group affiliations* (K. H. Wolff & R. Bendix, Trans.). Glencoe, IL: Free Press. (Original work published 1922)

Simpson, J. A., Gangestad, S. W., & Biek, M. (1993). Personality and nonverbal social behavior: An ethological perspective of relationship initiation. *Journal of Experimental Social Psychology, 29,* 434–461.

Size of floral industry. (2003). Retrieved February 18, 2003, from http://www.aboutflowers.com/press_b1.html

Slater, P. E. (1963). On social regression. *American Sociological Review, 28,* 339–358.

Snow, D. A., Leahy, P. J., & Schwab, W. A. (1981). Social interaction in a heterogeneous apartment: An investigation of the effects of environment upon behavior. *Sociological Focus, 14,* 309–319.

Snyder, M., Berscheid, E., & Glick, P. (1985). Focusing on the exterior and the interior: Two investigations of the initiation of personal relationships. *Journal of Personality and Social Psychology, 48,* 1427–1439.

Solomon, G. F. (1985). The emerging field of psychoneuroimmunology: With a special note on AIDS. *Advances, 2,* 6–19.

Spanier, G. B., & Thompson, L. (1984). *Parting: The aftermath of separation and divorce.* Beverly Hills, CA: Sage.

Spitzberg, B. H., & Cupach, W. R. (1998). *The dark side of close relationships.* Mahwah, NJ: Lawrence Erlbaum Associates.

Spitzer, A., Bar-Tal, Y., & Golander, H. (1995). Social support: How does it really work? *Journal of Advanced Nursing, 22,* 850–854.

Sprecher, S. (1988). Investment model, equity, and social support determinants of relationship commitment. *Social Psychology Quarterly, 51,* 318–328.

Sprecher, S., & Felmlee, D. (1992). The influence of parents and friends on the quality and stability of romantic relationships: A three-wave longitudinal investigation. *Journal of Marriage and the Family, 54,* 888–900.

Sprecher, S., & Felmlee, D. (2000). Romantic partners' perceptions of social network attributes with the passage of time and relationship transitions. *Personal Relationships, 7,* 325–340.

Sprecher, S., Felmlee, D., Orbuch, T. L., & Willetts, M. C. (2002). Social networks and change in personal relationships. In H. T. Reis, M. A. Fitzpatrick, & A. L. Vangelisti (Eds.), *Stability and change in relationships* (pp. 257–284). Cambridge, England: Cambridge University Press.

Sprecher, S., & Regan, P. C. (2002). Liking some things (in some people) more than others: Partner preferences in romantic relationships and friendships. *Journal of Social and Personal Relationships, 19,* 463–481.

Squires, T., & Busuttil, A. (1995). Child fatalities in Scottish house fires 1980–1990: A case of child neglect? *Child Abuse and Neglect, 19,* 865–873.

Stack, S. (1990). New micro-level data on the impact of divorce on suicide, 1959–1980: A test of two theories. *Journal of Marriage and the Family, 52,* 119–127.

Stafford, L., & Canary, D. J. (1991). Maintenance strategies and romantic relationship type, gender, and relational characteristics. *Journal of Social and Personal Relationships, 8,* 217–242.

Stein, C. H., Bush, E. G., Ross, R. R., & Ward, M. (1992). Mine, yours and ours: A configural analysis of the networks of married couples in relation to marital satisfaction and individual well-being. *Journal of Social and Personal Relationships, 9,* 365–383.

Stern, D. N. (1985). *The interpersonal world of the infant: A view from psychoanalysis and developmental psychology.* New York: Basic Books.

Sternberg, R. J. (1986). A triangular theory of love. *Psychological Review, 93,* 119–135.

Sternberg, R. J. (1987). Liking vs. loving: A comparative evaluation of theories. *Psychological Bulletin, 102,* 331–345.

Sternberg, R. J. (1998). *Cupid's arrow: The course of love through time.* Cambridge: Cambridge University Press.

Storr, A. (1988). *Solitude: A return to the self.* New York: Free Press.

Straus, M. A., & Savage, S. A. (2005). Neglectful behavior by parents in the life history of university students in 17 countries and its relation to violence against dating partners. *Child Maltreatment: Journal of the American Professional Society on the Abuse of Children, 10*(2), 124–135.

Suitor, J., & Keeton, S. (1997). Once a friend, always a friend? Effects of homophily on women's support networks across a decade. *Social Networks, 19,* 51–62.

Sullivan, H. S. (1953). *The interpersonal theory of psychiatry.* New York: Norton.

Suls, J., & Wan, C. K. (1993). The relationship between trait hostility and cardiovascular reactivity: A quantitative review and analysis. *Psychophysiology, 30,* 615–626.

Sunnafrank, M. (1991). Interpersonal attraction and attitude similarity: A communication-based assessment. In J. A. Anderson (Ed.), *Communication yearbook 14* (pp. 451–483). Newbury Park, CA: Sage.

Surra, C. A. (1985). Courtship types: Variations in interdependence between partners and social networks. *Journal of Personality and Social Psychology, 49,* 357–375.

Surra, C. A., & Milardo, R. M. (1991). The social psychological context of developing relationships: Interactive and psychological networks. In W. H. Jones & D. Perlman (Eds.), *Advances in personal relationships* (Vol. 3, pp. 1–36). London: Jessica Kingsley.

Suttles, G. D. (1970). Friendship as a social institution. In G. J. McCall, M. M. McCall, N. K. Denzin, G. D. Suttles & S. B. Kurth (Eds.), *Social relationships* (pp. 95–135). Chicago: Aldine.

Swain, S. (1989). Covert intimacy: Closeness in men's friendships. In B. J. Risman & P. Schwartz (Eds.), *Gender in intimate relationships* (pp. 71–86). Belmont, CA: Wadsworth.

Swidler, A. (2001). *Talk of love: How culture matters.* Chicago: University of Chicago Press.

Talbani, A., & Hasanali, P. (2000). Adolescent females between tradition and modernity: Gender role socialization in south Asian immigrant culture. *Journal of Adolescence, 23,* 615–627.

Taylor, D., Dubé, L., & Bellerose, J. (1986). Intergroup contact in Quebec. In M. Hewstone & R. Brown (Eds.), *Contact and conflict in intergroup encounters* (pp. 93–106). Oxford, England: Blackwell.

Taylor, D. A. (1968). Some aspects of the development of interpersonal relationships: Social penetration processes. *Journal of Social Psychology, 75,* 79–90.

Terhell, E. L., Broese van Groenou, M. I., & Van Tilburg, T. (2004). Network dynamics in the long-term period after divorce. *Journal of Social and Personal Relationships, 21,* 719–738.

Terman, L. M., & Wallin, P. (1949). The validity of marriage prediction and marital adjustment tests. *American Sociological Review, 14,* 497–504.

Thibaut, J. W., & Kelley, H. H. (1959). *The social psychology of groups.* New York,: Wiley.

Thompson, E. A., Eggert, L. L., Randell, B. P., & Pike, K. C. (2001). Evaluation of indicated suicide risk prevention approaches for potential high school dropouts. *American Journal of Public Health, 91,* 742–752.

Thompson, R. A., & Wyatt, J. (1999). Values, policy, and resarch on divorce: Seeking fairness for children. In R. A. Thompson & P. R. Amato (Eds.), *The postdivorce family: Children, parenting, and society* (pp. 191–232). Thousand Oaks, CA: Sage.

Thornes, B., & Collard, J. (1979). *Who divorces?* London: Routledge & Kegan Paul.

Ting-Toomey, S. (1991). Intimacy expressions in three cultures: France, Japan, and the United States. *International Journal of Intercultural Relations, 15,* 29–46.

Titus, S. L. (1980). A function of friendship: Social comparisons as a frame of reference for marriage. *Human Relations, 33,* 409–431.

Todd, J., Mckinney, J. L., Harris, R., Chadderton, R., & Small, L. (1992). Attitudes toward interracial dating: Effects of age, sex, and race. *Journal of Multicultural Counseling and Development, 20,* 202–208.

Tönnies, F. (1957). *Community & society (Gemeinschaft und Gesellschaft).* (P. Loomis, Trans.). East Lansing, MI: Michigan State University Press. (Original work published 1887)

Trickett, E. J., & Buchanan, R. M. (2001). The role of personal relationships in transitions: Contributions of an ecological perspective. In B. Sarason & S. Duck (Eds.), *Personal relationships: Implications for clinical and community psychology* (pp. 141–157). Chichester, England: Wiley.

Trout, D. L. (1980). The role of social isolation in suicide. *Suicide and Life-Threatening Behavior, 10,* 10–23.

Tsiantar, B. (2005, April 11). The war on wrinkles. *Time, 165,* A16–17.

Tucker, M. B., & Mitchell-Kernan, C. (1995). Social structural and psychological correlates of interethnic dating. *Journal of Social and Personal Relationships, 12,* 341–361.

U.S. weight loss and diet control market. (2002). Retrieved January 14, 2003, from http://www.marketdataenterprises.com/studies.html#LOSS

Udry, J. R. (1981). Marital alternatives and marital disruption. *Journal of Marriage and the Family, 43,* 889–898.

Umberson, D. (1987). Family status and health behaviors: Social control as a dimension of social integration. *Journal of Health & Social Behavior, 28,* 306–319.

Van Duyn, M. (1990). *Near changes: Poems.* New York: Knopf.

VanderVoort, L., & Duck, S. (2000). Talking about "relationships": Variations on a theme. In K. Dindia & S. Duck (Eds.), *Communication and personal relationships* (pp. 1–12). New York: Wiley.

Vangelisti, A. L., & Banski, M. A. (1993). Couples' debriefing conversations: The impact of gender, occupation, and demographic characteristics. *Family Relations: Journal of Applied Family & Child Studies, 42,* 149–157.

Vangelisti, A. L., Caughlin, J. P., & Timmerman, L. (2001). Criteria for revealing family secrets. *Communication Monographs, 68,* 1–27.

Vaughan, D. (1986). *Uncoupling: Turning points in intimate relationships.* New York: Oxford University Press.

Vera, H., Berardo, F. M., & Vandiver, J. S. (1990). Age irrelevancy in society: The test of mate selection. *Journal of Aging Studies, 4,* 81–95.

Verbrugge, L. M. (1977). The structure of adult friendship choices. *Social Forces, 56,* 576–597.

Veroff, J., Douvan, E. A. M., & Hatchett, S. (1995). *Marital instability: A social and behavioral study of the early years.* Westport, CT: Praeger.

Von Andics, M. (1947). *Suicide and the meaning of life.* London: W. Hodge.

von Kanel, R., Mills, P. J., Fainman, C., & Dimsdale, J. E. (2001). Effects of psychological stress and psychiatric diorders on blood coagulation and fibrinolysis: A biobehavioral pathway to coronary artery disease? *Psychosomatic Medicine, 63,* 531–544.

Vondra, J., & Garbarino, J. (1988). Social influences on adolescent behavior problems. In S. Salzinger, J. Antrobus & M. Hammer (Eds.), *Social networks of children, adolescents, and college students* (pp. 195–224). Hillsdale, NJ: Lawrence Erlbaum Associates.

Vora, J. A., & Vora, E. (2004). The effectiveness of South Africa's Truth and Reconciliation Commission: Perceptions of Xhosa, Afrikaner, and English South Africans. *Journal of Black Studies, 34,* 301–322.

W. T. Grant Foundation. (1988). *The forgotten half: Non-college bound youth in America.* Washington, DC: Author.

Waldrop, J. (1990). Marketing motherhood. *American Demographics, 12*(5), 4.

Waldrop, J. (1992). Flowers for all seasons. *American Demographics, 14*(5), B02.

Walker, K. (1994). Men, women, and friendship: What they say, what they do. *Gender and Society, 8,* 246–265.

Waller, W. W., & Hill, R. (1951). *The family, a dynamic interpretation.* New York: Dryden Press.

Walster, E., Aronson, V., Abrahams, D., & Rottmann, L. (1966). Importance of physical attractiveness in dating behavior. *Journal of Personality and Social Psychology, 4,* 508–516.

Walther, J. B., & Boyd, S. (2002). Attraction to computer-mediated social support. In C. A. Lin & D. Atkin (Eds.), *Communication technology and society: Audience adoption and uses* (pp. 153–158). Cresskill, NJ: Hampton.

Wang, H.-Z., & Chang, S.-M. (2002). The commodification of international marriages: Cross-border marriage business in Taiwan and Viet Nam. *International Migration Review, 40*(6), 93–116.

Wapner, S., & Craig-Bray, L. (1992). Persons-in-environment transitions: Theoretical and methodological approaches. *Environment and Behavior, 24,* 161–188.

Waters, M. (1994). *Modern sociological theory.* London ; Thousand Oaks, CA: Sage.

Watts, D. J. (2003). *Six degrees: The science of a connected age.* New York: Norton.

Watzlawick, P., Beavin, J. H., & Jackson, D. D. (1967). *Pragmatics of human communication.* New York: Norton.

Weber, H. R. (2005, February 9). Roses are red, keeping profits in the black. *Tacoma News Tribune,* p. C8.

Wedding and honeymoon statistics. (2003). Retrieved February 18, 2003, from http://www.topweddinglinks.com/wedstatistics.html

Wedding costs on the rise in Shanghai. (2002, August 23).*Xinhua News Online.* Retrieved March 2, 2006 from http://news.xinhuanet.com/english/2002%2D08/23/content%5F536102.htm

Weigel, D. J., & Ballard-Reisch, D. S. (2002). Investigating the behavioral indicators of relational commitment. *Journal of Social and Personal Relationships, 19,* 403–423.

Weinstock, H., Berman, S., & Cates, W., Jr. (2004). Sexually transmitted diseases among American youth: Incidence and prevalence estimates, 2000. *Perspectives on Sexual and Reproductive Health, 36*(1), 6–10.

Weiss, R. L. (1980). Strategic behavioral marital therapy: Toward a model for assessment and intervention. In J. P. Vincent (Ed.), *Advances in family intervention, assessment, and theory* (Vol. 1, pp. 229–271). Greenwich, CT: JAI Press.

Weiss, R. L., Birchler, G. R., & Vincent, J. P. (1974). Contractual models for negotiation training in marital dyads. *Journal of Marriage and the Family, 36,* 321–330.

Wellman, B. (1979). The community question: The intimate networks of East Yorkers. *American Journal of Sociology, 84,* 1201–1231.

Wellman, B., Wong, R. Y., Tindall, D., & Nazer, N. (1997). A decade of network change: Turnover, persistence and stability in personal communities. *Social Networks, 19,* 27–50.

Wenger, G. C., & Jerrome, D. (1999). Change and stability in confidant relationships: Findings from the Bangor longitudinal study of aging. *Journal of Aging Studies, 13,* 269–294.

Werner, C. M., Altman, I., Brown, B. B., & Ginat, J. (1993). Celebrations in personal relationships: A transactional/dialectical perspective. In S. Duck (Ed.), *Social context and relationships* (pp. 109–139). Newbury Park, CA: Sage.

Westman, M. (2001). Stress and strain crossover. *Human Relations, 54,* 717–752.

What bosses think about corporate ethics. (1988, April 6). *Wall Street Journal*, p. 21.

Wheeless, L. R. (1976). Self-disclosure and interpersonal solidarity: Measurement, validation, and relationships. *Human Communication Research, 3,* 47–61.

Wheeless, L. R. (1978). A follow-up study of the relationships among trust, disclosure, and interpersonal solidarity. *Human Communication Research, 4,* 143–157.

White, H. C. (1970). *Chains of opportunity.* Cambridge, MA: Harvard University Press.

White, H. C. (1992). *Identity and control.* Princeton, NJ: Princeton University Press.

Wilmot, W. W., Carbaugh, D. A., & Baxter, L. A. (1985). Communicative strategies used to terminate romantic relationships. *Western Journal of Speech Communication, 49,* 204–216.

Wilson, L. L., Roloff, M. E., & Carey, C. M. (1998). Boundary rules. *Communication Research, 25,* 618–640.

Wilson, M., & Daly, M. (1993). Spousal homicide risk and estrangement. *Violence and Victims, 8,* 3–16.

Winch, R. F. (1958). *Mate-selection: A study of complementary needs.* New York: Harper.

Winn, K. I., Crawford, D., & Fischer, J. (1991). Equity and commitment in romance versus friendship. *Journal of Social Behavior & Personality, 6,* 301–314.

Wirth, L. (1938). Urbanism as a way of life. *American Journal of Sociology, 44,* 3–24.

Wiseman, J. P., & Duck, S. (1995). Having and managing enemies: A very challenging relationship. In S. Duck & J. T. Wood (Eds.), *Confronting relationship challenges* (pp. 43–72). Thousand Oaks, CA: Sage.

Wolin, S. J., & Bennett, L. A. (1984). Family rituals. *Family Process, 23,* 401–420.

Wood, J. T. (2000). Gender and personal relationships. In C. Hendrick & S. Hendrick (Eds.), *Close relationships: A sourcebook* (pp. 301–313). Thousand Oaks, CA: Sage.

Wood, J. T., & Inman, C. (1993). In a different mode: Recognizing male modes of closeness. *Journal of Applied Communication Research, 21,* 279–295.

Wright, D. R., & Fitzpatrick, K. M. (2004). Psychosocial correlates of substance use behaviors among African American youth. *Adolescence, 39,* 653–667.

Wright, L. B., Treiber, F. A., Davis, H., Strong, W. B., Levy, M., Van Huss, E., et al. (1993). Relationship between family environment and children's hemodynamic responses to stress: A longitudinal evaluation. *Behavioral Medicine, 19,* 115–121.

Wright, P. H. (1982). Men's friendships, women's friendships and the alleged inferiority of the latter. *Sex Roles, 8,* 1–20.

Wright, P. H. (1985). The acquaintance description form. In S. Duck & D. Perlman (Eds.), *Understanding personal relationships: An interdisciplinary approach* (pp. 39–62). London: Sage.

Wright, P. H., & Wright, K. D. (1995). Codependency: Personality syndrome or relational process? In S. Duck & J. T. Wood (Eds.), *Confronting relationship challenges* (pp. 109–128). Thousand Oaks, CA: Sage.

Wright, S. C., Aron, A., McLaughlin-Volpe, T., & Ropp, S. A. (1997). The extended contact effect: Knowledge of cross-group friendships and prejudice. *Journal of Personality and Social Psychology, 73,* 73–90.

Yang, J. (1994, July 18). New wedding trend. *Beijing Review, 37,* 24.

Yeh, H.-C., & Lempers, J. D. (2004). Perceived sibling relationship and adolescent development. *Journal of Youth & Adolescence, 33*(2), 133–147.

Youniss, J., & Smollar, J. (1985). *Adolescent relations with mothers, fathers, and friends.* Chicago: University of Chicago Press.

Zipf, G. K. (1949). *Human behavior and the principle of least effort.* Cambridge, MA: Addison-Wesley.

Author Index

Subject Index